MIT and the Transformation of American Economics

MIT and the Transformation of American Economics

Annual Supplement to Volume 46
History of Political Economy

Edited by E. Roy Weintraub

Duke University Press
Durham and London 2014

Printed in the United States of America
on acid-free paper. ISBN 978-0-8223-6812-0.
This is the 2014 supplement to
History of Political Economy, ISSN 0018-2702.

Contents

Introduction: Telling the Story of MIT Economics in the Postwar Period

E. Roy Weintraub

On October 3, 1940, Paul Samuelson's doctoral mentor, E. B. Wilson, wrote to him saying that he had heard that Samuelson, newly appointed as a Harvard instructor, had just received an offer to join the MIT faculty as an assistant professor of economics. In the letter, discussed in detail by Roger Backhouse in this volume, Wilson recalled that he himself, as a first-year assistant professor at Yale, had received an offer to go to MIT as an associate professor, had accepted the offer, and "was never sorry that I did it." He went on to say:

> I have thought a great deal about the situation in economics at Tech. When [Francis Amasa] Walker was President . . . the prospects for economics were extremely good. [Since Walker's death] the [economics] staff at Tech hasn't been notably statistical or mathematical and has in no way adequately capitalized in their instruction [on] the background of their students, which consists of 2 years of required mathematics, 2 years of required physics, 1 year of required chemistry, and a year of required mechanics. . . . It seems a much more powerful course on economics could be given if this background were thoroughly used. . . . I do think it shows extremely keen intelligence on the part of Tech [and Freeman] to try to get you. . . . What will happen at Tech I don't know but they are starting out well if they secure you.

Correspondence may be addressed to E. Roy Weintraub, Department of Economics, Duke University, Box 90097, Durham, NC 27708-0097; e-mail: erw@duke.edu.

History of Political Economy 46 (annual suppl.) DOI 10.1215/00182702-2716091

And in a follow-up letter dated October 14, Wilson concluded:

> I expect you would go ahead fast at Tech, perhaps fast enough so that you won't be thinking about going anywhere else as was indeed my own experience. If you stay there as the Tech continues to appoint persons like you to its staff then by the time you are in early middle life there may be a very great change in the instruction at Tech and the Tech may have a really distinguished research department as it now has in mathematics, physics, and chemistry.

Wilson's prediction, made in late 1940, was prescient. Samuelson did stay at MIT, and the department, bolstered by a number of appointments of technically strong scholars, became, by the late 1950s, one of the three or four most distinguished research departments of economics in North America. In another decade it would become the most highly regarded economics department in the world. The history of this process, and the important paper that provided the common background understanding for the conferees, was developed by Beatrice Cherrier (this volume) from multiple archival sources. At the same time, MIT's rise to prominence coincided with the remarkable transformation of American economics in the postwar period. Cherrier is the first historian of economics to take up the narrative challenge of situating the particular circumstances of MIT in the context of that transformation.

Over the past twenty-five years the Duke history of economics faculty, together with the collection development librarians (particularly Robert Byrd and Will Hansen) in the David M. Rubenstein Rare Book and Manuscript Library, have been gathering the papers of notable (mostly) twentieth-century economists in what is now called the Economists' Papers Project. Over time that archive has grown and become central to historical research on economics in the postwar period. The papers of Edwin Burmeister, Evsey Domar, Franklin Fisher, Duncan Foley, Lawrence Klein, Franco Modigliani, and Robert Solow, all MIT faculty or students, have attracted scholars from around the world. After Paul Samuelson's death in December 2009, his papers, by prior arrangement, came to the Economists' Papers Project and quickly became a magnet for historians of economics. In response, early in 2010 I was encouraged by my colleagues Bruce Caldwell, Neil De Marchi, Craufurd Goodwin, and Kevin Hoover to plan a conference in the *HOPE* annual conference series to examine the history of MIT economics. After a year's worth of conversations and e-mails, I invited a select group of scholars to consider MIT's role in the transformation of American economics in the postwar period. That conference, held April 26–28, 2013, at the R. David Thomas Conference Center at Duke University, was sponsored as usual by Duke University Press. However, the very generous financial support of the Alfred P. Sloan Foundation made possible the expansion of the "standard" *HOPE* conference into one that included a larger number of participants and papers. In the end the conferees learned that telling the story of MIT's role in the postwar period required attending to both the particular circumstances that shaped MIT and the various ways in which economics itself was changing.

The Historiographical Challenge

Stories in the history of science engage both narratives of continuity and narratives of disruptive change. Historians of economics, who have long employed such a distinction, appear to agree that the 1940s saw a major break between an older economics and a newer economics. Before World War II, even as economics encompassed diverse approaches, methodologies, and theories, most economists still employed the same kinds of tools, studied the same texts, examined and reexamined a stable canon, and shared common educational goals and practices. Rhetorically, they were indistinguishable. Aside from the early issues of *Econometrica* (and later the *Review of Economic Studies*), most books, journals, articles, and reviews published in the 1930s exhibited their literary nature even as they incorporated occasional geometric and descriptive statistical arguments. By the mid-1950s, in contrast, most prominent published works had a "scientific" character and featured mathematical or econometric arguments in support of conjectures and hypotheses. These changes were sufficiently well recognized at the time that the community of economists sought to impose new standards for those seeking professional credentials as economists.

Over the next half-century historians of economics sought to characterize this disruption and explain its sources and consequences. Different historians examined this transformation in different ways, not all of them consistent with one another. The historiography is additionally complicated because the 1940s are recent enough that a number of the central figures themselves provided accounts of the transformation to the historians. But as is true for many histories of contemporary science, the tension between historians' and participant observers' interests complicates the process of constructing compelling accounts of the postwar period. Telling the story of modern economics must begin by interpreting the discontinuity in both the body of economic knowledge and the image of economic knowledge held by economists in the postwar period.[1] But there are many interpretations.

If the specific task here is to tell MIT's story while employing (or rejecting) the discontinuity stories, it will be useful first to look away from MIT to describe how scholars have addressed the general history of the postwar period and the changes both in economic knowledge and in the community of economists between the 1930s and the 1950s. After framing those issues, we can better see how the conferees addressed the ways in which the MIT story is consistent with, and yet different from, those often-told tales.

Competing Narratives

There are three well-established narrative approaches to telling the story of how economics changed in the postwar period. Probably the oldest story of the transformation talks about the world before John Maynard Keynes's 1936 book *The General Theory of Employment, Interest, and Money* and the world after Keynes's book appeared. An old example of this is G. L. S. Shackle's 1967 volume *The Years of High Theory*. Certainly Lawrence Klein's *The Keynesian Revolution* ([1947] 1966), an extension of his doctoral thesis written at MIT under Paul Samuelson, contributed to this way of thinking, as did Keynes himself in his 1936 book, which opened by characterizing "classical" economists as every economist before him. Samuelson himself, who had learned Keynesian economics from Alvin Hansen at Harvard, was a member of a generation that saw, in Keynes's theory, a way out of the Great Depression. Thus by the time Thomas Kuhn's *Structure of Scientific Revolutions* appeared in 1962, economists had been referring to the Keynesian revolution for two decades and were able to appropriate Kuhn's arguments as fitting the Keynes case: the story became one in which the normal neoclassical science through the 1920s faced the crisis of the Depression, and Keynes's revolutionary paradigm-changing theory created a new kind of normal economic science by the 1940s. This story required that economics

1. The distinction between the body of knowledge and the image of knowledge was developed by the historian of mathematics Leo Corry (1996; following Yehuda Elkana) in his study of Bourbaki and algebra based on several of his earlier papers. I have employed it to discuss the interconnection of mathematics and economics in Weintraub 2002.

divided sharply into before and after Keynes. Even arguments about the changing nature of econometrics between the 1930s and 1950s, changes deplored by Keynes and his associates, have been cast in terms of this Keynesian revolution (Louça 2007). Similarly, the development of national income accounts by Simon Kuznets, James Meade, and Richard Stone was made necessary by, and facilitated, the Keynesian revolution, while wartime planning employed Keynesian categories, and statistical data collection post–World War II reflected these new features of economic life. The Keynesian revolution in this standard account produced a change in the nature of economic policy, as economists became embedded in governments as technicians and analysts. In the United States, the Employment Act of 1946 reified this transformation with the creation of the Council of Economic Advisers and the Economic Report of the President.

Several articles in this conference volume engage this master narrative to a greater or lesser degree. Perry Mehrling argues that the Keynesian allegiances of Samuelson and Modigliani generated a particular kind of monetary analysis and policy. The growth theory that grew from Robert Dorfman, Samuelson, and Solow's 1958 volume on linear programming, and Solow's 1957 paper, was neoclassical in the sense of the neoclassical synthesis, but that synthesis itself involved Keynesian theory, for it was that which was "synthesized" to neoclassical theory. This work at MIT is discussed in the articles of Verena Halsmayer and of Mauro Boianovsky and Kevin D. Hoover.

The Keynesian narrative both frames discussion of the transformation of economics and enables new kinds of inquiries. For example, important new work in economics would be located in those academic institutions that more quickly adopted Keynesian ideas. Assimilation of Keynesian ideas at the textbook level created a new generation of elementary textbooks beginning with Lorie Tarshis's and Samuelson's, published in 1947 and 1948, respectively. This is the subject of Yann Giraud's article in this volume. The "new" economics can be traced back to Keynes and to those who surrounded him at Cambridge, at least according to historians with some connection to Cambridge. The complex but confusing relationship between these two Keynesian networks is the subject of Roger Backhouse's article deconstructing the Cambridge capital theory controversy.

A second framing narrative emerged from the important *HOPE* conference volume edited by Mary Morgan and Malcolm Rutherford titled *From Interwar Pluralism to Postwar Neoclassicism* (1998). A number of scholars had become dissatisfied with histories characterizing the twentieth-century transformation of economics in the United States as a struggle in which institutionalism lost adherents with respect to an ascendant neoclassicism. Scholars like Rutherford (2003) and Yuval Yonay (1998) began to reconstruct the interwar period as one of theoretical diversity. The lacunae in previously told stories were that neither institutionalism nor neoclassical economics had been monolithic. Demand theory and production theory and the theory of the firm had been contentious and contested in the interwar years. By the mid-1950s, however, they were settled chapters in intermediate and graduate microeconomics textbooks. For historians of economics, the emergent question was, "How did postwar microeconomics become stabilized?" "Keynes" could not be the answer to this question. From an interwar economics in which a large number of themes and threads in economic theory were not necessarily consistent with one another, the 1950s presented a coherent vision of what had become microeconomics. The stability of neoclassical economics became the end point to be explained. Accounts of that particular stabilization process became a more or less convincing set of arguments according to which historians narrated the transformation of economics. The most prominent of these arguments was that mathematical models and the use of econometric techniques to provide empirical tests of those models untangled the various theoretical bafflements, puzzlements, and conundrums. Simple geometric models and descriptive statistics no longer sufficed to establish an economist's claims. The postwar microeconomics was stabilized by the increased use of mathematics and statistics in economic analyses (Weintraub 1991, 2002). The role of models became more important, and the role of value judgments and ethical concerns became less important in undergraduate teaching, graduate curricula, and the socialization of new entrants into the economics profession. The postwar period witnessed a new rhetoric of economics. The articles in this volume by (again) Halsmayer and Harro Maas engage these important matters.

Perhaps the increased importance of more formal, more explicit models in this period was associated with the growing epistemological awareness, even self-consciousness, of economists in this time of methodological change. Samuelson's references to Percy Bridgman's "operationalism" and Karl Popper's "falsificationism" as presented to economists by Terence Hutchison required something theorylike, which in economics could only mean a model, to be subject to tests in order to claim scientific status (Morgan 2012). Despite the residual differences among national economics communities (Fourcade 2009), economics became an international discourse whose problems and answers were stabilized by an accepted set of techniques. Historians of economics working within this conceptual space would focus on the emergent methodologies associated with the new scientific economics and on the increased technical nature of the subject.

Since MIT's economics department was identified with this new technical economics, the conferees spent time detailing the paths along which these analyses changed the intellectual values and the rhetorical strategies of the community of economists in the postwar period. The articles by Andrej Svorenčík and Pedro Garcia Duarte, in particular, examine the movement of both people and ideas inside and outside the MIT economics department.

A third historiographical framework employed to explain the transformation of economics in the postwar period grew from political and sociological concerns. Stories told from this awareness recognized that prior to the war, economics had been connected in a disciplinary fashion to particular national traditions in countries that had been producing economics and economists. As a result of the wreckage of World War II, the United States became the dominant producer of non-Marxist economic analyses. America's hegemony stabilized economic discourse by replacing various national traditions with the emergent traditions of the American economics community. Stephen Meardon's article on Charles Kindleberger engages these matters. Only the United States had the resources to educate, hire, and train economists, and to publish research in economics on a massive scale. Over time, economics stabilized in the sense that disparate national traditions were submerged and marginalized with respect to an American mainstream economics. Many of those traditions lived on, of course, as heterodoxy. Two particular examples were the UK Post Keynesian group around Joan Robinson at Cambridge (Backhouse, this volume, "The Other Cambridge"), and the Austrian, neo-Austrian, and Chicago group around Friedrich Hayek that found a home among the small band of neoliberals connected to the Mont Pelèrin Society. Aside from Chicago economics, the heterodox traditions were not well regarded and in fact produced few if any serious connections to the reward structures of mainstream economics, and were not represented at MIT.

These three framing narratives of the postwar change in economics—the Keynesian revolution, the rhetorical stabilization of mathematical and econometric model-based economics, and the Americanization of economics—are of course neither mutually exclusive nor exhaustive. Thus there was open space in the last decade for constructing alternative narratives. Some work by a small number of historians of economics as well as some members of the larger science studies community built from the Americanization theme and had as one of its necessary implications that the economics discipline's postwar emphasis on building and analyzing models was, in Andrew Pickering's (1995) terms, a forced move and not a free move.[2] A few scholars strongly critical of both mainstream economics and mainstream economists went farther and characterized postwar economics as an intellectual disaster shaped and controlled by Cold War ideology. Philip Mirowski, particularly in his *Machine Dreams* (2002), and Sonja Amadae in her *Rationalizing Capitalist Democracy* (2003) argued that the contingency of the Cold War determined the nature and institutions of postwar economics. Of course no one denies that economists, brought into service during the war to analyze resource allocation problems—shipping paths, antiaircraft fire, convoy movements, antisubmarine warfare, logistics, military inventories, quality control of military production lines, and so forth—helped create a new kind of analysis soon to be termed operations research. But Mirowski and Amadae deride RAND, Cowles, and foundations such as Ford and Rockefeller as witting or unwitting contributors to the American Cold War project. From this fourth narrative's perspective, game theory, which would eventually unify large areas of what had become neoclassical economics, was military Cold War in origin and instantiated assumptions about human behavior that made it impossible to countenance disparate and more generous visions of human action. This historiography emphasizes the role of money flows from the military, grants, contracts, and personal networks of Cold Warriors in the emergent economics. In an article in this volume rejecting a number of Mirowski's claims, William Thomas examines how operations research developed at MIT. By establishing that it did not develop at all in MIT's economics department, Thomas refutes Mirowski's central claim.

A fifth narrative line, not often explored by historians of economics, likewise developed from the contingency of World War II. The sleepy backwater that was the American university prior to the war was transformed not only by the new world of Vannevar Bush and science funding connected to a Cold War interest but also by the most remarkable piece of social legislation in the immediate postwar period. The Servicemen's

2. A free move is an activity "in which scientists display choice and discretion [which are] aspects of human agency. . . . [A forced move is] where the discipline asserts itself . . . [and] where scientists become passive in the face of their training and established procedures" (Pickering 1995, 116).

Readjustment Act of 1944, known informally as the GI Bill, reshaped American higher education. Colleges and universities had been moribund during the Great Depression as they reduced staff and compensation and postponed thoughts of hiring new faculty and admitting more students. In the prewar period they had trained graduate students in such small numbers that there were few instructors available to teach the postwar flood of fee-paying undergraduates applying for admission.[3] It was at this time, for instance, that Lionel McKenzie, recently demobilized and facing a half year of unemployment before he could take up his Rhodes Scholarship to Oxford, used his Princeton master's degree in economics to secure a position teaching industrial economics to MIT undergraduates. New economists were needed as teachers, as government analysts, and as business economists. Economics graduate programs proliferated. The large numbers of undergraduate economics students forced changes in styles of instruction as well: tools and techniques were teachable in a way that a moral philosophy–based economics was not. Pedro Teixeira's article deals precisely with these matters, as does Giraud's. The GIs were on average older and more in need of workplace credentials than had been the stereotypical elites who were thought to populate the Ivy League establishments or the fraternity brothers and sorority sisters who inhabited many American state institutions before the war. These new students were also "better" than earlier cohorts: the best students from a large pool of applicants will be at least as good as the best students from the included smaller pool. This influx of students not only called forth a new generation of college teachers but also had profound implications for the kind of economics done. Universities became instrumental in securing employment for returning veterans fearful of being underqualified for employment. The returning veterans sought credentials and useful knowledge. A classical humanities–based education was a luxury that these older students could not afford. The demand for economics courses and for business courses exploded (Augier and March 2011). From a prewar liberal arts education that looked down on economics as a practical subject fit only for those unqualified by breeding or availability of leisure to study the humanities, postwar economics became an important academic discipline.

3. One example will suffice to tell the tale. The number of economics students at the University of Michigan jumped 120 percent in 1945–46, and jumped another 89 percent in 1946–47, peaking at 9,100 students in 1947–48. Prewar, that university had produced on average two PhDs in economics per year since 1920, which meant that there was no supply of classroom-ready economics teachers after 1945 (Brazer 1982, 206–7).

While there have been few sustained contextualizations of the changes in postwar economics that draw extensively on these educational and institutional matters, and fewer still by historians of economics, two recent contributions along these lines have drawn some attention from both historians and economists. The sociologist Marion Fourcade (2009) examined the professional discipline of economics in the United States, Britain, and France from the 1890s to the 1990s, and wove the different social and educational institutions of each country into her narrative of change in economics. More recently, scholars have engaged with an excellent discussion of these issues with respect to business education. The organization theory scholar Mie Augier and the education theorist James March, in their *Roots, Rituals, and Rhetorics of Change: North American Business Schools after the Second World War* (2011), tell a new story of a changing economics in the postwar period through a history of the growth of business schools in that period. Many of the topics alluded to in the various historiographies of economics were present as well in business education, and the prewar-postwar break was even more significant in business than it had been in economics. But of course the fate of economics and business education were intertwined.

The MIT economics department was not insulated from more general challenges that faced both universities and the community of economists. Its response to the profession's shifting away from history is the subject of Peter Temin's article on the role of economic history in the MIT program. With respect to the discipline's response to past discrimination against black applicants to many graduate schools, and the resulting absence of black economists on research universities' faculties, MIT's attempts to address this were, despite good intentions, no more successful than those of other "top" economics departments. William Darity Jr. and Arden Kreeger's article provides a detailed account of this attempt and its aftermath.

Any one or several or all of the five narratives—three older and two newer—can "explain" the growing importance of the MIT economics department in the postwar period. The Keynesian revolution? Paul Samuelson, check. The emergent technical nature of the discipline? The technical training of MIT students, nascent scientists and engineers, and a faculty brought in to teach such students, check. Cold War military funding and the engagement of economics faculty and institutions with both sources of support and professions of national need? The history of MIT and the Rad Lab, and the explosion of defense spending that moved through MIT in this period, check. The international hold of American economics and institutions in this period? The connection of a primarily technological institution to a postwar world hungry for the training in engineering and technology that MIT could provide, check. An influx of students on the GI Bill transforming both the mission and the nature of MIT as an institution? The creation of an actual economics program at MIT in exactly this immediate postwar period, and the stirrings that would create the Sloan School, check.

Paul Samuelson (2000), in fact, employed two of these narratives in his own accounting:

> Two factors explain our success. One, MIT's renaissance after World War II as a federally-supported research resource. Two, the mathematical revolution in macro- and micro-economic theory and statistics: this was overdue and inevitable—MIT was the logical place for it to flourish. What was not inevitable was that the MIT Economics Department maintained throughout its explosive development a deserved reputation for collegial amiability.

The idea that MIT emerged from "nowhere" in the 1930s to its place as one of the three or four most important sites for economic research by the mid-1950s would appear overdetermined with respect to these several narratives. It would not be inappropriate to develop the story of MIT's meteoric rise to prominence along any of these five narrative axes. And as the conference made clear, there is even a sixth narrative that supports any story of MIT's quick success, namely, that the immediate postwar period saw a collapse—in some places slower, in some places faster—of the barriers to the hiring of Jewish faculty in American colleges and universities. More than any other elite private or public university, particularly Ivy League universities, MIT welcomed Jewish economists. Both Backhouse's discussion of Samuelson's move to MIT, and my own article's discussion of the issue, opened this topic for the conference's consideration.

References

Amadae, S. M. 2003. *Rationalizing Capitalist Democracy: The Cold War Origins of Rational Choice Liberalism.* Chicago: University of Chicago Press.

Augier, M., and J. G. March. 2011. *The Roots, Rituals, and Rhetorics of Change: North American Business Schools after the Second World War.* Stanford, Calif.: Stanford University Press.

Brazer, M. C. 1982. "The Economics Department of the University of Michigan: A Centennial Retrospective." In *Economics and the World around It*, edited by S. H. Hymans, 133–275. Ann Arbor: University of Michigan Press.

Corry, L. 1996. *Modern Algebra and the Rise of Mathematical Structures*. Boston: Birkhauser.

Dorfman, R., P. Samuelson, and R. Solow. 1958. *Linear Programming and Economic Analysis*. New York: McGraw-Hill.

Fourcade, M. 2009. *Economists and Societies: Discipline and Profession in the United States, Britain, and France, 1890s to 1990s*. Princeton, N.J.: Princeton University Press.

Keynes, J. M. 1936. *The General Theory of Employment, Interest, and Money*. New York: Harcourt Brace.

Klein, L. R. (1947) 1966. *The Keynesian Revolution*. New York: Macmillan.

Kuhn, T. S. (1962) 1966. *The Structure of Scientific Revolutions*. Chicago: University of Chicago Press.

Louçã, F. 2007. *The Years of High Econometrics: A Short History of the Generation That Reinvented Economics*. New York: Routledge.

Mirowski, P. 2002. *Machine Dreams: Economics Becomes a Cyborg Science*. Cambridge: Cambridge University Press.

Morgan, M. S. 2012. *The World in the Model: How Economists Work and Think*. New York: Cambridge University Press.

Morgan, M. S., and M. Rutherford, eds. 1998. *From Interwar Pluralism to Postwar Neoclassicism*. Supplemental issue to vol. 30 of *History of Political Economy*. Durham, N.C.: Duke University Press.

Pickering, A. 1995. *The Mangle of Practice: Time, Agency, and Science*. Chicago: University of Chicago Press.

Rutherford, M. 2003. "American Institutional Economics in the Interwar Period." In *A Companion to the History of Economic Thought*, edited by W. Samuels, J. E. Biddle, and J. B. Davis, 360–76. Oxford: Blackwell.

Samuelson, P. A. 1948. *Economics*. New York: McGraw-Hill.

———. 2000. "Economics in MIT's Fourth School." *Soundings*, Fall. web.mit.edu/shass/soundings/issue_00f/fea_lum_pas_00f.html.

Shackle, G. L. S. 1967. *The Years of High Theory: Invention and Tradition in Economic Thought, 1926–1939*. Cambridge: Cambridge University Press.

Solow, R. 1957. "Technical Change and the Aggregate Production Function." *Review of Economics and Statistics* 39 (3): 312–20.

Tarshis, Lorie. 1947. *Elements of Economics*. Boston: Houghton Mifflin.

Weintraub, E. R. 1991. *Stabilizing Dynamics: Constructing Economic Knowledge*. New York: Cambridge University Press.

———. 2002. *How Economics Became a Mathematical Science*. Durham, N.C.: Duke University Press.

Wilson, E. B. 1940. Letters to Paul Samuelson: October 3, 1940, and October 14, 1940. Paul A. Samuelson Papers, Correspondence Series, "W" file, David M. Rubenstein Rare Book and Manuscript Library, Duke University.

Yonay, Y. P. 1998. *The Struggle over the Soul of Economics: Institutionalist and Neoclassical Economists in America between the Wars*. Princeton, N.J.: Princeton University Press.

Part 1
Beginnings

Toward a History of Economics at MIT, 1940–72

Beatrice Cherrier

In November 2011, Mario Draghi (PhD MIT, 1977) became president of the European Central Bank, thereby joining a group of central bank governors that also included Stanley Fischer (PhD MIT, 1969; MIT professor, 1973–79) and Ben Bernanke (PhD MIT, 1979). That same month, Lucas Papademos (PhD MIT, 1977) became Greece's prime minister. Earlier that year, as Austan Goolsbee (PhD MIT, 1995) left the directorship of the Council of Economic Advisers, the John Bates Clark Medal was awarded to a 1999 MIT PhD, Jonathan Levin, just as it was the two previous years—Esther Duflo, Clark medalist in 2010, and Emmanuel Saez, Clark medalist in 2009, both received their PhDs from MIT, also in 1999.[1] This elicited

Correspondence may be addressed to Beatrice Cherrier, Departement Carrières Sociales, IUT d'Alencon, Pole Universitaire de Montfoulon, 61250 Damigny, France, e-mail: beatrice.cherrier@gmail.com. This research has been made possible by a postdoctoral grant and a research fellowship from the Center for Political Economy at Duke University (CHOPE). I am especially grateful to E. Roy Weintraub, Roger E. Backhouse, and Yann Giraud for their enthusiasm, constant support, and numerous helpful suggestions. I have also benefited from helpful comments from Pedro Garcia Duarte, Paul Dudenhefer, Thomas Ferguson, Philippe Fontaine, Robert Solow, Andrej Svorenčík, Peter Temin, the participants in a CHOPE lunch seminar and workshop, in the INET "silos" conference, in HISRECO, in the Nijmegen History of Political Economy Workshop, and in the Cercle d'épistémologie économique, La Sorbonne. This work also owes much to the dedication of Will Hansen, Elizabeth Dunn, Nora Murphy, and the archivists of the Economists' Papers Project at Duke University and of the MIT Archives.

1. Levin was himself to be succeeded by Amy Finkelstein (PhD MIT, 2001) in 2012. Only four of the past seventeen Clark medalists were neither MIT PhDs nor MIT faculty.

History of Political Economy 46 (annual suppl.) DOI 10.1215/00182702-2716100

public comment from observers concerned that one institution should be in such a dominant position. At the same time, during the celebrations of MIT's 150th anniversary, a different tone was struck by MIT alumni and some of the thirteen Nobel Prize laureates in economics associated with the institution. They spoke of MIT's excellence in growth theory, macroeconomics, public economics, finance, development economics, urban economics, and energy and environmental economics, as well as of the leadership of Paul Samuelson, Robert Solow, Franco Modigliani, and Peter Diamond, among others.

MIT achieved this dominant position between 1940 and 1972. Although there had always been economists at MIT, they were, as late as the forties, no more than a small group providing service teaching to science and engineering students. In complete contrast, by the seventies, MIT was ranked top among the world's economics departments; it was MIT—not so much Harvard, Chicago, or Stanford—that lesser institutions sought to emulate. However, despite its acknowledged prominence, MIT economics experienced a crisis in the seventies, to which it responded by becoming more like other institutions, a task made easier because other institutions had sought to copy much of MIT's way of doing economics.[2] Given its importance in the history of postwar economics, one would have expected historians to have written extensively about economics at MIT. However, this has not been the case, perhaps because when attention started to be paid to postwar economics, it was the University of Chicago that attracted the most publicity. MIT merely comes into discussions of specific fields. In the context of finance, for instance, Perry Mehrling (2005, 192–95) has identified it with "the neo-Keynesian troika" of Samuelson, Solow, and Modigliani. As a result, it has been left to MIT insiders to identify what might have been distinctive about MIT. For example, Paul Krugman ([1995]), who graduated with a PhD from MIT in 1977, described the MIT style as involving "small models applied to real problems, blending real-world observation and a little mathematics to cut through to the core of an issue."[3]

Some lessons can be nevertheless learned from recent historical work on Chicago (compiled in Van Horn, Mirowski, and Stapleford 2011). It has shown the importance of paying attention not simply to a particular eco-

2. For a quantitative identification of two distinct periods in MIT history, see Svorenčík, this volume.

3. References to an MIT "style" can be found in Solow 2006, 662; Modigliani (in Solow 2007); Diamond 2010; Stiglitz 2001; and Merton 1997. See also David Colander's (1998, 5–6) contradicting definition of MIT's approach.

nomics department but to relationships between economists in different departments and between economists and other social scientists. Attention has also been drawn to the variety of forces that shaped the interactions of economists, such as the workshop, institutional strategies, and funding, and to the importance of an institution's perception of its own identity and role. Three features are especially salient in the development of economics at MIT: the variety of institutions within the Institute in which economics was considered a relevant subject, long before the Department of Economics became dominant; the importance of the engineering context on the research style and subjects, the curricula, and the recruitment of graduate students and faculty; and the close interwining of scientific and educational concerns in every decision made during the period.[4]

This article tells the story of the rise of an economics department within an engineering school up to the early seventies. In section 1, I explain how the recruitment of Samuelson in 1940 fostered the establishment of a small community of economists within the Institute, which was itself undergoing major transformations, and how the war opened the door to the development of the humanities and the social sciences at MIT, to psychology and political science as much as to economics.[5] Section 2 describes how a "new economics" was shaped during the fifties, one still influenced by the demands of engineers, scientists, and business students, and somewhat eclipsed by the promising interdisciplinary research programs emerging in the newly founded Center for International Studies. In section 3, I show how, in the context of the increased professionalization of the discipline, MIT economists instantiated the vision of Samuelson and Solow, worked to make their graduate program the most appealing in the country, and gained wide public visibility as policy-oriented scientists. Section 4 details how, beginning in the midsixties, MIT's apparently flourishing community was internally and externally challenged, and how the reforms implemented in reaction to those challenges led to a normalization and standardization of its programs.

4. Throughout this article, I use the term *MIT* to refer to the community of scholars doing economics at MIT, and the term *Institute* for "Massachusetts Institute of Technology," understood as the institution as a whole.

5. The information on recruitment at the MIT Department of Economics and Social Science between 1933 and 1970 is taken from "Economic Department Academic Staff, 1933–1965 and 1969–1971," Collection AC394, "Department of Economics Records, 1947–1982," Institute Archives and Special Collections, Hayden Library, MIT (hereafter AC394). To minimize the number of footnotes, materials from archival and oral history sources are usually referenced in footnotes at the end of each paragraph only.

1940–50: Establishment

Economics for Scientists, Engineers, and Managers

In contrast to older traditional economics departments such as Chicago or Harvard, it was not until the thirties that a "department of economics and social science" was created at MIT. President Karl Compton and Provost Vannevar Bush were moving the Institute away from practical engineering training to science-based research (see Lecuyer 1992 and Teixeira, this volume). They reformed the university structure by creating three distinct schools (science, engineering, and architecture) and two divisions (humanities, and industrial cooperation and research), introduced a heavy dose of fundamental sciences into the undergraduate curriculum, and added several renowned faculty to the physics and biology departments to foster the science-based technological research that they believed would interest foundations such as the Rockefeller and government agencies such as the Tennessee Valley Authority. By the late thirties, the Institute hosted around twenty-five hundred undergraduate and four hundred graduate students. It had always attached great importance to economics and business as part of the training of engineers, and among the major industrial patrons of these years was Alfred P. Sloan, who lavishly funded an educational program in business and engineering. In line with Sloan and Institute executives' beliefs that "the engineer of the future will be vitally concerned with relations between labor and management" (PR 1940, 89), an industrial relations section was established within the Department of Economics and Social Science in 1937.[6] Its purpose was to perform research on hiring policies, collective bargaining, and so forth (PR 1939, 135–37). The department also taught quality control, statistics, money and banking, corporate finance, and labor problems, and as a result, Economic Principles was made compulsory for engineering juniors.[7]

The department head, Ralph Freeman, was eager to advance Compton's vision of a science-oriented research university. Together with Rupert McLaurin, a Harvard business school PhD whose fund-raising acumen had just got him a huge grant from the Rockefeller Foundation for the

6. The material borrowed from the *Reports to the President* published by MIT beginning in 1871 and archived online at libraries.mit.edu/archives/mithistory/presidents-reports.html is referred to as PR and date of issue.

7. Samuelson to Garnsey, December 11, 1943, papers, box 32, folder "general correspondence," Paul Samuelson Papers, David M. Rubenstein Rare Book and Manuscript Library, Duke University. The date of this arrangement is not known with certainty. Samuelson wrote that "it has been in effect for many years now," which suggests it predated his recruitment to MIT.

study of technological changes, and several other industrial fellowships, he began hunting for promising recruits (Brown and Solow 1983). Paul Pigors and Charles Myers were brought in to staff the Rockefeller project, and in September 1940 assistant professor and statistician Harold Freeman advised McLaurin to lure Samuelson from Harvard (Backhouse, this volume, "Samuelson's Move"). Samuelson helped set up a graduate program in industrial economics in 1941, its first graduate being Lawrence Klein (PhD, 1944). The program was briefly discontinued during the war, but when the returning veterans began to crowd the Institute corridors in 1945, the seeds for the rise of economics at MIT were sown.

Bringing the Humanities and the Social Sciences into the Curriculum

As student numbers expanded to 3,750 undergraduates and 1,950 graduates after the war (PR 1949, 26; see also Giraud, this volume), the administration changed the kinds and number of courses students were required to take. It was increasingly felt that many students would become managers and economists, and that they should be trained accordingly. Already in the early forties, the chemical engineering department, finding that its recruits lacked a basic knowledge of social and economic matters, required that all students take economics, psychology, and sociology courses. Such a requirement was formally integrated into the undergraduate curriculum in 1944. Students could take two introductory courses in economics during their junior year, then specialize in psychology, labor relations, or industrial economics. A "course XIV" was also established in 1946 and attracted sixty students by 1949 (PR 1949, 149). It allowed science and engineering students to pursue an economics or international relations major together with their scientific studies. Course XIV was the only program in which students could take up to 50 percent of their courses in something other than engineering or the hard sciences. In 1947 the graduate program in industrial economics reopened, and in 1949, when fifty students were doing graduate work in the department, the business school opened an "advanced studies program for executives." With these various programs, and introductory economics made compulsory by most engineering departments, by 1950 most of the 3,750 MIT undergraduates were enrolled in at least one economics course.

As a consequence of the 1949 Committee on Educational Survey, chaired by the chemical engineer Warren K. Lewis, the humanities and social sciences at MIT were formally recognized with the establishment of a humanities school within the Institute and the requirement that the science and engineering curriculum comprise 80 percent science courses and 20 percent humanities courses. Freshmen and sophomores would take a common humanities core, and juniors would then choose between three social science sequences: one in international relations, one in industrial relations, and one in economics. The latter comprised the two introductory courses that most engineering departments had already made compulsory and a set of electives to be chosen between National Income, Economics of Patents and Inventions, Public Finance, and Banking and Finance. This was the first time that MIT undergraduates were presented with a consistent sequence in economics.[8] The curriculum also reflected both the growing demand for training and the enhanced visibility of psychology triggered by the war.[9] To meet the requirements of the new curriculum, the Department of Economics and Social Science also recruited its first specialist in international relations, Norman J. Padleford.

Several economists were recruited to meet the increased teaching needs.[10] Robert Bishop (PhD Harvard, 1949) became assistant professor in 1949, fiscal specialist Cary Brown (PhD Berkeley, 1937) transferred from the division of tax research of the United States Treasury in 1947, and international economist Charles Kindleberger (PhD Columbia, 1937) arrived in 1948 after helping frame the Marshall Plan; they were joined by industrial economist Morris Adelman (PhD Harvard, 1948). In 1949 Robert Solow (PhD Harvard, 1951) was hired to meet the increasing need for teaching in statistics at both the undergraduate and the graduate levels. Although the bulk of research was still conducted by the industrial section in the late forties, the reputation of MIT economics was strengthened by Samuelson's prestige inside and outside the Institute. *Foundations of Economic Analysis* (1947) was immediately recognized as a watershed, and Samuelson was awarded the John Bates Clark Medal the same year. Those prizes, together with his Guggenheim fellowship in 1948 and the creation

8. Note that no humanities or economics undergraduate major existed at MIT until the midsixties.

9. One of the leading figures in psychology at MIT was Kurt Lewin, who had transferred from Harvard in 1946 to participate in the newly created Tavistok Institute and soon created a "Research Center for Group Dynamics" (PR 1945, 142) and an associated PhD program. Attracting students such as Leon Festinger, its main areas of research were industry, community life, minority problems, and relations between economics and culture (PR 1946, 149). After Lewin's sudden death in 1947, Alex Bavelas founded a laboratory in communication theory in 1949.

10. Note that a large portion of these recruits were of Jewish descent, a rarity in the American academic landscape at the time. See Weintraub, this volume, "MIT's Openness."

of course XIV, were the only events related to economics reported in the student weekly newspaper, the *Tech*, in these years. Economists received constant support from Compton and his successor, former vice president James Killian. They not only provided the funding but also supported Samuelson when the Keynesian content of his highly successful textbook, *Economics* (1948), was attacked (see Giraud, this volume).

1951–58: Expansion

The Center for International Studies, the Sloan School, and the Development of Interdisciplinary Social Sciences at MIT

The expansion of economics at MIT during the fifties was driven by the transformation of the Institute's organizational structure and interests. After the recruitment of Joseph C. R. Licklider, a psychologist specializing in information technology and psychoacoustics, and of cognitive psychologist George A. Miller, psychology became an independent section within the Department of Economics and Social Science in 1952.[11] Also of great impact on the composition of the department faculty was the creation of the Center for International Studies (CIS) in 1952.[12] The Ford Foundation offered the Institute a $1 million grant to turn "Project Troy"—aimed at making the Voice of America radio a technical and political tool to help America fight Soviet propaganda—into a permanent interdisciplinary institute to deal with "the problems of policy and action arising out of the international position of the United-States" (PR 1953, 83). Max Millikan, a former CIA member recruited in 1950 by the Department of Economics and Social Science, was appointed chairman. The CIS had close (yet undisclosed) ties to the CIA and the defense department, for whom it ran classified projects.

As a research body attached to the School of Humanities, the CIS had neither faculty nor an educational project of its own, with the consequence

11. This administrative move gave more independence to psychologists for the management of their research projects, undergraduate courses, and graduate program (PR 1952, 77).

12. Histories of the Center for International Studies can be found in Blackmer 2002 and Gilman 2003. On the administrative status of the CIS within the Institute, see PR 1969. In particular, the center was not allowed to recruit its own faculty. All its members had to be recruited by the Department of Economics and Social Science. In 1955 the CIS was awarded $75,000 for general purposes by the Ford Foundation (compared with $15,000 for the department), $212,500 for Indian studies (compared with $4,250), and $18,500 for research projects conducted by Brown and Samuelson; in 1957, Ford granted another $150,000 for development studies.

that its members had to be hired by an MIT department and work with that department's faculty to create courses within existing curricula. The students' rising concern with international relations ensured the success of its dedicated undergraduate sequence. Research programs on Soviet studies and international communication were immediately launched, chaired by MIT historian Walt Rostow and communication specialist Ithiel de Sola Pool (PhD Chicago, 1952), respectively. With the addition of sociologist Daniel Lerner, political science gained enough momentum to become an independent section in 1956. A third CIS program dealt with the economic development of several countries deemed vulnerable to communism, and this spurred the recruitment of several economists in 1953 with the status of "visiting professors." Paul Rosenstein-Rodan from the International Bank for Reconstruction and Development was to work on Italy, while Wilfred Malenbaum from the Department of State would concentrate on India. Everett Hagen, formerly at the University of Illinois and senior economic adviser to the government of Burma, was hired to focus on Indonesia, assisted by Benjamin Higgins from McGill University. These additions were seen as an opportunity to orient the curriculum toward preparing engineers for foreign service. As for research, their various contributions were unified by a common focus on the issue of growth. In addition to Hagen and his team, Rostow was working on a systematic description of the successive stages of growth and the conditions for economic takeoff (productive investment, development of manufacturing sectors, and free trade, leading to high mass consumption). His modernization theory was published in 1960 under the title *The Stages of Economic Growth: A Non-Communist Manifesto*. Development economics became a doctoral field in 1955.

Meanwhile, the industrial relation (IR) section, enlarged by the promotion of graduate student George P. Shultz to assistant professor in 1952 and the recruitment of John Coleman, was in the process of becoming a joint structure of the economics and social science department and the business school. Thanks to a $5 million grant from Sloan, the business school became the School of Industrial Management, the fifth school of the Institute, in 1952, and was endowed with a graduate program. Business school officials had endorsed the same vision as that advanced by the Graduate School of Industrial Administration at Carnegie, in which management techniques were to become more scientific if underpinned by economic concepts. Accordingly, the school drafted economists to upgrade its curriculum. By 1954 one-third of the theses written by Sloan fellows were supervised by economists from the IR section (PR 1954), and most economists (Solow, Freeman, and Adelman, among others) were teaching business students new quantitative techniques such as statistics and operations research.[13] As repeatedly emphasized in *Reports to the President*, "much of the research of the [economics] Department bears directly on the interests of the School [of Industrial Management]—research on the economics of particular technologies; on the problems of measurement of productivity and output; on the contribution of technical progress to economic growth; on the origin and growth of new enterprises." When the members of the business school moved to the newly acquired Sloan Building at the far end of the campus at the beginning of 1953, the Department of Economics and Social Science left Hayden Library, where humanities was located, and moved to the same building.

Forging a "New Economics"

In 1950, MIT neoclassical economists were a small group closely connected with Harvard, where most of them had done their graduate work. These contacts continued, and the connection with Harvard was used to attract visitors.[14] For example, Bishop and Adelman collaborated with Harvard economists on studies of monopoly, size, and antitrust laws. However, it was in the fifties that MIT economics began to acquire its own identity, associated not only with Samuelson and, increasingly, Solow but also with Kindleberger and Evsey Domar (recruited in 1958 to teach comparative economic systems and Soviet economics). Although Samuelson's and Solow's approaches to modeling were quite different from each other (see Backhouse, this volume, "The Other Cambridge"), their intellectual heritage, skills, and sustained collaboration led them to devise a "new economics." They spent part of the fifties working on linear programming for RAND, producing a book with Robert Dorfman (see Halsmayer, this volume).[15] As was the case with CIS economists, most of their research was converging on growth issues. In the thirties Samuelson had already

13. On the diverging intellectual path taken by business schools in the postwar era, see Khurana 2007. On the diverging conceptions of operations research in these years, see Thomas, this volume.

14. To convince Hendrik Houthakker to visit MIT, Solow argued that "we have plenty of contact with the Harvard people, like Orcutt, Duesenberry, Dorfman, etc." (Solow to Houthakker, January 21, 1957, box 55, folder H1, Robert Solow Papers, David M. Rubenstein Rare Book and Manuscript Library, Duke University [hereafter cited as RSP]).

15. On the linear programming book, see Backhouse 2012. They were indeed working in close connection with Harvard circles. Samuelson taught one joint course on monopolies with Edward Chamberlin.

published papers that investigated the functioning of an ideal capital market and the behavior of the interest rate, and he had applied linear programming to dynamic models in a 1949 RAND memo. While teaching input-output analysis to engineering students, Solow came up with his collapsed-production function, identified a steady state depending on population growth and technical progress and a convergence path defined by capital accumulation, and subsequently estimated the total factor productivity (Solow 1956, 1957; for a detailed account, see Halsmayer, this volume). Further analysis of efficient capital accumulation paths resulted in the first turnpike theorem. Gradually, a distinctive style of doing economics emerged, one that Samuelson labeled the "neoclassical synthesis" in the third edition of *Economics* in 1955 (Giraud, this volume). Along the guidelines set in *Foundations*, it relied on modeling microeconomic behavior as maximization under constraints and macroeconomic behavior as the interaction of aggregate demand and aggregate supply, imperfect competition, and the use of comparative statics. It became characterized by the use of mathematical yet simple models aimed at understanding a few aspects of a situation and was applied to a wide range of economic issues: trade (Samuelson 1948b), welfare economics, consumer behavior (Samuelson 1938), capital theory, and public expenditure (Samuelson 1954). As a small, tractable, and simplifying mathematical model on a key social issue (Halsmayer, this volume; Boianovsky and Hoover, this volume), Solow's growth model quickly became the epitome of the approach some MIT economists were developing in the fifties.[16]

A Community Built through the Development of the Curriculum

The ambition of MIT economists was not merely to develop a new economics but also to spread it. This was achieved through textbook writing

16. On Samuelson's new economics, see Feiwel 1982; Weintraub 1991; McCloskey 2002; and Mirowski 1989. Characterizations of the MIT style can be found in Mehrling 2005, 192–95; and Mirowski 2006. Despite the diverging interests and methods of these various groups of MIT economists and social scientists, there did not seem to be any fight for control, recruitment, or curriculum issues similar to those seen at the Harvard social relations department in the forties between the followers of Talcott Parsons and those of Pitirim Sorokin (for a detailed account, see Johnston 1998). As later attested by Millikan (Report, February 18, 1964, box 1, AC394) and Samuelson 2007, the reason for this peaceful cohabitation might be found in the constant stream of position openings and the growth in the number of students in the fifties and sixties, which enabled every group of social scientists to hire its own specialists and create its own undergraduate courses and graduate programs.

and Solow's and Samuelson's editorial responsibilities at *Econometrica*. Most important, their idea was to train students in the set of skills that they believed were essential to perform good economics, so that they would be placed in other top departments and further spread the MIT style. "We view ourselves as net exporters of finished economists," Solow wrote Domar, then at Johns Hopkins, in 1956.[17] Twenty to twenty-five graduate students were allowed to enroll each year, so that there were, for instance, sixty-seven students in residence in 1956. The graduate population was different from that at other universities, if only because of the Institute's requirement that every graduate student had to have taken one full-year college course in mathematics and one in physics.[18] Some had come to MIT to study mathematics (Diamond 2007) or physics, and switched after a semester, to enroll in graduate work in economic theory and statistics, international economics, industrial relations, industrial economics, economic history, or development economics. In the midfifties Solow was supervising, among others, John Kareken on the policymaking process in trade unions, then on monetary theory; Ronald Jones on international trade theory; Louis Lefeber at the CIS on external economies and transportation; and Alain Enthoven at RAND. Samuelson was advising his student Dick Kruizenga to take into account Brownian movement in his theoretical and institutional study of the put and call market. Robert Mundell was working on international trade under the supervision of Kindleberger. The graduate students' first two choices for thesis supervision were Solow, who supervised close to seventy students (between 1954 and 1997), including ten in the late fifties, and Kindleberger, who had trained around fifty graduates by 1980, including fifteen in the fifties. By comparison, Samuelson supervised twenty-three dissertations between 1948 and 1978, including eight in the fifties.

The training of undergraduates was not neglected. Although Samuelson was not much personally involved, the careful revision of his *Economics* textbook every three years enabled him to ascertain as well as anticipate and eventually influence the evolution of what was standard fare in the undergraduate education of economics students. His widely used textbook,

17. This "crowding-out effect" strategy, as Andrej Svorenčík (this volume) calls it, was very successful. Not many departments trained mathematical yet policy-oriented economists in those years, and MIT graduate cohorts were much smaller than Harvard's or Chicago's, which eased their placement. For detailed analysis of MIT graduates in the postwar period, see also Teixeira, this volume, and Duarte, this volume.

18. HUG 4517.5, General Correspondence, box 19, Wassily Leontief Papers, Harvard University.

which was thus a major tool to define and standardize the way economists were trained (see, e.g., Skousen 1997, 139), was the basis for the two elementary economics courses, labeled 14.01 and 14.02. They followed it closely, and it was supplemented by a book of readings assembled with the help of Bishop and Coleman. The general orientation of the undergraduate program was to introduce the student to macroeconomics first. Course 14.01 covered notions of scarcity, supply, and demand, but the bulk of it was devoted to national income accounting, income determination, unemployment, monetary theory, and economic growth. Course 14.02 focused on consumer theory, the theory of firms, equilibria, capital theory, and micro policies. A core sequence was gradually shaped, which included two intermediate courses, Price and Production and Economic Fluctuations and Growth, as well as a course on elementary statistics and one on the structure of the American economy. The other subjects were determined by the interests of the then small number of faculty interested in undergraduate teaching. For instance, Kindleberger proposed a course in international trade, Brown in public finance, and Domar in comparative economic systems.

Complying with humanities requirements, some eight hundred undergraduate students took economics courses at MIT, yet no one majored in economics. Moreover, the audience for course XIV, with its half science or engineering sequence and half economic studies, was floundering.[19] In 1958 a committee chaired by Brown concluded that the professional visibility of the program would be improved if the electives chosen were grouped in three fields. "General economics" would comprise courses such as Money and Banking, Public Finance, International Trade, and Labor Economics. The "industrial and labor economics program," with its emphasis on industrial economics, labor relations, and industry courses, would appeal to the future industry policymaker, broker, an economist in the research department of a trade union, a consultancy firm such as A. D. Little, or an industrial economist at the State Department, the World Bank, and so forth. The third option, "quantitative economics," would focus on the acquisition of technical skills in econometrics, statistical theory, pro-

19. After the end of veterans' quotas in 1949, enrollment dramatically fell from eighty-four students registered in 1949 to twenty-seven in 1952–53, only to improve slightly afterward. The quality of students was poor, and the program was perceived by MIT students as "designed for those students that are so frustrated by Newton, Faraday and Co. that they can't even cope with Course XV [Business and Engineering Administration], or for reluctant engineers that really should be in the ivory towers up the river" (*Tech*, January 17, 1947). For online editions of the *Tech*, go to tech.mit.edu/browse.html.

gramming and decision theory, and sequential analysis, among other related topics. The main organizers of this sequence, Samuelson and Solow, thus drew on the mathematical background of their audience and "their ability to move into more advanced things more quickly" (Diamond 2007), to bring their most recent research into the curriculum.[20]

1959–66: Emancipation and Success

A Student-Oriented Department

By the time the MIT graduate program achieved wide recognition in the early sixties, competition among economic departments had grown steadily, a consequence of the sweeping movement of professionalization described by Marion Fourcade (2009). MIT economists therefore envisioned recruitment as a privileged way to remain at the cutting edge of economic research, as attested by the arguments put forth during the recruitment of Franklin Fisher, a Harvard student in mathematical economics working on a priori information and time-series analysis, who had just accepted a position at the University of Chicago. Solow underlined that "Fisher could be compared only with Griliches of Chicago, Jorgenson of Berkeley, and Nerlove of Stanford in his age group. I think I would add Ned Phelps of Yale. . . . These are the stars of the 30–35 age group in American economics. . . . With so many departments expanding all around the country, and only this small pool of first-class people to bid for, it's no surprise that prices get bid up fast." The same considerations prevailed during the recruitment of Diamond: "To maintain our position in the pecking order [of economics departments], we simply must nab one or two of the top young economists in each succeeding generation; and among those, the economic theorists are the most important. . . . Any connoisseur will tell you that there are only four young mathematical economic theorists under the age of 30 worth talking about in the world. Diamond is one; McFadden of Berkeley, Mirrlees of Cambridge, and Weizsacker of Heidelberg are the others. If I could, I'd want to hire them all."[21]

While Diamond was perceived as the leader of the next generation of MIT theorists, Fisher was the architect of the development of econometrics

20. "Course XIV Undergraduate Economic Program," undated report (probably 1958 or 1959), AC394, box 2; PR 1958, 1959.

21. Solow to Bishop, October 26, 1964, box 52, RSP; Solow to Brown, May 16, 1966, box 52, RSP.

at MIT, with the help of Edwin Kuh (PhD Harvard, 1955), who had been on a joint appointment with the business school since 1959.[22] Fisher set up an econometrics course available to both undergraduates and graduates, and taught mathematical economics and advanced economic theory to graduates. As PhD requirements evolved from a monograph to a three-essay format in the sixties and seventies, all second-year students were asked to write an econometric essay.[23] The faculty was increasingly involved in undergraduate education: beside those traditionally concerned, Solow, Domar, and Kindleberger, the department welcomed a stream of young economists willing to improve its course offerings: Richard Eckaus, a former CIS student (PhD MIT, 1954) and specialist on India, proposed courses in development economics; Albert Ando (PhD Carnegie, 1959) taught macroeconomics, and 1964 recruit Stephen Marglin (PhD Harvard, 1963) and Karl Shell (PhD Stanford, 1965) continued the tradition of MIT economic theory through popular lectures as well as through theoretical work. Course XIV consequently achieved more recognition. From the low point of thirty-five students in 1960–61, enrollment reached seventy-eight in 1964–65. The success of the graduate school was even greater, with three hundred applications in 1964. The number of faculty had barely risen, from twenty-two to twenty-five between 1959 and 1964. As in the fifties, only twenty-five to thirty students were selected to enroll in the graduate program, bringing the total number of graduate students to about a hundred around 1965. The faculty's educational strategy was paying off: virtually every former MIT student insisted on mentioning the open door policy, the quality of teaching, the lack of hierarchy, the limited number of graduate students (who, moreover, were all encouraged to collaborate with each other), the sophisticated placement system (see Duarte, this volume); Solow alone wrote hundreds of supportive recommendation letters (see, e.g., Shell 2001, 708; Shiller 2006). Duncan Foley (2004, 191–92), recruited in 1966 after completing a PhD thesis on general equilibrium at Yale, reflected that, if he was allowed to bring general equilibrium into the curriculum despite the theoretical reservations of most MIT economists, it

22. At the 1967 Christmas party of the economics department, Peter Temin and Duncan Foley parodied the Arthurian legend of the Round Table in a script to be played by students, where Arthur (Frank Fisher) tried to set up a new elite economics department that would preserve theory, and Lancelot (Diamond) represented the young knight who, it was hoped, would "rescue theorems from rape and pillage at the brutal hands of Midwestern PhDs" ("Shawmut Follies" [1967], box 2, AC394).

23. Conversations with Peter Temin and Jim Poterba at the 2013 *HOPE* conference. The first-year essay was in economic history.

was because "they were so student oriented and interested in making sure that people would come through the department with what they needed to play leading roles in the discipline" (see also Diamond 2007, 562).

On the whole, students were drawn to the consistency of the intellectual program. Economic theory, micro and macro, was perceived as the strong point of the program, but there was no permanent responsibility of the kind that Milton Friedman and Gary Becker held at Chicago on the introductory price theory course.[24] Mathematical Approach to Economics was the only course that Samuelson had been teaching on a regular basis since 1954. Economic analysis and advanced theory were taught by Shell, Fisher, Samuelson, and Solow. Monetary economics was the realm of Modigliani, whom the faculty had contemplated hiring since 1957 and who finally joined the business school in 1962, but Samuelson sometimes replaced him. Dominant research agendas were discernible in thesis subjects. In particular, the sixties were the golden age of growth theory (Stiglitz 2001), as exemplified by the dissertations written by Diamond (PhD, 1963) and David Levhari (PhD, 1964), both under the supervision of Solow (see Boianovsky and Hoover, this volume). The recruits of the early sixties largely contributed to thesis supervision: Fisher trained forty-three students in his career (1962–93), twenty-three of whom wrote their dissertations in the sixties and early seventies. When he left MIT in 1973, Kuh had supervised fifteen students, and between 1964 and 1970 Ando directed around ten students. This sense of overall consistency was not only intellectual but also deeply rooted in the close-knit social community the faculty had built. "This is a small department, which had decided not to get any bigger," Solow explained in 1963. Besides the famous daily faculty lunch, many of its members lived in Concord, a western suburb of Boston. Brown, Solow, Kuh, and Fisher came to MIT in a carpool that cemented their friendship and was the place, it was said, where all departmental decisions were made. Contrasting the Harvard and MIT circles a few years later, Kenneth Arrow aptly summarized the general atmosphere at both institutions. "The Massachusetts Institute of Technology sticks very

24. On the role of the graduate introductory price theory course in the making of a distinct Chicago intellectual tradition, see Hammond 1999. The situation was different with technical courses: Fisher, Shell, Kuh, and Harold Freeman had been in charge of the mathematics-statistics-econometrics courses during the sixties. Also, the graduate program offered a range of field courses that could be taught by only one faculty member. Between 1960 and 1965, Brown taught fiscal economics, Eckaus taught development economics, Domar was in charge of Soviet studies, and Kindleberger was in charge of international economics. The titles and content of these courses were revised every year.

much to a closer unity. . . . The Harvard image, even at the graduate level, draws a different kind of student than say, MIT, one more humanistically and critically inclined. . . . It was immediately noticeable to me upon coming here [Harvard] that my contacts with my colleagues were somehow less frequent and more formal than they had been at Stanford. I know the M.I.T. Department well, and they are very different. There is constant informal contact there. When the faculty have close relations with each other, they tend also to be in close relation with graduate students," he wrote.[25]

Economics Becomes an Independent Department

A second element at work in the professionalization of the social sciences was the specialization of knowledge, embodied in the American departmental structure. The presence of psychologists and political scientists in the Department of Economics and Social Science had fostered very little interdisciplinary work outside the CIS, and the two disciplines became independent in 1964 and 1965, leaving economists on their own.[26] Such fragmentation took the CIS farther away from the department. In 1960 Everett Hagen and Paul Rosenstein-Rodan became full professors, but Benjamin Higgins and Wilfred Malenbaum left and were not replaced. The department requirement that a thesis be written onsite was not suitable given the long and frequent journeys of the CIS's graduate students to India, Indonesia, or Europe, and administrative problems for thesis validation became more and more frequent. Also, the CIS's interests in national security, military affairs, and communist studies drew it closer to political scientists than to economists, who did not share its recent interest in agri-

25. Student report on the graduate curriculum, March 27, 1966, box 2; "Changes for Fall 1965," May 2, 1965, box 2; "Changes for Spring 1966," box 2; AC394. Solow to Bishop, October 26, 1965, box 52, folder B4, RSP. Solow to Brown, May 16, 1966, box 52, folder B4, RSP. Solow to Patterson, January 18, 1963, box 53, folder B7, RSP; Solow to Fisher, April 6, 1967, box 55, RSP. Solow 2007. Peter Temin, e-mail to author, May 10, 2013. Arrow to Derek Bok, April 5, 1975, box 35, Kenneth Arrow Papers, David M. Rubenstein Rare Book and Manuscript Library, Duke University.

26. Interestingly, the 1963 PR mentions that "the Political Science Section is at present at a considerable physical distance from the Economics Section, but this will change upon completion of the recently authorized new structure behind the Sloan Building. This contemplated move reflects in part the fact that the Economics and Political Science Sections have a closer relationship (largely through their common connection with the Center for International Studies) than either has with the Psychology Section." On the importance of campus geography in the development of a university's research, see the introduction to Fourcade 2009 on Berkeley.

culture in underdeveloped countries or Latin American development problems. As pointed out by Max Millikan in a 1964 report, "The research interests of the faculty [of the Department of Economics] have its center of gravity nearer the domestic than to international economic problems."[27]

A Distinctive Style on the Public Scene

To some extent, Millikan's characterization was correct. The sixties were the golden age of neo-Keynesian macroeconomics at MIT. Samuelson and Solow had published their famous estimation of the Phillips curve in 1960. Solow actively looked for empirical evidence contradicting Milton Friedman's theory of lags in government reaction with the help of his student John Kareken (Kareken and Solow 1963), and Modigliani and Ando (1965) challenged Friedman and Chicago graduate student David Meiselman's testing of the relative stability of the velocity of money and of the Keynesian multiplier (Friedman and Meiselman 1963). But the sixties were also the moment when MIT economists' influence on the policymaking process became visible. Such policy orientation was not new. From the forties onward, the *Reports to the President* exhibited long lists of "outside activities": Brown consulted for the United States Department of the Treasury (1951) and the Committee for Economic Development (1954), Samuelson provided advice to the Treasury and the Bureau of the Budget, Adelman was a member of the attorney general's committee, and Shultz served as specialist on labor economics on the staff of the president's Council of Economic Advisers in 1956. The scale of this involvement with the policy process changed when Samuelson became John Kennedy's adviser during the 1960 presidential campaign and when Solow subsequently joined the Council of Economic Advisers at the request of Walter Heller and James Tobin in 1962.[28] From that moment on, MIT economists engaged more in public debates while insisting on remaining experts devoid of political intentions.[29] Solow formed a close friendship with Columbia sociologist Daniel Bell, who founded the *Public Interest* with Irving Kristol in 1965. Solow's relationship with Bell enabled him to play an important role in the

27. Report from Millikan, February 18, 1964, box 1, AC394.

28. There, he worked on the establishment of formal wage and price "guideposts" to prevent inflation and of tax cuts to stimulate demand.

29. See, in this volume, Giraud's presentation of Samuelson's self-characterization as "middle-of-the-road" and Maas on his war work and subsequent influence on his technical approach to economics.

early editorial line of that journal on economic questions. In the same vein, Samuelson agreed to be the voice of "new economics" in a weekly column for *Newsweek* in 1966, alternating with Friedman and Henry Wallich, who represented the free enterprise and center viewpoints, respectively.[30] This focus on policy was an essential characteristic of the MIT style. If Diamond was meant for MIT, Solow claimed, it was because of "his interest in certain applied problems, especially public finance and fiscal policy. . . . He will contribute to the atmosphere of rigor-with-policy relevance that we have been trying to maintain."[31]

This quotation also shows that, during the sixties, MIT economists increasingly thought of themselves as having a distinctive identity. When Fisher was courted by Harvard in 1966, Solow wrote him that the faculty needed him "to keep the special MIT flavor alive in theory and econometrics." This self-awareness largely derived from interactions—and confrontations—with other intellectual communities. In other words, this MIT identity was as much built from the outside as from the inside. MIT economists were neoclassical, but for Chicago monetarists, they were primarily neo-Keynesians, who held the functioning of markets as flawed, requiring the implementation of macroeconomic, industrial, and antitrust policies. As confrontations became more numerous in academic journals and newspapers and on radio and TV, Solow joked that Friedman could suspect "an organized MIT vendetta" from the "MIT Mafia." They were Keynesians, but for their overseas Cambridge colleagues, they had betrayed John Maynard Keynes's theoretical insights and his methods (see Backhouse's article on the Cambridge controversy, this volume). For in the sixties, it was Cambridge, rather than Harvard, that was MIT's doppelgänger and rival. Spending some time in Britain had been a tradition for MIT faculty and students since Samuelson's visit in 1949. Brown spent a year at Cambridge in 1957; Solow in 1962–63; Fisher and Stiglitz, then graduate students, in 1965; and Diamond in the summer of 1967. In turn, MIT welcomed Frank Hahn in 1956–57, and Amartya Sen and Joan Robinson in 1961. These visits and the significant correspondence on technical progress, the aggregation of capital inputs, and the shape of production functions and the associated impulse to label economists as Keynesian or neoclassical exhibited by Nicholas Kaldor, Robinson, Harry Johnson,

30. When Samuelson stopped writing his column, the *Newsweek* editor replaced him with Lester Thurow, an MIT colleague from the business school.

31. Solow to Brown, May 16, 1966, box 52, folder B4, RSP. On the monetarist versus neo-Keynesian dispute, see Hammond 1996.

Hahn, Samuelson, and Solow helped MIT faculty and students to understand that in this developing controversy, they were considered a distinct and unified intellectual community. While MIT members' methodological and intellectual stances were far from identical (Backhouse, this volume, "The Other Cambridge"), in a published response to Robinson, Samuelson realized that they were identified as an "MIT school." In the same vein, Solow wrote Sen that

> I'm afraid I got a little annoyed in Cambridge last year by the indiscriminate use of "Keynesian" as an adjective meaning "mine" and "neoclassical" to mean "yours." To the extent that "neoclassical" describes the belief that a capitalistic economy tends automatically to full employment, I am not neoclassical and neither is James Meade. To the extent that "neoclassical" means a belief that you need a plausible microeconomics that allows for some kind of near optimizing behavior under whatever market conditions prevail, then it is not in the slightest incompatible with being Keynesian.[32]

Expansion beyond Departmental Boundaries

In these years of public exposure and growing self-awareness, research was not solely conducted at the department. As relationships with the CIS weakened, relationships with the business school flourished, so much so that boundaries between the two institutions gradually faded. The geographic proximity had created a common identity. "It doesn't really matter much whether he works through the Economic Department or the School; we're in the same building," Solow wrote a prospective student in 1963. In 1960 Howard Johnson, newly appointed dean of the business school, announced his intention to "seek their [the economics department's] concurrence for every economics appointment made by the school." Besides Kuh, Abraham Siegel, a labor economist at the department since 1958, also became a joint appointment faculty in 1964, two years after Modigliani had joined the business school.[33] The department's economists found the intellectual atmosphere at Sloan congenial: "Our school of industrial management represents a rather different tradition from the Harvard Business School, more technically oriented, more concerned with training

32. Solow to Sen, October 26, 1964, box 60, folder S7, RSP.

33. Siegel was dean of the business school between 1981 and 1987. He was succeeded by Lester Thurow (PhD Harvard, 1964), also recruited at the department in 1968.

people skilled in analytical methods than in training businessmen," Solow wrote, emphasizing the "quantitative approaches in the theory of the firm" and the "heavy dose of course work in economics" that students would find in the business school's master's degree. Indeed, in the midsixties, 25 percent of the business graduate students were former undergraduate economics majors, and a large number were supervised by economics department faculty. Above all, it was common research interests that drew the department and the business school together. Samuelson shared with Sloan researchers a deep interest in commodity trading, and the idea of using Brownian movement to model stock price variation loomed large in their community at that time. Paul Cootner, an MIT PhD (1953), had returned to the business school in 1959 to teach finance. In 1964 he compiled the work of his colleagues, including Sid Alexander, Richard Eckaus, Hendrik Houthakker (then visiting professor), and Edwin Kuh, on subject of random walks in a book. The following year, Samuelson (1965) published an article in which he formalized the idea that random walks characterize the behavior of an ideal financial market where anticipations are perfect.[34]

By 1965 the MIT graduate school had made its way to the top of US economics department rankings, sharing first place with Harvard. It was the first choice of students earning a Woodrow Wilson or National Science Foundation fellowship, the two main sponsors of graduate studies in those years. No less than George Akerlof, William Nordhaus, Robert Hall, Martin Weitzman, Robert Gordon, Eytan Sheshinski, Joseph Stiglitz (PhDs, 1966–67), and Jagdish Bhagwati (PhD, 1967) were doing graduate work there, all but two with Solow. That year, the word *industrial* was dropped from the title of the graduate course, and most important, course XIV eventually became an undergraduate economics major.

1966–72: Challenges and Reformation

From Synthesis to Disciplinary Fragmentation

The decision to make course XIV an economics major led to a steady rise in enrollments. The number of students willing to study economics

34. Solow to Don Roper, September 19, 1962, box 59, RSP; Solow to H. L. Ryan, November 26, 1962, box 59, RSP; Solow to Vernon Ruttan, April 15, 1963, box 59, RSP. On the ties between the department and the business school, see also PR 1954, 1961 (p. 13). On the history of finance at MIT, see Poitras 2006; Jovanovic 2008; Mehrling 2005; Bernstein 1992, chap. 6; and Fox 2009, chap. 4.

within a curriculum hitherto designed for scientists and engineers doubled in two years, reaching around 150 in 1969. At the same time, the number of undergraduates taking economics courses as part of their scientific or humanities curriculum was around 1,200, after a peak of 1,450 in 1967. Apparently, the graduate school was also flourishing. MIT succeeded in luring some of its best graduate students into faculty positions: besides Diamond, Peter Temin and Bhagwati (PhDs, 1964 and 1967, both with Kindleberger) were recruited in 1967. Robert Hall was director of graduate studies in the early seventies, and Weitzman returned from Yale in 1972. A stream of young economists supplemented them: Harvard labor economist Michael Piore; Miguel Sidrauski, who had worked on the effects of money on long-run growth at Chicago; Northwestern Africanist John Harris; and Cambridge development economist Pranab K. Bardhan all arrived immediately after completing their PhDs in 1967. The same year, Columbia welfare economist Jerome Rothenberg accepted a joint appointment with the Department of City and Regional Planning. Political economist Lester Thurow (PhD Harvard, 1964) and the young Cornell econometrician Robert Engle arrived at MIT in 1969. This rapidly brought the faculty to thirty members in 1972. They were teaching a hundred graduate students, among whom were Avinash Dixit (PhD, 1968) and Stanley Fischer (PhD, 1969), who, like fellow graduate Robert Merton (PhD, 1969), were working on lifetime portfolio choice (Mehrling 2005). Fellow graduates also included Richard Schmalensee and Robert Shiller (PhDs, 1970 and 1972, both with Modigliani). These graduate students were attracted by the strong theoretical sequence offered in macroeconomics and microeconomics, a cutting-edge combination of subjects taught by the old guard as well as the recent additions to the department. In the early seventies, students first took the microeconomics sequence in which Foley, Hall, Samuelson, Solow, Diamond, and Fisher taught price theory, welfare and mathematical economics, uncertainty, linear programming, and general equilibrium. A macroeconomic sequence taught by Solow, Hall, Foley, Modigliani, and Diamond would then introduce students to Keynesian static macroeconomics, intertemporal general equilibrium and financial markets, inflation and Phillips curves, econometrics models of the United States, monetary economics, and fiscal economics. The econometrics sequence had also been redesigned in 1968, with the creation of separate graduate and undergraduate courses, with Fisher teaching theoretical econometrics and Kuh introducing students to applied econometrics with the help of the TROLL (Time-shared Reactive On-Line Laboratory) software that he was developing.[35]

Yet from the midsixties on, MIT economists experienced a period of self-doubt, beginning with the lost battle to recruit Kenneth Arrow. His decision to go to Harvard, in 1966, was a huge blow for the faculty. Solow, Fisher, Domar, and Brown exchanged incredulous letters.[36] Harvard further tried to tempt away Fisher and Carl Christian von Weizsäcker, a promising German mathematical economist who was spending every spring term at MIT. At a moment when the termination of the Woodrow Wilson fellowship was announced, doubts about the financial attractiveness of the Institute were on everyone's mind. In the 1967 *Reports to the President*, Brown complained about the "aggressive response by other institutions in the financial support offered to graduate students and in the retention and expansion of faculty." In the same move, some economists expressed concerns over MIT's ability to keep up with new theoretical developments. The neoclassical synthesis was increasingly shattered (see Blanchard 2008). The continuous attacks against Friedman and monetarism, Samuelson's and Solow's questioning of the natural rate of unemployment hypothesis, and Peter Temin's (1976) critical examination of Friedman and Schwartz's *Monetary History* did not curb the spread of monetarist ideas in a context of stagflation, and the emerging theory of rational expectations was an even greater threat to come. The macroeconometric forecasting model developed by Modigliani in association with Ando (then at the University of Pennsylvania) and the Federal Reserve Board between 1967 and 1973, aimed at bringing together the work of several MIT economists (Brown and Ando's study of countercyclical fiscal policy, Kareken and Solow's analysis of lags, etc.), was not as successful as expected. From Israel, Fisher wrote Solow: "One view of our depart-

35. "Committee on the Undergraduate Economic Program: Final Report with Recommendations," 1968 or 1969, box 2, AC394. "Subcommittee on Graduate Subjects of Instruction," Brown to G. C. Williams, February 1, 1968, box 2, AC394. "Economics Graduate Students," Eckaus, January 29, 1968, box 2, AC394. "Memorandum from Franklin Fisher," January 24, 1968, box 2, AC394; "Committee on Curricula," Brown to R. R. Randlett, February 1, 1968, box 2, AC394. "A Proposal for Reorganizing the Graduate Program," Hall, January 1, 1971, box 2, AC394; "The Graduate Program in Economics, 1972–1973," box 2, AC394.

36. Arrow explained that "there are two basic reasons for my final decision. One has to do with my perhaps somewhat dilettantish intellectual interests. I like to be close to historians, political scientists and sociologists as well as economists, and apart from strictly professional interests, I have always enjoyed close association with people in the humanities. Doubtless these interests will detract from my work as an economist but I like them and need them" (Arrow to Solow, March 30, 1968, box 52, RSP).

ment (expressed in an extreme and biased way) is as follows. You and Paul are heavily committed ideologically to the neo-classical synthesis (whatever that is). As a result, we are unable to recognize good unorthodox work and future development in economics (and especially theory) will largely come from outside MIT."[37]

Solow's response to Fisher emphasized the promises of the young recruits: "Peter Diamond and Peter Temin will help a lot. Miguel Sidrauski may develop very well. . . . The department has agreed to go for another econometrician if we can find a young star. . . . I think the prospects are good that we can remain the Duffy Tavern's of economics, where the elite meet to eat." Indeed, even as the dream of building a neoclassical synthesis was encountering serious difficulty, these young economists found that the "Bob Solow view" of doing economics (Foley 2004, 192) and the "toy models" developed by Samuelson in the previous decades were suitable for the development of a range of subfields. A thriving area was public economics. After Samuelson's 1954 article on public expenditures, Brown had kept the interest alive at MIT. When Diamond, whose interest in optimal taxation was aroused by teaching an undergraduate course in that field at Berkeley (Diamond 2007), came back to the Institute, he and Brown set up a graduate sequence together. The next summer, Diamond began to work on optimal income taxation with James Mirrlees during a summer stay at Cambridge, and by the end of 1967 they had written their articles on the production efficiency result and the extension of the Ramsey rule to include distributional concerns (Diamond and Mirrlees 1971a, 1971b). Their use of duality set a new research agenda for the emerging field of public economics (Atkinson and Stiglitz 1980). With Foley and Sidrauski interested in fiscal and monetary policy, Thurow analyzing poverty, crime, and manpower, and Piore studying the links between manpower, training, and the labor market, by the late sixties MIT was hosting a substantial group of public economists. To assess the impact of monetary and fiscal policies on growth, several of them were trying to integrate money into consumption functions with the help of overlapping generations models. Diamond had taken up Samuelson's (1958) consumption-loan model to enrich growth models, and the idea was further extended to multiasset accumulation by Shell, Stiglitz, and Sidrauski (1969). Thanks to the effort of Jerome Rothenberg, urban economics also became a major subfield by the early seventies. Two urban economists, Ronald Grieson

37. Fisher to Solow, March 30, 1967, box 55, RSP; Solow to Fisher, April 6, 1967, box 55, RSP.

and Duncan McRae (a joint appointment with the Department of Urban Studies and Planning), were recruited, and several public economists and econometricians, in particular Robert Engle, participated in associated projects. As relations with the CIS were growing increasingly cold, the department was developing its own brand of development economics. Baghwati conducted research on exchange controls and liberalization, and he was also editing a readings book on foreign aid. Domar was in charge of the analysis of communist countries (PR 1970). Rosenstein-Rodan and Eckaus produced case studies of Chile, and John Harris pursued his study of East Africa. These research programs were directly reflected in the evolution of the curriculum. Under the leadership of Rothenberg, the department developed a teaching collaboration with the transportation system division of the School of Engineering, and urban economics eventually became a new doctoral field. A graduate sequence in development economics was set up under the leadership of Eckaus and Bhagwati, with the participation of Domar and Weitzman, while Temin and Kindleberger launched a course in economic history. The fifteen theses Adelman directed in that period also reflected a sustained interest in industrial economics.

The Challenge of Relevance

The challenges of the sixties were not only driven by scientific considerations. Like other universities, MIT had to face the social agitation resulting from the Vietnam War, the civil rights movement, the feminist movement, and the rise of the New Left. In 1966 the ties between the CIS and the CIA came under public scrutiny. During a meeting of the International Studies Association, Senator Wayne Morse (1966) warned his audience against blind confidence in purportedly ideologically free academic research in political science and international relations, explicitly targeting the CIS. Journalists from the *New York Times*, the *Boston Herald*, and the *Nation* relayed the information. CIS alumnus Marglin and MIT graduate student Tom Weisskopf were working in Delhi at that time, and the Indian officials they were working with immediately terminated their relationships with them. MIT economists, who had hoped to recruit those two promising development economists, interpreted their subsequent move to Harvard as a consequence of this "unhappy Indian accident." Worried that their objectivity would be doubted, the department's faculty also issued a collective statement calling for a reexamination of the funding of economics at MIT and asking for the termination of the CIA contracts. Adelman complained that his research on energy, already suspect in those European countries where oil was a strategic commodity, would be further hindered by the association of MIT with the CIA. Domar similarly pointed out that his long-standing association with Russia and various Western economies would be compromised. As the Vietnam War escalated, the MIT radical students and faculty hid, for several months, a drafted student who had gone AWOL (Nisonoff, quoted in Mata and Lee 2007). In November 1968 demonstrators invaded the Hermann Building where the CIS was located. The following spring, classes were suspended in the wake of the demonstrations against the Cambodian invasion. In the name of the MIT faculty and graduate students, Solow drafted a letter to Paul McCracken, chairman of the Council of Economic Advisers. He claimed that they were "horrified, saddened and angered by the Administration's desperate decision to invade Cambodia" and urged him to "oppose any continuation of the war, both publicly and in your private dealings with the president."[38]

Stagflation and the energy crisis soon added to the social troubles, resulting in a direct challenge to the economics undergraduate and graduate curricula. The New Left was on the rise, and in September 1968 radical economists founded the Union for Radical Political Economics. At MIT some instructors began to question the content of the introductory economics courses as well as Samuelson's *Economics*, arguing that they did not provide an introduction to Marxist economics and that reading material from Robert Heilbroner, John Kenneth Galbraith, and Paul Baran and Paul Sweezy should be introduced into the curriculum. Students repeatedly circulated petitions asking for new types of evaluations rewarding creativity. They criticized the compartmentalization of courses and complained about the view that graduate students were merely "an input into a process the goal of which is to maintain the prestige of the MIT economics department and to spread the adoption of its approach to economics." Solow's claim that the MIT style was oriented toward policy relevance notwithstanding, MIT programs were perceived as too theoretically oriented and remote from real-world issues. Stanley Fischer (2004)

38. "MIT and the CIA, again," Ed Kuh, June 14, 1966, box 1, AC394. "A Statement of the Relationships between the Center for International Studies at the Massachusetts Institute of Technology and the Central Intelligence Agency," undated. Kindleberger to D. L. M. Blackmer, February 10, 1967, box 1, AC394.

remembers that in the late sixties, it was Friedman's Chicago, not MIT, that was seen as the right place to apply economics to real issues (see also Shiller 2006, 655). Underlying these protests was a demand for greater relevance that was spreading throughout the profession. Emerging from economists' promises to focus on a few basic economics principles and their various applications to real-world issues, "issue-oriented" introductory courses were implemented throughout the country (Fleury 2012). At MIT, attempts were made to revise the content of the two introductory economics courses. In 1974 Temin wrote in a memorandum that the courses should be "oriented toward problems of current interest—such as pollution regulation, the role of women in the labor force, government regulation of industry, the energy crisis, the current food shortage, income distribution, the monetarist debate, wage and price controls." Also, it was decided that micro would precede macro so as to introduce economics through those problems that are most apparent to the noneconomist and in particular to the engineer. Also, from 1969 on, supplementary readings were introduced to reading lists: articles from *Challenge*, the *Public Interest*, and *Public Policy*, as well as articles by Galbraith. The study of these articles was meant to "improve the students' understanding of econ concepts by showing him applications and provide factual background for the analysis of economic problems." Also, the use of problem sets was generalized.[39]

To meet the demand for greater relevance, MIT economists also turned back to their engineering tradition. On the model of the sustained collaboration with the Department of Urban Studies and Planning, Adelman and Paul Joskow (PhD Yale, 1972) collaborated with the newly created Energy Laboratory to conduct studies on the oil and nuclear industries and on the regulation of public utilities (PR 1974, 226, 337–40), and two joint appointments in 1974 brought the number of economic faculty members with appointments in other departments to eleven out of thirty-two: Ann Friedlaender served jointly with the Department of Civil Engineering, and Lance J. Taylor jointly with the Department of Nutrition and Food Science (PR 1974, 227). The interest of the Institute as a whole and the broad concerns of engineers therefore influenced the research interests of economists at MIT (PR 1969).

39. Letter to students, February 1, 1971, box 2, AC394; "Committee on the Undergraduate Economic Program: Final Report with Recommendations," 1968 or 1969, box 2, AC394; "Curriculum Development—14.01 and 14.02—Summer 1969," box 2, AC394. "14.01–14.02 Proposed Revisions," by Peter Temin, October 18, 1974, box 1, AC394.

Conclusion: A Surviving MIT Style of Doing Economics?

By the time the social troubles had calmed down, MIT had normalized its curricula, recruitment processes, and research programs. Although the Institute's unique identity was apparent in the development of certain subfields, the department's evolution was now governed by the same forces influencing other leading departments in the country. The undergraduate and graduate programs had lost their specificity, while the use of mathematical tools had been accepted as the essence of economists' methodology. Attempts to build intellectual systems such as the neoclassical synthesis (but also general equilibrium theory or simultaneous equations systems in econometrics) were being challenged everywhere, and MIT was becoming less identifiable with a specific intellectual content.

Today's observer is thus left with a paradox. From the inside as well as from the outside, MIT economics is still endowed with a distinctive identity. Yet the features it is associated with—technicality, a Keynesian or at least interventionist bent, the use of toy models to draw policy-relevant conclusions—seem to describe modern economics as it is done everywhere. This paradox is a direct consequence of the agenda set by these first overlapping generations of MIT economists, from Solow and Samuelson to Diamond and Fisher: to devise and spread a "new economics." This story has shown how new modeling strategies emerged equally from everyday discussions in cars, classrooms, and corridors; were enabled and reinforced by the peculiar demands of an engineering institute; spread through published writings; and immediately communicated in constantly evolving curricula and textbooks, public testimonies and advice, and newspaper columns. It is such a system that explains the dominance of MIT economics today.

References

Atkinson, A., and J. Stiglitz. 1980. *Lectures in Public Economics*. New York: McGraw-Hill.

Backhouse, R. 2012. "Paul Samuelson, RAND, and the Cowles Commission Activity Conference, 1947–1949." Working paper, version 2, October.

Bernstein, P. 1992. *Capital Ideas: The Improbable Origins of Modern Wall Street*. Hoboken, N.J.: John Wiley & Sons.

Blackmer, D. L. M. 2002. *The MIT Center for International Studies: The Founding Years, 1951–1969*. Cambridge, Mass.: MIT Center for International Studies.

Blanchard, O. 2008. "Neoclassical Synthesis." In *The New Palgrave Dictionary of Economics*, edited by S. N. Durlauf and L. E. Blum. 2nd ed. London: Palgrave Macmillan.

Brown, C., and R. Solow. 1983. *Paul Samuelson and Modern Economic Theory*. New York: McGraw-Hill.

Colander, D. 1998. "Confessions of an Economic Gadfly." In *Passion and Craft: Economists at Work*, edited by M. Szenberg, 93–107. Ann Arbor: University of Michigan Press.

Cootner, P., ed. 1964. *The Random Character of Stock Market Prices*. Cambridge, Mass.: MIT Press.

Diamond, P. 1965. "National Debt in a Neoclassical Growth Model." *American Economic Review* 55:1126–50.

———. 2007. "An Interview with Peter Diamond." *Macroeconomic Dynamics* 11:543–65.

———. 2010. "Interview." MIT150 Oral History Project. mit150.mit.edu/infinite-history-a-z.

Diamond, P., and J. Mirrlees. 1971a. "Optimal Taxation and Public Production I: Production Efficiency." *American Economic Review* 61 (1): 8–27.

———. 1971b. "Optimal Taxation and Public Production II: Tax Rules." *American Economic Review* 61 (3): 261–78.

Dorfman, R., P. Samuelson, and R. Solow. 1958. *Linear Programming and Economic Analysis*. New York: McGraw-Hill.

Feiwel, G. R. 1982. Introduction to *Samuelson and Neoclassical Economics*, edited by G. R. Feiwel, 1–29. Boston: Kluwer.

Fischer, S. 2004. "An Interview with Stanley Fischer," by O. Blanchard. *Macroeconomic Dynamics* 9 (2): 244–62.

Fleury, J.-B. 2012. "The Evolving Notion of Relevance: A Historical Perspective to the 'Economics-Made-Fun' Movement." *Journal of Economic Methodology* 19 (4): 427–37.

Foley, D. 2004. "Duncan K. Foley." In *The Changing Face of Economics: Conversations with Cutting Edge Economists*, edited by D. Colander, R. Holt, and J. B. Rosser. Ann Arbor: University of Michigan Press.

Fourcade, M. 2009. *Economists and Societies: Discipline and Profession in the United States, Britain, and France, 1890s to 1990s*. Princeton, N.J.: Princeton University Press.

Fox, J. 2009. *The Myth of the Rational Market: A History of Risk, Reward, and Delusion on Wall Street*. New York: Justin Fox Harper Business.

Friedman, M., and D. Meiselman. 1963. "The Relative Stability of Monetary Velocity and the Investment Multiplier in the United States, 1897–1958." In *Commission on Money and Credit: Stabilization Policies*, 165–268. Englewood Cliffs, N.J.: Prentice-Hall.

Gilman, N. 2003. *Mandarins of the Future: Modernization Theory in Cold War America*. Baltimore: Johns Hopkins University Press.

Hammond, J. D. 1996. *Theory and Measurement: Causality Issues in Milton Friedman's Monetary Economics*. Cambridge: Cambridge University Press.

——. 1999. *The Legacy of Milton Friedman as Teacher.* Cheltenham: Elgar.

Johnston, B. 1998. "Social Relations Department at Harvard: A Case Study in Hegemony and Disintegration." *American Sociologist* 29 (3): 26–42.

Jovanovic, F. 2008. "The Construction of the Canonical History of Financial Economics." *History of Political Economy* 40 (2): 213–42.

Kareken, J., and R. M. Solow. 1963. "Lags in Monetary Policy." In *Stabilization Policies: Commission on Money and Credit*, 3–7. Englewood Cliffs, N.J.: Prentice-Hall.

Khurana, R. 2007. *From Higher Aims to Hired Hands: The Social Transformation of American Business Schools and the Unfulfilled Promise of Management as a Profession.* Princeton, N.J.: Princeton University Press.

Krugman, P. [1995]. "Incidents from My Career." www.princeton.edu/~pkrugman/incidents.html.

Lecuyer, C. 1992. "The Making of a Science Based Technological University: Karl Compton, James Killian, and the Reform of MIT, 1930–1957." *Historical Studies in the Physical and Biological Sciences* 23 (1): 153–80.

Mata, T., and F. S. Lee. 2007. "The Role of Oral History in the Historiography of Heterodox Economics." In *Economists' Lives: Biography and Autobiography in the History of Economics*, edited by E. R. Weintraub and E. L. Forget. *History of Political Economy* 39 (supplement): 154–71.

McCloskey, D. 2002. "Other Things Equal: Samuelsonian Economics." *Eastern Economic Journal* 28 (3): 425–30.

Mehrling, P. 2005. *Fischer Black and the Revolutionary Idea of Finance.* Hoboken, N.J.: John Wiley & Sons.

Merton, R. 1997. "Autobiography." The Sveriges Riksbank Prize in Economic Sciences in Memory of Alfred Nobel. nobelprize.org/nobel_prizes/economics/laureates/1997/merton-autobio.html.

Mirowski, P. 1989. *More Heat Than Light: Economics as Social Physics, Physics as Nature's Economics.* Cambridge: Cambridge University Press.

——. 2006. "Twelve Theses concerning the History of Postwar Neoclassical Price Theory." In *Agreement on Demand: Consumer Theory in the Twentieth Century*, edited by P. Mirowski and D. W. Hands. *History of Political Economy* 38 (supplement): 343–79.

Modigliani, F., and A. Ando. 1965. "The Relative Stability of Monetary Stability and the Investment Multiplier." *American Economic Review* 55 (4): 693–728.

Morse, W. 1966. "Dangers in Government Sponsorship of Research on Foreign Policy and Foreign Areas." *Background* 10 (2): 123–30.

Poitras, G., ed. 2006. *Pioneers of Financial Economics.* Vol. 2. Cheltenham: Elgar.

Rostow, W. W. 1960. *The Stages of Economic Growth: A Non-Communist Manifesto.* Cambridge: Cambridge University Press.

Samuelson, P. A. 1938. "A Note on the Pure Theory of Consumer's Behaviour." *Economica* 5 (17): 61–71.

——. 1947. *Foundations of Economic Analysis.* Cambridge, Mass.: Harvard University Press.

——. 1948a. *Economics: An Introductory Analysis.* New York: McGraw-Hill.

——. 1948b. "International Trade and the Equalization of Factor Prices." *Economic Journal* 58 (230): 163–84.
——. 1954. "The Pure Theory of Public Expenditure." *Review of Economics and Statistics* 36 (4): 387–89.
——. 1958. "An Exact Consumption-Loan Model of Interest with or without the Social Contrivance of Money." *Journal of Political Economy* 66 (6): 467–82.
——. 1965. "Proof That Properly Anticipated Prices Fluctuate Randomly." *Industrial Management Review* 6 (2): 41–49.
——. 2007. "Interview." MIT150 Oral History Project. mit150.mit.edu/infinite-history/paul-samuelson.
Samuelson, P., and R. Solow. 1960. "The Problem of Achieving and Maintaining a Stable Price Level: Analytical Aspects of Anti-Inflation Policy." *American Economic Review* 50 (2): 177–94.
Shell, K. 2001. "An Interview with Karl Shell," by Stephen E. Spear. *Macroeconomic Dynamics* 5:701–41.
Shell, K., J. Stiglitz, and M. Sidrauski. 1969. "Capital Gains, Incomes, and Saving." *Review of Economic Studies* 36 (1): 15–26.
Shiller, R. 2006. "An Interview with Robert J. Shiller," by John Y. Campbell. *Macroeconomic Dynamics* 8:649–83.
Skousen, M. 1997. "The Perseverance of Paul Samuelson's *Economics*." *Journal of Economic Perspectives* 11 (2): 137–52.
Solow, R. 1956. "A Contribution to the Theory of Economic Growth." *Quarterly Journal of Economics* 70 (1): 65–94.
——. 1957. "Technical Change and the Aggregate Production Function." *Review of Economics and Statistics* 39 (3): 312–20.
——. 2006. "Interview." In *Modern Macroeconomics: Its Origins, Development, and Current State*, edited by Brian Snowdon and Howard R. Vane, 660–72. Cheltenham: Elgar.
——. 2007. "Interview." MIT150 Oral History Project. mit150.mit.edu/infinite-history/robert-m-solow.
Stiglitz, J. 2001. "Autobiography." The Sveriges Riksbank Prize in Economic Sciences in Memory of Alfred Nobel. nobelprize.org/nobel_prizes/economics/laureates/2001/stiglitz-autobio.html.
Temin, P. 1976. *Did Monetary Forces Cause the Great Depression?* New York: Norton.
Van Horn, R., P. Mirowski, and T. A. Stapleford, eds. 2011. *Building Chicago Economics: New Perspectives on the History of America's Most Powerful Economics Program*. Cambridge: Cambridge University Press.
Weintraub, E. R. 1991. *Stabilizing Dynamics: Constructing Economic Knowledge*. Cambridge: Cambridge University Press.

MIT's Openness to Jewish Economists

E. Roy Weintraub

MIT emerged from "nowhere" in the 1930s to its place as one of the three or four most important sites for economic research by the mid-1950s. Other articles in this volume provide a variety of narratives of how this occurred. Here I point out that the immediate postwar period saw a collapse—in some places slower, in some places faster—of the barriers to the hiring of Jewish faculty in American colleges and universities. And more than any other elite private or public university, particularly Ivy League universities, MIT welcomed Jewish economists.[1]

Correspondence may be addressed to E. Roy Weintraub, Department of Economics, Duke University, Box 90097, Durham, NC 27708-0097; e-mail: erw@duke.edu. Earlier versions of this article were presented in 2012 at Berlin's Humboldt University and Duke University, and in 2013 at HES/AEA meetings in San Diego. In addition to the *HOPE* 2013 conferees, particularly Roger E. Backhouse, the author received very helpful comments from Lorraine Daston, Paul Davidson, Till Düppe, David Hollinger, Evelyn Forget, Tiago Mata, Robert Solow, the late Barbara Solow, and Glen Weyl.

1. There is no substantial article or monograph-length discussion of anti-Semitism and the economics profession. For the most part, this necessitates reliance not only on secondary sources beyond those familiar to historians of economics but also on sketchy primary sources. A more detailed study than this one would examine different US economics faculties and their histories, and the histories of their institutions with respect to anti-Semitism. Thus the present discussion, although it will in passing contrast the MIT experience with that of other economics departments, is by no means systematic in scope.

History of Political Economy 46 (annual suppl.) DOI 10.1215/00182702-2716109

Another Narrative

Through 2012, twenty-nine of the first sixty-eight Nobel laureates in economics (43 percent) were Jewish, as were 63 percent of the John Bates Clark Medal winners. One might suppose that historians of economics had interrogated this startling fact. Feminist historians of economics have long written about the underrepresentation of women economists. Afro-American historians of economics have written freely and effectively about the underrepresentation of Afro-American economists. One might reasonably expect, by symmetry, that historians would be as interested in the *over*representation of a particular identifiable group. This, however, has not occurred.

The difficulty is real and reflects a strange sensibility. The first economist to write about these matters was Thorstein Veblen (1919) in a paper called "The Intellectual Pre-eminence of Jews in Modern Europe" in *Political Science Quarterly*. Veblen sought to explain what he regarded as the overrepresentation of "the chosen people" in the sciences and in fields of scholarship and intellectual inquiry. His own argument was that habits of scholarship and learning within the community set the stage for young Jews, breaking free of the ties of their established diaspora communities, and living among the gentiles, to bring a skeptical and inquiring mind-set to the intellectual problems on which they worked, and that mind-set was particularly suited to the kinds of scientific explanations that the modern age seemed to need.

Since Veblen, twentieth-century discussion of the place of Jews in the learned professions has proceeded without any contributions from historians of economics. In contrast, intellectual historians such as David Hollinger have examined questions about the role of Jews, and anti-Semitism, in the academic community in the United States. Hollinger's (1993, 1996, 2004, 2006) discussions about anti-Semitism in the pre–World War II period and the secularization of universities from the war onward, which permitted the rapid influx of Jewish scholars after World War II, are well known. Intellectual historians, and historians of the university, have seen fit to raise these questions and to seek both data and insight. Social scientists, writing in primarily Jewish publications, have written about the role of Jews in American universities. The works by Seymour Martin Lipset and Everett Carl Ladd Jr. (1971) and Lewis S. Feuer (1982) are typical. These studies are apparently unknown to historians of economics. Historians of physics like Daniel Kevles ([1971] 1995) have for many years written about the place of Jews in their own histories of scientific communities.

If one examines the work of economists and historians of economics, I am aware of exactly one article written by a sometime historian of economics, Mark Perlman, that addresses this subject, and that article appeared not in an economics journal or a history of economics journal but in the journal *Judaism*. Titled "Jews and Contributions to Economics: A Bicentennial Review," Perlman's (1996) article was surely a study both from the personal and from the historical dimension, as his father, Wisconsin's Selig Perlman, was an extremely important figure in the history of the American economics profession. Mark Perlman takes up a number of issues, including the anti-Semitism that characterized the American economics community through World War II. He has tales of this kind of prejudice as representing the exclusionary nature of the economics profession. Often he recounts anecdotes told by the subjects of the exclusion themselves.

Roger Backhouse, in this volume, deconstructs the famous story of how Paul Samuelson, a newly appointed Harvard instructor with an offer of an assistant professorship from MIT, was not encouraged about his chances to secure a similar position at Harvard in the next year or two. Harvard's departing chairman Harold Burbank's dislike of Jews was well known—he also disliked mathematical economics and Keynesian economics,[2] which disqualified Samuelson three times over.

Or consider a personal story. My father, Sidney Weintraub, who had been teaching at St. Johns University (then) in Brooklyn, was recruited in late 1949 by both Indiana University and the University of Pennsylvania. At that time Penn had half of one Jew, Simon Kuznets, on its tenured economics faculty, since his appointment was shared with statistics (Weyl 2011). As my father was given the permanent appointment at Pennsylvania in fall 1951 after one year as a visiting professor, Kuznets was already negotiating with Johns Hopkins University to join its faculty. It was in this period that Irving Kravis, a student of Kuznets's, was considered for a tenured appointment to the economics department at Penn *in anticipation of Kuznets's departure*.[3] The department had gone from one-half to one and one-half tenured Jews with my father, but adding another was seen as moving too quickly by some, even though Kravis's appointment was finally approved.[4]

2. Robert Solow pointed out that this meant that Samuelson's, and his, future at Harvard was dim (letter to the author, October 2013).

3. Kuznets, as is well known, left Johns Hopkins for Harvard very quickly because the Johns Hopkins president, a notorious anti-Semite, did not want Kuznets on his faculty.

4. There were a few Jewish faculty members in other departments of the Wharton School at that time, one of whom was Joseph Rose of the transportation department.

This episode appears, like many other episodes, as a curiosity when it surfaces in one or another account. But there has been no systematic collection of such accounts, no systematic examination of the exclusionary habits of the economics profession through the end of the interwar period. The mathematics community has not been shy in welcoming historians of mathematics who explore these topics (Reingold 1988). Why have historians of economics walked away from such matters? One would have expected this to be well known and taught in almost all histories of economics and lectures in history of economics courses. It of course has not been so treated.

Anti-Semitism and the Universities in the 1930s

Before the Second World War, Jews were hardly to be found on the faculties of American colleges and universities. In a comprehensive study of Jewish academics in the United States, which appeared in 1971 in the *American Jewish Year Book*, Seymour Martin Lipset and Everett Carl Ladd Jr. (1971, 90–91) wrote:

> Overt anti-Jewish prejudice within academia seemingly was at a high point in the 1920s and 1930s, when large numbers of the children of immigrants began to enter college. This pressure led many schools to impose quotas on the admission of Jews to both undergraduate and professional schools. A. Lawrence Lowell, as president of Harvard, and Nicholas Murray Butler, then president of Columbia, openly defended Jewish quotas. And as late as 1945 Ernest M. Hopkins, then president of Dartmouth, justified the use of a [Jewish] quota at his institution on the grounds that "Dartmouth is a Christian college founded for the Christianization of its students."

Quotas for Jewish students emerged in the 1920s as applications of Jews to Ivy League schools exploded. Immigrant children competed for access to the elite schools. The College Board examination and the high school transcript had been the tools by which applications were accepted or rejected. Thus the schools changed the rules. As is well known (Karabel 2005), Harvard, Yale, and Princeton began using "a good character" and "leadership ability" as admissions requirements. How to assess these attributes? Interview the student applicants and determine just how Jewish they looked and sounded. German Jews, good; Sephardim, good; Ashkenazi—

not so good. Nothing needed to be written down in explanation of the rejection to the applicant, although as Jerome Karabel found, the admissions records from that period revealed exactly what was happening.

> These restrictions carried over even more intensely to faculty appointments. Ludwig Lewisohn reported in his *Memoirs* how he was prevented from teaching English; Edward Sapir was told by his graduate-school professors that as a Jew he could not expect an appointment and would have to go to Canada. Lionel Trilling recalled in an article in *Commentary* that he was the first to be appointed to the English Department in Columbia; the Harvard Law School did not appoint another Jew after Felix Frankfurter until 1939. . . . The City College of New York became one of the first schools to open its doors to Jews, but even CCNY was charged with discrimination at the beginning of the 1930s. (Lipset and Ladd 1971, 90–91)

Even accounting for the historical connection of many colleges and universities, particularly the elite schools, to religious denominations, the low number of Jewish faculty is startling. In his article on the social history of Jewish academics in the United States, Lewis S. Feuer (1982, 455) pointed out that "by the mid-twenties there were still probably less than 100 Jews among the college and university professors in the liberal arts and science faculties in the United States." He went on to quote from a 1927 article that had appeared in a Yale undergraduate publication, the *Reflex*:

> With very few exceptions, the Jewish university professor in America is non-existent. Of course, every major American university will point out that it has one or two Jewish professors. For instance, Yale, Princeton, Chicago University, the University of Wisconsin, Johns Hopkins, Michigan University, and the Universities of Texas and Georgia each have one: Harvard has 3; Berkeley 2; Columbia 2; St. Louis, 5; New York University, none; College of the City of New York, 4 and so forth. (S. M. Melamed, quoted in Feuer 1982, 455)

Feuer's article is a long and detailed examination of interwar anti-Semitism. He argued that even in New York City, home to the largest concentration of Jews in the United States,

> as late as April, 1930, the institution which had the largest Jewish student body in the world had not a single Jewish professor. That institution was not the City College of New York which had in monumental

> sentimentality been called the internal "proletarian Harvard." Rather it was the down-town Washington Square College of New York University, where 93% of the seven thousand students were Jews, 8% more than the City College. If all the departments were included in the enumeration, there were estimated to be more than fifteen thousand Jews at the downtown N.Y.U.—the world's largest undergraduate body of Jews. Yet in the entire college, the writer for the *Menorah Journal* could find only 8 Jewish teachers of whom 7 were assistants not destined for promotion. The one exception owed his job to his chairman who with remarkable tactical skill had managed to prevent a meeting between the instructor and the chancellor. (455–56)

Hiring economics faculty required vigilance about "Jewishness." Chicago was not immune to such practices. In a letter to Chicago's chairman, L. G. Marshall,[5] Harvard's Allyn Young recommended a man who was first in his Harvard class, who was "tops in erudition and cleverness," and who wrote a brilliant PhD thesis. He was said to be "loyal and a good and well-liked teacher of undergraduates." But "now you will ask, what's wrong? His name is A. W. Marget and he is one of the chosen people. More than that he looks it. . . . You might do worse than take him on a year's trial." Marget went to Minnesota.

For the most important economics faculty in New York, matters were no different. Eli Ginzberg (1990, 15) recalled that in the mid-1920s, the Columbia economics department "decided to add a theorist and the choice narrowed down to Jacob Viner or John M. Clark, both at the time of the University of Chicago. [Although Clark was hired, it was claimed, on his merits,] . . . one [cannot] discount the University's ambivalence about Jews (Viner was a Jew)." Yet after around 1930, Columbia began to change, if only slowly at the beginning of that decade. The economics department hired Joseph Dorfman in 1931. It replaced E. R. A. Seligman in 1930 with Leo Wolman, who was an official with the Amalgamated Clothing Workers' Union and the National Bureau of Economic Research. It also had graduate students in the late 1930s like Moses Abramowitz and students of Harold Hotelling like Milton Friedman and Kenneth Arrow. Columbia was not unique: "Jewish professors on university campuses in all subjects were estimated in 1935 as under 500" (Shapiro 1964, 380n116). And then the European émigrés arrived.

5. Young to Marshall, February 8, 1927, box 38, folder 1, University of Chicago Economics Department Archive.

Jewish Émigré Scholars

Albert Einstein and John von Neumann were more pulled than pushed to the United States by huge salaries and no teaching offered them by the Institute for Advanced Studies in Princeton in the early 1930s. In the period from Adolf Hitler's accession to the German chancellorship in 1933 and the first wave of restrictions on Jews, through the passage of the Nuremberg Laws in 1935, which deprived Jews of citizenship, and ending with the *Kristallnacht* pogrom of November 1938, the stream of Jewish scholars seeking to emigrate increased continuously. Adding to the flow was the *Anschluss* in Austria in March 1938 and the resulting elimination of Jews from public life and Viennese educational institutions.

The story of the effect of the émigrés on American science is well known (Rider 1984). The later role of physicists like Enrico Fermi, Léo Szilárd, Edward Teller, Stanislaw Ulam, and others on the Manhattan project made the refugee story vivid: "Between 1933 and 1941, more than a hundred of these [émigrés] joined the ranks of American physicists" (Weiner 1969, 190–91). Certainly the fact that physics was an international discipline, like mathematics, meant that the refugees were familiar with many American physicists before they arrived. Unlike economics, the natural and mathematical sciences were not shaped by national boundaries. One could more comfortably welcome those whose work was similar to one's own. There was more acceptance in the 1930s of hiring émigré Jews in the science and technology fields than there was in the social sciences and humanities. The story of the émigré economists was first addressed in the Austrian case by Earlene Craver and Axel Leijonhufvud (1987) and Harald Hagemann and Claus-Dieter Krohn (1999) for German-speaking economists more generally, as well as by Fred Scherer (2000), although stories of particular individuals in biographies and memoirs (e.g., Franco Modigliani, Karl Menger, Oskar Morgenstern) make up a distinct genre. Following the lead of England, where Lionel Robbins and William Beveridge were actively seeking to bring refugee scholars to universities, in the United States such efforts were loosely coordinated. Of special importance in this rescue operation was the Rockefeller Foundation, which had, in economics, been supporting a number of centers in Europe doing research on business cycles. Its close connection with these more "scientific" economists, bringing them to the United States on traveling fellowships, for instance, provided the foundation's officers with good intelligence on the deteriorating situation in Germany and Austria and other countries, especially for Jewish scholars. It also accounts for the greater than usual mathematical training of many of the émigré economists (Jacob Marschak, Tjalling Koopmans, Abraham Wald, Menger, Morgenstern, Gerhard Tintner, William Fellner, etc.).

Since some of the victims of the Nazi purges had worked under fellowships and grants from the Rockefeller Foundation, a certain moral pressure for action was inescapable. Joseph Schumpeter of Harvard made an appeal on behalf of Jacob Marschak, the "most brilliant" scholar on his list of displaced economics professors, but Schumpeter added that "all of them have on the one hand had strong claims to human sympathy and would on the other be very useful acquisitions to any university" (letter from Schumpeter to Rockefeller Foundation, April 19, 1933, quoted in Lamberti 2006, 162).

These efforts led, over the 1930s, to the movement of some Jewish scholars into irregular and short-term positions in schools that had been closed to Jewish faculty for decades. For instance, at Harvard the astronomer Harlow Shapley (father of the game theorist Lloyd Shapley) worked tirelessly to gather names on petitions to the Harvard administration, and the Harvard Corporation, to provide refugee scholars with some kind, any kind, of appointment to permit them to establish their scholarly careers in the United States, and thus after a few years to be able to gain regular academic positions at Harvard or elsewhere.

> By the fall of 1939, Harvard had appointed 16 émigré professors to permanent faculty positions and 7 in other regular faculty positions. Shapley was successful in convincing the administration to allow 14 jobless refugee scholars, who were in transit or close to the age of retirement, the use of the university's facilities without faculty status. The Harvard Corporation agreed to their appointment as "research associates" on the condition that their stipends would come from outside funds. Shapley raised the money through appeals to the wealthy Petschek and Warburg families and other Jews. (Lamberti 2006, 174)

Thus over the 1930s, more and more Jewish refugees were assisted in relocating their scholarly activities to the United States. "The test for the success of the programs of the Rockefeller Foundation and Emergency Committee was the progress made by their grantees in obtaining tenured professorships. . . . Between 1933 and 1945, the [separate and separately run] Emergency Committee gave grants to 145 colleges and universities, which subsidized in part the faculty salaries of 277 exiled scholars, of whom 207 came from Germany and 31 from Austria" (177).

An unintended consequence of these assistance programs for Jewish scholars fleeing Nazi rule was the softening of objections to having American-born Jews on the faculties of those US colleges and universities that had been so clearly anti-Semitic up through World War II. As faculties were more open to Jews, Jewish undergraduates began to see that academic careers, closed to them earlier, were possible in the United States. Paul Samuelson, Robert Solow, Milton Friedman, Martin Bronfenbrenner, Arthur Bloomfield, Lawrence Klein, Sidney Weintraub, Kenneth Arrow, and others who had entered graduate school before 1945 had many more opportunities than did those of the preceding generation. In 1941 Alvin Johnson, president of the New School and director of the Emergency Committee, overoptimistically reported that "his 'extensive communication by word and by letter with American scholars' had convinced him that 'academic anti-Semitism is decidedly on the decline.' There was 'hardly a single respectable university that has not welcomed to its faculty Jewish émigré scholars'" (quoted in Lamberti 2006, 181).

A "fourth generation" of Jewish scholarship and science in the United States, rising with the advent of the Second World War, grew to flourish during the years of postwar crises. The conflict with the Soviet Union—political, ideological, and military—required the aid of scientists ranging from physics to political science and from mathematics to sociology and on a scale that the United States had never known; "experts" in foreign languages and areas hitherto deemed too recondite for Americans were summoned to conduct an ideological debate in several continents. The barriers against Jews in the university world were dismantled almost completely (Feuer 1982, 464).

These changes were well recognized both at the time and later. Although the period appears to be one of continuous progress to a more open, less discriminatory, environment for faculty hiring, it certainly was not so in fact. Liberal arts college faculties did not rush to recruit Jews and Catholics. Discriminatory barriers to hiring women and Afro-Americans were to persist for many decades, and in some measure persist today. Even though Jews and Catholics saw more openness in the universities, their success was not to be any beacon of hope for women or Afro-Americans.

MIT's Unique Openness to Jewish Economics Faculty

Paul Samuelson, in an interview with MIT's *Soundings*, recalled how the economics program took shape after his arrival in 1940.

> Ralph Freeman, Rhodes Scholar and Canadian World War I artillery officer in the British Army, had absolute powers then as Head. By courtesy he deferred to our professional votes on new appointments and one by one we added stars to our team: Robert Bishop, E. Cary Brown, Charles Kindleberger, Morris Adelman, Max Millikan, Walter Rostow, Paul Rosenstein-Rodan, Robert Solow, Evsey Domar, Franco Modigliani and other early tenured acquisitions, as if led by an Invisible Hand. Statistician Harold Freeman [who was Jewish] in the background guided our recruitment judgments. (Samuelson 2000)

If one takes into account the fact that Samuelson was not encouraged to remain at Harvard, his description of MIT's hiring is startling. Adelman, Millikan, Rostow, Rosenstein-Rodan, Solow, Domar, and Modigliani were all, like him, Jewish. Freeman's department was able to recruit so well, and so quickly, not only because of Samuelson's growing renown (he was the first Clark medalist, in 1947), but because the department and university were remarkably open to the hiring of Jewish faculty at a time when such hiring was just beginning to be possible at Ivy League universities.

With respect to other schools, as points of comparison to MIT, consider the University of Wisconsin. This progressive liberal bastion was, as noted above, the home institution of Selig Perlman. In Mark Perlman's article, there is a discussion of his father's struggles as the only Jew in that department. Mark Perlman briefly alludes to the so-called Milton Friedman affair in 1940–41. In *The Economists* (1976, 58–59), Leonard Silk writes that "an ugly note of anti-Semitism crept into the controversy. Selig Perlman, a distinguished labor historian, was the only Jew on the Wisconsin faculty and some members of the department felt that one was enough. Further, Friedman was 'from New York,' 'from the East,' 'from Chicago' and was thus regarded as kind of an interloper."

Robert Lampman (1993, 120), who edited the book *Economists at Wisconsin*, reports that Friedman wrote to him "on December 5, 1990, to share his reflections on his Wisconsin year. . . . 'I did not at the time regard anti-Semitism as the major factor involved in the affair and I do not now. . . . However, a minor subtheme was indeed anti-Semitism.'" In fact, it was not until 1947 that Martin Bronfenbrenner and Eugene Rotwein were hired into the economics department. As two Jewish PhDs from Chicago, they made Perlman less of an outlier.

In contrast to the University of Wisconsin, the University of Michigan appeared to have no similar issues about appointing Jews. This was, in some respects, related to the fact that the chair of its economics department from 1927 to 1954 was Isaiah Leo Sharfman, who came to the United States in 1894 from Ukraine and became a citizen with his father's naturalization in 1903. He had gone to Boston Latin School and took an undergraduate degree and a law degree from Harvard. Arriving at the University of Michigan in 1912, he remained there until retirement. With such an obvious, and apparently well-loved, Jewish presence at the University of Michigan's department, there appeared to be no serious issues over recruiting Jewish faculty in the 1940s. With Harold Levinson and Wolfgang Stolper arriving in the late 1940s and Lawrence Klein arriving in 1950, the department bore no resemblance to Ivy League departments (Brazer 1982).

Lest this judgment appear overstated, consider Yale University. Eugene V. Rostow (1931, 45) wrote in an undergraduate publication there that

> the bold fact remains, in spite of all official disclaimers, that there's not one Jew on the faculty of Yale college, and only a few, of great repute, scattered through the scientific graduate and professional schools. The younger men on the faculty recognize the situation, and confess themselves powerless. Apparently, nothing can be done, and even the most liberal dare not be sanguine. Yale College is closed to the Jewish teacher, the graduate school only recently and hesitantly opened.

A historian (Oren 2000, 128–29) recently noted that the most insular of all the Yale faculties was that of

> Yale College proper. As of 1929, neither a Jew nor a known Catholic had ever achieved a full professorship in the college. Not until after the end of the Second World War would a Jew be granted tenure. Jewish students were occasionally warned by their professors not to waste their time in graduate school, since academic careers were not open to them.

As mentioned earlier, the University of Pennsylvania did not hire a Jew for a full-time position in economics until 1950. Dartmouth hired its first Jewish economics professor, Daniel Marx, in 1941 and its second, Martin Segal, in 1958. As late as 1964 they remained the two Jews among the twenty-one economics teachers there.[6]

6. I thank Tom Velk, who provided the documentation for this statement about 1964, his first year on the Dartmouth economics faculty: www.e-yearbook.com/yearbooks/Dartmouth_College_Aegis_Yearbook/1965/Page_371.html.

Why MIT Was Different

Several articles in this volume have stressed the particular nature of MIT in identifying the difference between its economics department and, say, the Harvard and Yale economics departments. The fact that MIT was an institute of technology, training (in the 1940s) engineers, architects, and scientists exclusively, had real consequences. As some other articles in this volume point out, the mission and identity of the school shaped the instruction that was provided to students studying economics. Those articles do not, however, explore the nature of the differences between this kind of science and engineering faculty and faculties in liberal arts institutions. Engineers and scientists are socialized differently from philosophers, literary scholars, and historians. This difference has been the subject of endless discussion and, in the American context, was a central theme in *The Education of Henry Adams*. The role of humanities faculty in the elite American universities, the Ivy League (Harvard, Yale, Princeton, Dartmouth, Brown, Cornell, Columbia, and Pennsylvania), the Little Ivies (Williams, Wesleyan, and Amherst), and the Seven Sisters (Radcliffe, Mount Holyoke, Vassar, Smith, Pembroke, Barnard, and Wellesley), was to educate the children of the American upper and upper-middle (professional) class. They were implicitly charged with educating the elite for leadership, not the masses for employment. Teaching their students the best works of the "Western Tradition," familiarizing them with a traditional education to uphold their unique place in American life, required (they believed) that they represent those traditions themselves. The schools "knew" that there was no possibility that an immigrant Jew whose parents had fled the Pale of Settlement could have an ear for the poetry of Emily Dickinson, a thrill in the novels of James Fenimore Cooper, or a pride in the biographies of George Washington and Thomas Jefferson. What did the Ashkenazi know of Teddy Roosevelt's Rough Riders? Calling attention to such matters in public, as C. P. Snow did in England in his Rede Lectures, almost always agitates "humanists." Nevertheless, the universalist notions that pervade the sciences, the idea that there is one physics community, one mathematics community, one electrical engineering community, and so forth do not transfer to the field of history: the presuppositions that shape the intellectual life of a historian in Japan are not those that shape the intellectual boundaries of the Civil War historian in the United States, even as cohomology theorists in Japan and in the United States are similarly trained and socialized.

It was long recognized that the occasional presence of Jewish faculty in a university's professional schools did not bear on their absence in that same university's liberal arts college. Yale had Jewish faculty in its medical school, while it did not in its college of liberal arts before the late 1940s (Synnott 1979). This was true for most other Ivy League institutions as well. Great professional schools were not in the business of passing on the dominant culture of American elites to the students they trained. When Columbia worried whether Lionel Trilling could possibly teach Shakespeare given that Shakespeare was not part of his cultural heritage, no such issue was raised in the appointment of Isidor Isaac Rabi to the Columbia physics department. Replicating the elites, the implicit mission of the arts and science faculties of the Ivy League colleges like Harvard, Yale, Princeton, and Dartmouth, was not relevant to the Harvard, Yale, and Dartmouth Schools of Medicine. The Johns Hopkins president might rail against having Simon Kuznets on his economics faculty, but he was not about to purge Jews from his School of Medicine. At MIT, where the science and engineering faculty defined the institution, and shaped the instructional mission of the economics department, the issue of Jewish faculty and their lack of "culture" could not arise because there was in fact no college of arts and sciences.

Explaining MIT's rise to prominence in economics is thus a matter of balancing a number of factors, some internal to the evolving intellectual norms of the community of economists, some connected to the evolving nature of MIT as a university, and some connected to the larger institutions and concerns of postwar America. People matter too. Any account of MIT's growing importance in the 1940s that fails to discuss the brilliance and energy of Paul Samuelson and Robert Solow would be an impoverished one indeed. But if to write history is to engage with the local and contingent contexts of the subject examined, any history of MIT's emergence among economics departments that left out any mention of its unique openness to hiring Jewish faculty in the first postwar decade would be likewise impoverished.

References

Brazer, M. C. 1982. "The Economics Department of the University of Michigan: A Centennial Retrospective." In *Economics and the World around It*, edited by S. H. Hymans, 133–275. Ann Arbor: University of Michigan Press.

Craver, E., and A. Leijonhufvud. 1987. "Economics in America: The Continental Influence." *History of Political Economy* 19 (2): 173–82.

Feuer, L. S. 1982. "The Stages in the Social History of Jewish Professors in American Colleges and Universities." *American Jewish History* 71 (4): 432–65.

Ginzberg, E. 1990. "Economics at Columbia: Recollections of the Early 1930s." *American Economist* 34 (2): 14–19.

Hagemann, H., and C.-D. Krohn, eds. 1999. *Biographisches Handbuch der deutschsprachigen wirtschaftswissenschaftlichen Emigration nach 1933* (*Biographic Handbook on the Emigration of German-Speaking Economists after 1933*). 2 vols. Munich: K. G. Saur.

Hollinger, D. A. 1993. "How Wide the Circle of the 'We'? American Intellectuals and the Problem of the Ethnos since World War II." *American Historical Review* 98 (2): 317–37.

———. 1996. "Science as a Weapon in *Kulturkämpfe* in the United States during and after World War II." In *Science, Jews, and Secular Culture: Studies in Mid-Twentieth Century American Intellectual History*, 155–74. Princeton, N.J.: Princeton University Press.

———. 2004. "Rich, Powerful, and Smart: Jewish Overrepresentation Should Be Explained Instead of Avoided or Mystified." *Jewish Quarterly Review*, n.s., 94 (4): 595–602.

———. 2006. "Why Are Jews Preeminent in Science and Scholarship? The Veblen Thesis Reconsidered." *Cosmopolitanism and Solidarity: Studies in Ethnoracial, Religious, and Professional Affiliation in the United States*, 135–53. Madison: University of Wisconsin Press.

Karabel, J. 2005. *The Chosen: The Hidden History of Admission and Exclusion at Harvard, Yale, and Princeton*. New York: Houghton Mifflin.

Kevles, D. J. (1971) 1995. *The Physicists: The History of a Scientific Community in Modern America*. Cambridge, Mass.: Harvard University Press.

Lamberti, M. 2006. "The Reception of Refugee Scholars from Nazi Germany in America: Philanthropy and Social Change in Higher Education." *Jewish Social Studies: History, Culture, Society* 12 (3): 157–92.

Lampman, R. J., ed. 1993. *Economists at Wisconsin: 1892–1992*. Madison: Board of Regents of the University of Wisconsin System.

Lipset, S. M., and E. C. Ladd Jr. 1971. "Jewish Academics in the United States: Their Achievements, Culture, and Politics." *American Jewish Year Book* 72:89–128.

Lyman, S. M. 1994. "A Haven for Homeless Intellects: The New School and Its Exile Faculties." *International Journal of Politics, Culture, and Society* 7 (3): 493–512.

Oren, D. A. 2000. *Joining the Club: A History of Jews and Yale*. 2nd ed. New Haven, Conn.: Yale University Press.

Perlman, M. 1996. "Jews and Contributions to Economics: A Bicentennial Review." In *The Character of Economic Thought, Economic Characters, and Economic Institutions*, 307–17. Ann Arbor: University of Michigan Press.

Reingold, N. 1988. "Refugee Mathematicians in the United States of America, 1933–1941: Reception and Reaction." In *A Century of Mathematics in America, Part 1*, edited by P. Duren, R. A. Askey, and U. C. Merzbach, 1:175–200. Providence, R.I.: American Mathematical Society.

Rider, R. E. 1984. "Alarm and Opportunity: Emigration of Mathematicians and Physicists to Britain and the United States, 1933–1945." *Historical Studies in the Physical Sciences* 15 (1): 107–76.

Rostow, E. V. 1931. "The Jew's Position." *Harkness Hoot* 23 (2): 45–59.
Samuelson, P. A. 2000. "Economics in MIT's Fourth School." *Soundings*, Fall. web.mit.edu/shass/soundings/issue_00f/fea_lum_pas_00f.html.
Scherer, F. M. 2000. "The Emigration of German-Speaking Economists after 1933." *Journal of Economic Literature* 38 (3): 614–26.
Shapiro, J. J. 1964. "Jewish Culture: Transplanted and Indigenous." In *The American Jew: A Reappraisal*, edited by O. I. Janowsky, 373–84. Philadelphia: Jewish Publication Society.
Silk, Leonard. 1976. *The Economists*. New York: Basic Books.
Synnott, M. G. 1979. *The Half-Opened Door: Discrimination and Admissions at Harvard, Yale, and Princeton, 1900–1970*. Westport, Conn.: Greenwood Press.
Veblen, T. 1919. "The Intellectual Pre-eminence of Jews in Modern Europe." *Political Science Quarterly* 34:33–42.
Weiner, C. 1969. "A New Site for the Seminar: Refugees and American Physics in the Thirties." In *The Intellectual Migration: Europe and America, 1930–1960*, edited by D. Fleming and B. Bailyn, 190–234. Cambridge, Mass.: Belknap Press of Harvard University Press.
Weyl, E. G. 2011. "Introduction: Simon Kuznets, Cautious Empiricist of the Eastern European Jewish Diaspora." In *Jewish Economies Volume II: Development and Migration in America and Beyond—Simon Kuznets*, edited by E. G. Weyl and S. Lo, xv–lvii. New Brunswick, N.J.: Transaction.

Paul A. Samuelson's Move to MIT

Roger E. Backhouse

It is hard to imagine the post-1945 rise of MIT economics without Paul Samuelson (see Cherrier, this volume). In the opinion of MIT president James Killian, "The growth to greatness of the Economics Department . . . at M.I.T. . . . can be attributed to the fame of Paul Samuelson and other scholars in the Department . . . who found satisfaction in being members of a team which included Samuelson."[1] The twenty-five-year-old economist, considered by many the star of his cohort at Harvard, had been recruited in 1940; by the age of thirty-two he had published his widely acclaimed *Foundations of Economic Analysis* (1947), the American Economic Association (AEA) had awarded him its first Clark medal, and he had turned down the offer of a position at Chicago (see Maas, this vol-

Correspondence may be addressed to Roger E. Backhouse, University of Birmingham, Edgbaston, Birmingham B15 2TT, UK; e-mail: reb@bhouse.org.uk. This article was written as part of a project, supported by a Major Research Fellowship from the Leverhulme Trust, to write an intellectual biography of Paul Samuelson, in which several points made herein will be examined at greater length. I am grateful to the Leverhulme Trust for its support. I wish to thank Beatrice Cherrier, Steven G. Medema, Henry Rosovsky, Robert Solow, E. Roy Weintraub, and participants in a seminar at the Center for the History of Political Economy at Duke University, as well as conference participants, for helpful comments on earlier drafts. In the reference list, works in *The Collected Scientific Papers of Paul A. Samuelson* are also cited as "CSP n:m," where *n* is the volume and *m* the article number. Quotations from the papers of E. B. Wilson are reproduced courtesy of the Harvard University Archives and the estate of E. B. Wilson.

1. J. R. Killian to Paul A. Samuelson and enclosed draft, April 19, 1984, Paul A. Samuelson Papers, David M. Rubenstein Rare Book and Manuscript Library, Duke University, box 42 (K [1969–88, 1 of 2]). Hereafter cited as PASP, box (folder).

History of Political Economy 46 (annual suppl.) DOI 10.1215/00182702-2716118

ume). The following year he published an introductory textbook, *Economics* (1948), that framed the way the subject was taught for a generation. Given Harvard had traditionally recruited from its own PhD students and that Samuelson wanted to stay, its failure to retain him seems a monumental miscalculation, leading to speculation about why he moved, for in answering that question one comes close to explaining why MIT's economics came to eclipse Harvard's.

The most commonly heard explanation is anti-Semitism. As E. Roy Weintraub (this volume, "MIT's Openness") explains, MIT's economics department welcomed Jews, whereas anti-Semitism was unquestionably rife at Harvard. Samuelson's explanation of his move was simply that MIT made a better offer—not only did he get a higher rank and access to research grants at MIT, but he got a telephone and a secretary, luxuries not available to all Harvard professors. However, later in life he talked openly about the anti-Semitism he experienced as a graduate student. His resentment surfaced privately in a "Roll of dishonor" he wrote for his friend Henry Rosovsky, in which department chair Harold Burbank came out on top, followed by Edward Chamberlin. Even his mentors, Joseph Schumpeter and E. B. Wilson, were not free of prejudice.[2] Later, Samuelson committed an account of anti-Semitism to print in a Festschrift for Mark Perlman, eight years younger but who had experienced anti-Semitism, and whose father had carved out a career as a labor economist at a time when there were even fewer Jews in the academy.[3] Samuelson wrote of Burbank in uncompromising terms.

> Burbank suffered fools gladly, but not Jews. . . . Faced with a plethora of unsavory talent, H. H. B. solved his dilemma by confining the best of them to a ghetto of assistants in statistics and accounting under W. L. Crum and his satellite Edwin Frickey. Because Burbank had almost absolute pitch in his distaste for talent, such names as R. A. Gordon, Abram Bergson, Joe Bain and Lloyd Metzler made this a legion of honor. Metzler, a boy from Kansas with a German-sounding name, used to sing hymn duets with Marion Crawford—such as, "Jesus wants me for a

2. P. A. Samuelson to Henry Rosovsky, September 26, 1989, PASP, box 63 (Rosovsky).

3. Even years after the letter to Rosovsky, despite having the opportunity to do so in a piece marking the fiftieth anniversary of *Foundations* that expressed his contempt for Burbank (Samuelson 1998), he stated simply that he chose to go to MIT "without malice" (1377). He does no more than hint, through referring to his "Protestant wife" (which could as easily imply that he was Roman Catholic as that he was Jewish), that this absence of malice referred to anything other than prejudice against economic theory.

> sunbeam." But as has been said, an anti-semite can smell out the last nine of the six Jews who have entered the room. (Samuelson 2002, 51)

However, in this account, Samuelson conflated anti-Semitism, an aversion to talent, and hostility to economic theory, recalling that Burbank once said to him, "Samuelson, you are narrow. Keynes and Hawtrey are narrow. Don't take up economic theory until after you are fifty. This is what our great Allyn Young used to say."[4] The view that Burbank and the majority of his colleagues were hostile to Samuelson because he was smart was echoed by another Harvard student, Wolfgang Stolper, who quoted Schumpeter as having said, "I could understand it if it were anti-Semitism; but it is just that he [Samuelson] is better than they are."[5] Robert Solow, who experienced Harvard a few years later, expressed the view that being a Keynesian was also fatal to Samuelson's chances at Harvard (so too were being a Jew and being smart).[6]

The present article reconstructs the events surrounding Samuelson's recruitment by MIT. After two years' coursework, Harvard had made him a junior fellow. His three-year appointment, during which he published a long string of articles on mathematical economics, came to an end in the summer of 1940, and he had to decide his future. On June 19 he was offered a one-year position as "Instructor in Economics and Tutor in the Department of Economics," and in September he began his teaching career. However, on October 10, MIT offered him a position as an assistant professor, asking Harvard for permission to make the offer because MIT wanted him to start immediately. The Harvard faculty held a meeting to discuss this, at which Schumpeter threatened to resign if nothing was done to retain Samuelson, but no competing offer was forthcoming, and Samuelson moved to MIT. The sources (mainly correspondence) are incomplete, but they are sufficient to paint a picture that, like most historical stories, turns out to be much more complex than the conventional one.

1. MIT's Offer

Around the beginning of December 1939, during his final year as one of Harvard's junior fellows, Samuelson received a letter from Harold Freeman, who had been a student with Samuelson from 1936 to 1938 and was now an associate professor at MIT. Asking Samuelson not to divulge its

4. Note that this list includes Jews and non-Jews.
5. W. Stolper to Paul A. Samuelson, February 12, 2002, PASP, box 71 (Stolper [1]).
6. R. M. Solow to Roger E. Backhouse, February 28, 2013, in author's possession.

contents, as the letter was entirely unauthorized, he explained that the professor who taught economic theory and business cycle theory was ill and might need to "rest up." "Would you mind telling me," Freeman asked, "if you would be interested in a position here next year and if so, under approximately what terms?"[7] Samuelson replied on December 5 that his appointment as a junior fellow was over at the end of the academic year and that he was interested in exploring all the alternatives open to him "at Harvard and elsewhere." Explaining that he had become interested in business cycle theory, and that he had been working on this subject with Alvin Hansen in the new Littauer Center (where, with John Williams, he was running the Fiscal Policy seminar), Samuelson suggested that they arrange an interview.

In subsequent recollections, Samuelson credited Harold with responsibility for his move. Harold persuaded the department head, Ralph Freeman (no relation), that not only was Samuelson a good scholar but he would work with others. When Ralph asked whether Paul was a cooperator, Harold replied, "Is Samuelson a cooperator? Why the man writes joint articles" (Samuelson 1996, 16). The basis for this claim was the article that Samuelson had written with his fellow student Russ Nixon. Samuelson also said that it was Harold who talked him into taking the job.

When Samuelson replied to Harold Freeman at the beginning of December 1939, he was still thinking in terms of his option at Harvard being to apply for a renewal of his junior fellowship.[8] However, he chose not to apply for that, and in September 1940 he took up the instructorship that he had been offered in June.[9] On leaving Chicago, where he had been an undergraduate, Samuelson chose to ignore the advice of his teachers to go to Columbia, opting instead for Harvard for his graduate work, for he was attracted by the idea of a traditional New England university. He wanted to stay at Harvard, and although Samuelson's friends might have expected him to be made an assistant professor, an instructorship was a significant offer. In the 1930s Harvard was not the wealthy institution it is today, and it relied extensively on instructors and had a comparatively small number of permanent faculty who had what was generally considered a high teaching load involving much individual supervision of undergraduates (see McCraw 2007, 226–27). In addition, James Conant, Harvard president

7. H. A. Freeman to Paul A. Samuelson, December [4], 1939, PASP, box 31 (Freeman).

8. The maximum term for a junior fellowship was six years, and his appointment had been for three.

9. The Society of Fellows has no record of his application for renewal. There is no evidence on the reasons.

since 1933, was making vigorous attempts to improve Harvard's academic standing by appointing eminent outsiders to professorial positions and making internal promotions more difficult. Furthermore, though Harvard might be reluctant to promote people, it offered salaries that were high in relation to those offered elsewhere.[10]

However, despite Harold Freeman having identified likely teaching needs at the end of the previous year, no offer was forthcoming until several MIT faculty had been drafted for national defense purposes, and there was an urgent need to appoint someone very quickly. So on very short notice, on October 10, MIT president Karl Compton offered Samuelson an assistant professorship, at a salary of $3,000 per year.[11] Samuelson recalls that while he was considering the offer, Rupert Maclaurin, who was trying to build up MIT's economics department, phoned him daily, dangling before him the prospect of research funds, including money offered by the businessman Roger Babson to support the study of the implications for economics of Isaac Newton's law of action and reaction.[12]

These circumstances explain the unusual timing of the offer to Samuelson, just a month into the new academic year. The circumstances were sufficiently unusual that Ralph Freeman, anxious to behave properly in the matter, contacted the head of Harvard's department, by then Edward Chamberlin, to ask permission to make the offer, no doubt explaining that MIT had been forced into doing so by the exigencies of preparing for war. This was the first, though far from the last, way in which Samuelson's career was significantly affected by the military situation. Chamberlin apparently called a department meeting, at which Freeman's request was considered and, apparently, the possibility of immediately recommending Samuelson for a five-year instructorship was discussed; however, nothing came of this, and Chamberlin gave MIT permission to make an offer to Samuelson.[13]

10. This is illustrated by a letter to the historian Arthur Schlesinger Sr. in which Wilson pointed out that the $5,000 salary that the sociologist Talcott Parsons had been offered as a full professor at the University of Wisconsin was no higher than what he earned as an assistant professor at Harvard with the same teaching hours. In 1937 Elizabeth Boody (later Schumpeter) was earning $3,000 as a research associate (McCraw 2007, 237).

11. K. T. Compton to Paul A. Samuelson, October 10, 1940, PASP, box 53 (MIT).

12. P. A. Samuelson, in a document I am calling "the Hurwicz 1940–41 year when MIT launched its graduate degree 'rocket'" (Samuelson's word), PASP, box 39 (Hurwicz).

13. This is inferred from Wilson's correspondence with Samuelson and Compton (E. B. Wilson to Paul A. Samuelson, October 3, 1940, Edwin Bidwell Wilson Papers, Harvard University, HUG4878.203 box 35 [S] [hereafter cited as EBWP, box]; Wilson to Karl T. Compton, November 13, 1940, MIT, Office of the President, AC4 box 239 [10]).

2. E. B. Wilson and the Need to Develop Economics at MIT

Samuelson's mentor at this time was Edwin Bidwell Wilson, a polymath who had worked as a mathematician and physicist, who in 1922 had moved from MIT to become professor of vital statistics in Harvard's Institute of Public Health. He had taught Samuelson statistics and mathematical economics, and was closely involved with some of the papers that Samuelson was writing. Wilson had long been concerned about Samuelson's employability because Samuelson was too mathematical for most economics departments, Wilson's letters to economists at other universities inquiring about possible openings having drawn a blank. On October 3, when he learned about MIT's impending offer, he wrote to Samuelson about the decision the latter had to make.

Though he went on to say that he did not want to make Samuelson's decision for him, Wilson drew clear parallels between his own experience and the situation Samuelson was in. Samuelson's decision, just after he had started teaching at Harvard, reminded Wilson of the fact that his offer from MIT came in his first year at Yale. Wilson said that he had never regretted his decision to move, "although there were many people at Yale who couldn't understand why I should change from Yale to M.I.T. under any circumstances and although I was very happy at Yale and perhaps better situated socially there than at M.I.T."[14] Wilson might now be at Harvard, but he knew what it was like to give up a much-prized position at an Ivy League university to go to MIT, and, difficult as his decision had been, he had no doubt that it had been correct. Wilson, who for three years had been copresident of MIT, then changed his tone to that of an MIT insider, saying that he had thought a lot about economics at "Tech." After the death of Francis A. Walker, first president of the AEA, and president of MIT from 1881 to 1897, economics had not been given the support it should have been. In particular, the mathematical and statistical side of economics had not been developed: the faculty at MIT had failed to take advantage of the fact that because it was an engineering school, its students were all required to have two years of mathematics, physics, and chemistry, with many of them having studied applied mechanics and thermodynamics (a subject that Wilson and Samuelson had discussed at length). If Samuelson went to MIT, he could take advantage of his situation there.

14. Wilson to Samuelson, October 3, 1940.

Realizing that Samuelson would find it difficult to break away from a department that included mathematical economists, including himself and Leontief (not to mention Schumpeter, who was an enthusiast for mathematical economics even though he did not do mathematical economics himself), Wilson wrote about the transformation that had taken place at MIT during his time there: despite having thought he would be going into "utter mathematical darkness," MIT's mathematics department had developed into one of the best research departments in the country. This had been the result of appointing a group of able young people; though he could not be certain that this would happen in economics if Samuelson went to MIT, he noted that "they are starting out well if they secure you."

Wilson then sought to weigh Samuelson's prospects at MIT and Harvard. He thought that there was a very good chance that Samuelson would be offered a permanent position at MIT and that having the title of professor would also make it easier to get offers elsewhere. In contrast, there was great uncertainty about whether Samuelson would get tenure at Harvard: recent decisions had made it much harder for young people to get tenure, Harvard was well stocked with economic theorists (at least in relation to its teaching needs), and Harvard had shortages of people in other fields that were becoming very important, such as agricultural economics. On the other side of the balance, Samuelson would enjoy being at Harvard, and he would, Wilson thought, very likely be offered a five-year instructorship the following year. Samuelson's knowledge of economic theory would make it possible for him to work up some other branch of economics, increasing his chances of advancement. There were arguments on both sides, but the balance was weighted heavily in favor of going to MIT.

On October 14, presumably after Samuelson had accepted Compton's offer, Wilson wrote again. Now that Samuelson made up his mind, Wilson's tone changed, and he explained much more explicitly than in his previous letter why he thought Samuelson's decision was the correct one. He laid out a vision of the advantages that could accrue to both MIT and Harvard from Samuelson's move and the development of MIT. He began by reviewing the history of mathematics, physics, and geology in Cambridge, Massachusetts, arguing that if one had adjacent yet different departments covering the same discipline, "there was enough difference in the environment and in the problems which came to the staff so that the combined departments undoubtedly covered the ground more widely than it would have been covered at either institution if the department there had been as large as the two departments combined and there had been no department at the other school."[15] He then applied the same argument to economics.

> Now I see no reason why there should not be some kind of fraternization between the Tech department of economics and the Harvard department whether in Cambridge or at the Business School as there was 30 years ago between the departments of geology (which may continue for ought I know) and as there is between the departments of physics in the two institutions. It seems to me clear that economics at Tech because it is at Tech will be kept closer to practical applied problems than in Cambridge though perhaps no more so than at the Harvard Business School. One reason there has not been very much influence of the Tech department on Harvard or of Harvard on Tech is because the department at Tech has been rather weak. For a long time the department of physics was weak and buzied itself only with teaching and with rather low-grade practical research. For a long time there was no research done in mathematics worthy of the name. I think one of the good things about your going to Tech will be not only that the department is thereby greatly strengthened on the theoretical side but that you have a chance to broaden yourself out on certain types of application and that moreover this appointment may be but the beginning of a real interlocking in interest between the departments.[16]

Wilson was thus assuring Samuelson that he had made the right decision to go to MIT, not just for himself but also for Harvard. Going to MIT would pull Samuelson's research in new directions—it was still very much an engineering school—but because of the synergy that would result from having two strong but different departments, at Harvard and MIT, economics in Cambridge would be stronger than if Samuelson were to stay at Harvard and MIT were to remain weak.

3. MIT as the Place for a Mathematical Economist

The timing of MIT's offer helps explain why the Harvard department chair's action was controversial: though Ralph Freeman's request was in a sense a courtesy and could hardly have been refused, Chamberlin

15. E. B. Wilson to Paul A. Samuelson, October 14, 1940, EBWP, box 35 (S).
16. Wilson to Samuelson, October 14, 1940.

consulted the whole department before giving MIT permission to make the offer. Compton wrote on November 12 that he had heard that this had caused a disturbance: "I heard by the grapevine route . . . that there was subsequently a little disturbance over the matter in the minds of some members of the department."[17] This was presumably when Wilson heard about Samuelson's offer and when Schumpeter had threatened to resign over Harvard's failure to make an offer sufficient to keep Samuelson.

Responding to Compton's anxiety about MIT having behaved properly, Wilson explained what had happened.

> Heads of departments at Harvard have very limited authority. They are really only chairmen and are according to the rules limited to a three year term although the rules are very often not followed in practice. Thus when your professor Freeman checked relative to Samuelson with Professor Chamberlin, Chamberlin could only represent his own attitude except as he called a special meeting of the department and took a vote on the matter. When some members of the department heard that Samuelson was likely to go to MIT they made a serious attempt to get the department to take some action which would keep Samuelson at Harvard. . . . The discussion was entirely friendly to MIT and to Samuelson.[18]

Wilson then explained how this decision was consistent with Harvard's own teaching needs: "Of course Professor Chamberlin would never have encouraged Professor Freeman to make an offer to Samuelson if it weren't for the fact that we are overloaded, so overloaded with high-grade people in economic theory that there really isn't much prospect that we can make a permanent position for a young fellow for a good many years especially as we are under-staffed in agricultural economies, in labor, and in social security and for that matter in economic history."

Harvard's teaching needs reinforced Wilson's conviction that MIT was the right place for Samuelson, about which he had written to Compton earlier in the month. In a letter that dealt mostly with other matters, Wilson added a paragraph that began by reassuring Compton that he had made the right decision in recruiting Samuelson: "I note with great satisfaction that you have taken on Samuelson in economics. He is one of the

17. K. Compton to Edwin Bidwell Wilson, November 12, 1940, MIT, Office of the President, AC4 box 239 (10).

18. E. B. Wilson to Karl T. Compton, November 13, 1940. Note that, despite the three-year rule, Burbank was chair for a decade and resumed the position later in the 1940s.

ablest young fellows I have ever met. I am sure he will have a distinguished career whether he stays with you or goes elsewhere."[19] Echoing what he had said to Samuelson three weeks earlier, he held out a vision of what could happen to economics at MIT.

> It seems to me that it is particularly appropriate for MIT to have in its department of economics persons who understand science and mathematics. Your students come to their economics with two years of mathematics, two years of physics, a year of chemistry and are simultaneously taking for the most part either physical chemistry or thermodynamics. It would seem to me that if the instruction in economics could be given in a way to use to the full the advantage of this long scientific training of your students it should be possible to give those students in one year a broader and deeper course of economics than can be given to ordinary economic students in two years.

Significantly, Wilson then explained that this was not just his own view, for he had discussed this with at least one of his Harvard colleagues:

> In this opinion Leonard Crum agrees. Neither of us would mean that such a course should be in mathematical economics as such. My great trouble in teaching advanced economics at Harvard is to get the young economists to realize the importance of definitions, of consistency, and of logic. Even those who know considerable mathematics don't seem to know how to use it for scientific purposes.

Wilson was thus laying before Compton a vision of how MIT might develop its economics through building on what were, he believed, Samuelson's strengths, and in a way calculated to make sense to MIT's physicist president.

In coming to the conclusion that Samuelson's profile was not a good fit with Harvard's teaching needs, it is important to realize the extent to which he was then regarded as a very narrow specialist. Hard as this is to imagine today when academic economics is dominated by the use of mathematics, "mathematical economics" was then considered a specific field of economics—one specialization among many and, moreover, one whose importance had not yet been established. In 1940, 70 percent of articles on economic theory in the AEA used no mathematics at all (Backhouse 1998,

19. E. B. Wilson to Karl T. Compton, November 5, 1940, MIT, Office of the President, AC4 box 239 (10).

93). Immediately after Samuelson defended his thesis, at the beginning of 1941, Wilson, one of the examiners, wrote to him urging that he should revise the text so as to make it accessible to "good economic theorists who are not primarily mathematical economists," an end that required considerable rewriting and expansion of the text. Such rewriting would both make it clearer what they could learn from Samuelson's results and "help them to appreciate the value or rigorous mathematical economics of which not a few of them are rather sceptical."[20] The thesis might be accessible to himself, or to John Hicks and Roy Allen, but beyond such readers its audience was limited. Implying that Samuelson might not necessarily wish to remain at MIT, Wilson explained that if he became known as a "general theoretical economist" he might find "first class positions" opening up all over the country.

At this time, as Schumpeter (1954, 23) explained, many applied fields were defined in relation to policy problems: agriculture, labor, transportation, public utilities, control of industry, and public finance. To teach such fields, it was necessary, to an extent perhaps not true today when theory has spread much farther, to venture into facts and institutions. This was an area in which Samuelson was still considered weak, even by Wilson, who supported him so strongly. There were few positions in mathematical economics, and Wilson believed that in order to get a position, it would be necessary for Samuelson to prove that he could teach weak, nonmathematical students. When, in May 1939, he had urged Burbank to give him a section of weak students on the introductory course, he admitted that "perhaps he [Samuelson] doesn't know much concrete economics." While this concession to Burbank might have involved an element of diplomacy, Wilson could be more frank with Lawrence Henderson. In a letter recommending Lloyd Metzler for the Society of Fellows, he wrote, "You may want me to compare him a little with Samuelson. As I see it he is nothing like the mathematician that Samuelson is though he has an adequate command of mathematics for an economist. As I see it he knows his economic phenomena and institutions a good deal better than Samuelson did when you took him on and is a better statistician."[21]

Although the comparison is with Samuelson as he had been in 1937, it remains an unfavorable judgment on his knowledge of concrete phenomena and was reinforced by comments about the narrowness of Samuel-

20. E. B. Wilson to Paul A. Samuelson, January 14, 1941, EBWP, box 37 (S 1941).

21. E. B. Wilson to Lawrence J. Henderson, January 31, 1940, EBWP, box 34 (H).

son's work: "I doubt whether he [Metzler] has a so highly specialized technique or is working or would be willing to work in so narrow a field as that of mathematical economics." Wilson even expressed the view that Metzler might end up being more influential than Samuelson, because "although he understands mathematical economics he can express himself, and prefers to express himself so far as possible in English." The implication was that Samuelson stayed within the confines of mathematical economics, choosing not to express himself in language that nonmathematical economists, let alone the weak students on which Wilson thought he should be allowed to develop his teaching skills, could understand. MIT, where university entrance requirements meant that Samuelson would never encounter students innocent of math and science, was the right place for him.

Although it might have been used to cover other reasons, the argument that Samuelson's profile did not fit Harvard's teaching needs was more than a justification for a decision made on other grounds. In April 1941 Wilson wrote to Chamberlin at length about the need to bring on young people in applied fields: "There is no use of over-building theory and under-building agriculture, history and other items."[22] He urged Chamberlin to get together with Burbank and Crum to plan a strategy for coping with a situation where they had a small staff and rapid turnover.

Arguments about teaching needs could be used to cover not only anti-Semitism but hostility to Keynes. Though Wilson shows no signs of having engaged with this work—he was no Keynesian, believing in sound finance—Samuelson had, as his 1939 letter to Ralph Freeman pointed out, begun to work with Hansen on problems of the cycle, taking seriously some of Keynes's ideas.[23] As is well known, though many of the younger economists at Harvard were enthusiasts for Keynes, with the exception of Hansen, the older generation was not. Hansen had been appointed as an exponent of "institutionalist" theories of the cycle by a department that expected him to remain more critical of Keynes than what turned out to be the case.[24] Though Schumpeter and Wilson would not have considered Samuelson's Keynesianism a problem, others would have done so. Burbank, whose course on public finance Samuelson described as a course

22. E. B. Wilson to Edward H. Chamberlin, April 16, 1941, EBWP, box 36.

23. See Samuelson 1939a, 1939b. The wording is carefully chosen, for the question of Samuelson's conversion to Keynesianism is complex and beyond the scope of this article.

24. Mehrling 1997 provides the most substantial discussion of the evolution of Hansen's ideas.

against public finance, would certainly have objected to his Keynesianism: in 1940–41, the year in which Samuelson had started teaching, it was, according to Solow, common gossip that those teaching sections on Ec. A were not allowed to mention the *General Theory*.[25] Chamberlin, department chair for the critical meeting, was opposed to Keynes, as was Crum (and if Samuelson was right, Frickey would have supported Crum). Williams and Leontief would presumably have been more open-minded, though neither was Keynesian. It was not until after the Second World War that Harvard made tenured appointments to Keynesian economists.

A further problem that, along with several other factors, could have been decisive on its own arose from the broader problem of Harvard's reliance on a large number of instructors on fixed-term contracts. This came to a head in 1936–37 when the department recommended that two instructors, John Walsh and Alan Sweezy, have their contracts renewed for a further three years with prospect of renewal, but that Conant's administration, in its bid to raise academic standards, would offer no more than a nonrenewable two-year extension (see Keller and Keller 2001, 66–68). Walsh and Sweezy were popular teachers, but Conant thought that they had not published enough. Though Conant insisted that the reason was their poor publication records, he was accused of political discrimination against economists who held radical political views.[26] On the advice of Walter Lippmann, then chair of the department's visiting committee, and in response to a petition from 131 faculty members, Conant set up a committee of senior professors, the so-called Committee of eight, to look into the matter.[27] The committee found that there had been no political bias, but that Walsh and Sweezy had not had a fair review and should be given a three-year extension as the department had recommended. However, Conant would not alter his decision, and the two ended up resigning. The following year Conant tasked the committee to produce recommendations for tenure procedures, and it came up with the rule of "up or out" in six years. Young people were to be offered instructorships for no more than six years, after which they either received tenure as associate professors or were asked to leave. It was proposed to abolish the rank of assistant professor. The report might not have become official university policy, but it was consistent with Conant's attitudes, and to do other than follow estab-

25. R. M. Solow to Roger E. Backhouse, February 28, 2013.

26. Conant's view was that their views were not particularly radical (Keller and Keller 2001, 67).

27. Craufurd Goodwin discusses this in an unpublished manuscript on Walter Lippmann.

lished procedures might reopen controversy. This alone could explain why even Wilson thought that Samuelson should be treated like anyone else and should wait his turn for promotion.

> The question has been raised of course as to whether the department of economics would at this time recommend you for a 5 year instructorship. I think you are pretty safe in counting on your getting a recommendation next spring for such an appointment if you don't get it now. For myself I agree in the main with Mr. Lowell's policy, as I understand it, which was the policy at Yale in the days when I was there, that able young people had to take their chances of getting what they wanted at the proper times and that a call to another institution shouldn't lead the university to make any future promises in advance of the regular time. I believe that as you advance in the academic world as you surely will you may yourself come to the conclusion that this is on the whole a sound policy no matter whether in your particular instance at the moment the university commits itself to a 5 year appointment for you or does not.[28]

4. Conclusions

There is no reason to doubt that both anti-Semitism and skepticism about the mathematical economics Samuelson was doing motivated some members of Harvard's faculty. Hostility to Keynesian economics was sufficiently strong that his work on the business cycle would not have been helpful. There seems to be no reason to doubt that Samuelson was justified in describing Burbank as anti-Semitic and that he was not alone in holding such views. (Burbank had been instrumental in Leontief's appointment, though the latter's Jewish ancestry was then unknown.)[29] It is, therefore, impossible to pick out one factor and to say that it was *the* cause of Harvard's failure to make an offer that was sufficiently attractive to induce Samuelson to stay. Anti-Semitism was woven into the fabric of academic institutions, and, as is usually the case, motivations could be hidden behind legitimate reasons.

One of the main problems was that Harvard's economics department had a large proportion of nontenured staff, few of whom could expect to achieve tenure. This was compounded by Conant's belief, supported by

28. Wilson to Samuelson, October 3, 1940.

29. Though his criticisms were different, Lippmann was also very critical of Burbank, believing that he should be replaced as department chair. McCraw (2007, chap. 12) discusses Burbank's role in bringing Schumpeter and Leontief to Harvard.

Lippmann, that building up the department required the appointment of exceptional economists from outside the university. The cases of Walsh and Sweezy had resulted in a system that applied rigid rules, with a widely publicized report having been published only the previous year. An improved offer to Samuelson to match the one he had received from MIT would have involved making a special case that the administration might have been reluctant to make for fear of reigniting controversy. It was not even clear, in 1940, that Samuelson would be the strongest candidate for any permanent position that became vacant. In the eyes of many he was an exceptional candidate, but mathematical economics was widely considered a narrow specialism in which Harvard already had ample expertise (Leontief backed up by Wilson and Schumpeter). Harvard had to teach large numbers of undergraduates, most of whom lacked both the ability and the training to study mathematical economics.[30] Burbank's resistance to letting Samuelson teach introductory economics meant that he had been unable to demonstrate his ability to teach general economics. As a junior fellow he had no need to teach, but Burbank had resisted Wilson's plea that he should be allowed to do so in order to improve his career prospects, and in 1940 even Wilson harbored doubts about whether Samuelson could communicate with economists outside the few who were trained in mathematics.

As far as Samuelson was concerned, he found it hard to drag himself away from his cherished Ivy League ambitions. Rupert Mclaurin's phoning Samuelson sufficiently often for him to remember it as being every day must have reflected a concern that Harvard might make Samuelson a counteroffer that would cause him to stay. It was a difficult decision for Samuelson because although a significant number of the faculty were appalled by discrimination, Harvard remained an institution that did not welcome Jews. If he remained, he would face continuing political battles over colleagues and students even if his own position were secure, something that would not be known for several years. In complete contrast, if he moved to MIT, not only would he have a more secure position with a higher salary, a research grant, better facilities, and students who could engage with his research, but he could leave such battles behind him and focus on academic matters.

Later in his life, Samuelson was clearly troubled by a letter in which Wilson, his revered mentor, had advised Talcott Parsons that one should

30. Wilson's continued concern about the imbalance of expertise in the department after Samuelson left demonstrates that it was perceived to be a long-term problem.

not appoint a Jew to a position in which their progress would eventually be blocked.[31] He came to realize that the letter did not imply that Wilson personally held anti-Semitic views, even if he had been complicit in anti-Semitism, and was prepared to exonerate him. However, what is remarkable is that Samuelson failed to point out that Wilson had also outlined, both to him and to MIT president Compton, a vision of what might be achieved at MIT should Samuelson go there.[32] Wilson, with his extensive network of contacts in the natural sciences and at MIT, would have been well aware that MIT was being transformed from an undergraduate engineering school into a full-fledged research university, Compton having been instrumental in increasing the level of fundamental science in the curriculum (see Kaiser 2010, chap. 3). Economics at MIT had lagged behind, and Wilson could see that Samuelson could help bring about a transformation in MIT's economics comparable with what Compton had done with MIT's engineering. Wilson's familiarity with mathematics, physics, and geology also led him to see that there could be benefits, even to Harvard, if economics at MIT were strengthened, turning Cambridge into a much stronger center for economics than Harvard could ever establish on its own. His case was so strongly argued that there seems little reason to doubt that he genuinely believed that Cambridge economics would be stronger with Samuelson at MIT than if he remained at Harvard, and that he had expressed this view to at least one of his Harvard colleagues.

Samuelson was not forced to leave Harvard. As he consistently claimed, he had the choice of remaining at Harvard, but, in his words, "revealed a preference for MIT" (Samuelson 1998, 1377). He was an ambitious young man in a hurry, aware that openings in his highly specialized field were very limited, who received an attractive offer and was actively courted by his new department. His mentor advised him that to abandon his cherished Ivy League ambitions would not compromise his career: to the contrary, moving to MIT might be the best choice for himself and for the Harvard to which he had become attached. As other articles in this volume make clear, Wilson's judgment turned out to be correct: MIT proved to be a highly supportive environment, free of the prejudices that surrounded Samuelson at Harvard, and it did prove possible to use his position at MIT dramatically to strengthen economics in Cambridge.

31. E. B. Wilson to Talcott Parsons, May 12, 1939, PASP Box 72 (Swedberg).

32. Samuelson also appears to have forgotten that by 1940 Chamberlin had replaced Burbank as department chair.

Historians have recognized the complexity of the ways in which anti-Semitism permeated decision making in Ivy League universities in this period. It was undoubtedly one factor behind Samuelson's decision. However, an equally important factor, usually overlooked, is that the Samuelson who was deciding whether to accept MIT's offer was not the same Samuelson as the AEA's first Clark medalist in 1947. In the intervening seven years he had transformed himself from a mathematical economist *pur sang*, known for a few highly technical articles, into a generalist, known as much for his Keynesianism as for his mathematics, who could communicate with students and even with the general public. This transformation started at Harvard, when he began to work with Hansen, but it was completed only after he moved to MIT, escaping the difficult Harvard environment, and became caught up in wartime activities.

There is a final twist to this story. Samuelson's move to MIT may have been a side effect of preparations for war. If it had not lost faculty to war work, MIT would not have had a vacancy at that point. This circumstance would have been a further factor making it impossible for Harvard not to accede to MIT's request without good reason, and would presumably have made it that much more difficult for Harvard to justify making promises that would clearly have been motivated only by the need to stop Samuelson from going to where he was most needed. Such pressures were obviously nowhere near as strong as they would have been once the United States had entered the war, but they may nonetheless have been significant.

References

Backhouse, R. E. 1998. "The Transformation of U.S. Economics, 1920–1960, Viewed through a Survey of Journal Articles." In *From Interwar Pluralism to Postwar Neoclassicism*, edited by M. S. Morgan and M. Rutherford. *History of Political Economy* 30 (supplement): 85–107.

Kaiser, D., ed. 2010. *Becoming MIT: Moments of Decision*. Cambridge, Mass.: MIT Press.

Keller, M., and P. Keller. 2001. *Making Harvard Modern: The Rise of America's University*. Cambridge, Mass.: Harvard University Press.

McCraw, T. K. 2007. *Prophet of Innovation: Joseph Schumpeter and Creative Destruction*. Cambridge, Mass.: Belknap Press of Harvard University Press.

Mehrling, P. 1997. *The Money Interest and the Public Interest: American Monetary Thought, 1920–1970*. Cambridge, Mass.: Harvard University Press.

Samuelson, P. A. 1939a. "Interactions between the Multiplier Analysis and the Principle of Acceleration." *Review of Economics and Statistics* 21 (2): 75–78. CSP 2:82.

——. 1939b. "A Synthesis of the Principle of Acceleration and the Multiplier." *Journal of Political Economy* 47 (6): 786–97. CSP 2:83.
——. 1947. *Foundations of Economic Analysis*. Cambridge, Mass.: Harvard University Press.
——. 1948. *Economics*. New York: McGraw Hill.
——. 1966. *The Collected Scientific Papers of Paul A. Samuelson*, edited by J. E. Stiglitz. Vol. 2. Cambridge, Mass.: MIT Press.
——. 1996. "On Collaboration." *American Economist* 40 (2): 16–21. CSP 7:583.
——. 1998. "How *Foundations* Came to Be." *Journal of Economic Literature* 36 (3): 1375–86. CSP 7:586.
——. 2002. "Pastiches from an Earlier Politically Incorrect Academic Age." In *Editing Economics: Essays in Honour of Mark Perlman*, edited by H. Lim, U. S. Park, and G. C. Harcourt, 47–55. London: Routledge. CSP 7:593.
——. 2011. *The Collected Scientific Papers of Paul A. Samuelson*, edited by J. Murray. Vol. 7. Cambridge, Mass.: MIT Press.
Schumpeter, J. A. 1954. *A History of Economic Analysis*. New York: Oxford University Press.

Part 2
Connections

The Early Years of the MIT PhD Program in Industrial Economics

Pedro Garcia Duarte

Immediately after World War II graduate education in economics in the United States expanded substantially with the dramatic transformation of higher education brought about by the Readjustment Act (GI Bill) of 1944 (see also Weintraub, this volume, introduction).[1] The increase occurred both by expanding the size of existing graduate programs and by creating new, competing ones. The MIT PhD program in industrial economics was born in 1941 with the help of the newly hired Paul Samuelson,

Correspondence may be addressed to Pedro Garcia Duarte, Dept. Economia, FEA-USP, Av. Prof. Luciano Gualberto, 908, Butantã, São Paulo, SP – Brazil 05508-010; e-mail: pgduarte@usp.br. I am very grateful to E. Roy Weintraub for all his encouragement and constructive criticism of an early version of this article. I thank very much Peter Temin for comments and clarifications kindly offered, as well as those of Richard Eckaus and Donald L. M. Blackmer. I am obliged to an anonymous referee who provided me with important feedback that helped me revise this article (which had previously benefited from comments by participants at the 2013 *HOPE* conference and at the seminar at Cedeplar [UFMG, Brazil]), and to Nora Murphy (MIT Institute archivist), Laurie Scheffler (Center administrator and assistant to the director of the MIT Center for International Studies), and William R. Massa Jr. and Nancy F. Lyon (Yale archivists), for their kind help with different institutional information. I gratefully acknowledge financial support from CNPq (Brazil).

1. The expansion of the economics graduate education is impressive, as Howard R. Bowen (1953, 29) noted: "For example, since the end of World War II (academic years 1945–46 through 1951–52), about 1,800 Ph.D.'s have been awarded by American universities. The magnitude of this figure can be appreciated when it is realized that this post-war crop represents nearly one-third of all the doctorates in economics ever awarded in this country. In all the years prior to 1945–46 fewer than 4,000 doctorates had been granted."

History of Political Economy 46 (annual suppl.) DOI 10.1215/00182702-2716127

discontinued during the war (Cherrier, this volume), and then reenacted for a sizable expansion that transformed it into one of the most important programs in the United States.

The immediate postwar period witnessed not only a considerable expansion of economics graduate education but also its reformulation. This occurred as economics was going through important changes, informed by its mathematization (cf. Mirowski 2002; Weintraub 2002), by the stabilization of a neoclassical way of doing economics (Morgan and Rutherford 1998), by the advancement of econometrics and the "Keynesian revolution" (both stressed by Barber 1996), and by the ultimate Americanization of economics (see Weintraub, this volume, introduction).[2] This period also witnessed the proliferation of different subfields in economics and the rearrangement of their positions (in terms of importance) in graduate education.

Given all this, the changing economics graduate education in the United States, with its increasing emphasis on technical training, was part and parcel of the broader changing face of the economics profession in the postwar period. The centrality that the MIT PhD program acquired makes it an important case study of the transformation of American economics more generally, as the new training offered by MIT to economists not only followed larger changes in US academe but also contributed to them. Pondering the rise to prominence of the MIT economics department, Samuelson (2000) emphasized two elements, concluding that the department was the place that nurtured a "revolution" in postwar economics: "One, MIT's renaissance after World War II as a federally-supported research resource. Two, the mathematical revolution in macro- and micro-economic theory and statistics: this was overdue and inevitable—MIT was the logical place for it to flourish."

More than a logical place, MIT was historically important to the changes taking place in economics, and history is hardly inevitable. MIT became the place not only for the "mathematical revolution" in economics but also for a new graduate training that emerged in the United States partly as a response to that very "revolution." My aim here is to scrutinize the formative years of the MIT PhD program in economics, mostly the 1940s and 1950s, contextualizing it as much as possible with what was going on else-

2. The Keynesian factor was very present in Samuelson's attempt to write his textbook, *Economics*. It was understood to be an MIT product with unacceptable Keynesian ideas by Samuelson's critics, the very same ideas criticized with respect to Lorie Tarshis's textbook, as discussed by Yann Giraud (this volume).

where in US graduate economics education at the time. I look at the student and faculty bodies, advisers and advisees and where the latter got their first jobs, and try to have a sense of the theses and fields in order to better understand the distinctive features of the program and of its products.

1. Economics Faculty and Major Advisers

The Department of Economics and Social Science at MIT was home for different groups of social scientists other than economists before they all created their own departments.[3] The department was relatively small in the early 1940s and, also because of its newly created PhD program in industrial economics, had professors with different backgrounds. Moreover, from 1945 to 1947, it offered an additional PhD program in group psychology. Of the seventeen regular professors (including all levels) at the department in 1945, six of them were professors of economics, five were professors of psychology, three were professors of industrial relations, and the others were professors of international relations, human relations, and statistics.

Ten years later, in 1955, the relative number of economists was roughly the same, but the department had an even greater variety of professors: there were nine professors of economics out of the twenty-six regular professors, five professors of psychology (counting two that were professors of social psychology)—a much smaller ratio than in 1945—three of industrial relations, and several others, including statistics (two), political science (five), sociology (one), and history (one).[4] The appearance of political scientists is explained by the introduction, in 1955, of political science at MIT under the economics department.[5] In the 1950s the department once

3. The Department of Economics, Statistics, and Political Science was established in 1903, and in 1907 it became the Department of Economics and Statistics. In 1934 it became the Department of Economics and Social Science, and Department of Economics only in 1965. For simplicity I shall not make these distinctions here and just refer to it as the economics department, although these changes are important for marking the evolution of social sciences at MIT and the ultimate specialization of the department in economics only (when the other social sciences finished creating their own departments). Curiously, Samuelson (2000) even mentioned that the department of "Humanics" at MIT was "temporarily merged into economics for administrative tidiness" (perhaps in the 1940s).

4. This information comes from the *MIT Bulletin* (course catalogs) for each of the years mentioned, available online at dome.mit.edu/handle/1721.3/81660 (accessed January 15, 2013).

5. Political science at MIT grew out of the Center for International Studies (CIS) and was part of the attempt to include social sciences in the engineering and science curricula. It became an independent department only in 1965 (web.mit.edu/polisci/about/history/index.html [accessed February 25, 2013]). For a discussion of the CIS, see Cherrier, this volume.

again offered two PhD programs: one in industrial economics and, from 1958 to 1965, another in political science.

In the early years MIT had two presidents, Karl Compton (1930–48) and James Killian (1948–59). Compton tried to improve the status of social sciences at MIT, helping it enlarge its sense of mission to include the social, economic, and political implications of science and technology (Blackmer 2000). In this period just two chairmen led the expansion of the MIT economics department: Ralph Evans Freeman (1933–58) and Robert L. Bishop (1958–64).[6] Instrumental to this expansion were the fundraising efforts of W. Rupert Maclaurin (professor of economics at MIT since 1936 and son of Richard C. Maclaurin, MIT president from 1909 to 1920) and the substantial power and independence that Compton gave him as first director of the industrial relations section of the department.[7]

In this period the MIT economics faculty rose from thirteen members (including assistant, associate, and full professor) in 1944 to thirty in the year Freeman stepped down, in 1958, reaching thirty-six in the following year under Bishop. The department hired professors from major producers of PhDs in the postwar years, such as Harvard, Columbia, and Chicago. The ties with Harvard were particularly strong, as I show with a look at major MIT advisers.

The evidence on the size of the faculty body should be complemented by another aspect of the MIT economics department at this time: the use of different kinds of collaborators to teach courses and aid with research. Besides all ranks of professors (assistant, associate, full, emeritus) and visiting professors, the department had five other types of collaborators: teaching fellow, lecturer, instructor, research assistant, and research associate. Figure 1 shows the change over time in the number of professors (assistant, associate, and full), visiting professors, instructors, research assistants, and research associates. In the 1940s the faculty was small, but there were a great number of collaborators. Over time, the faculty increased and research assistants and associates decreased, vanishing by the mid-1950s.

6. Bishop had Edgar Cary Brown as his successor, who in turn had another long chairmanship, from 1964 to 1982 (though not as long as Freeman's).

7. Samuelson (2000) described this period as follows: "Compton it was who turned MIT from the best engineering school in the world to the best place for science and engineering. Operating as loose cannon on the deck was W. Rupert Maclaurin. . . . Rupert inherited his father's green begging hand and President Karl Compton gave him a loose rein. Ralph Freeman . . . had absolute powers then as Head." Besides the industrial relations, the two other sections of the economics department were psychology and political sciences, established in 1951 and 1956, respectively. Biographical information on W. Rupert Maclaurin comes from Godin 2008.

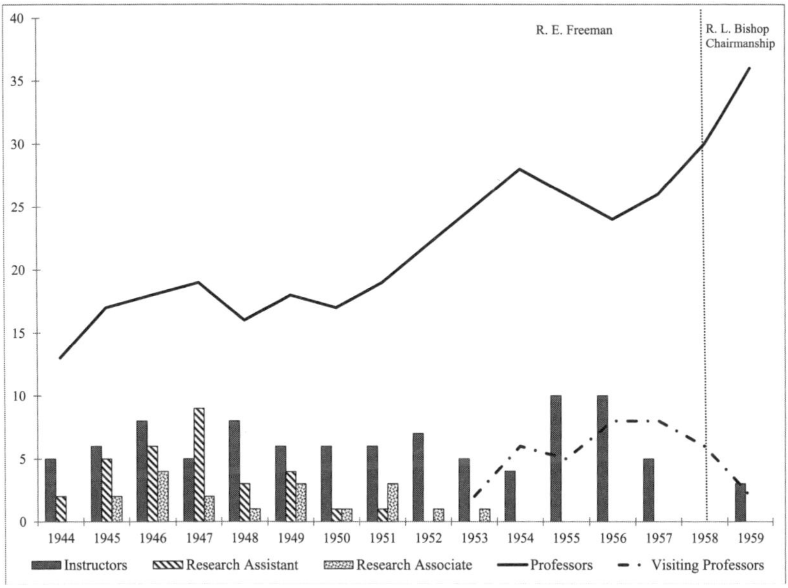

Figure 1 MIT economics faculty and collaborators. The vertical axis represents the number of people. Source: *MIT Bulletin*, various years

The number of instructors was somewhat stable, with a reduction by the late 1950s. It was not very often that someone transitioned from one type of collaborator to another. Thus it is not the case, for instance, that the reduction in the number of research assistants and associates is equivalent to the increase in the number of instructors.

The teaching fellowship was given in this period to only four advanced PhD students (Lawrence Klein in 1944, Harold J. Leavitt in 1947, Hugh Gilbert Lovell and Jack D. Roger in 1950). As for lectureships, the department had for several years a single professional in this situation: Joseph N. Scanlon, an accountant working as director of the United Steel Workers of America who was the first to start as a lecturer at the MIT economics department in 1946, a position he held until his death in 1956. For three consecutive years, from 1952 to 1954, Scanlon had one lecturer colleague (a different person each year). After having one lecturer in the academic year of 1956, the department had two lecturers in 1957 and in 1959, and four in 1958. One lecturer was unique because subsequently he had a long career at MIT: Herbert A. Shepard was a PhD student who was also a research associate in 1949 and an instructor in 1950, the year he graduated.

He then was an assistant professor (of sociology) at the MIT economics department from 1951 to 1956, turning into a lecturer in the following year only and leaving the department afterward.

In contrast to the teaching fellows and lecturers, who were few, figure 1 shows that there were several research assistants, instructors, and research associates. As was the case at Harvard in the 1930s (see Backhouse, this volume, "Samuelson's Move"), the MIT economics department also relied substantially on instructors: the average ratio of instructors to professors (including assistant, associate, and full professor) was around 1:3 from 1944 to 1955 (reaching a maximum of 1:2 in 1948). While several of these instructors were Harvard graduate students, fifteen of the fifty-six instructors (i.e., more than 25 percent) were advanced PhD economics students at MIT. The majority of the instructors stayed up to two years in this position (several serving for just one year).[8] Out of the fifty-six instructors at MIT in 1944–59, fourteen (25 percent) became a professor at MIT after a few years as instructors, as in the case of Robert L. Bishop, Alex Bavelas, Herbert A. Shepard, and Albert Ando, who all became important PhD advisers in the following years.[9] Nonetheless, the scale of the transition from instructor to assistant professor does not account fully for the expansion of the number of regular professors.

Visiting professors started arriving at MIT in 1953 and became very numerous in the second half of the 1950s, reaching a peak of eight in 1956 and 1957 (more than 30 percent of the number of regular professors in the department in these years). Most visitors in the 1950s were economics professors hired for particular projects by the Center of International Studies (CIS), an interdisciplinary center founded in 1952 and having at the time foundation-funded research on economic and political development called "international communication" (see Cherrier, this volume). Among the economics visiting professors were Daniel Lerner (1953–56); Paul Rosenstein-Rodan (1954–59); Wilfred Malenbaum, Everett E. Hagen, and Benjamin H. Higgins (1954–58); Frank Hahn and Evsey D. Domar (1956); Hendrik S. Houthakker (1957); and Robert H. Strotz (1958).[10] From

8. Among the thirty-three people who were instructors at MIT for only one year are James S. Duesenberry, Albert Ando, Guy H. Orcutt, Lionel McKenzie, and Warren Bennis, besides Herbert Shepard already mentioned.

9. Most of the instructors spent up to two years before becoming assistant professors. Two of them spent four or five years as instructors: James E. Boyce, who became assistant professor of international relations in 1953, and Jesse Harris Proctor, who became assistant professor of political science in the subsequent year.

10. Lerner, Rosenstein-Rodan, Malenbaum, Hagen, Higgins, Domar, and James C. Abegglen (visiting professor of psychology), W. Phillips Davison (visiting professor of political science),

Table 1 Main Advisers Arriving at MIT in the 1940s and the 1950s

	Percentage of Students Advised		
	1944–49	1950s	1960s
D. Brown	33.3	12.0	1.1
C. Myers	20.0	18.5	6.4
P. Samuelson	26.7	10.9	2.1
Group total	80.0	41.4	9.6
M. Adelman		8.7	8.5
R. Bishop		4.3	1.6
E. C. Brown		1.1	2.7
E. Domar		0	3.2
C. Kindleberger		14.1	13.3
E. Kuh		0	6.4
R. Solow		7.6	15.4
Group total		35.8	51.1
Grand total	80.0	77.2	60.7

Source: MIT Barton online catalog.

them, four became professors at the MIT economics department in this period: Lerner became a professor of sociology, and Rosenstein-Rodan, Hagen, and Domar became professors of economics.

The size of the economics department may perhaps be a weak indicator of the size of the PhD faculty, and I now look at the main advisers in 1944–59, when the number of economics PhDs awarded by MIT increased substantially (see Svorenčík, this volume). As the number of PhD students rose steeply from each of the first decades of the program to the next, I present in table 1 the percentage of graduated PhDs advised by each professor who was part of a group that arrived in the first two decades of the program (the 1940s and the 1950s).[11]

and Erik H. Erikson (visiting professor of communications) all came to MIT at the initiative of the CIS (more than 50 percent of visitors in this period). See Blackmer 2002, 73–75.

11. I am most grateful to Roger E. Backhouse for kindly sharing his data set (obtained from MIT) of students and advisers with me. It was complemented with a search at the theses section of the MIT Barton online catalog and with additional data on students' placements. In table 1, I included as one advisee a student who had a given professor as one of his advisers. So, in the case of a student who was advised by two professors, he enters as one student for each of them. But I do not include the other readers or members of the thesis committee in these data.

In the 1940s three professors advised (or co-advised) 80 percent of the fifteen PhDs who graduated from 1944 to 1949: Douglass V. Brown (Harvard PhD, 1932), Charles A. Myers (Chicago PhD, 1939), and Paul A. Samuelson (Harvard PhD, 1941), with the first two working on industrial relations. Samuelson advised Lawrence Klein, the first economics PhD from MIT, in 1944. So the PhD program was indeed small, and the advising was handled by just a few professors. Other advisers in that first decade include Dorwin P. Cartwright (Harvard PhD in psychology, 1940), professor of psychology and a leading figure in social psychology.[12] One of Cartwright's economics students in this period was Harold Harding Kelley, who later became an important psychologist.

In the following decade new advisers entered the scene and the strengthening of the economics identity of the department started, eventually leading to the migration of the industrial economics group to the Sloan School of Management. In addition to the three major advisers of the 1940s, five new names advised a significant percentage of the ninety-two PhDs who graduated in the 1950s: Charles P. Kindleberger (Columbia PhD, 1937), Morris A. Adelman (Harvard PhD, 1948), Robert M. Solow (Harvard PhD, 1951), Robert L. Bishop (Harvard PhD, 1949), and E. Cary Brown (Harvard PhD, 1948). Altogether, these eight professors advised roughly 77 percent of the PhDs who graduated from the economics department in the 1950s—with the group of the advisers of the 1940s still dominating that of the new advisers, a situation that was reversed in the 1960s. There are other important advisers displayed in table 1: Evsey Domar (Harvard PhD, 1947), hired at MIT in 1958, and Edwin Kuh, who was another Harvard PhD (1955) hired at MIT in 1959, both of whom became active advisers in the 1960s.

With new professors being hired in the subsequent decades, table 1 shows the life cycle of an adviser, and the slow reduction in the percentage of students advised over time (when it is not the case that the adviser leaves MIT for another job). Solow was different in this respect, as he increased his share of students advised and also remained an active adviser for a longer period (see also Svorenčík, this volume). Solow was instrumental in changing the direction of scholarship in the PhD program toward economics and away from management and industrial relations.

12. Cartwright was a cofounder, with Kurt Lewin, of the MIT Research Center for Group Dynamics, where most of his students developed their work. A year after Lewin's death, this center moved to the University of Michigan in 1948 allegedly because of funding difficulties (www.rcgd.isr.umich.edu/history/ [accessed January 10, 2013]).

Table 2 MIT Advisers and the Number of Students Advised

MIT Advisers		Number of MIT Advisees				
Graduated Elsewhere	*University and Year*	1944–49	1950–59	1960–69	1970–79	1944–2009
D. Brown	(Harvard, 1932)	5	11	2	0	18
C. Kindleberger	(Columbia, 1937)	0	13	25	10	49
C. Myers	(Chicago, 1939)	3	17	12	1	34
P. Samuelson	(Harvard, 1941)	4	10	4	8	26
M. Adelman	(Harvard, 1948)	0	8	16	10	35
R. Solow	(Harvard, 1951)	—	7	29	25	77
F. Fisher	(Harvard, 1960)	—	—	13	25	54
Graduated from MIT	*Adviser and Year*					
H. Shepard *	(A. Bavelas, 1950)	—	6	0	0	6
P. Diamond	(R. Solow, 1963)	—	—	0	8	41
P. Temin *	(C. Kindleberger, 1964)	—	—	0	10	20
J. Bhagwati *	(C. Kindleberger, 1967)	—	—	0	10	12
S. Fischer	(F. Fisher, 1969)	—	—	0	13	52

*First placement after graduating was at MIT.
Source: MIT Barton online catalog.

With the new generation of advisers (also with ties to Harvard), in the 1960s, arrived a group of former MIT students who became intimately associated with the image of the economics department: Peter Diamond (PhD, 1963), Peter Temin (PhD, 1964), and Jagdish Bhagwati (PhD, 1967), with the last two having MIT as their first placement after graduating (either the economics department, in the case of Bhagwati, or the business school, in the case of Temin).[13]

To have a sense of the size of the student body advised by each professor, table 2 reports the number of students advised by decade by a selection of

13. The advisers arriving in the 1960s who graduated from Harvard were Franklin Fisher (1960), Michael Piore (1966), and Lance Taylor (1968). The MIT economics department used to hire some of its own students. The first such occurrence in the 1940s and 1950s was George P. Shultz, a student of Douglass Brown, who graduated in 1949 and did not advise graduate students at MIT. Others in this situation were George B. Baldwin (a student of Charles Myers), Romney Robinson (advised by Paul Samuelson), and Warren Bennis (a student of Herbert Shepard). The MIT advisers in this period who were MIT alumni also include Richard Eckaus (1954). For family trees of MIT advisers who graduated from MIT, as well as other data on faculty and students, for the entire period 1944–2011, see Svorenčík, this volume.

major MIT advisers, some of whom obtained their PhDs elsewhere and others who graduated from MIT.[14] The second column shows the year that advisers obtained their PhDs and either the university from which they graduated (in the case of those with a PhD from other institutions) or their advisers (for the MIT students).

Three things stand out in table 2. The first, already noted, is that several MIT advisers graduated from Harvard, which was the leading producer of economics PhDs at the time (cf. Bowen 1953, 209–10; Barber 1996, 18). The second is that if we identify both the number of students directly advised by a particular professor and those advised by someone who was his student as one important aspect of the influence of that professor in the graduate program, it seems fair to state that Kindleberger was a very important adviser in the early period. Not only did he advise a significant number of students over time, but he was also the adviser of two professors, Peter Temin and Jagdish Bhagwati, who later on advised a significant number of MIT students themselves. Robert Solow and Franklin Fisher come after Kindleberger in this dimension: both advised a great number of students and each one had a prominent student become an important adviser at MIT, Peter Diamond and Stanley Fischer, respectively. Finally, Samuelson advised a relatively small number of students in comparison with other professors. But this certainly does not decrease his importance as a teacher, academic interlocutor, and magnet for students and visitors going to MIT (for praise from some of his prominent students, see Dixit 2012, 23–24; and Szenberg, Gottesman, and Ramrattan 2005, 24–26, 99–108).

Given that I have identified the major advisers in the early decades of the PhD program, it is interesting to have an idea of their main lines of research. To this end, I looked at the theses of their advisees to have a sense of the kinds of works these advisers supported. Through the theses' titles and fields to which their students were affiliated immediately after graduating, and using the list of the fields of specialization in economics of the time, I tried to identify broad lines of research associated with MIT advisers.[15]

Several of the main advisers had a clear orientation toward industrial relations and business administration, with most of their advisees writing on these themes: Douglass Brown, Charles Myers, and Herbert Shepard.

14. The data in this table, as in table 1, include students' advisers and coadvisers.

15. The information about fields in economics comes from the American Economic Association directory of members and handbooks from several years.

The first two were professors of industrial relations; Shepard was professor of sociology at the MIT economics department. Some of the thesis titles advised by Brown, Myers, and Shepard are illustrative: "The Purchasing Power Theories of Trade Unions," "Industrial Relations in the British Coal Industry," "Management, Labor, and the Concept of Control," "Some Problems of Negotiated Pension Plans," "Relationships between Business Activities and Social and Civic Activities of Executives: A Case Study in Wellesley, Massachusetts," and "Aggregate Employee Productivity under the Scanlon Plan."

Kindleberger (a professor of economics) advised mostly on international economics (sometimes with a historical approach), though also covering a few other areas such as income and employment theory, economic systems, economic growth, and monetary economics and business fluctuations. Some of the thesis titles advised by Kindleberger in this period are "A Study on the Theory of International Economic Organization," "New Zealand and Cyclical Dependence, 1920–1939," and "The Natural Resource Content of the United States Foreign Trade, 1870–1955." Morris Adelman (professor of economics) supervised students working on themes of industrial organization, such as "Coaxial Cable and Radio Relays in Long Distance Telephone Lines," "Economies of Scale in the Operation of Crude Oil Pipe Lines," and "Internal Transfer Pricing and Vertical Integration in the Automotive Assembly Industry."

Finally, the department had Paul Samuelson and Robert Solow, who each advised a diverse set of works, including monetary and business fluctuations, price theory, public finance, international economics, investment and security markets (finance), mathematical methods and econometrics, and economic growth.

We can now go to the other side of the graduate program, the students, and see not only the substantial increase in the size of the PhD program and the placement of these students, but also the important changes in the very conception of a PhD degree in the United States in the 1950s.

2. MIT PhD Students

Although economists in the United States were a heterogeneous group with a lower prestige among the general public as compared with other professions (Bowen 1953, 33), they acquired increasing importance in American society. The professionalization of American economics went hand in hand with the redefinition of the PhD into "an *academic* credential providing evidence of specialized *scholarly* competence" in practical and scientific matters (Fourcade 2009, 72).[16]

The greater social importance of economists combined with the "technicalization of economics" (Bowen 1953, 103) raised concerns with the form, standards, and nature of the graduate program in economics in the 1940s and the 1950s. These issues included the list of courses offered, the nature of the graduate work and of a PhD thesis, the interinstitutional diversity among graduate programs in the United States, the duration of a PhD program, and job prospects for an economist with a PhD degree.

The changes taking place in economics motivated the American Economic Association (AEA) to sponsor a study of the economics profession in 1951–52. Howard Bowen (at Williams College when the report was published) led a group of representatives from the Carnegie Institute of Technology (G. L. Bach), University of Chicago (Milton Friedman), University of Michigan (I. L. Sharfman), and Duke University (Joseph J. Spengler).[17] Their effort involved interviewing chairmen, professors, and graduate students, and visiting several institutions, as well as compiling data on different graduate programs. The group produced a long study published in the *American Economic Review* in 1953 (Bowen 1953), with a detailed analysis of the economics graduate education, data on its evolution, and discussions on future trends and recommendations. Bowen was clear about two things: first, that the AEA sponsored and published the study but did not attempt "to give official sanction to the report or to the recommendations contained therein," and second, that he directed the study and was "solely responsible for the conclusions and recommendations" (iii).

I want to highlight here two main issues from that report: first, the proposal for a core in the PhD training, and second, a new understanding of the nature of the PhD thesis. With respect to the first, the view held at the

16. Marion Fourcade (2009, 96–114) discusses "the academic roots of public expertise" in the United States.

17. Bowen obtained his PhD from the University of Iowa in 1935 and was a professor of economics (and dean) at the University of Illinois from 1947 to 1952, when he moved to Williams College. At Illinois he became dean in 1947 with a mandate "to stimulate research and scholarship, to improve teaching, to bring curricula up to date," among other issues discussed by Winton Solberg and Robert Tomilson (1997). The authors show how Bowen was forced to resign as dean in 1950 after a harsh conflict (known as the Bowen controversy) initiated by reforms he implemented. This controversy, they argue, also reflected a clash between free market ideologies and Keynesian ideas associated with Bowen and others. Just before resigning as a dean, he was appointed chair of the ad hoc committee that started working in 1951 after obtaining a Rockefeller Foundation grant to finance it (Bowen 1953, iii).

time was that the economics undergraduates had very uneven backgrounds and no great intellectual independence and maturity when they entered graduate school (Bowen 1953, 3–4, 7). According to Bowen, this led to a widespread understanding that a graduate program should "require knowledge of fundamentals [economic theory, economic history, history of ideas, and research techniques] and breadth of understanding" from its students and emphasize scholarship (40): the idea being that the graduate training is just one of a sequence of steps in their careers (instead of being its pinnacle) and they are just learning the rudiments of their profession that they will further develop when practicing it.

Bowen then expressed his views on "the standards to be met by a Ph.D. candidate" (42) that would respect the diversity of interests, capacities, skills, and differences among universities that characterized economics back then.[18] Among the several issues that were part of these standards was the idea of a common core, coupled with the realization of comprehensive exams to test the students' proficiency, and with the organization of the subsequent graduate training in major and minor fields—when students would further acquire both breadth and specialization.

What should be the content of a common core to be required of all PhD students? Bowen sent questionnaires to professors, who agreed in general that this core should be required, and a "near-agreement" emerged on "only one subject, namely, economic theory" (104)—though the very understanding of what constituted economic theory was not completely clear, as Bowen discussed (106, 109–11). Other subjects that had strong support for inclusion in the core were statistics, economic history, history of economic thought, and monetary and banking theory (105–6).

Given that economics training would proceed through core courses, comprehensive exams, and fields, and that economics was understood to have become more technical, it follows that graduate students were expected to demonstrate the mastering of techniques. Therefore, it is not surprising to see the desire to change the nature of a PhD thesis, which was already an integral part of the requirements of economics graduate programs. A thesis would still have to be "an important and original contribution to knowledge" (153), but no longer would it "deal with problems that are too comprehensive," which used to imply massive tomes with more of a synthesis of "other economists' ideas rather than reports of original

18. Bowen (1953, 41) considered that imposing "uniform and detailed minimal standards" would neither be possible nor be desirable in economics.

research" (156). Students should instead research "a specific and limited problem" (157). Bowen thus welcomed the tendency of having dissertations of article length provided that did not compromise quality and "adequate documentation and description of methodology" (156). After all, doctoral dissertations are not to be considered "the student's final creative effort" (157).[19]

An important side to the discussion on the format and requirements of a PhD thesis is the role that mathematics (and the use of models) assumed in economics in the postwar period. In the late 1940s and 1950s public discussions about the use of mathematics in economics were roiling the profession (see summary and references in Koopmans 1957, 172–78). MIT voices were strongly heard in this debate, particularly from Samuelson (1952, 1954) and Solow (1954), two of the major advisers there. They joined other economists like Robert Dorfman (1954) and Tjalling Koopmans (1957) in stressing that mathematics is a language and a powerful tool to be used by social scientists, and that it plays the same role in economics as it does in physical science and engineering.

While Samuelson (1952, 56) repeated Willard Gibbs's statement he had used in his 1947 book *Foundations of Economic Analysis*, "Mathematics is a language," Solow (1954, 373) stated something that, according to him, nearly all academic economists know: "It would be tedious and trite to review here exactly what mathematics is and what it does. My own position is that it is simply an immensely powerful and efficient device or vocabulary for thinking about certain kinds of problems."

The role of mathematics in the training of social scientists was broader and very important in this period, to the point that the Social Science Research Council established a committee to address this issue (Social Science Research Council 1956).[20] The committee justified its mission by the demand for a new curriculum in mathematics for social scientists created by the "recent developments in various fields of social science" (82), being indisputable that social scientists "ought to study mathematics" (83).

19. Indeed, as Bowen (1953, 48) summarized, "we cannot hope to make every Ph.D. into a Wesley Mitchell or a J. M. Keynes. We can, however, insist that they know something about the basic methods of research in economics and that they are able to apply these methods in relatively limited research situations."

20. The Committee on Mathematical Training of Social Scientists of the Social Science Research Council worked during 1954–55 and was chaired by the mathematician William G. Madow, professor at the University of Illinois at Urbana-Champaign. It included a diverse set of five other members: another mathematician (working on operations research), a historian, a psychologist, a statistician, and the economist Jacob Marschak (then at the University of Chicago).

While it recommended policies for a special undergraduate curriculum in mathematics for social science students (understood to be a joint responsibility of the mathematics and social science departments), the committee was clear that this would affect the graduate training in social sciences as well: "It will be necessary for many years to provide opportunities in graduate schools and summer sessions for the mathematical training of those who do not obtain satisfactory mathematical training while in college" (83).

Finally, with respect to the social role of the PhD degree in the United States, Marion Fourcade (2009, 77) argues that it served "as a key instrument of both professional standardization vis-à-vis outside markets *and* disciplinary, intellectual standardization inside." For Bowen (1953, 179), the PhD was no longer "a union card for college teaching" conferred after long gestation to older college teachers "seasoned by years of practical experience":

> If . . . the Ph.D. is regarded not as something to be awarded in middle life after some of the most productive years have passed, but as something to be given to a young person who has mastered the basic knowledge and techniques of economics and who shows ability and promise, then the argument for the long period becomes much less persuasive. I lean strongly toward the latter concept of the degree.

It is against this broad background that we should look to the substantial increase in the economics graduate education in the postwar period in the United States. In the case of the MIT program, the number of economics PhDs who graduated each year skyrocketed (see Svorenčík, this volume): if the average number in the 1940s was 2.5 students per year, it went to 18.8 in the 1960s.[21] This increase at MIT accompanied similar trends in other economics graduate programs such as Yale's (with an average of 3 students per year in the 1940s, and 12.6 in the 1960s), despite the fact that some of them were older and more established than MIT's.[22] Even other newer programs, such as the one that Rochester implemented after hiring

21. The MIT economics department explicitly stated in the *MIT Bulletin* (1944–45, 72) of the early 1940s that a small group of graduate students would be admitted to the PhD program "who can be given an individual type of instruction"; that language had been abandoned by 1946.

22. The data on Yale come from the *Yale Book of Numbers*, 1701–1976 and 1976–2000, oir.yale.edu/1701-1976-yale-book-numbers [accessed March 1, 2013]). The data for 1976, missing in these books, were obtained from an archivist at Yale's Manuscripts and Archives, who consulted the *Graduate School Report of the Dean*.

Table 3 Major Producers of Economics PhDs, 1945–51

Rank	Institution	Percentage of PhDs awarded 1945–46 through 1950–51	Number of PhDs awarded 1945–46 through 1950–51
1	Harvard	17.1	257
2	Columbia	8.8	132
3	Chicago	6.3	95
4	Wisconsin	6.1	92
5	Cornell	4.5	68
6	Illinois	4.4	66
7	Minnesota	3.2	48
8	Iowa	3.1	46
9	New York	3.1	46
10	Ohio State	3.1	47
	Total	59.7	897

Source: Bowen 1953, 209–10, 214.

Lionel McKenzie, were not much smaller than MIT's: in 1958 McKenzie reported that Rochester had five doctoral students (while MIT had nine), and that he expected to have thirteen in 1959 (MIT had eighteen), and "add about five to eight students each year for the three years following 1959–60" (MIT reached nineteen students in 1963).[23]

In the postwar period, a handful of universities produced a substantial number of PhDs, which constituted a group of the ten big producers that awarded roughly 60 percent of all PhD degrees in economics. As table 3 shows, among them, Harvard, Columbia, Chicago, and Wisconsin awarded almost 40 percent of all PhD degrees, as reported by Bowen (1953, 209–10, 214). In contrast to these top ten institutions, MIT awarded only twenty-one PhDs in the same years (1945–46 through 1950–51), which corresponded to only 1.4 percent of the economics PhDs awarded in the period (Bowen 1953, 210). The figures for Yale, Princeton, Northwestern, Duke, and Pittsburgh—programs that had existed at least since the mid-1920s—according to Bowen, varied from fourteen to twenty-four PhDs awarded (0.9 percent to 1.6 percent).[24] These institutions ranked higher than many

23. Letter to Thomas H. Carrol, July 15, 1959, box 7, folder "Outgoing Correspondence 1959," Lionel McKenzie Papers, David M. Rubenstein Rare Book and Manuscript Library, Duke University.

24. Instead of the twenty-four students reported by Bowen for Yale, the *Yale Book of Numbers* registers twenty-seven PhDs in this period.

others that awarded from one to ten PhDs in these five years. So, despite being a new program, the MIT doctorate in industrial economics managed to attract a good number of students from the start.

In terms of the graduate courses in economics that MIT offered to its students in the 1940s and 1950s, all of them were elective. It was not unusual, then, to have undergraduate and graduate students attending these courses at MIT and several other universities, an issue analyzed by Bowen (who emphasized the need to have separate courses dedicated to master's and to doctoral students). Looking at the courses listed as being "primarily for Graduate students" in the *MIT Bulletin* for the years 1945 and 1955, we can produce the list presented in table 4.

One interesting aspect is that this list reflects the changes in the faculty body and the broad research interests indicated in the previous section. Together with an increase in the number of courses offered (from thirty in 1945 to forty-four in 1955), the graduate program in industrial economics kept its identity. However, there was a relative reduction in psychology courses and an increase in economics courses, with new areas now covered, such as economic history, economic development, economic growth, economics of innovation, national income, money and banking, and fiscal policy.

In terms of formal requirements, the MIT graduate school specified four: one major field concluding with a general examination, one minor field in an area distinct from the major (with the idea that the minor would contribute to the development of professional leadership rather than improving technical competence), proficiency in two scientific modern foreign languages, and the thesis in the major field. From the beginning, the PhD program at MIT required that students have some understanding of all fields offered, which included economic theory. However, students would choose four fields to compose their major and their general examination—and here economic theory was not mandatory but just one option among many. In 1948 the number of fields for the examination increased to six.[25] In 1951 things changed: now students would be examined in five

25. The fields listed from 1944 to 1947 were economic theory, sociopsychological theory, industrial relations, industrial organization and price policy, economics of technological change, statistical method and theory, economic history, and the state in relation to industry. In 1948 the list changed: "Possible fields include Economic Theory, Labor Economics and Labor Relations, Industrial Organization and Price Policy, the Economics of Innovation, Human Relations in Industry, Methods in Human Relations, Statistical Method and Theory, Fiscal Policy and Economic Fluctuations, International Economics and Relations, Economic and Industrial History, and others" (*MIT Bulletin* 1948, 93).

Table 4 Graduate Courses Offered by the MIT Department of Economics

	1945–46	
No.	*Subject*	*Instructor*
Ec17	Economic Analysis	Samuelson
Ec18	Economic Analysis	Samuelson
Ec19	Mathematical Approach to Economics	Samuelson, H. A. Freeman
Ec24	Schools of Economic Thought	D. V. Brown, Bissell
Ec26	Business Cycles	Samuelson
Ec37	Advanced Economic Statistics	H. A. Freeman, Samuelson
Ec47	Investment Finance	D. S. Tucker
Ec48	Investment Analysis	D. S. Tucker
Ec59	International Economics	R. E. Freeman
Ec66	Seminar in Industrial Relations	Pigors
Ec67	Seminar in Labor Problems	D. V. Brown
Ec68	Seminar in Labor Problems	D. V. Brown
Ec721	Psychology of Perception and Action	Cartwright
Ec735	Advanced Group Psychology	Bavelas
Ec75	Laboratory in Research Methods	Lippitt
Ec76	Laboratory in Research Methods	Lippitt
Ec77	Seminar in Topological Psychology	Lewin
Ec781	Social Psychology of Change	Radke
Ec782	Social Psychology of Change	Radke
Ec791	Advanced Psychological Seminar	Lewin, Radke
Ec792	Advanced Psychological Seminar	Lewin
Ec793	Advanced Psychological Seminar	Lewin
Ec794	Advanced Psychological Seminar	Lewin
Ec82	Government Control of Industry	Thresher
Ec91	Economics Seminar	R. E. Freeman
Ec92	Economics Seminar	R. E. Freeman
Ec93	Industrial Economics Seminar	D. V. Brown
Ec94	Industrial Economics Seminar	D. V. Brown
Ec95	Social Science Seminar	McGregor
Ec96	Social Science Seminar	Knickerbocker
	1955–56	
No.	*Subject*	*Instructor*
14.673	Labor-Management Relations and Public Policy	D. V. Brown, Shultz
14.681	Seminar in Personnel Administration	Pigors
14.682	Seminar in Personnel Administration	Pigors
14.691	Research Seminar in Industrial Relations	Myers
14.692	Research Seminar in Industrial Relations	Myers

Table 4 *(continued)*

1955–56		
No.	*Subject*	*Instructor*
14.693	Collective Bargaining and Union-Management Cooperation	Scanlon
14.694	Seminar in Union-Management Cooperation	Scanlon
14.772	Industrial Sociology Seminar	Shepard
14.774	Social Psychology Seminar	Bavelas
14.775	Analysis of Behavior Seminar	Licklider
14.776	Analysis of Behavior Seminar	Licklider
14.784	Psychological Theory Seminar	Bavelas
14.791	Reading Seminar in Social Science	—
14.792	Reading Seminar in Social Science	—
14.116	Economic and Financial Policies III	Adelman
14.121	Economic Analysis	Bishop
14.122	Economic Analysis	Samuelson
14.132	Schools of Economic Thought	Bishop
14.151	Mathematical Approach to Economics	Samuelson
14.161	Economic History	W. W. Rostow
14.162	Economic History	W. W. Rostow
14.171	Theory of Economic Growth	Rosenstein-Rodan
14.172	Research Seminar in Economic Development	Millikan
14.174	Non-Economic Factors in Economic Growth	Hagen
14.191	Economics Seminar	R. E. Freeman
14.192	Economics Seminar	R. E. Freeman
14.195	Reading Seminar in Economics	—
14.196	Reading Seminar in Economics	—
14.271	Problems in Industrial Economics	Adelman
14.272	Government Regulation of Industry	Adelman
14.281	Economics of Entrepreneurship and Innovation	Maclaurin
14.282	Economics of Innovation Seminar	Maclaurin
14.291	Industrial Economics Seminar	—
14.292	Industrial Economics Seminar	—
14.382	Economic Statistics	Solow
14.391	Research Seminar in Economics	Solow
14.451	National Income	Millikan
14.461	Monetary and Banking Problems	R. E. Freeman
14.472	Fiscal Policy	E. C. Brown
14.481	Business Cycles	Solow
14.581	International Economics	Kindleberger
14.582	International Economics	Kindleberger
14.671	Problems in Labor Economics	Myers, Shultz
14.672	Public Policy on Labor Relations	—

Source: *MIT Bulletin*, 1945 and 1955.

fields (with two or three designated as primary and requiring "more intensive preparation than the other two or three, which are designated as secondary"), and they must "demonstrate an elementary knowledge in Statistics and have taken one graduate subject in Economic History" (*MIT Bulletin* 1951, 107).[26] This situation remained the same until 1957, when economic theory became compulsory for all students, who would be examined in five fields: economic theory was a required primary field for everybody, and the same requirements for statistics and economic history applied as before.[27]

Given that the MIT PhD program was on the rise, with new advisers gaining prominence (among them important economists), and with important changes taking place in the graduate training in the United States, it is interesting to see the role of mathematics and the use of models in the theses at MIT. Without examining in detail each thesis produced in the early years, we can have an indirect indication of how MIT was contributing to the move toward shorter and narrowly defined theses through the number of thesis pages. The evidence presented in table 5 and figure 2 is that there was a reduction in the median length of MIT theses, with a simultaneous increase in the dispersion of such length.[28] Given that shortening the length and narrowing the focus of PhD theses were most likely developing slowly over time, I present statistics on page numbers of theses advised by all advisers in each decade, the 1940s, the 1950s, and the 1960s.

In figure 2 is the distribution of the number of pages across the theses defended in the three first decades. The general movement is interesting: a reduction of the occurrence of "very short" theses (say, up to 100 pages) and a standardization of the median number of pages around 230 pages. With respect to the "very big" theses (say, above 500 pages), there was a tendency for a reduction of their occurrence, but over time even very few massive theses were produced (above 900 pages). As recorded in the last

26. The list of fields was almost the same as that of 1948 (with "Economic Fluctuations and Their Control" replacing "Fiscal Policy and Economic Fluctuations"), which remained unchanged until 1956.

27. "Other possible fields include national income and fluctuations, industrial organization and policy, economics of innovation, international economics, economic development, labor economics and labor relations, human relations in industry, economic history, statistical theory and methods, and others" (*MIT Bulletin* 1957, 133).

28. The page numbers used in figure 2 and table 5 come from the MIT online catalog. This information was available for roughly 98.5 percent of the theses defended in this period.

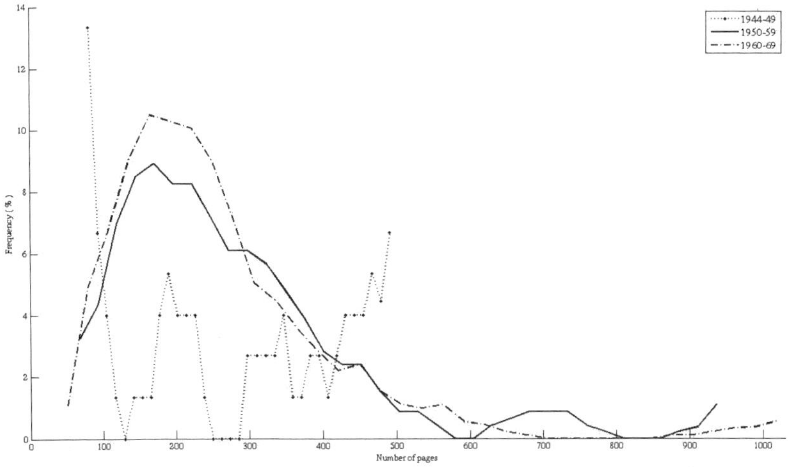

Figure 2 The distribution of the number of pages of PhD theses in each of the three first decades of the MIT program. Source: MIT online catalog

row of table 5, the median (and the minimum) number of pages reduced monotonically from 322 (81) in the 1940s to 224 (51) in the 1960s, while the maximum number of pages followed the reverse path. This table also identifies the statistics of thesis length for a group of main advisers.

It is significant that the median length of the theses advised by the professors working on industrial economics, industrial organization, and business administration—Douglass Brown, Myers, and Adelman (though this does not apply to Shepard)—is higher than those advised by several economists.[29] In particular, Samuelson and Solow, so instrumental in the training (and advising, in the case of Solow) of MIT students and in the defense of mathematics in economics, advised relatively shorter theses (small median number of pages together with overall small standard deviation). Therefore, as the economists gained importance over time as advisers, they changed the standard length for PhD theses.

After graduation, what were the job opportunities for MIT economists? I once again focus on 1944–59 and try to identify the placement of the PhD students. In table 6 are the major advisers of this period, the number of students advised (counting for each professor only the students whom

29. The biggest thesis in each decade was advised either by Douglass Brown or by Myers.

Table 5 Number of Pages of PhD Theses, by Decade and by Main Advisers

	1944–49					1950–59					1960–69				
	Theses	Median	Std. Deviation	Minimum	Maximum	Theses	Median	Std. Deviation	Minimum	Maximum	Theses	Median	Std. Deviation	Minimum	Maximum
D. Brown	5	398	111.9	173	491	9	241	72.1	140	357	2	268	149.5	118	417
C. Myers	2	451	13.5	437	464	16	345	197.2	125	937	14	302	211.8	94	1,018
P. Samuelson	4	270	71.3	204	370	9	225	55.8	108	290	3	100	34.2	97	171
M. Adelman						8	376	166.0	84	700	16	272	125.7	117	599
R. Bishop						4	213	11.2	195	226	3	245	67.1	112	262
E. C. Brown						1	192	5	203	104.3	178	455			
C. Kindleberger						13	190	94.6	152	469	24	244	101.4	113	560
M. Millikan						2	232	92.0	140	324	5	224	70.3	153	344
H. Shepard						6	199	80.9	123	365	—	—	—	—	—
R. Solow						7	186	74.0	134	378	27	148	71.3	51	385
A. Ando											9	207	74.9	115	362
E. Domar											6	250	282.3	147	966
R. Eckaus											9	251	104.2	83	372
F. Fisher											13	204	154.3	72	551
E. Kuh											12	245	117.3	129	514
F. Modigliani											5	148	98.8	141	399
All advisers	15	322	139.6	81	491	92	243	152.1	68	937	183	224	145.3	51	1,018

Note: The first column in each decade, "Theses," indicates the number of theses advised by a given professor for which information about page numbers was available.
Source: MIT online catalog.

he served as primary adviser), and the percentage of the students of each adviser whose placement information was available ("placement coverage"). Of those students whose placement was identifiable, I indicated the kind of placement they had: in the private sector, in academe (not including business schools), in business schools, in the government and international agencies (International Monetary Fund and United Nations), and in other sectors (research institutes, foundations, Cowles Commission, etc.). Interesting patterns are shown in table 6.[30]

One noteworthy characteristic is that for most advisers the majority of their students (whose placement information was available) went to academic positions. The exception was Douglass Brown, a professor of industrial relations, whose students mostly went to the private sector. The other professors whose students went to the private sector were Adelman and Myers, both advising on industrial economics and business administration, and Samuelson. To the business schools went students of the industrial relations professors, Douglass Brown and Myers, and of Bishop. And six of the nine advisers listed had students going to governments and international agencies.

The overall placement pattern of MIT economists followed somewhat the employment trends of the time in the United States: Bowen (1953, 1) indicated that the majority of economists were employed in higher education, followed by the government and the business sector. Jobs for economists with a PhD degree in the government had increased greatly in previous decades, while the business sector hired only a very small, though steadily growing, share of economists. This is roughly the picture we get in the first row of the bottom section of table 6 with all advisers, but with more MIT students going to the private sector than to the government as compared with the data from Bowen. When we look at all advisers in two subperiods, the 1940s and the 1950s, we see that the private sector was much more important in the first period, employing almost the same as academe. However, in the 1950s the importance of academic jobs skyrocketed while the private sector shrank to the level of the government (which stayed roughly constant in these periods). This overall trend between these two decades is also observed in two of the three major advisers who arrived in the 1940s (not shown in the table): Myers and

30. Walter Isard (Harvard PhD in economics, 1943), listed as an adviser, was first a research fellow and lecturer at Harvard (1943–53), then a professor associated with the Center for Urban and Regional Studies that was part of the MIT School of Architecture. Isard advised theses cataloged as from the economics department.

Table 6 Main Advisers and the Placement of Their Advisees

			Placement Distribution				
MIT Advisers	Number of Advisees, 1944–59	Placement Coverage (%)	Private Sector	Academe (not Business School)	Business School	Government and It'l Agencies	Other
M. Adelman	8	88	14.3	71.4	0.0	0.0	14.3
R. Bishop	4	100	0.0	50.0	25.0	25.0	0.0
D. Brown	14	86	50.0	16.7	16.7	8.3	8.3
W. Isard	3	100	0.0	66.7	0.0	33.3	0.0
C. Kindleberger	13	100	0.0	84.6	0.0	15.4	0.0
C. Myers	19	89	5.9	64.7	23.5	5.9	0.0
P. Samuelson	13	100	15.4	69.2	0.0	7.7	7.7
H. Shepard	6	67	0.0	75.0	0.0	0.0	25.0
R. Solow	7	100	0.0	100.0	0.0	0.0	0.0
All Advisers							
1944–59	107	88	12.8	62.8	10.6	7.4	6.4
1944–49	15	87	30.8	38.5	7.7	7.7	15.4
1950–59	92	88	9.9	66.7	11.1	7.4	4.9

Source: Data obtained from MIT by Roger E. Backhouse.

Samuelson advised students who went significantly more to academe in the 1950s than their students who graduated in the 1940s (Douglass Brown, in contrast, kept sending half of his students to the private sector in the two decades).

A few additional issues emerge when we look at placements of students of each of the major advisers. First, it was common to have students as instructors at the MIT economics department either prior to their thesis defense or immediately after graduation (in which case I also looked at their employment after this position). Second, several of the major advisers had at least one student staying at MIT after graduation: Myers, Douglass Brown, Shepard, Adelman, Samuelson, and Bavelas.[31] Third, three students, one advised by Max Millikan (first chairman of the Center for International Studies who advised only two students in this period) and two by Solow (out of his seven advisees), went to the CIS.

In terms of institutions that hired MIT students more frequently, a few are worth mentioning: Rice Institute (one student advised by Kindleberger and two by Adelman), business schools (mostly Berkeley, but also Columbia, Chicago, University of Pennsylvania, Minnesota, Pittsburgh, and others), Minnesota and Northwestern (each hired three students, with two additional students going to the linguistics department and the transportation center at Northwestern), and Michigan State University (two students advised by Myers, and one of Brown's students whose second appointment was there). The University of Michigan was also a place where MIT students went (with some of them going to the Department of Industrial Relations), and Brandeis University hired two students advised by Samuelson. RAND Corporation and the Cowles Commission each hired just one MIT economist in 1944–59 (advised by Solow and Samuelson, respectively).

Given the small scale of the MIT program in the formative years, the number of students who went to particular sectors or institutions is significant. And the wide range of the job network for MIT economists is an interesting aspect of a graduate program that was on the rise.

31. Samuelson had another advisee whose second appointment was at MIT: Eckaus, who graduated in 1954 and was associated with the CIS and its director in 1957, and who stayed at Brandeis University from 1951 to 1961, going to MIT in 1962. During his time at Brandeis, Eckaus received an offer from Rochester (thanks to Samuelson's recommendation to Lionel McKenzie) that he eventually declined (letter from Samuelson, April 1, 1957, box 6, folder "1957 Letters at Mich., includes Debreu on eq. paper" and letter from Eckaus, February 14, 1958, box 6, folder "Lionel W. McKenzie (incoming) Sept. 1957–Sept. 1958," Lionel McKenzie Papers, David M. Rubenstein Rare Book and Manuscript Library, Duke University).

3. Concluding Remarks

As the social importance of economists in the United States in the postwar period increased and as American higher education expanded after the GI Bill, a new graduate training in economics started to take shape. There was an expansion of the existing programs and the creation of new ones, together with the reformulation of the nature of that training. Economists became increasingly seen as technicians who should take core courses and show proficiency in techniques applied to narrowly defined problems in shorter theses. PhD degrees would now be awarded to young people who would perfect their techniques in practice after graduation.

The PhD program in industrial economics at MIT was part of the general expansion of graduate education in the United States. It originated from the need to give engineers and scientists an education in social sciences (Cherrier, this volume). And the program found its way to face and to contribute to the changes in economics and economists' training of the time. It went through a substantial expansion in the first two decades, a pattern shared with other universities, with an increase in the number of students and of professors. Overall, the MIT economics program had close ties with Harvard, the biggest producer of PhDs at the time and a neighboring institution: multiple Harvard PhDs served as instructors, and, more importantly, several became active advisers at MIT. The program kept its industrial relations identity, but gradually emphasized training in several fields of economics and reduced the role played by psychology. The home of social sciences at MIT, the economics department offered in two periods a second PhD program: group psychology (1945–47) and political science (1958–65).

From the advisers' side, we see that not only Samuelson but also Myers and Douglass Brown were very important in the first decade of a program with a clear industrial relations identity. In the subsequent years other professors entered this group and started reshaping the program with a stronger economics identity: Kindleberger, Fisher, Solow, and Adelman. The first three, in turn, advised students who later became distinctive MIT advisers: Temin, Bhagwati, Diamond, and Fischer.

MIT professors like Samuelson and Solow were active voices in the broader discussion on the role of mathematics in the social sciences that was so prominent in the late 1940s and the 1950s. Together with other professors of economics they helped standardize a shorter length of PhD thesis produced at MIT and gave their contribution to the broad changes in graduate economics education that were taking place in the United States in this period.

As for the students, in addition to the courses they had available, we saw that their placement was wide, but clearly connected to the kind of work they produced and advisers they had. The private sector absorbed more of those students working in industrial economics and business administration (advised by Douglass Brown and Myers), and in industrial organization (Adelman). Business schools hired mostly students in industrial economics. Nonetheless, the majority of jobs that MIT graduates landed were in universities, such as Rice Institute, Minnesota, Northwestern, and Michigan State University, among others.

Despite being new, the MIT PhD program managed to attract a good number of students from its beginning, but it was not among the major producers of PhDs in economics. However, it was not alone in this situation: it had the good company of several other programs already well established, like Yale's, Princeton's, and Northwestern's. The MIT program eventually managed to increase its relative importance in the production of doctorates in economics and became a leading institution contributing to the Americanization of economics.

References

Barber, William J. 1996. "Postwar Changes in American Graduate Education in Economics." In *The Post-1945 Internationalization of Economics*, edited by A. W. Coats. *History of Political Economy* 28 (supplement): 12–30.

Blackmer, Donald. 2000. "Fifty Years on—plus ça change . . . ?" *Soundings*, Fall. web.mit.edu/shass/soundings/issue_00f/fea_lum.html (accessed September 10, 2013).

———. 2002. *The MIT Center for International Studies: The Founding Years, 1951–1969*. Cambridge, Mass.: MIT Center for International Studies.

Bowen, Howard R. 1953. "Graduate Education in Economics." *American Economic Review* 43 (4, pt. 2, suppl.): ii–xv, 1–223.

Dixit, Avinash. 2012. "Paul Samuelson's Legacy." *Annual Review of Economics* 4:1–31.

Dorfman, Robert. 1954. "A Catechism: Mathematics in Social Science." *Review of Economics and Statistics* 36 (4): 374–77.

Fourcade, Marion. 2009. *Economists and Societies: Discipline and Profession in the United States, Britain, and France, 1890s to 1990s*. Princeton, N.J.: Princeton University Press.

Godin, Benoît. 2008. "In the Shadow of Schumpeter: W. Rupert Maclaurin and the Study of Technological Innovation." *Minerva* 46 (3): 343–60.

Koopmans, Tjalling C. 1957. *Three Essays on the State of Economic Science*. New York: McGraw-Hill.

Mirowski, Philip. 2002. *Machine Dreams: Economics Becomes a Cyborg Science*. Cambridge: Cambridge University Press.

MIT Bulletin. Various years. Cambridge, Mass.: MIT. dome.mit.edu/handle/1721.3/81660.

Morgan, Mary S., and Malcolm Rutherford, eds. 1998. *From Interwar Pluralism to Postwar Neoclassicism*. Supplemental issue to volume 30 of *History of Political Economy*. Durham, N.C.: Duke University Press.

Samuelson, Paul A. 1952. "Economic Theory and Mathematics—an Appraisal." *American Economic Review: AEA Papers and Proceedings* 42 (2): 56–66.

———. 1954. "Some Psychological Aspects of Mathematics and Economics." *Review of Economics and Statistics* 36 (4): 380–86.

———. 2000. "Economics in MIT's Fourth School." *Soundings*, Fall. web.mit.edu/shass/soundings/issue_00f/fea_lum.html (accessed September 10, 2013).

Social Science Research Council. 1956. "Recommended Policies for the Mathematical Training of Social Scientists: Statement by a Committee of the Social Science Research Council." *Econometrica* 24 (1): 82–86.

Solberg, Winton U., and Robert W. Tomilson. 1997. "Academic McCarthyism and Keynesian Economics: The Bowen Controversy at the University of Illinois." *History of Political Economy* 29 (1): 55–81.

Solow, Robert M. 1954. "The Survival of Mathematical Economics." *Review of Economics and Statistics* 36 (4): 372–74.

Szenberg, Michael, Aron Gottesman, and Lall Ramrattan. 2005. *Paul A. Samuelson: On Being an Economist*. New York: Jorge Pinto Books.

Weintraub, E. Roy. 2002. *How Economics Became a Mathematical Science*. Durham, N.C.: Duke University Press.

MIT's Rise to Prominence: Outline of a Collective Biography

Andrej Svorenčík

For over half a century, the MIT economics department has been one of the most influential economics departments in the world. Not only thirteen Nobel laureates but also "many of world's leading central bankers and policy makers have roots that trace back" to MIT (Hilsenrath 2012). In support of this claim, the *Wall Street Journal* listed fifteen doctorate holders or former MIT faculty who were either classmates or in student-adviser relationships (Hilsenrath 2012).[1] However, MIT started training academic economists only in the 1940s, later than its rivals Harvard, Chicago, Columbia, and Cambridge. True, MIT's rapid ascent might be explained by resorting to the traditional view of the history of economic thought as a succession of great minds and their seminal ideas. MIT economists

Correspondence may be addressed to Andrej Svorenčík, Department of Economics, University of Mannheim, L7, 3-5, 68131 Mannheim, Germany; e-mail: svorencik@uni-mannheim.de. I would like to thank Beatrice Cherrier, Roger E. Backhouse, Marek Hlavac, and James Poterba for their comments on a preliminary draft, and Will Thomas for our discussion about his prosopographic research on the American postwar physics elite. The idea for the present article appeared when I had the opportunity to discuss Cherrier's early version of her article (this volume) presented at the HISRECO conference in 2010 in Paris. I would also like to thank Paul Pieper for sharing the MIT-relevant part of the source data of his 1999 paper. Jan Zilinsky provided invaluable help in obtaining some records from the MIT Archives. The usual disclaimers apply.

1. The article mistakenly claims that Mario Draghi, the European Central Bank chief, was supervised by Stanley Fischer. However, my data and a check of his dissertation suggest that his only supervisor was Franco Modigliani.

History of Political Economy 46 (annual suppl.) DOI 10.1215/00182702-2716136

undisputedly provide ample evidence for this approach. Yet it disregards the role of the networks within which economists operate, their ideas diffuse, and gain scientific credit. In this article I advocate an alternative view that the history of economics is largely the history of groups of economists, and the emphasis should be placed on their networks such as departments. To this end, inspired by *collective biography*, or *prosopography*, a method successfully employed by historians, this article takes a first step toward a collective biography of the MIT economics department.

Among historians of economics, "Chicago Economics" has become an industry on its own (Van Horn, Mirowski, and Stapleford 2011; Emmett 2010). Yet historians have largely ignored MIT, which equals—and very likely exceeds—Chicago's influence among academic economists. Moreover, MIT's influence in the current world of central banking exceeds any other economics department. According to the *Wall Street Journal*, it is "MIT engineers" who have been wielding power in central banks around the world during the recent economic crisis. While the present volume attempts to mitigate this acute historiographical lacuna, this article promises a rigorous empirical basis for a new understanding of MIT's transformative influence on American and world economics. Furthermore, prosopographic research allows turning received knowledge about MIT for which there is no reference except for, say, anecdotes into reliably demonstrated evidence.

Collective biography (prosopography) is an established historiographical method that identifies and draws relationships between various people within a specific, well-defined historical or social context by collecting and analyzing statistically relevant biographical data (Keats-Rohan 2007).[2] It is particularly well suited for identifying hidden hierarchies or relationships that remain elusive when the focus is on the most prominent members of a group. The prosopographic method provides an interpretative framework for understanding academic communities that is novel to

2. The literal meaning of prosopography is the "description of external/material individual characteristics" (Verboven, Carlier, and Dumolyn 2007, 37). However, prosopography as a historiographical method goes beyond a mere collection of such characteristics, as its goal is to identify often unrecognized relations. It is the study of biographical details of individuals in aggregate, *not a biography of groups*. Therefore the alternative term *collective biography* is somewhat misleading. The classic treatment of prosopography was delivered by Lawrence Stone (1971, 1987). Steven Shapin and Arnold Thackray (1974) advocated that prosopographic research could reform notions of "the scientist" and "the scientific community." Some of the many applications of prosopography to history of science include Söderqvist and Silverstein 1994, and Bellhouse et al. 2009.

the history of economics.[3] It might be particularly useful given the dramatic expansion in the numbers of economists in the postwar era.

Typically, collective biography is applied to overcome the scarcity of historical data. In contrast, in an MIT collective biography one examines a period that is much richer in relevant biographical data.[4] This allows more than an investigation of sociocultural background and academic peregrinations of students and faculty that is typical of prosopographies of early academic institutions like medieval universities. It shifts the focus to networks of patronage and academic genealogies.[5]

Patronage and genealogies are closely connected, and an analysis requires the reconstruction of a target population of students and faculty and also of the adviser-advisee relationship. The implicit assumption in this article is that the adviser-advisee relationship is the most important in defining the network of patronage. True, there might be faculty who do not supervise a particular student, but influence her in class or her research. However, in the post–World War II period, each step of the academic career cycle such as the job market, promotion reviews, and, to a lesser extent, attribution of scientific credit heavily relies on advisers' letters of recommendation.[6] On an individual level, being supervised by a particular adviser informs in no small part others' prior beliefs about the nature, quality, and context of the student's research. On a collective level, such beliefs are also formed by the student's affiliation to a particular department. Together, they form the student's academic identity through shared

3. The literature on quantitative analysis of economists and the economics profession typically includes bibliometric analysis; content analysis of publications; and rankings of individuals, departments, and so forth. For a survey covering this field until the late 1990s, see Backhouse, Middleton, and Tribe 1997. However, only two history of economics papers come close to prosopographic research. Both investigated whether the decline of institutional economics can be explained through lower rates of graduates staying in academe. Malcolm Rutherford (2006) chose to follow the career paths of students of John R. Commons, a key interwar institutionalist. Jeff Biddle (1998), on the other hand, investigated the decline of institutionalism through a comparison of career paths of PhDs at the University of Wisconsin and in several other departments who graduated in the interwar period.

4. For a discussion of data-intensive research, databases, and implications for history of science including further references, see Strasser 2012.

5. Interest in academic genealogies is not new. The online *Mathematics Genealogy Project* inspired similar endeavors in artificial intelligence, chemistry, linguistics, and philosophy. Randall Collins, in his 1998 book *The Sociology of Philosophies*, successfully utilized them to uncover, as the back-cover copy reads, "patterns of intellectual networks and their inner divisions and conflicts."

6. This is not to say that the academic career cycle is not evolving. However, the nature of its change is not investigated in this article.

training, experiences, practice of economics, and personal networks that extend beyond graduate school and have led to characterizations of MIT or Chicago economists. This can be visualized through academic family trees that I construct in this article for MIT. These identities, especially of influential departments, have become the subject of considerable attention by historians of economics, including in this volume, who use the rubrics of MIT style, MIT economics, or MIT economists. These issues are well known in the sociology of science literature (Collins 1998) and in science and technology studies (e.g., Knorr-Cetina 1999; Latour and Woolgar 1986), but also in sociology in general (Wetherell 1998).

The first section of this article analyzes the available data and lays out the evidence about MIT. The first two subsections address MIT's graduate students and faculty. The third subsection zooms in on the adviser-advisee relationship and constructs a partial academic family tree. Once these basic prosopographic characteristics are established, subsection 4 adds various relational structures to demonstrate the growing importance of MIT over time. In the second section I introduce the high retention conjecture as a possible explanation for MIT's rapid rise to prominence. The concluding section synthesizes the structure and the ways of operation of the MIT network and outlines future research avenues.

1. Evidence

1.1. MIT Students

The first step toward an MIT collective biography is to establish the size of the MIT population. It consists of both PhD students and faculty from the beginning of the MIT doctoral program in 1941. My investigation ends with the year 2011. This article is based on a complete data set of MIT graduates that includes the year of graduation, names of adviser(s), and title of dissertation—all laboriously obtained directly from MIT's library records.[7] These records are unique in their scope, as I was unable to retrieve such data from library records for any other major US economics department.

Observation 1: For 1944–2011, 1,316 MIT economics PhDs are recorded. The first PhD degree was conferred on Lawrence Klein in 1944,

7. I do not include PhD degrees awarded by the MIT Sloan School of Management. Since the establishment of its doctoral program in 1964, 671 doctorates were conferred until 2011, but only a small fraction of them were in economics or were (co)supervised by faculty from the economics department.

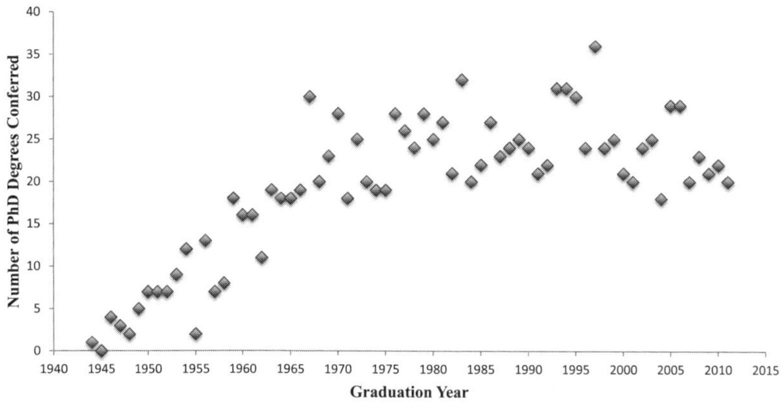

Figure 1 Number of economics PhDs awarded at MIT, by year, 1944–2011. All data are from MIT library records and the author's computations based on them.

who was supervised by Paul Samuelson. Figure 1 depicts the evolution of the number of degrees awarded.

Observation 2: Two distinct periods can be observed in this figure. First, until about 1970 the number of graduates rose steadily. Second, from 1970 onward the number of graduates has hovered around twenty-four per year; the fluctuations around this number likely reflect external economic conditions influencing student enrollment. Until the 1990s the modal duration of graduate studies was four years; the MIT program reached a saturation point by the mid- to late 1960s.[8]

In the first twenty years, 1944–64, 185 doctorates were completed. This many students finish now during an eight-year period. Put differently, by 1972 the number of economists with a degree from MIT doubled. In comparison, in the 1950s Harvard was churning out 34 doctorates, Wisconsin over 25, and Berkeley and Columbia around 19 doctorates annually. Only in the 1970s did MIT join these departments as one of the largest programs in the United States (Scott and Anstine 1997, 313).

There is only one case of a joint thesis, and for each author it is counted individually.[9] Another peculiarity is a thesis with a coauthor, and the coau-

8. The four-year modal duration was suggested by a referee.

9. This happened in 1967 when D. Carter and G. Nicholas were jointly supervised by Karl Shell. Their dissertation was titled "On the Use of a Non-Linear Criterion Function in Development Programming Models."

thor defended a separate thesis.[10] According to library records, 945 students had one supervisor; 333, two supervisors; and 38, three supervisors. All theses are counted individually. However, shared supervision is divided in equal parts. For instance, Susan Athey, the 2007 Clark medalist and MIT faculty member from 1995 to 2001, was involved in supervising four graduate students, and her total supervision share was 1.83 students—the result of three half supervisions and a one-third supervision. In my interpretation, Athey influenced four MIT doctorates, but the actual strength of her influence was 1.83 students. I refer to these measures as *extensive* and *intensive supervision measures*. I give preference to the intensive supervision measure, as I implicitly assume that the each cosupervisor has an equal impact on a student. The available data do not allow establishing who had the decisive influence on a student.[11]

Observation 3: Theses with two supervisors became common in the second half of the 1980s; there were just seven cases prior to 1985. Theses with three supervisors became popular only in the 2000s; there were just four cases prior to 2000. In consequence, unlike in the early years, supervisors in the past two decades have a much lower intensive supervision than extensive one.[12]

1.2. MIT Faculty

Observation 4: In all, 165 distinct advisers supervised 1,316 MIT PhDs.[13] There are 33 supervisors who advised at least 1 percent of all

10. The dissertation titled "Informational Aspects of Securities Markets" was written by Robert Ward Vishny and supervised by Eric Maskin and Franklin Fisher (1985). Two out of three essays were coauthored with Andrei Shleifer, who defended a separate thesis.

11. I checked several theses that are available online. For those with several supervisors, the primary supervisor is not indicated.

12. James Poterba became an assistant professor at MIT in 1982 and served as associate department head between 1994 and 2006 (except 2000–2001). He recalls that "for most of the period over which I've been at MIT, the primary function of the third advisor was to read the completed dissertation, to determine whether it met the standards for acceptance, and to provide some advice to the student on where the various parts of the dissertation might be submitted for publication. I believe that there would be three faculty names on the dissertation in this case, but the third reader, as I suggested, would have had a relatively minor role in the advising process. More recently, however, we have seen a number of students with three actively involved advisers. I can't hazard a guess of how common that is, and I don't think there is any way to determine this based only on department records—the dissertation would still have three faculty signatures" (e-mail to author, May 27, 2013).

13. Names of advisers of thirteen students were missing from the library records. They were obtained through direct inquiry with the department and the MIT Archives.

students.[14] Table 1 orders them according to their intensive supervision—a measure that modifies extensive supervision by accounting for cosupervision. The second column indicates the year of the first recorded graduation of a student by the particular adviser—even though the adviser may have joined the department a few years earlier. The third column indicates the year of the last recorded graduation of a student by the particular adviser in the period I am examining; many of those advisers may still be on the faculty and may or may not still be supervising students.

Observation 5: There are only nine supervisors who supervised more than 3 percent of students (intensive count). In total, they have supervised 468.98 students, or 36 percent of all doctorates. As the length of supervision tenure differs among supervisors, one could normalize their performance. However, this does not change the results in table 1 significantly.

Observation 6: Of the nine most active supervisors, from the mid-1950s until the mid-1970s Robert Solow is the dominant figure, with Kindleberger and somewhat later Franklin Fisher being important. Rüdiger Dornbusch dominated the second half of the 1970s and the 1980s. His influence extended well throughout the 1990s until his premature death in 2002. With the 1990s came the prominence of James Poterba and Olivier Blanchard. Daron Acemoglu dominates the 2000s.

Labeling a particular period according to one or two leading supervisors requires the consideration of the total number of students produced. For instance, Charles Kindleberger and Charles Meyers dominated the 1950s with 13 and 14 supervisions, respectively. Douglass Brown, Morris Adelman, Paul Samuelson, and Robert Solow supervised from 8 to 10.5 theses in that period.

Observation 7: Table 2 depicts advisers who supervised at least six theses in 1944–69 (i.e., at least two 2 percent of theses written then). At the very beginning Brown, Meyers, and Samuelson were leading these efforts. Kindleberger and Adelman joined in the early 1950s and Solow in the mid-1950s. In the 1960s both Solow and Kindleberger clearly led the supervision efforts. The second half of the 1960s saw an increase in the number of active supervisors.

Observation 8: In the 1970s Kindleberger decreased his supervision activity, and the decade was dominated by Robert Solow and Franklin Fisher, with 24.50 and 23.83 supervisions, respectively. The 1980s

14. As the graduation rate is not constant in time, faculty in earlier periods did not have that many supervision opportunities. I later show that this was compensated by the smaller (supervising) faculty size.

Table 1 Most Active MIT Supervisors, according to Intensive Measure of Supervision

Name	Supervising From	Supervising Until	Intensive Supervision	Extensive Supervision
Robert Solow	1954	1997	72.5	76
Rüdiger Dornbusch	1977	2002	69.33	86
Olivier Blanchard	1985	1999	52.66	76
James Poterba	1985	2010	51.5	66
Franklin Fisher	1962	2003	49.83	55
Charles Kindleberger	1951	1980	47.5	48
Stanley Fischer	1975	1994	47	50
Jerry Hausman	1976	2010	39.33	54
Daron Acemoglu	1995	2011	39.33	73
Charles Myers	1946	1980	35.5	37
Morris Adelman	1952	1982	33.33	34
Peter Diamond	1973	2010	28	38
Michael Piore	1969	2000	26.33	29
Paul Samuelson	1944	1978	25.5	26
Richard Eckaus	1965	1997	24	25
Lance Taylor	1976	1989	24	24
Paul Krugman	1981	2000	23.5	28
Abhijit Banerjee	1995	2011	22.5	46
Paul Joskow	1976	2005	21.5	28
Glenn Ellison	1994	2007	20.33	36
Ricardo Caballero	1995	2011	19.33	35
Franco Modigliani	1967	1985	19	19
Peter Temin	1972	2005	17.83	21
Jonathan Gruber	1994	2011	17.66	30
Esther Duflo	2000	2011	16.66	34
Henry Farber	1980	1993	16	16
Joshua Angrist	1998	2011	15.83	34
Douglass Brown	1947	1966	16.5	18
Edwin Kuh	1962	1973	15	15
Evsey Domar	1960	1984	15	15
Jerome Rothenberg	1968	1979	14	14
Jagdish Bhagwati	1970	1981	13	13
David Autor	2003	2011	13	27

Source: All data are from MIT library records and the author's computations based on them.
Note: Names in italics indicate Nobel laureates and in bold a PhD degree from MIT.

Table 2 The First Twenty-Five Years of MIT's Graduate Program and Distributions of Graduates according to Supervisors Who Supervised at Least Six Students

Year	Adelman	Ando	Bishop	Brown	Domar	Eckaus	Fisher	Kindleberger	Kuh	Millikan	Myers	Samuelson	Shepard	Solow	Sum per Year
1944												1			1
1946				1							1	2			4
1947				1.5							0.5	1			3
1948				1											1
1949				1							1				2
1950				3.5							1.5				5
1951				1.5				2			2.5	1			7
1952	1		1								3		1		6
1953	1			2								1	2		6
1954	1			1				1		1	1	3	2	1	11
1955	1			1											2
1956				1				3			1	2.5		3	10.5
1957	1							1			1	2	1	1	7
1958	1		2					2		1					6

Table 2 *(continued)*

Year	Adelman	Ando	Bishop	Brown	Domar	Eckaus	Fisher	Kindleberger	Kuh	Millikan	Myers	Samuelson	Shepard	Solow	Sum per Year
1959	2		1	1				4			4			2	14
1960	1	1	1	1	1			3			2			4	14
1961	2	1.5			2			0.5		1	1	1		1	10
1962	2	1			1		1		1						6
1963		3	1					3				1		6	14
1964	1	3					1	3		1	4	1		1	15
1965		1				1	2	4	1	1	1	1		2	14
1966	2			2		2	2	1	1	2	2			4	18
1967	1			2	1	3	1	4	3		3			7	25
1968	2					2	1	4	4					3	16
1969	4		1	2	1	1	5	1	2		1				18
Total	**23**	**10.5**	**7**	**22.5**	**6**	**9**	**13**	**36.5**	**12**	**7**	**30.5**	**17.5**	**6**	**35**	**235.5**

Source: All data are from MIT library records and the author's computations based on them.

witnessed a transition toward Rüdiger Dornbusch and Stanley Fischer, with 27 and 29.5 supervisions, respectively. In both decades the two leading supervisors mentored twice as many PhDs as the other faculty members.

In the 1990s Poterba, Blanchard, and Dornbusch with 33.50, 28.83, and 27.83 supervisions, respectively, led these efforts, but the gap between the other supervisors tripled. The 2000s have only one leading faculty member, Daron Acemoglu, with 32.33 supervisions. However, in this period a large group of nine faculty members with around 13 supervisions each emerged.

Observation 9: Thirty-one out of 165 supervisors received their doctorates from MIT. These faculty members (I refer to them as *second-generation advisers*) were involved in supervising 479 students (37 percent of all MIT students), and their intensive share was 346.1 students. Together with their advisers they form a group of forty-nine faculty, or 30 percent of faculty, and they effectively supervised 851.91 students, or 65 percent of all graduates. The extensive supervision measure is 1,140 students, or 87 percent of all graduates.

Observation 10: The complete MIT population thus consists of 1,316 PhD holders (including 31 who returned to MIT as supervisors), and 133 advisers, that is, 1,449 individuals total.

True, there might be MIT faculty who have not supervised any students—most likely because of a short period of activity at MIT or visiting status. That is, for instance, the case of Mervyn King, the current governor of the Bank of England, who was a visiting professor at MIT in 1983–84 and shared an office with Ben Bernanke. However, the proposed way to count faculty adds many supervisors who supervised no more than one student, likely indicating external status. That is, for instance, the case of David Laibson, a professor at Harvard, who cosupervised one student at MIT.

Observation 11: There are twenty-six advisers with an intensive supervision measure of less than one student and thirty-six advisers who supervised just one student. They include three advisers who were MIT students themselves (David Laibson, Dimitrios Vayanos, and David Cutler). If we exclude these 62 advisers, then there would be just 103 advisers responsible for the supervision of MIT students or 74 advisers if second-generation advisers are excluded as well. Once details on the job histories of all 165 supervisors are established, a better decision whom to count as MIT faculty can be made.

Observation 12: A rapid intake of new supervising faculty took place in the first half of the 1950s—Charles Kindleberger's first student graduated in 1951, Morris Adelman's and Robert Bishop's in 1952, Walt Rostow's in 1953, and Robert Solow's in 1954. There was a lot of fluctuation in the 1960s, despite longtime figures such as Fisher, *Richard Eckaus*, and Franco Modigliani.[15] In the 1970s faculty who joined stayed much longer and remained the dominant force until the early 1990s (e.g., Michael Piore with a first graduate in 1969; *Jagdish Bhagwati* in 1970; *Peter Diamond* and *Peter Temin* in 1972; Stanley Fischer in 1975; Jerry Hausman, Paul Joskow, and Lance Taylor in 1976; Rüdiger Dornbusch in 1977; and *Paul Krugman* in 1981). The 1980s resemble the 1960s—the new leading supervisors *Olivier Blanchard* and James Poterba had first students in 1985. Both the 1990s and the 2000s experienced an increase in new faculty, and half of them are still active at MIT (i.e., they supervised a thesis in 2010 or 2011).

1.3. Adviser-Advisee Relationship

Observation 9 stated that there are thirty-one second-generation advisers. Table 3 lists them and highlights three groups—two small ones started by Solow and Dornbusch, and a large one that originated from Kindleberger, Maskin, and Fisher and now is connected through students.

Observation 13: While there are no discernible patterns in terms of graduation year among these thirty-one faculty, in terms of the start of their supervision work there are two five-year periods marked by their concentrated arrival at MIT. The first period took place during 1972–76 and the other 1991–95. In each, six former graduates were hired. The first period also suggests Solow's strong position in the department in the 1960s, as three second-generation advisers who were hired were supervised by him. The same holds for Fisher and the 1970s.

Observation 14: There are three distinct groups of second-generation advisers—two originating by Solow and Dornbusch each with three students. The third comprises fifteen second-generation advisers. For them, it is possible to draw a joint family tree of their academic progeny, as depicted in figure 2.[16] Academic family trees allow visualizing the adviser-advisee network and the variety of meanings that one can attach to it. It presents formal connections between immediate advisers and her advisees. It also presents often intellectual connections (academic lineage) that

15. Names in italics in this paragraph denote second-generation MIT supervisors.

16. Unlike in familial genealogy, academic genealogy allows for multiple academic "parents," and therefore the form of the family tree is a lattice rather than a tree.

Table 3 List of MIT Advisers Who Are MIT Graduates

Name	MIT PhD	Adviser(s)	Active at MIT From	Until
Herbert Shepard	1950	Bavelas	1952	1957
Paul Cootner	1953	Rostow	1963	1965
Richard Eckaus	1954	Samuelson	1965	1997
Peter Diamond	1963	Solow	1973	2010
Ann Friedlaender	1964	Ando	1975	1989
Peter Temin	1964	**Kindleberger**	1972	2005
Martin Weitzman	1967	Solow	1976	1987
Robert Hall	1967	Solow	1975	1981
Jagdish Bhagwati	1967	**Kindleberger**	1970	1981
Stanley Fischer	1969	**Fisher**	1975	1994
Richard Schmalensee	1970	**Fisher**	1980	1998
Paul Krugman	1977	Dornbusch	1981	2000
Olivier Blanchard	1977	**Fischer**	1985	1999
Francesco Giavazzi	1978	Dornbusch	2008	2011
Drew Fudenberg	1981	**Maskin**	1989	1994
Jean Tirole	1981	**Maskin**	1986	1995
Whitney Newey	1983	Hausman	1993	2010
Nancy Rose	1985	Joskow, Fisher	1994	2011
Jeremy Stein	1986	Hart	1994	1997
Roland Benabou	1986	**Tirole, Blanchard**	1991	1994
David Scharfstein	1986	Maskin, Hart	1993	1995
Ricardo Caballero	1988	**Temin, Blanchard**	1995	2011
Simon Johnson	1989	Dornbusch	2002	2006
David Cutler	1991	Poterba	1997	1997
Glenn Ellison	1992	**Fudenberg**	1994	2007
Dimitrios Vayanos	1993	**Tirole**	2001	2001
David Laibson	1994	**Blanchard**	2010	2010
Esther Duflo	1999	Banerjee, Angrist	2000	2011
Amy Finkelstein	2001	Poterba, Gruber	2008	2010
Guido Lorenzoni	2001	Caballero	2008	2011
Pol Antràs	2003	Ventura, Acemoglu	2005	2010

Source: All data are from MIT library records and the author's computations based on them.
Note: The names in bold belong to the largest group for which a joint family tree can be drawn.

can run through several generations.[17] The academic family tree also depicts professional relations. Other students such as those who gained prominent positions in central banks can be added to the tree to demonstrate the close ties between MIT and particular nonacademic institutions.[18]

Observation 15: Currently the longest line of direct MIT descent ends with Guido Lorenzoni, who can claim up to three generations of MIT-educated advisers and four complete generations of advisers working at MIT. Further similar growth of the tree can be expected soon from the academic descendants of Glenn Ellison, who has been a prolific MIT supervisor and has two generations of MIT-affiliated advisers.[19]

The family tree in figure 2 excludes the separate branches that originate with Solow and Dornbusch. Three students of Solow joined MIT—Diamond (PhD, 1963; 28/38 supervisions during 1973–2010), Robert Hall (PhD, 1967; 7/7 supervisions during 1975–81), and Martin Weitzman (PhD, 1967; 4.5/5 supervisions during 1976–87). Solow also trained central bankers such as Charles Bean, the deputy director of the Bank of England (PhD, 1981).

Rüdiger Dornbusch supervised Paul Krugman (PhD, 1977; 23.5/28 supervisions during 1981–2000); Francesco Giavazzi (PhD, 1978; 1.66/4 supervisions during 2008–11); and Simon Johnson (PhD, 1989; 1.5/3 supervisions during 2002–6). Dornbusch also supervised the former governors of Chile and Cyprus—Jose de Gregorio and Athanasios Orphanides, both received degrees in 1990.

1.4. Markers of MIT's Preeminence

Now that the MIT population and the adviser-advisee relationships are reconstructed, various relational structures can be superimposed on them. I use the Clark Medal and Economics Nobel Memorial Prize awards, positions in the executive committee of the American Economic Associa-

17. For example, the thesis research topics of Fisher and Blanchard are more closely related than those of Lorenzoni and Temin. To investigate the intellectual connection one would, however, need to add the research topics that the researchers were involved with (theses, joint articles).

18. For instance, Fischer's students Ben Bernanke (PhD, 1979), Daniel Wilcox (PhD, 1986; Federal Reserve Economic Research), and William English (PhD, 1987; Federal Reserve Monetary Affairs); Blanchard's student Michael Gibson (PhD, 1993; Federal Reserve Bank Supervision); or Hart's student Jeremy Stein (PhD, 1986; Federal Reserve).

19. I do not address the issue of the meaning or impact of having two to three generations of ancestors from the same department.

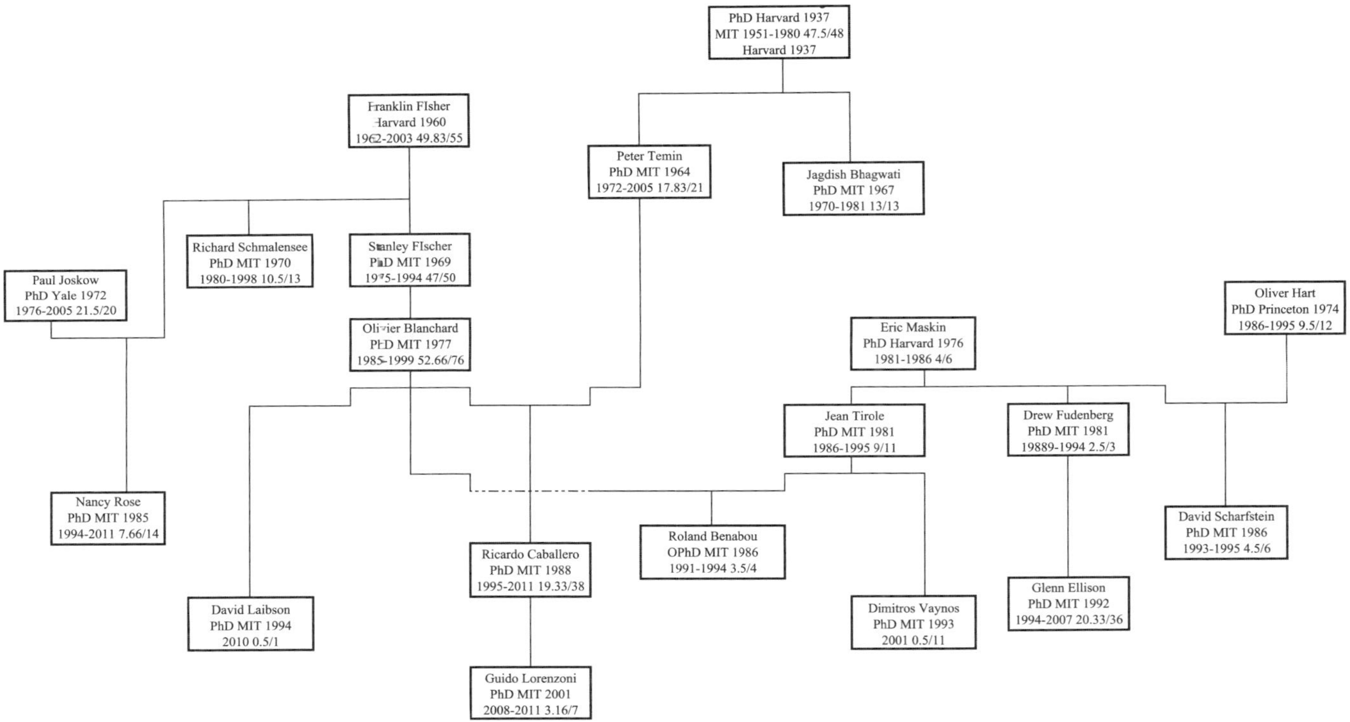

Figure 2 Family tree of MIT advisers who graduated from MIT (second-generation advisers). Each box contains full name, place and year of doctorate, and active years of supervision at MIT with the intensive and extensive measures of supervision. The dotted line is used in the case of two lines crossing each other—i.e., Tirole and Blanchard jointly supervised only Benabou, not Caballero. All data are from MIT library records and the author's computations based on them, supplemented with information from online CVs and Blaug and Vane 2003.

Table 4 MIT-Affiliated Clark Medalists

	MIT Faculty at the Time of Award of the Clark Medal		
PhD from MIT	Yes	No	**Sum**
Yes	4 Fisher 1973, Krugman 1991, Duflo 2010, Finkelstein 2012	6 Klein 1959, Stiglitz 1979, Shleifer 1999, Rabin 2001, Levitt 2003, Saez 2009	**10**
No	4 Samuelson 1947, Solow 1961, Hausman 1985, Acemoglu 2005	2 Summers 1993, Athey 2007	**6**
Sum	**8**	**8**	**16**

Source: www.aeaweb.org/honors_awards/clark_medal.php.

tion, and membership in the Council of Economic Advisers as such topologies. They shed more light on the rise of MIT to the top economics department in the world.

Observation 16: Out of twelve MIT-affiliated Nobel laureates, eight served as supervisors at MIT. Five of these supervisors appear in table 1 (most active supervisors). The other three laureates are Eric Maskin, Daniel McFadden, and Robert Engle, with intensive supervision measures of 4, 9.5, and 1, respectively.

Observation 17: Out of thirty-five Clark medalists until 2012, sixteen (47 percent) have some affiliation with MIT. Table 4 breaks them down according to whether they graduated from MIT or were faculty at MIT at the time of the award. Only two Clark medalists—Lawrence Summers and Susan Athey—can be excluded from the count; neither one was an MIT graduate or on the faculty at the time of the award. MIT's dominance in the Clark Medal category is particularly conspicuous in the period 1999–2012, when all nine awardees had a connection with MIT. Only the most recent winner, Raj Chetty (2013), has no MIT connection.

Observation 18: For eleven MIT economists with either of these two awards, it is possible to draw a joint academic family tree (figure 3).

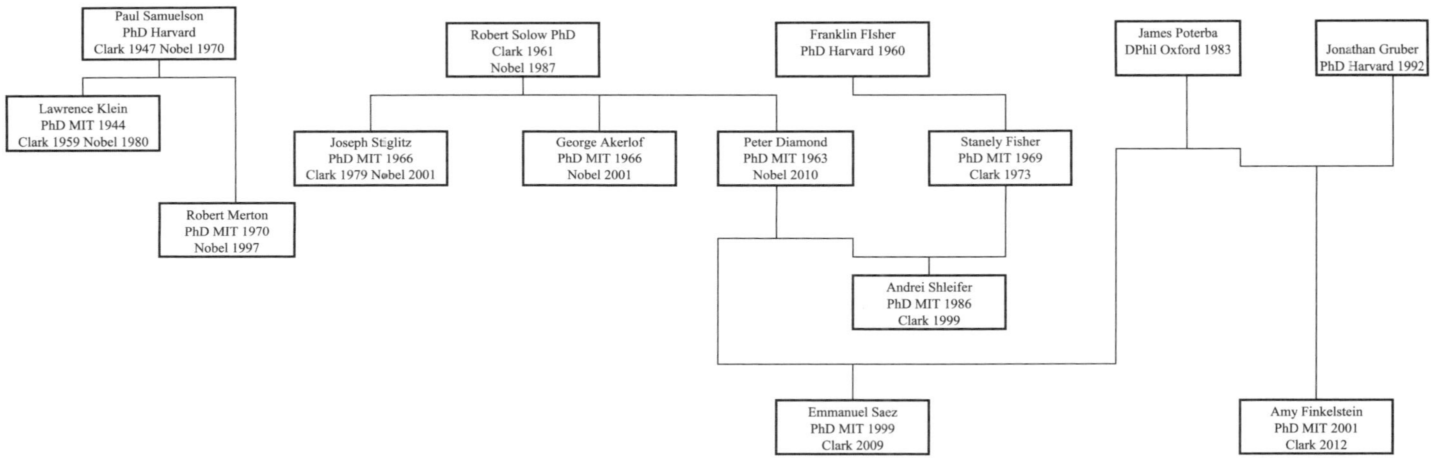

Figure 3 Academic family tree of MIT Clark medalists and Nobel laureates. Each box contains information on the person's PhD and, if received, information on Clark and Nobel awards. Emmanuel Saez was jointly supervised by Peter Diamond and James Poterba; Andrei Shleifer by Diamond and Franklin Fisher. All data are from MIT library records and the author's computations based on them, supplemented with information from online CVs and Blaug and Vane 2003.

Table 5 AEA Vice Presidents' Educational Backgrounds (PhD)

1950–2013		1980–2013	
University from Which PhD Was Received	Number	University from Which PhD Was Received	Number
Harvard	24	MIT	18
MIT	19	Harvard	15
Chicago	12	Chicago	8
Yale	8	Yale	7
Columbia	8	Princeton	5
Princeton	6		

Source: Research conducted by the author and Kevin D. Hoover.
Note: The order is according to most frequent origin of their PhD degrees.

My joint work with Kevin D. Hoover on the leadership hierarchy of the American Economic Association adds further insights into MIT's rise to preeminence. We analyzed the educational background and job history of all members of the executive committee of the AEA—presidents, vice presidents, and elected members—216 distinct officers from 1950 until 2013. One of my main conclusions is that these data reveal a rapid growth of MIT's standing. In 1950–2013, only five AEA presidents graduated from MIT with a PhD, compared with ten for Harvard, eight for both Columbia and Chicago, and seven for Wisconsin. In terms of employment at the time of election, only four presidents worked at MIT. However, most importantly, four out of the five MIT-educated presidents were in office only after 1980.

Observation 19: MIT's representation among AEA vice presidents is even more revealing. Until 1980 only one MIT-educated economist was elected as an AEA vice president. In contrast, eighteen have been elected since 1980. That is a 27 percent share of all vice presidents in that period (table 5). On average, it took 26.5 years after graduation from MIT to be elected.

MIT-educated economists also lead in the counts of elected members of the AEA executive committee (six members elected with a three-year tenure). For 1950–2013, MIT graduates were second behind Harvard, and their share of all elected members was 20 percent. In the shorter period 1980–2013, their share rose to 34 percent and outperformed Harvard. In terms of current employment at the time of election, MIT leads in both periods.

While these markers suggest an early rise of MIT academic preeminence, it is not clear whether it was accompanied by coeval success in gaining high positions in the government. Membership in the Council of Economic Advisers is one such position. Since its establishment in 1946 until 2011, only seventy-six economists have served on its executive board. A number of other MIT members, such as Solow, were also senior economists at the council.

Observation 20: Sixteen MIT PhD graduates served on the Council of Economic Advisers—a share of 21 percent. The first to join was William Nordhaus in 1977. In 1977–2011, MIT economists made up 34 percent of the council. Robert Solow supervised one-third of them.[20] Table 6 lists their tenures.

2. High Retention Conjecture

All the effort in this article so far has only indirectly tackled the core question of MIT's history—why did MIT rise to preeminence so quickly? And all my observations so far address a related question—how did MIT rise to preeminence so quickly? Analyzing the career paths of MIT students, particularly those who stayed in academe, might provide a possible explanation.

A study by Paul Pieper and Rachel Willis from 1999 provides a tantalizing piece of evidence that, in conjunction with my previous results, suggests a high retention of MIT graduates in academe compared with other leading departments. They surveyed 3,291 faculty members of 121 economics PhD-granting institutions in the United States in the academic year 1991–92. MIT, they found out, was the second-most frequent doctoral origin of these economists after Harvard, and 213 faculty positions were held by MIT graduates. Analyzing their unpublished data, 204 can be identified as graduates of the MIT economics department.[21] They further reported that Harvard had 233, Chicago 184, Berkeley 174, Stanford 150, Yale 132, Wisconsin 130, Minnesota 115, Princeton 112, and Columbia 100 graduates active in American academe (Pieper and Willis 1999,

20. The fact that Solow served at the council as a senior economist suggests an obvious reason why so many of the council's appointed members with MIT backgrounds have been his students.

21. The remaining nine faculty received their PhDs from other departments such as mathematics (e.g., Robert Aumann), political science, urban studies and planning, and so forth. I did not have access to individual data of other PhD-granting institutions.

Table 6 MIT Graduates as Members of the Council of Economic Advisers

Name	Position	Date Took Office	Date Left Office	Advisers	Graduation Year
William D. Nordhaus	Member	March 1977	February 1979	Solow	1967
Stephen M. Goldfeld	Member	August 1980	January 1981	Ando	1963
Richard L. Schmalensee	Member	October 1989	June 1991	Fisher	1970
Alan S. Blinder	Member	July 1993	June 1994	Solow	1971
Laura D'Andrea Tyson	Chair	February 1993	April 1995	Domar	1974
Joseph E. Stiglitz	Member	July 1994	June 1995	Solow	1966
Joseph E. Stiglitz	Chair	June 1995	February 1997	Solow	1966
Jeffrey A. Frankel	Member	April 1997	March 1999	Dornbusch	1978
Rebecca M. Blank	Member	October 1998	July 1999	Farber	1983
Martin N. Bailey	Chair	August 1999	January 2001	Fisher, Solow	1972
Mark B. McClellan	Member	July 2001	November 2002	Poterba	1993
N. Gregory Mankiw	Chair	May 2003	February 2005	Fischer	1984
Kristin J. Forbes	Member	November 2003	June 2005	Ventura, Dornbusch	1998
Ben S. Bernanke	Chair	June 2005	January 2006	Fischer	1979
Matthew J. Slaughter	Member	November 2005	March 2007	Krugman, Brainard	1994
Donald B. Marron	Member	July 2008	January 2009	Joskow	1994
Christina Romer	Chair	January 2009	September 2010	Temin, Dornbusch	1985

Source: www.whitehouse.gov/administration/eop/cea/about/Former-Members (accessed January 13, 2013).

Note: Joseph Stiglitz is mentioned twice, once for when he became a member, once for when he became chair.

Table 7 Top Ten Locations of MIT Graduates in the Academic Year 1991–92 and Comparison of These Departments with 2012–13

	MIT Graduates 1991–92		
Department	All	Those Who Graduated after 1980	MIT Graduates 2012–13 and (All Faculty)
Berkeley	17	9	14 (66)
MIT	13	5	11 (45)
Princeton	9	4	10 (58)
Harvard	7	6	13 (66)
Columbia	7	3	7 (58)
Yale	6	1	10 (48)
UCLA	6	3	3 (43)
UCSD	6	2	6 (58)
Boston University	6	3	5 (48)
Boston College	6	1	6 (36)

Source: Data for the first two columns were obtained from unpublished source data of Pieper and Willis 1999 and the last column from the faculty lists on departmental websites and my database of MIT graduates.
Note: The numbers in parentheses in the last column denote the total size of faculty in 2012–13. Not all departments list their emeritus faculty separately.

82).[22] All these institutions had begun conferring doctorates in economics earlier than MIT, and, as noted in observation 2, MIT joined other largest programs only in the 1970s. By 1992 there were 820 MIT minted economists, and almost one-fourth were active in American academe in 1992.[23]

Observation 21: One can conjecture that MIT has had the highest ratio of graduates among American graduate programs who stay in academe.[24] Over time this would lead to a higher share of MIT students in American academe than their share of all PhDs produced in the United States.

Observation 22: The 204 MIT graduates were located at seventy different departments, with eighty-three (41 percent) located at just ten departments (see table 7). Almost one-fifth, thirty-seven in total, of MIT

22. All other programs had fewer than one hundred graduates active as faculty. It is safe to conclude that the numbers for other departments include some graduates of other departments than just economics.

23. The issue of graduates leaving the United States for academic positions abroad and regular faculty positions at American non-PhD-granting institutions is not addressed in the Pieper and Willis paper. The term *American academe* needs to be understood in this limited sense.

24. Small graduate programs that produce few doctorates might have a higher academic retention, but among equally large programs, I contest, MIT has the highest rate.

graduates worked on UC campuses (or forty when Stanford is included in a California contingent). Another large group is the Boston area, with thirty-three MIT graduates active there in 1992. Although the clement California weather or ties to the Boston area might play a role in the high concentration in those areas, examining the temporal distribution of graduation years of the MIT graduates at these ten departments unravels another aspect. Of these eighty-three MIT graduates, eighty graduated after 1960, sixty after 1970, and thirty-eight after 1980.

It would be premature to conclude that the 1980s mark a period when MIT definitely reached to all top departments—its students were sought after everywhere. More data would be needed to determine whether the surge in the 1980s is a result of taking 1992 as a reference point (i.e., these departments might have been hiring MIT students in earlier decades, but they might have moved to different departments), or whether it is just an artifact of the stabilization of number of annual PhD output in the 1970s. However, the last column of table 7 suggests relative stability in the number of graduates placed at the top destinations in 1992 in comparison with 2012.

3. Conclusions

The results of prosopographic research do not have the same narrative quality of archive-centered research affording rich histories such as Beatrice Cherrier's (this volume) "Toward a History of Economics at MIT, 1940–72." Nevertheless, even utilizing only a fragment of the plethora of the dispersed, yet available, biographical data allows drawing a number of preliminary conclusions about social and intellectual relationships that rich histories cannot avoid dealing with. Let me highlight and combine some of the most salient observations about the MIT economics department:

- **Large community**: Conclusions about MIT should be based on the total number of MIT economists rather than the small number of well-known figures. By 2011, 1,449 economists can claim the membership in the group—1,316 MIT PhD holders and 133 supervising faculty without a PhD from MIT (observations 1, 4, and 10)
- **Concentration and self-replication**: Within the department, a small circle of advisers has emerged who have supervised a disproportionally large portion of students, and from the late 1960s on such supervisors very likely graduated from MIT itself. Hence economists like

Solow, Kindleberger, Fisher, Fischer, Dornbusch, Poterba, Blanchard, and Acemoglu have left an indelible mark on MIT graduates and created subgroups in the MIT network (observations 9, 11, and 13–15).

- **High retention**: Compared with other leading economics departments, a higher proportion of MIT graduates has stayed in academe, strengthening and extending the influence of MIT economists (observations 21–22).
- **Lagged recognition**: Beginning with the late 1970s, MIT students started receiving the highest honors of the profession. Their representation among Clark medalists (50 percent), Nobel laureates, AEA executive committee members (27 percent of AEA vice presidents since 1980), and Council of Economic Advisers (one-third since 1977) grew rapidly since then. However, MIT faculty were whispering into the ears of princes a decade or two earlier (e.g., Samuelson, adviser to Presidents Kennedy and Johnson) (observations 16–20).

Hence the emerging picture of MIT reveals a fairly large community of economists who are trained largely by a few key advisers mostly trained at MIT as well. Apart from this self-replication, MIT has a large share of graduates who remain in academe, thus leaving MIT with a disproportionate share of American faculty. Since the 1970s, MIT dominance is ubiquitous.

Unsurprisingly, these conclusions raise further questions. For instance, Paul Samuelson is not revealed as a central figure.[25] He is not among the most active supervisors, not even in the early days of MIT. His students (with one brief exception) do not return to MIT like the students of Solow and Fisher. To understand why that is so and how he extended his influence, one might need to turn to archives and other sources (e.g., courses taught, informal advising). However, there are other questions that can be dealt with by the collective biography method. Collecting data on supervisors of the faculty who did not receive their doctorates at MIT is likely to reveal additional second-generation links among MIT advisers and likely to connect the family tree depicted in figure 2 with the students supervised by Solow and Dornbusch and also with leading figures such as Samuelson and Modigliani. Hence a more precise identification of subgroups within MIT clustered around various key faculty members could be established. Such analysis will demonstrate the interaction with other top

25. A similar case is Franco Modigliani.

departments such as Harvard, MIT's closest neighbor. A number of key faculty got their doctorates at Harvard—such as Samuelson, Kindleberger, and Fisher—and many graduates found their first jobs there, suggesting deep ties between the two departments. Collecting data on job histories of MIT graduates will reveal typical career trajectories of MIT economists in academe, business, or government. Analyzing how MIT graduates have dispersed in time could highlight (1) how its graduate program's standing rose and also the dynamics of the economics academic job market; (2) the crowding-out conjecture; (3) the level of successful penetration of leading governmental and international economic policy agencies and central banks. Apart from well-known figures such as Ben Bernanke, Mario Draghi, Stanley Fischer (Bank of Israel governor), Jeremy Stein (Federal Reserve governor), and Olivier Blanchard (IMF chief economist), one can expect to find many MIT graduates at lower-level positions. It remains an open question how soon they started obtaining these jobs. In short, answers to all these and related questions are certain to provide a prosopography, an empirical collective biography, of MIT.[26]

References

Backhouse, R. E., R. Middleton, and K. Tribe. 1997. "Economics Is What Economists Do, but What Do the Numbers Tell Us?" Paper presented at the annual History of Economic Thought conference, University of Bristol, September 3–5.

Bellhouse, D. R., E. M. Renouf, R. Raut, and M. A. Bauer. 2009. "De Moivre's Knowledge Community: An Analysis of the Subscription List to the Miscellanea Analytica." *Notes and Records of the Royal Society of London* 63:137–62.

Biddle, J. 1998. "Institutional Economics: A Case of Reproductive Failure?" *History of Political Economy* 30:108–33.

Blaug, M., and H. R. Vane. 2003. *Who's Who in Economics*. 4th ed. Cheltenham: Elgar.

Collins, R. 1998. *The Sociology of Philosophies: A Global Theory of Intellectual Change*. Cambridge, Mass.: Belknap Press of Harvard University Press.

Emmett, R. B. 2010. *The Elgar Companion to the Chicago School of Economics*. Cheltenham: Elgar.

26. Data on close to one hundred unique members of the MIT population have been already gathered for this purpose. The design of an MIT-specific database is under way. It should allow importing data from web-based or pdf-based forms that are going to be distributed among the living MIT members utilizing various social and alumni networks. Thus self-reporting will eliminate much transcription of data related to living members of MIT, as well as speed up the project and allow future scaling up.

Hilsenrath, J. 2012. "MIT Forged Activist Views of Central Bank Role and Cinched Central Bankers' Ties." *Wall Street Journal*, December 12.

Keats-Rohan, K. S. B. 2007. *Prosopography Approaches and Applications: A Handbook*. Oxford: Unit for Prosopographical Research, Linacre College, University of Oxford.

Knorr-Cetina, K. 1999. *Epistemic Cultures: How the Sciences Make Knowledge*. Cambridge, Mass.: Harvard University Press.

Latour, B., and S. Woolgar. 1986. *Laboratory Life: The Construction of Scientific Facts*. Princeton, N.J.: Princeton University Press.

Pieper, P. J., and R. A. Willis. 1999. "The Doctoral Origins of Economics Faculty and the Education of New Economics Doctorates." *Journal of Economic Education* 30:80–88.

Rutherford, M. 2006. "Wisconsin Institutionalism: John R. Commons and His Students." *Labor History* 47:161–88.

Scott, F. A., Jr., and J. D. Anstine. 1997. "Market Structure in the Production of Economics Ph.D's." *Southern Economic Journal* 64:307–20.

Shapin, S., and A. Thackray. 1974. "Prosopography as a Research Tool in History of Science: The British Scientific Community, 1700–1900." *History of Science* 12:1–28.

Söderqvist, T., and A. M. Silverstein. 1994. "Participation in Scientific Meetings: A New Prosopographical Approach to the Disciplinary History of Science: The Case of Immunology, 1951–72." *Social Studies of Science* 24:513–48.

Stone, L. 1971. "Prosopography." *Daedalus* 100:46–79.

———. 1987. *The Past and the Present Revisited*. London: Routledge and Kegan Paul.

Strasser, B. J. 2012. "Collecting Nature: Practices, Styles, and Narratives." *Osiris* 27:303–40.

Van Horn, R., P. Mirowski, and T. A. Stapleford. 2011. *Building Chicago Economics: New Perspectives on the History of America's Most Powerful Economics Program*. Cambridge: Cambridge University Press.

Verboven, K., M. Carlier, and J. Dumolyn. 2007. "A Short Manual to the Art of Prosopography." In *Prosopography Approaches and Applications: A Handbook*, edited by K. S. B. Keats-Rohan. Oxford: University of Oxford.

Wetherell, C. 1998. "Historical Social Network Analysis." *International Review of Social History* 43:125–44.

Negotiating the "Middle-of-the-Road" Position: Paul Samuelson, MIT, and the Politics of Textbook Writing, 1945–55

Yann Giraud

Several historical contributions have emphasized the role that the MIT economist Paul Samuelson played in disseminating Keynesian ideas in the United States through his 1948 textbook, *Economics: An Introductory Analysis*.[1] Samuelson's success in doing so, it is said, lay partly in his ability to introduce John Maynard Keynes's conceptions in a larger framework that encompassed the older neoclassical tradition prevailing in economics before World War II. On the policy side, this *neoclassical synthesis*, a term Samuelson coined in 1955 in the third edition of his text, presents itself as a middle ground between laissez-faire and governmental planning, arguing that free markets and private initiative need to be supplemented by state intervention to ensure economic efficiency. Nevertheless, because the range of economic policies embodied in this framework is large enough to be subject to conflicting interpretations, many scholars have also tried to locate retrospectively in *Economics* evidence that Samuelson's middle

Correspondence may be addressed to Yann Giraud, THEMA/Université de Cergy Pontoise, 33 Bd du Port, 95011 Cergy-Pontoise Cedex, France; e-mail: yanngiraud@gmail.com. I benefited from the material help of the David M. Rubenstein Rare Book and Manuscript Library at Duke University. This research has been partly funded by the History of Recent Economics Scientific Coordination Network (GDRE CNRS 711). I thank Roger Backhouse, Beatrice Cherrier, Pedro Duarte, Paul Dudenhefer, Philippe Fontaine, Harro Maas, and E. Roy Weintraub, as well as the participants of the History of Postwar Social Science workshop at the London School of Economics and the ASSA meeting in San Diego, for their comments and suggestions on an earlier version of this article.

1. See Elzinga 1992; Pearce and Hoover 1995; and Colander and Landreth 1996.

History of Political Economy 46 (annual suppl.) DOI 10.1215/00182702-2716145

ground is in fact ideologically biased. Defenders of Samuelson, on the other hand, have argued that whatever may be found ambiguous in his policy recommendations only reflects his adopting a scientific stance, something that the author himself described on several occasions, which I examine further in this article, as a "middle-of-the-road" position.[2]

The object of the present article is not to side with either the critics or the eulogists, or to locate in Samuelson's textbook some signs of his "true" political positioning. Instead, I am interested in the making of the text itself and in the way it was revised and defended in its early years. More specifically, using archival materials,[3] I describe how the various political pressures Samuelson faced while preparing his book for publication affected its content. The central thesis of this article is that Samuelson's "middle-of-the-road" position is the result of a political negotiation, something that he had to come up with to balance conflicting views on economic policy and address his critics. Of course, Samuelson was not acting alone in this process; he had to discuss and collaborate with MIT officials, his editors at McGraw-Hill, other economists, and the various reviewers of his work, and proceed to subsequent editorial changes.

In various autobiographical pieces, Samuelson himself has mentioned or hinted at these political elements.[4] However, to my knowledge, no historical contribution so far has fully attempted to substantiate Samuelson's claim and to provide a larger narrative of the context surrounding the making, the editing, and the revising of *Economics*. What has not been studied, in particular, is the influence of the political context on the making of the textbook and Samuelson's ethos. Although Samuelson first intended to write a policy-oriented textbook with a strong Keynesian inclination, the changes he introduced, while keeping most of the substance, made it a more theoretically inclined text whose policy recommendations were presented in a softened fashion.

1. Samuelson's Arrival at MIT and the Writing of "Modern Economics"

Samuelson was appointed assistant professor at MIT in October 1940 after MIT lured him with a better offer than Harvard, where he had been

2. For unsympathetic appraisals of *Economics*, see Linder 1977, Skousen 1997, and Nelson 2001. On the hagiographic side, see Gottesman, Ramrattan, and Szenberg 2005.

3. Paul A. Samuelson Papers, David M. Rubenstein Rare Book and Manuscript Library, Duke University; hereafter cited as PASP.

4. See Samuelson 1997 and Samuelson et al. 1999.

a graduate student and junior fellow, was prepared to make (see Backhouse, this volume, "Samuelson's Move"). Soon after his arrival, he helped develop a graduate program in economics and supervised Lawrence Klein's PhD dissertation. Then he had to cease momentarily these activities to join the Radiation Laboratory in 1944, where, in the mathematics and statistics group, he conducted research on fire control problems. Samuelson's commitment to wartime science also included his participation in the elaboration of Vannevar Bush's influential report *Science, the Endless Frontier* (July 1945), whose aim was to secure the funding of American science in the early postwar period while preventing too much state intervention in this domain.[5] More relevant to the genesis of *Economics* was the work Samuelson had done as early as 1941 under the supervision of his friend and mentor Alvin Hansen for the National Resources Planning Board (see Backhouse 2011). Created in 1933 by Harold Ickes and chaired by Frederic Delano, President Franklin Roosevelt's uncle, the NRPB issued a few reports in the early forties showing how governmental planning could help ensure full employment in the aftermath of the war. The work Samuelson undertook for these reports was fairly technical, but it undoubtedly established his reputation as an applied economist while allowing him to encounter the statistical material he would include in his textbook. In addition, Hansen's influence made him more outspoken as a political Keynesian, leading him to write a series of articles for the *New Republic* and the *Washington Post* in 1945 in favor of the Full Employment Bill, which was to be voted on by the US Senate.

When Samuelson returned to the Department of Economics and Social Science in October 1945 as an associate professor, MIT was faced with some important demographic changes. Following the adoption of the GI Bill, which helped war veterans pursue higher education, there was a dramatic increase of students in American universities. Many of those who chose to study engineering were likely to occupy executive positions in businesses or in the administration after graduation. The consequence, as shown in Kaiser 2010, was that the training of engineers at MIT had to change dramatically. The war experience had shown that the boundaries between pure technique and political relevance were blurry, and engineers,

5. On *Science, the Endless Frontier*, see Hollinger 1990. Bush's report was specifically written against the claim, famously made by the West Virginia senator Harley Kilgore, that science should by organized by the state toward democratically determined needs. Bush's victory over Kilgore was a landmark in the emergence of "laissez-faire communitarianism" in American science.

therefore, should be taught the human consequences of their work. Actually, the introductory economics course, Ec11, had been compulsory for all engineering students for many years. Accordingly, the economics class was expected to provide the students with a complete picture of the American economy and a toolbox to confront the issues of the day. The difficulty in teaching such a course was made worse by the absence of an introductory text that would combine solid theoretical content with some statistical information presented in an appealing way for nonspecialists. The leading principles textbooks of the time were austere and almost devoid of actual data on the economy, while the textbooks devoted to nonspecialists were often poor on the analytical side.[6] According to Samuelson (1997), this is why Ralph Freeman, chair of the department, asked him to write an introductory text to fill the void. What began as a mimeographed document intended for his students at MIT soon transformed into a full textbook when Samuelson got a publishing contract with McGraw-Hill.[7]

Even so, pedagogical concerns alone could not explain why Samuelson, a prolific technical writer, would spend months working on an undergraduate textbook. There was also a more political agenda involved in his decision. Following his experience as a wartime planner and as a columnist for the *New Republic*, Samuelson was in search of a new way to spread the economics of Keynes to the public. In addition, there was a growing interest among publishers in releasing such a text. This was clearly reflected in Samuelson's correspondence with his former PhD student, Lawrence Klein, whose main project at the time was to write a Keynesian essay drawn from his dissertation. In April 1945 Klein wrote to him: "A book salesman from Prentice-Hall . . . proposed to me to write an introductory textbook on the economics of full employment, but when I read your mimeographed notes, I decided you could actually do a much better job by carrying on from there. The salesman thought that there would be a good market for such a book now."[8] Samuelson's answer, although quite elusive about his own project, was that "there [was] a real need for more than one text book on this subject."[9] A few weeks later, as he may have

6. On economics textbooks before World War II and a comparison with their postwar counterparts, see Solow 1997 and Giraud 2010.

7. According to Kenneth Elzinga (1992), Samuelson chose McGraw-Hill as his publisher because it had previously published Joseph Schumpeter's *Business Cycles*. Although the company was not particularly well known as a publisher of economic texts at the time, it was already a leader in the marketing of textbooks devoted to engineering students (see Burlingame 1959).

8. Klein to Samuelson, April 9, 1945, PASP, box 45, folder "Klein, Lawrence R."

9. Samuelson to Klein, April 17, 1945, PASP, box 45, folder "Klein, Lawrence R."

secured a contract with McGraw-Hill in the meantime, he made his intent clearer to his former student: "To my shame I am putting in some time writing an elementary one semester text book along the lines we discussed. Don't breathe it to a soul."[10]

This preliminary version, titled "Modern Economics: An Introductory Analysis of National Income and Policy," included thirteen chapters, some of which analyzed the determination of the national income and the causes of unemployment. Still, it also included a quite detailed introduction to the theory of supply and demand and, more surprisingly, an incursion into business management, including some elements of accounting and a 1941 business report—which was removed in subsequent revisions of the text.[11] Samuelson's manuscript differed from preexisting texts not only in method but also in the way it addressed political issues. Besides the inclusion of up-to-date economic analysis, large portions of text commented on the respective merits of the free market system and government interventions to alleviate unemployment and poverty. Samuelson's statements were written in a discursive manner uncharacteristic of a mathematical economist. Concerning the economic analysis itself, two features of this early manuscript stood in sharp contrast to the preexisting literature: first, there was the emphasis on income distribution and inequalities, with the Lorenz curve used twice in the corresponding chapter, along with a passing reference to Karl Marx's class struggle; second, whereas Samuelson made it clear in the beginning of the text that the capitalist system in which most of his analysis was located worked well most of the time, a large portion of the subsequent analysis was devoted to unemployment and the way government intervention could help things out, drawing on wartime experience.

By 1946 Samuelson had written a more advanced draft version of his textbook, which had now adopted its definitive title: "Economics: An Introductory Analysis." The table of contents listed twenty-eight chapters, of which only eighteen were included in the mimeographed version. This manuscript was divided into four sections: "Basic Economic Concepts and National Income," "The Level and Fluctuations in the National Income," "The Economics of Full Employment"—which included the study of supply and demand—and "The Economics of Progress." This final section was supposed to include two chapters, one titled "The War

10. Samuelson to Klein, July 24, 1945, PASP, box 45, folder "Klein, Lawrence R."

11. "Modern Economics: An Introductory Analysis of National Income and Policy," 1945, PASP, box 91.

and Postwar Reconstruction" and the other "Basic Trends in the American Economy," but neither was included in the manuscript at this stage.[12]

This second preliminary manuscript was printed as a mimeograph and distributed to all MIT students. It was apparently so successful that it was soon used outside MIT by a few neighboring institutions willing to provide a vibrant introduction to economics to their students.[13] However, Samuelson's insistence on the drawbacks of imperfect competition and involuntary unemployment as characteristic of the failures of the "free enterprise system" in this manuscript provoked the anger of some local businessmen, who tried to influence its content and prevent its publication.

2. The Virulence of Conservative Attacks on Samuelson's Manuscript

In 1947 Walter J. Beadle, a business executive working for DuPont in Wilmington, Delaware, and a member of the MIT Corporation, chaired a visiting committee, whose mission was to appraise the content of courses taught in the Department of Economics and Social Science at MIT.[14] Its attention focused on Ec11 and its accompanying manuscript, which circulated among the various members of the committee and outside referees for appraisal. This followed Ralph Freeman's suggestion that Samuelson himself wanted someone at MIT to review his text before its publication by McGraw-Hill. The reaction of the readers, however, was less than enthusiastic. A June 1947 report by a Mr. Peterson, an economist at the First National Bank of Boston, found Samuelson's approach to be "neither sufficiently objective nor complete." "Apparently," he wrote, "the author believes that some managed capitalism is necessary and presents theories along these lines as established facts without presenting alternative theories or points of view."[15] Building on this report, Beadle wrote to Freeman a letter listing all of Samuelson's statements about the economy that he

12. "Economics: An Introductory Analysis," second preliminary edition, PASP, box 91.

13. A 1947 letter from Professor Chelsie C. Bowland of Brown University suggests that the text may have been available at the time for others to use, although Samuelson's answer was that he wanted to keep the last available copies in preparation for the published version and correct some imperfections, for reasons I examine later (Bowland to Samuelson, November 25, 1947, PASP, box 12, folder "B—General Correspondence 1939–1951").

14. The MIT Corporation was created in 1862 and includes businessmen, scientists, civil servants, and professionals from both the Boston area and other US states. Some of them hold a lifetime membership. Beadle sat there as an MIT alumnus.

15. Peterson, "Economics, an Introductory Analysis," Report, June 26, 1946, PASP, box 80, folder "Criticism of the Textbook."

believed should be reconsidered, either because they "could not be justified by a consideration of all the facts" or because they seemed "open to serious question." One example of the latter was the following: "Sometimes the mistakes which a flock of independent competitors make—for instance in all overbuilding as in 1929, or in continually entering the already overcrowded grocery store business—could have been avoided by advanced centralized planning." Appealing to the authority of another textbook writer, Fred Fairchild of Yale, whose latest edition of his *Elementary Economics*, written with Edgar Furniss and Norman Buck, was to be published in 1947, Beadle concluded: "If [Samuelson] approaches the matter as objectively as a professor in an engineering school approach[es] a problem of this kind, I am hopeful that the text which is eventually to be published will attain recognition everywhere as reflecting credit on both M.I.T. and the author."[16]

The letter was passed on to Samuelson, who replied amicably. Thanking Beadle for his "very constructive letter," Samuelson assured him that it would be possible "to reword six out of ten of [his] selected quotations," while "three other had already been changed in revised versions." He also provided Beadle with a list of scholars who had commented on previous drafts of his textbook, without citing any name but mentioning that one of them was "Fairchild's successor in public finance instruction." Noting that his manuscript had also been "criticized by both conservatives and radicals," Samuelson concluded: "What I do wish to avoid is a departure from a middle-of-the-road position, as compared to my present generation of economists. And I am sure that your comments have been most helpful in this respect."[17]

Simultaneously, Beadle had chosen to address similar concerns to MIT president Karl T. Compton. Noting that Samuelson lacked "the knowledge and capacity to make himself effective outside the narrow area of mathematical economics," Beadle expressed his hope that "under adequate administrative supervision the Institute may be able to bring him to maturity."[18] Frank Chesterman, another committee member, voiced his discontent to Compton more virulently:

16. Beadle to Freeman, July 15, 1947, PASP, box 80, folder "Criticism of the Textbook." It should be noted that Fairchild was not only one of Samuelson's competitors in the textbook market but also an economist who had adopted an opposite political stance to that of Samuelson and was often quoted in the press as a virulent opponent to postwar planning (see Backhouse 2011).

17. Samuelson to Beadle, July 31, 1947, PASP, box 80, folder "Criticism of the Textbook."

18. Beadle to Compton, July 15, 1947, PASP, box 87, folder "MIT Archives Photocopies 1 of 3."

> I am astonished to find that a teacher of economics at M.I.T. shall enunciate some of the absurd thinking which is quoted in Walter's letter to you. It is perfectly obvious that the young man is socially-minded if not strictly communistic. It would be a terrible reflection on M.I.T. if the book in its present condition were published. . . . I question whether Samuelson is a member of the subversive societies we hear so much about because his line of reasoning and method of expressing his thoughts are those of that group.[19]

Having read Samuelson's reply and dissatisfied with what he saw as mere cosmetic adjustments from him, Beadle strengthened his position and extended his criticism. In another letter to Compton, he assessed that "more drastic correctives would be required with respect to the teaching of economics at the Institute" and that the economics department should be "subject to severe censure for having permitted the text, in the form in which the Committee reviewed it, to be passed out to the students of Ec 11 and used as a basis for classroom instruction."[20]

The virulence in Beadle's letter prompted Compton to write an equally straightforward response: "There is no question that every member of our Economics department is a wholehearted advocate of the free enterprise system. . . . Professor Samuelson has taken your criticisms and suggestions in excellent spirit and has modified a number of parts of his manuscript where this was not inconsistent with his own beliefs."[21] Although there was no doubt that Compton and Vice President James Killian Jr. were both fully committed to Samuelson and his home department, the author felt it necessary to provide the MIT president with more justification about his methodology: "The book is in no sense a 'left-wing' work; and I have never, myself, been connected with left-wing organizations of any kind, or with organizations working with such groups, or—for that matter—with any labor organizations whatsoever. . . . The methods of analysis used are those that have been employed by 90 per cent of the active academic economists under the age of 50 over the last decade."[22] Following this letter and in regard to what he saw as inadmissible pressures

19. Chesterman to Compton, July 21, 1947, PASP, box 87, folder "MIT Archives Photocopies 1 of 3."

20. Beadle to Compton, August 6, 1947, PASP, box 87, folder "MIT Archives Photocopies 1 of 3."

21. Compton to Beadle, August 6, 1947, PASP, box 87, folder "MIT Archives Photocopies 1 of 3."

22. Samuelson to Compton, August 7, 1947, PASP, box 80, folder "Criticism of the Textbook."

from Beadle and his allies, Compton issued a more explicit statement: "If either your committee or I were to go beyond suggestion, advice and criticism in respect to the views or publications expressed by any member of the faculty the institution would be wrecked. There would be wholesale resignations irrespective of whether or not other members of the staff felt that the criticisms were justified."[23]

In consequence, the discussion moved to the larger question of whether an intervention by the MIT Corporation on the publications of a faculty member should be seen as a violation of academic freedom. Not all of the visiting committee members agreed. Charles Spencer and Ellis Brewster, for instance, believed that the visiting committee should not interfere with the book's content, even though they were critical of Samuelson's views. That Beadle was partly disavowed by his colleagues did not put the MIT president at ease. Killian, in particular, feared that Beadle might want to go public about his claims, which would probably harm MIT's reputation. Consequently, Compton and Killian decided to release a statement about the position of MIT toward academic freedom in the economics department. It asserted that the policy on appointments and teaching in economics was the same as in any other field, namely, that "it seeks . . . to give the student a scholarly treatment of the subject which stimulates and trains him to do his own thinking . . . and which encourages him to reach his own conclusions of all relevant facts and points of view."[24]

Yet Beadle's persistence in criticizing Samuelson's *Economics* did not vanish. The recent publication of a new textbook, *Elements of Economics* by the Stanford economist Lorie Tarshis, which was severely criticized in the conservative press for its Keynesian inclination, did nothing to dissipate the feeling among MIT benefactors that some kind of socialistic conspiracy was brewing in American academe. For Beadle's superior Lammot DuPont, Tarshis's textbook was "an aggravated example of what [Samuelson had] done in a milder way," which was bad enough to justify that Compton be disturbed.[25] That the American Economic Association

23. Compton to Beadle, August 8, 1947, PASP, box 87, folder "MIT Archives Photocopies 1 of 3."

24. Statement, August 28, 1947, PASP, box 87, folder "MIT Archives Photocopies 1 of 3."

25. DuPont to Beadle, September 12, 1947, PASP, box 87, folder "MIT Archives Photocopies 1 of 3." On the controversy over Tarshis's textbook and its subsequent failure, see Colander and Landreth 1996. In the existing literature, as well as in Samuelson's own reminiscences (Samuelson 1997; Samuelson et al. 1999), it has often been stated that the two textbooks were quite similar in content but that Samuelson's scientific credentials served as a bulwark against criticisms, allowing for a more successful output. This story, as the present narrative shows, needs some qualification.

awarded Samuelson the very first John Bates Clark Medal in December 1947 represented a welcome assistance for the MIT president. Both Compton and Killian never failed to mention this fact when they responded to the critics.[26] For a short period, the pressures loosened up.

3. Changes, Increased Criticisms, and Further Changes

Once published, *Economics* was a smashing success. Advance orders were so high that McGraw-Hill printed forty-five thousand copies, an exceptional run for an economics text at the time. In August 1948 Samuelson wrote to Compton: "The book has been adopted for use at such institutions as Yale, Princeton, Harvard, Duke, Columbia, Purdue, etc. In terms of royalties it has been a profitable venture beyond my fondest expectations."[27] Compared with the 1946 manuscript that Beadle and his allies had read, however, the final version of *Economics* included a few editorial changes. These revisions did not represent a drastic departure from the overall pro-interventionist message of the initial manuscript, yet some controversial aspects had been toned down. For instance, the passage that Beadle had mentioned in his first letter to Freeman had been rephrased as the following:

> But sometimes the mistakes which a flock of independent competitors make—for instance in all overbuilding as in 1929, or in continually entering the already overcrowded grocery store business—would be lessened in an economy characterized by planning. (Of course, fallible bureaucrats might perpetrate a series of planning errors of their own, and new problems of individual liberty would be introduced.) (Samuelson 1948, 39)

Samuelson's efforts to find a reasonable middle ground to address the political issues of the day while providing a good introduction to technical economics is something that most of the younger generation of economists appreciated, as exemplified by the Columbia professor Albert Gailord Hart's (1948, 912) review for the *American Economic Review*:

26. Killian almost immediately sent a letter to Beadle, attaching the notification Samuelson had received from the American Economic Association about the award (Killian to Beadle, December 15, 1947, PASP, box 87, folder "MIT Archives Photocopies 1 of 3").

27. Samuelson to Compton, August 31, 1948, PASP, box 1, folder "MIT Archives Photocopies, 1 of 3."

> The supreme merit of the book, to my taste, is a systematic effort to find points of contact between different points of view which students and their neighbors in society may hold. Samuelson's own policy position is middle-of-the-road. . . . In consequence of this tone of reasonableness and tolerance, his book should prove congenial to teachers and students over a wide range to right and left of Samuelson's own political position.

However, one early reviewer disagreed. For the conservative economist Lewis Haney, Samuelson's textbook had a "snappy style" and "drop[ped] to wisecracks at times," making "the inferior student (and teacher) feel good." The "economics of Keynes" it incorporated broke "with the evolutionary development of economics as science" (Haney 1948, 221). Having written these comments in the *Annals of the American Academy of Political and Social Science*, Haney subsequently published a column in the *L.A. Examiner*, calling on readers to write to the publishers and to "the trustees of various colleges in which the book is said to be used."[28] Haney's call to arms was one instantiation of a larger campaign against Samuelson's textbook launched by a group of economics columnists writing in conservative periodicals. One such publication was the *Educational Reviewer*, in which Charles Kraemer, a professor of business administration at Wagner College, had written a widely circulated attack on *Economics*. According to Kraemer, Samuelson's method was characteristic of a group of "econometricians" who tried to use mathematical formalism "to justify their national planning control."[29]

Kraemer's review, as Haney suggested, provoked reactions of letters sent to Killian, who had by now succeeded Compton as MIT president,[30] as well as to James McGraw Jr., Samuelson's publisher. To the latter, Beadle's colleague Lammot DuPont wrote: "The name of the publisher of this book is so close to the name of your company that I assume there must be some connection. Understanding that the book is still being published and sold, I cannot understand how you can permit it, knowing your feeling for

28. Haney Comment on "Economics" book, *L.A. Examiner*, January 20, 1950, PASP, box 80, folder "Criticism of the Textbook."

29. Charles L. Kraemer, Review of *Economics: An Introductory Analysis*, *Educational Reviewer*, October 15, 1949, PASP, box 80, folder "Criticism of the Textbook." It is notable that, like many of these reviews, this one barely quoted Samuelson's text. The only quote in Kraemer's review was "socialist Britain (1948) has more civil liberties than did the United States in the 1920s era of rugged individualism" (Samuelson 1948, 590).

30. Compton resigned in October 1948 to become chairman of the MIT Corporation, which then elected Killian as his successor.

free private enterprise."[31] McGraw's answer to DuPont signaled that Samuelson's publisher was well aware of the situation at MIT:

> As you know, there are wide differences in opinion between recognized authorities in the many fields of science and technology served by our Book Company just as there are such differences among the members of university and college faculties, including that of Massachusetts Institute of Technology. . . . In matters of this sort, I think the friend to whom you refer in your letter [i.e., Beadle] did exactly right when he got the authorities at the Massachusetts Institute of Technology to prescribe required reading material that would complement the presentation in Professor Samuelson's text. That is an eminently proper way to deal with differences of opinion in such matters.[32]

Beadle and his allies, conscious that they would not manage to alter much of the content of *Economics*, had turned their attention to issues of diversity in the economics curriculum. Their view was that Ec11 should include a wide variety of readings supplementing Samuelson's text and expressing different points of view—meaning others than those in favor of governmental intervention in the economy. For Beadle, this was a way to counteract Compton's and Killian's defense of academic freedom, by defining freedom not as the freedom for the researcher to express his own opinions but, rather, as the freedom for students to benefit from the largest range of existing opinions in order to forge their own views on economic subjects. These issues resurfaced as the campaign against Samuelson's *Economics* in the conservative press gained increasing importance. In particular, Benjamin Namm's (1950) critique in *Collier's Weekly* did not go unnoticed. Namm was a New York merchant and an officer of the United States Chamber of Commerce. The chamber had decided to investigate the issue of "subversive teaching" in colleges and to take to task anyone who would question the ability of the free enterprise system to solve the economic problems of the day. Admittedly, commentators such as Namm had little credit as economists, but they had an audience, and some of their readers, astonished by what they read about an MIT professor, wrote to Killian in good faith to know if there was any truth in these

31. DuPont to McGraw Jr., December 30, 1949, PASP, box 1, folder "MIT Archives Photocopies 1 of 3."

32. McGraw Jr. to DuPont, January 25, 1950, PASP, box 87, folder "MIT Archives Photocopies 1 of 3."

statements. Although the MIT president was prone to reject these allegations every time they appeared, his endorsement of Samuelson's textbook did not go as far as saying that he agreed with its policy conclusions. Killian's responses to alarmed MIT supporters consisted in asserting that many MIT faculties, including himself, often disagreed with Samuelson's policy advice but that because his analysis relied on the latest developments in the field, it was the surest way to let the students exert their own freedom of thought. Accordingly, Killian wrote Samuelson: "I do feel there are many businessmen with a thoroughly honest and liberal outlook who are troubled about what they feel to be the Keynesian outlook and who have gained the impression that colleges have succumbed to one-sided propaganda. . . . Do you agree that there is an opportunity to do something constructive about this situation rather than remain always on the defensive?"[33] Samuelson's answer was a clear qualification of the argument that what he taught was Keynes's doctrine:

> I myself think that much of what is called Keynesianism is incorrect and in need of qualification. Much of my text is concerned with such qualifications and criticisms. . . . I myself rarely use the words Keynesianism and have repeatedly deplored the formation of "schools of thought" in economics. I accept and use whatever parts of the analysis of saving and investment, income-determination, and inflation that Keynes and anybody else has contributed—so long as the analysis seems to add to our knowledge of the facts of economic behavior.[34]

Despite Samuelson's willingness to explain his position whenever necessary, the matter got worse in 1951, as suspicious inquiries multiplied after the publication of William Buckley's *God and Man at Yale*, which criticized liberal education and quoted from Samuelson's textbook. To Freeman, Killian confessed: "Everywhere I go now practically, business people speak to me about [Samuelson's book]." John Burchard summarized the situation: "The President is in a terribly difficult position on this. He takes the beating. He has no desire, I am sure, to do anything but find a good affirmative position. I myself do not think the affirmative position could be made by simply getting some classical economist (if indeed one now exists)."[35] There was another way, however, to bring classical econo-

33. Killian to Samuelson, August 29, 1950, PASP, box 87, folder "MIT Archives Photocopies 1 of 3."

34. Samuelson to Killian, August 30, 1950, PASP, box 53, folder "MIT."

35. Burchard to Freeman, March 1, 1951, PASP, box 87, folder "MIT Archives Photocopies 2 of 3."

mists into the classroom, hence the revived idea of a readings volume that would incorporate some other texts and particularly those advocating an unconstrained free enterprise system and accordingly critical of governmental intervention. Freeman, in a letter to Killian, referred to the existence of "a small book of readings" that MIT students were required to purchase and that presented "different points of view."[36]

In the meantime, similar measures had been taken at McGraw-Hill in response to the increased attacks on *Economics*. John Taylor, the editor in charge of college textbooks, had ordered a detailed memorandum responding to all the critiques addressed to Samuelson. The resulting document reported all the quotations in Kraemer that had been taken out of context and recommended counterbalancing them with a series of quotations from Samuelson that "stress[ed] the values of capitalism and free-enterprise, and show[ed] his basic opposition to socialist and welfare-state tenets." The report also reproduced portions of Hart's review in the *American Economic Review*, mentioning the passage on Samuelson's "systematic effort to find points of contact between different points of views."[37] At the same time, during the summer and the fall of 1951, Taylor and Samuelson concretized the publishing of the supplementary readings volume. Their correspondence made it clear that *Readings in Economics* was not the sole idea of the editor but a joint decision between McGraw-Hill and the MIT economics department. The making of this volume, indeed, involved three other economists at MIT: Robert Bishop, John Coleman, and Cary Brown—although the latter would not appear as a coeditor of the published version. As soon as November 1951, before the volume was published or even completed, Freeman referred to it in a letter to Killian:

> As I indicated to you in a recent conversation, a group of the Department staff is preparing a new book of readings to supplement the textbook which we use in Economic Principles. . . . As you will observe, the projected book of readings aims to present a variety of points of views ranging from radical to conservative, from Marx and Engels to

36. Freeman to Killian, May 9, 1951, PASP, box 87, folder, "MIT Archives Photocopies 1 of 3."

37. "Discussion of the textbook entitled 'Economics: an Introductory Analysis' by Paul A. Samuelson," report to John Taylor, PASP, box 80, folder "Criticism of the Textbook." It is possible that the author of this report was Hans Apel, a professor at the University of Bridgeport (Conn.). Apel spent a considerable amount of time battling his institution's decision to drop *Economics* in the wake of Kraemer's 1949 review. He subsequently collaborated with McGraw-Hill on this matter and, as a member of the American Association of University Professors, participated in the writing of a code of ethics designed to support academic freedom (see Backhouse 2013).

> Pope Leo XIII. There are also readings from classical economists such as Adam Smith, Ricardo and Bastiat. Articles criticizing recent government policies are included as well as various opinions on the economics of the defense program.[38]

Killian immediately made use of this material in order to respond to criticisms. To one Pittsburgh businessman, he wrote: "Included in the various readings . . . are such documents as 'Meaning of Competition,' published by the National Association of manufacturers, Crawford Greenewalt's 'Dupont and the Problem of Bigness in Industry,' Hayek's 'The Road to Serfdom,' and the Standard Oil Company of New Jersey's report, 'A Stockholders Meeting.'"[39] All these texts were included in the version McGraw-Hill released in 1952, as well as a series of left-wing texts, such as an excerpt from Marx and Friedrich Engels's *Communist Manifesto*. The editors stated in the volume's introduction that they had included "arguments *for* and *against* various policies and viewpoints" to provide "an enhanced and informed appreciation of the merits of the American economy" (Samuelson, Bishop, and Coleman 1952, vi).

As for the textbook itself, it was revised to help prevent further criticisms. In particular, Samuelson and his editors at McGraw-Hill took great care in changing most of the passages quoted in Buckley's book. These paragraphs were simply omitted in the second edition or their wording was reworked to soften the argument, replacing, for instance, a passage on the defects of *free* competition by another one criticizing *perfect* competition. These changes in the second edition did not go unnoticed. Alvin Hansen, undoubtedly one important influence on Samuelson in the writing of the first edition, was now quite critical of the new presentation his former protégé had made of macroeconomic policies. In December 1954 he wrote to Samuelson, expressing his dissatisfaction with the way that the issue of public debt was treated in *Economics*. Hansen's argument was that Samuelson insisted too much on the detrimental effects of public debt and therefore undermined its favorable redistributive aspects and its ability to serve as a cushion for the financial system during depressions. He wrote: "I feel strongly that your analysis is not altogether well-balanced and indeed, at points, leaves the reader with unsound conclusions."[40] In his answer to

38. Freeman to Killian, November 19, 1951, PASP, box 87, folder "MIT Archives Photocopies 1 of 3."

39. Killian to D. M. Gray, November 20, 1951, PASP, box 87, folder "MIT Archives Photocopies 1 of 3."

40. Hansen to Samuelson, December 14, 1954, PASP, box 36, folder "Hansen, Alvin H."

Hansen, Samuelson conceded that he should give "appropriate (or even *equal*) weight to the many advantages that the debt's existence implies to our present-day economy."[41] Yet he also notified Hansen that his third edition was in press, and that he would not be able to take these remarks into account at this stage. It is in this edition that Samuelson famously came up with the *neoclassical synthesis* label, a term he introduced several times in the text, but more preeminently at the end of chapter 18, on the treatment of public debt. In Samuelson's own words, the neoclassical synthesis embodied not only a theoretical result—that the new Keynesian theory of income determination underwrote rather than disqualified the old neoclassical price theory—but also a policy principle: "By means of appropriately reinforcing monetary and fiscal policies, our mixed enterprise system can avoid the excesses of boom and slump and can look forward to healthy progressive growth" (Samuelson 1955, 360).

These changes in *Economics*, together with the publication of the *Readings* volume, put a final note on the questioning of Samuelson's legitimacy as a textbook author and as a teacher of introductory principles at MIT. While conservative criticisms remained quite frequent until the early 1960s, they were counterattacked ferociously by everyone at MIT. In 1961 even Beadle asserted to one of the remaining skeptics that "Samuelson [had] made real improvements from a business standpoint in each of the five editions that [had] now been published."[42]

4. The "Middle-of-the-Road" Position: Between Rhetoric, Political Consciousness, and Economic Expertise

There are several ways to interpret the preceding account of the making and subsequent revising of Samuelson's *Economics*. One interpretation would be to see *Economics* as a project doomed to failure: the writing of a "truly" Keynesian textbook. What the story shows, indeed, is that Samuelson's textbook was at first a policy-oriented manual, with the clear objective of promoting the demand management policies that the author had been witnessing since the early 1940s by working at the National Resources Planning Board with Alvin Hansen. In 1945 this project was deemed viable for a variety of reasons: from an academic point of view, these policies

41. Samuelson to Hansen, January 3, 1955, PASP, box 36, folder "Hansen, Alvin H."

42. Beadle to Willard J. Rockwell, November 14, 1961, PASP, box 87, folder "MIT Archives Photocopies 3 of 3."

and the theoretical apparatus that justified them were the rage among younger economists; from a pedagogical point of view, teaching the economics of full employment and its consequences for the economy was the best way to raise the interest of students, especially newcomers and non-majors stemming from the GI Bill; from a publisher's point of view, finally, there was the need for a new generation of economics textbooks that would treat the latest advances in the field in an accessible way. All these reasons, mutually reinforcing one another, allowed for a successful textbook. Yet because of the conservative attacks that occurred at a very early stage and grew in virulence in the early 1950s, Samuelson's textbook was rephrased and reshaped in a way that would soften its pro-interventionist message and mix it with the older, neoclassical analysis. If we see the preceding story in that fashion, then, there is an obvious feeling that something got lost in the process. Accordingly, it might be tempting for those willing to adopt a moral interpretation of the past to see it as the story of Samuelson's abandonment of his political convictions in pursuit of career objectives. In this interpretation, the "middle-of-the-road" position that Samuelson put forward would be considered a mere rhetorical device, something he would have come up with to justify the reversal of his initial left-wing position in favor of a more balanced view.

However, the archives suggest a different, subtler interpretation. In 1949 Samuelson received an invitation from Evans Clark, a liberal philanthropist and director of the Twentieth Century Fund, to advise on the composition of a committee devoted to devising a basic economics course for high school students. Samuelson replied: "My own limited experience makes me think that a committee of recognized authorities who are known to be middle-of-the-road people is better than a committee that tries to arrive at a mean balancing somebody at one extreme against somebody at the other extreme."[43]

What we see emerging in Samuelson's response to Clark is the figure of the economic expert, who is able to acknowledge the various political positions but is not taking a stand when giving policy recommendations. Therefore, it is also possible to interpret the preceding narrative as an important episode in the construction of the image of the economist as expert in the postwar period (see also Maas, this volume). Although Samuelson clearly intended his textbook as a policy-relevant treatise, there is no reason to think that he ever quite considered his own policy orientation as strongly partisan from a political point of view—at most, he considered himself a

43. Samuelson to Evans Clark, October 10, 1949, PASP, box 72, folder "T—General Correspondences, 1938–1968."

liberal Democrat whose beliefs were compatible with his scientific practice.[44] Then he soon realized that the groups of people whose criticisms he was facing had their own policy agenda, one that he viewed as much more crudely ideological than his. Moreover, these critics projected their own political prejudices onto the textbook, arguing that it was Samuelson who was the ideologically committed one. Having to deal with this rather strange culture as a textbook author, Samuelson's main concern in revising his text was to show that his policy recommendations were not tied to predetermined political convictions. The "middle-of-the-road" position emerged as a way to respond to these critics, by stepping *aside* rather than *against* them.

Far from being anecdotal, therefore, the controversies that surrounded the publication of *Economics* in its early years should rather be seen as foundational in the identity of what historians are trying to identify as "MIT economics," which Robert Solow once defined as "an atmosphere of rigor-with-policy-relevance" (see Cherrier, this volume). More generally, they should invite us to reconsider from a historical viewpoint the relationship between *politics* and *policy*.

References

Backhouse, Roger E. 2011. "Entering Hansen's New World: Paul Samuelson, the Young Keynesian, 1938–47." Working paper.

———. 2013. "Hans Apel, Samuelson's Economics and Academic Freedom, 1950–57." Working paper.

Burlingame, Roger. 1959. *Endless Frontiers: The Story of McGraw-Hill*. New York: McGraw-Hill.

Cherrier, Beatrice. 2011. "The Lucky Consistency of Milton Friedman's Science and Politics, 1933–1963." In *Building Chicago Economics: New Perspectives on the History of America's Most Powerful Economics Program*, edited by Robert van Horn, Philip Mirowski, and Thomas Stapleford, 335–67. Cambridge: Cambridge University Press.

Colander, David C., and Harry Landreth, eds. 1996. *The Coming of Keynesianism to America: Conversations with the Founders of Keynesian Economics*. Cheltenham: Elgar.

Elzinga, Kenneth G. 1992. "The Eleven Principles of Economics." *Southern Economic Journal* 58 (4): 861–79.

Fairchild, Fred R., Edgar S. Furniss, and Norman S. Buck. 1947. *Elementary Economics*. 5th ed. New York: Macmillan.

44. In this respect, Samuelson's views on the separation between science and politics did not strongly differ from those of his most famous opponent within the neoclassical orthodoxy, Milton Friedman (see Cherrier 2011)

Giraud, Yann. 2010. "The Changing Place of Visual Representation in Economics: Paul Samuelson between Principle and Strategy, 1941–1955." *Journal of the History of Economic Thought* 32 (2): 175–97.

Gottesman, Aron A., Lall Ramrattan, and Michael Szenberg. 2005. "Samuelson's *Economics*: The Continuing Legacy." *Quarterly Journal of Austrian Economics* 8 (2): 95–104.

Haney, Lewis H. 1948. Review of *Economics: An Introductory Analysis*, by Paul A. Samuelson. *Annals of the American Academy of Political and Social Science* 260:221–22.

Hart, Albert G. 1948. Review of *Economics: An Introductory Analysis*, by Paul A. Samuelson. *American Economic Review* 38 (5): 910–18.

Hollinger, David A. 1990. "Free Enterprise and Free Inquiry: The Emergence of Laissez-Faire Communitarianism in the Ideology of Science in the United States." *New Literary History* 21 (4): 897–919.

Kaiser, David. 2010. "Elephant on the Charles: Postwar Growing Pains." In *Becoming MIT: Moments of Decision*, edited by David Kaiser, 103–21. Cambridge, Mass.: MIT Press.

Linder, Marc. 1977. *The Anti-Samuelson*. With the help of Julius Sensat Jr. 2 vols. New York: Urizen Books.

Namm, Benjamin H. 1950. "Would You Enter a Door Marked 'Socialism'?" *Collier's Weekly*, April 29, 34–49.

Nelson, Robert H. 2001. *Economics as Religion: From Samuelson to Chicago and Beyond*. University Park: Pennsylvania State University Press.

Pearce, Kerry A., and Kevin D. Hoover. 1995. "After the Revolution: Paul Samuelson and the Textbook Keynesian Model." In *New Perspectives on Keynes*, edited by Allin F. Cottrell. *History of Political Economy* 27 (supplement): 183–216.

Samuelson, Paul A. 1948. *Economics*. New York: McGraw-Hill.

———. 1952. *Economics*. 2nd ed. New York: McGraw-Hill.

———. 1955. *Economics*. 3rd ed. New York: McGraw-Hill.

———. 1997. "Credo of a Lucky Textbook Author." *Journal of Economic Perspectives* 11:153–60.

Samuelson, Paul A., Robert L. Bishop, and John R. Coleman, eds. 1952. *Readings in Economics*. New York: McGraw-Hill.

Samuelson, Paul A., Harold W. McGraw Jr., William D. Nordhaus, Orley Ashenfelter, Robert M. Solow, and Stanley Fischer. 1999. "Samuelson's *Economics* at Fifty: Remarks on the Occasion of the Anniversary of Publication." *Journal of Economic Education* 30 (4): 352–63.

Skousen, Mark. 1997. "The Perseverance of Paul Samuelson's *Economics*." *Journal of Economic Perspectives* 11 (2): 137–52.

Solow, Robert M. 1997. "How Did Economics Get That Way and What Way Did It Get?" *Daedalus* 126 (1): 39–58.

Tarshis, Lorie. 1947. *Elements of Economics*. Boston: Houghton Mifflin.

Serving the Institute and the Discipline: The Changing Profile of Economics at MIT as Viewed from Textbooks

Pedro Teixeira

Textbooks reflect the state of a science.
They also help shape the development of a science.
—Paul A. Samuelson and William Nordhaus,
New York Times (February 19, 1985)

Textbooks have been an important vehicle for disseminating scientific ideas and became a particularly prominent issue with the emergence of mass higher education in the second half of the twentieth century (Trow 2010; Meyer and Schofer [2006] 2009). With the rapid rise in enrollments, there was a need to rethink teaching methods for an expanding and more diverse student cohort. Moreover, the standardization of curricula and teaching tools was also regarded as an effective way to ensure minimum standards and a coordinated and systematic approach to the various areas of a discipline or field. In economics, as in many other disciplines, a great number of teachers assign a textbook as core reading (many assign only a textbook), and these influence the views of future professionals by shaping

Correspondence may be addressed to Pedro Teixeira, CIPES, Rua 1° Dezembro 399, 4450-227 Matosinhos, Portugal; e-mail: pedrotx@fep.up.pt. I thank the participants at the 2013 *HOPE* conference for their comments and suggestions, and Roy Weintraub for his advice and encouragement. I am also grateful to Robert Solow for his comments on an earlier draft. In the collection of data I have benefited from excellent research assistance by Ricardo Biscaia. This research has been financially supported by the FCT (Fundação para a Ciência e a Tecnologia).

History of Political Economy 46 (annual suppl.) DOI 10.1215/00182702-2716154

the ways in which students are introduced to the discipline and its various specialized fields.[1]

The rapidly expanding student cohort and increasing number of institutions and programs created demand for textbooks on a large scale, and certain developments in the publishing industry made this financially attractive because of the potential economies of scale (see Coser, Kadushin, and Powell 1985; and Thompson 2005).[2] Thus the industry became much more professionalized in developing those products, namely, by identifying those in each field who could be regarded by their peers as reliable and authoritative sources. Authorship of textbooks therefore became a proxy for a significant recognition among peers, and the financial incentives made it attractive for many leading academics to accept what was time-consuming work, and not necessarily a priority in their research-oriented careers.

Although they are often presented to students as objective, impartial, and factual, textbooks are shaped by their social, cultural, and ideological contexts (Apple and Christian-Smith 1991; Altbach et al. 1991).[3] In recent years there has been a growing interest in the history of science in the study of textbooks and their multiple roles (Vicedo 2012b; see also Giraud, this volume). The traditional view regards them as boring, dogmatic, and conservative (Kuhn 2012), although recent work on the history of science has noted that they have played an important role in internalizing concepts and tools (Kaiser 2005a). In those fields in which the disciplinary developments became very technical, textbooks (and other ancillary pedagogical instruments) were recognized as very relevant in familiarizing students with those new techniques, especially by focusing on applications, techniques, and procedures rather than on theoretical foundations and assumptions. This seems to be a particularly relevant issue in postwar economics because of the growing degree of formalism and technicality (see, e.g., Blaug 2003; Fourcade 2009), aspects that are usually associated with the MIT economics department.

In this text I look at the postwar evolution of MIT economics by exploring the role of textbooks in the consolidation of the department's position internally (within MIT) and externally (within the economics discipline).

1. For an analysis of this in the case of American history, see Kornblith and Lasser 2005.

2. According to some recent indications, the market for college textbooks in the United States may be worth $4 billion (Chevalier and Goolsbee 2009).

3. For recent illustrations of these in economics, see Clawson 2002 and Kalmi 2007.

I analyze the different roles played by writing textbooks and the profile of those textbooks with respect to field (macro, micro, labor, etc.) and level of course (introductory, intermediate, advanced). I also investigate the evolution in terms of different generations of economists trained in or associated with the MIT Department of Economics. Finally, I try to identify certain characteristics in those textbooks that may help us to confirm or rethink our views about the type of economics developed by that group of economists. In the first section I briefly analyze the emergence and development of the economics department within a context in which the role of MIT moved from an institution of advanced vocational training to a research-based university, thus broadening its scope to encompass the social sciences and humanities. In the second section I analyze the involvement of economists associated with MIT (either as faculty members or as former graduates) in the production of economics textbooks. In the concluding section I present some reflections about the relevance of teaching and teaching-related publications in understanding the development of economics at MIT.

The Changing Profile of Economics at MIT

During the second half of the nineteenth century a new wave of higher education institutions developed in the United States, largely propelled by the so-called Morrill Act of 1862 (Thelin 2004). In Massachusetts this led to the creation of MIT, founded in 1861 in Boston as a private institution, and the state's Agricultural College (which was founded in Amherst in 1863 [Freeland 1992]). MIT was from the beginning more closely associated with the mechanical arts and was supposed to combine practical education with broader training, seeking to distinguish itself both from more classical modes of training and from narrow vocational training.[4] From the outset, MIT was created on a dynamic tension between basic science and more applied and technical education, which throughout its history would prove to be sometimes an asset and sometimes a weakening and divisive issue. However, MIT slowly followed the drift toward a stronger research orientation that was becoming visible at other major private universities (Geiger 1986, 1993). In that process MIT also broadened its focus to include social sciences and the humanities.

4. On the details of the foundation of MIT and its initial years, see Stratton and Mannix 2005, Kaiser 2010, and Etzkowitz 2002.

The changes at MIT had a significant impact on the role of economics there.[5] The growing emphasis on research purposes and graduate education, coupled with the broadening of MIT's original disciplinary focus, created an opportunity in the postwar decades for economics at MIT to expand and to strengthen its research credentials. The changes of the 1940s facilitated the development of the PhD program created in 1940, whose focus showed an attempt to link the program with the core disciplines at MIT and to differentiate it from PhD programs in economics at other research universities. The development of the economics department also led to the establishment of a new undergraduate program of studies in economics and engineering, in 1946. The expansion in these programs was regarded as an important step in legitimizing the department within MIT, by playing an increasing role in MIT's educational activities.

The role and position of economics at MIT has changed since the creation of the first courses in the early twentieth century, and this has been framed by developments in MIT at large. These changes meant not only that economics could play a greater role in the life of MIT but also that expectations about its contribution could be changed. In the first period (until the late 1950s) the emphasis was still very much on teaching and the need to justify the congruence of the department with MIT's profile; hence, the department focused more on graduate education and research, using its growing reputation in economics to strengthen its institutional position and reputation. With the growing postwar involvement of MIT with graduate education and basic research, the department also benefited from its success on those fronts and could consolidate its profile internally as a small but respected department within the institution.

The position of the department within MIT also seemed to be relevant to the former's prevailing attitude in the postwar decades toward innovative research in economics. In the words of Duncan Foley (2006, 193), one of the leading faculty members in the late 1960s and early 1970s, "MIT wasn't a place to do new stuff, it wasn't they weren't interested in new stuff. They were. But the level at which new stuff had to be presented had to be very mature, ready for prime time, and they were not very patient about nurturing new approaches over the long term." This was visible in the reaction of some of its leading members toward the work that people such as the late Gary Becker were doing. Becker often reported what he perceived as initial strong hostility to his work and that MIT was one of

5. For more details on this, see Cherrier, this volume.

the places harboring particularly critical views about it (see Becker's interview in Swedberg 1990).[6]

Criticisms of the expansion of disciplinary boundaries were not uncommon among other mainstream departments in the 1960s and 1970s, although it is hard to avoid seeing this as partly shaped by the institutional culture and position of the department. The economics department had been developed within an institution dominated by engineering and science; this in turn had shaped the teaching portfolio, in which economics was often regarded in connection with practical training. Moreover, although MIT favored interdisciplinary collaboration, a research agenda that could be perceived as dominating other social sciences would not necessarily contribute to that reputation and would potentially create further difficulties with the other social sciences. Hence forays into such work would be regarded as too idiosyncratic and unhelpful in strengthening the position of the department within the school and MIT at large.

The particular position of the economics department vis-à-vis its internal and external interlocutors has contributed to a situation in which the department seemed to be more interested in consolidating its internal prestige through the reputation of a strong degree of technicality and its recognition among the mainstream of the discipline. The consolidation of the position of the MIT economics department had to be strengthened internally (as a small department in an institution focused on sciences and engineering) and externally (in relation to other much older and more institutionally visible departments of economics). I look at that process by analyzing the role of the department in the production of textbooks during the second half of the twentieth century. Notably, I explore the extent to which economists at MIT gave particular attention to this type of academic output, reflecting MIT's traditional emphasis on teaching and didactic concerns. On the other hand, I explore how this could be regarded as an instrument to consolidate the department's reputation among its disciplinary peers. Finally, I examine whether, over time, the motivations associated with the writing of textbooks may have changed, potentially becoming more of a reflection of MIT economists' reputation among those disciplinary peers.

6. In his review of Becker's *Human Capital*, Solow stated that he considered it a good book, despite being motivated by a research fad. He concluded his review with an ironic remark: "A good mind can produce some order out of even a messy question" (Solow 1965, 553). The dominant figures of Solow and Samuelson remained skeptical toward that kind of work in the ensuing decades (see, e.g., Samuelson 1985 and Solow's interview in Swedberg 1990).

Economists and Textbooks at MIT: From Teaching to Reputational Issues?

In recent years there has been growing interest among historians of science in exploring the multiple roles of textbooks in order to analyze the evolution of scientific ideas (Vicedo 2012b; Warwick 2003). This corresponds to abandoning a view, disseminated particularly by authors such as Thomas Kuhn (2012), that textbooks are merely didactic and truncated presentations of scientific developments and play a passive role in those scientific and intellectual developments (Kaiser 2005a; Vicedo 2012a). Instead, we can explore the role of textbooks in pedagogical and training practices and how these contribute to understanding how professionals and researchers acquire knowledge of their discipline and specialized fields, or trace the development of ideas and how they are presented or omitted over time in different textbooks (see Kaiser 2005b). This corresponds to a view that emphasizes the importance of pedagogical history for the history of science, by looking at what was taught and how, and what the mechanisms of reproduction of scientific and technical culture were (Warwick 2003; see also Duarte, this volume, and Svorenčík, this volume).

Textbooks are important for analyzing the role played by MIT's economics department because of their relevance not only to the dissemination of certain scientific theories but also to the diffusion of certain views about a field or discipline. This includes the emphasis on certain competences and skills and how textbooks may become oriented toward the internalization of certain methodological and epistemological aspects of a certain discipline. Textbooks are even relevant in how they contribute to popularizing certain aspects of vocabulary and syntax associated with different generations of scientific language (Kuhn 2012). Thus they are an important vehicle to reconstruct how MIT economists have shaped the views of successive generations of economists about economics, its purpose, and its modes of reasoning.

In this section I look at textbooks by economists associated in some way with MIT, either because they were trained there or because during part or most of their careers they were affiliated with MIT's economics department. I start with the postwar generation of MIT professors, which includes some of the best-known economists associated with the department, and then move to a younger generation of economists trained in the

1960s who were also relevant members of the department in the 1960s and 1970s. Finally, I look at a sample of well-known contemporary economists who have past or present links with MIT. The analysis aims at identifying the role of MIT economists as authors of textbooks and the part this has played in influencing the training and thinking of several generations of economists. The analysis also explores the extent to which economists associated with the MIT economics department played a particularly strong role in this regard.

Textbooks and the Older Generation of MIT Economists (1945–60)

The most frequent association of an economist affiliated with the economics department at MIT is certainly that of Paul Samuelson and his introductory textbook in economics, the first edition of which was published in 1948, and which would become one of the most popular textbooks in economics in the second half of the twentieth century (with nineteen editions up to 2009: in 1951, 1955, 1958, 1961, 1964, 1967, 1970, 1973, 1976, 1980, 1985, 1989, 1992, 1995, 1998, 2001, 2005, 2009). According to Samuelson (1997, 2004) this followed a suggestion by MIT chairman Ralph Freeman that he write an elementary text (for a more complex account of that process, see Giraud, this volume). Among the various aspects that have been highlighted about Samuelson's approach in his textbooks, two are worth underlining in this discussion of textbooks and MIT economists. The first is that he tries to claim a central position in the discipline, emphasizing a synthetic view that combines neoclassical and Keynesian economics. The second is the emphasis on technicality and on economics as a technically complex subject that has to be communicated to students, notably by showing its practical, social, and policy relevance.

Although the textbook was a significant instant success, being adopted by more than fifty universities and colleges in its first year, it also faced some resistance in the department. In the annual report of 1948 the head of the department noted that the visiting committee of the department had studied the undergraduate curriculum, with particular attention to economic principles, and recommended the use of additional material to supplement the textbook. The department followed the recommendation and introduced a set of readings presenting viewpoints somewhat different from those of Samuelson.[7] The success of Samuelson's textbook led him to several other ventures in similar volumes. In 1952 he published his *Readings in Economics* (with another six editions in 1955, 1958, 1964, 1967, 1970, and 1973). Then, in the late eighties, he published two textbooks, *Macroeconomics* and *Microeconomics*, that tried to build on his reputation as a textbook author and to follow curriculum and market trends leading to increasing specialization in the textbook market (each of these has had seven editions: 1989, 1992, 1995, 1998, 2001, 2005, 2010).

Among the leading postwar figures of the economics department, there is hardly anyone comparable with Samuelson in terms of textbooks, although there are a few other cases of authors of successful textbooks. One is Charles P. Kindleberger, who studied for his PhD at Columbia (1939) and joined MIT in 1948 (where he would stay until his retirement in 1981). In 1953 he published the first edition of his *International Economics*, which had seven editions (1953, 1958, 1963, 1968, 1973, 1978, 1982), and in 1958 he published his *Economic Development* (with two more editions—in 1965 and 1977).[8] One interesting aspect of Kindleberger's textbooks is the same emphasis on economics and technicality. Thus in the preface to the first edition of *International Economics*, the author states that his approach is different from the institutional and historical approaches to international trade. Moreover, although he considers that historical and institutional illustrations may be relevant, they are subordinated to a theoretical approach that gives preeminence to economics and its technical approach to international trade.[9]

Later in life, Kindleberger (1992, 178) recognized the importance and intellectual and academic rewards of writing a textbook, such as organizing and improving one's knowledge of the subject, keeping up with progress in the field, and disseminating knowledge. He also found that textbook writers

7. Interestingly, the president of MIT between 1948 and 1959, James Killian (1985, 203), who saw the recruitment of Samuelson as the turning point in the life of the economics department, had a high regard for his textbook, placing it alongside Francis Amasa Walker's (MIT's third president) as two examples of the influence and acclaim achieved by a few textbooks. In his memoirs he dedicates a few pages not only to the textbook but also to the way it was received in economics, and notably to the criticisms it faced because of its Keynesian approach. It is also interesting to note how relevant he regarded the role of textbooks to be, not only in reflecting the state of the art in science, but also in shaping it.

8. To this could be added *Manias, Panics, and Crashes: A History of Financial Crises* (with three editions: 1978, 1989, 1996): although not planned as a textbook, it saw extensive use as a basic reference.

9. This justification disappears in the following editions, suggesting that he no longer felt the need for justification.

enjoyed a high degree of recognition among their academic peers. However, he did not regard it as intellectually satisfying, since it was writing for students rather than one's peers, and corresponded more to collating the advances in the field rather than to making them (Kindleberger 1991, 136). Moreover, writing textbooks was also a task requiring painstaking work, and he did not seem to regard it as a major aspect of his intellectual achievements.

Another leading figure in the department who wrote textbooks was Charles Myers, who had moved to MIT in 1939 after finishing his PhD at Chicago, and who stayed in the department until the end of his career. His main textbook was *Personnel Administration: A Point of View and a Method* (written with Paul Pigors), which had nine editions (1947, 1951, 1956, 1961, 1965, 1969, 1973, 1977, 1981). With the same coauthor, in 1952 he published a companion volume (*Readings in Personnel Administration*). In the 1960s he published two volumes that were extensively used as references in labor relations: *Industrialism and Industrial Man: The Problems of Labor and Management in Economic Growth*, with Clark Kerr, John Dunlop, and Frederick Harbison (1960); and in development economics and the economics of education, *Education, Manpower, and Economic Growth: Strategies of Human Resource Development*, also with Harbison (1964). Labor relations was also the topic of the text published by George P. Shultz in 1953, *Labor Problems: Cases and Readings* (with John Coleman).[10]

Among the heads of department of the period, Ralph Evans Freeman (1933–58), Robert Lyle Bishop (1958–64), and Edgar Cary Brown (1964–82), there are a few examples of published textbooks, although none very significant.[11] Several other important figures in the department wrote books that were not necessarily planned as textbooks, but which often became introductory and reference volumes to a certain field or topic, especially at the graduate level.[12] The other leading figure of the postwar period

10. Shultz served as secretary of labor for Eisenhower, moving afterward to Chicago.

11. Freeman published his *Economics for Canadians* in 1928, followed ten years later by *The Economic Process* (written with Floyd Armstrong). Bishop published *Readings in Economics* (1952) with Samuelson and Coleman, following the criticisms of Samuelson's textbook.

12. This was the case with Robert Solow's *Growth Theory: An Exposition* (1970). In the case of growth, mention should also be made of Rostow's *Process of Economic Growth* (1952, 1962) and *Stages of Economic Growth: A Non-Communist Manifesto* (1960); Domar's *Essays in the Theory of Economic Growth* (1957); and Richard Eckaus, who edited two important volumes in 1973, one with Jagdish Bhagwati (*Development and Planning*) and the other with Paul Rosenstein-Rodan (*Analysis of Development Problems*), and the year before this published an introductory textbook, *Basic Economics*, and *Contemporary Issues in Economics*. For more details on growth economics at MIT, see Boianovsky and Hoover, this volume.

who wrote textbooks was Franco Modigliani, although these were written at a later stage of his career.[13] Thus, in the case of Modigliani, the writing of textbooks can be regarded more as a reflection of his prestige in those topics. This contrasts with Samuelson or Kindleberger, in whose cases the writing of textbooks contributed, in parallel, to cementing their (rising) reputation in economics.

Textbooks and the Younger Generations of MIT Economists (1960s–80s)

In the sixties MIT's economics department was attaining significant recognition within both MIT and the economics profession, and this was reflected in a rather successful period for its graduate program (see Modigliani 2001; Kindleberger 1991). This period was often considered its golden age with regard to the quality of the students, several of whom would join the faculty either immediately after completing their degrees or after a few years working elsewhere (although several would then move elsewhere).[14] Among the group of MIT graduates of the 1960s, we find the names of Stanley Fischer (1965), Peter Diamond (1962), Peter Temin (1964), Ann Friedlaender (1964), and Robert Merton and Richard Schmalensee (both 1970). All spent a significant part (or even most) of their subsequent academic careers at MIT, and a few became well-known authors of textbooks. Among this group, Stanley Fischer is probably the one most associated with textbooks. He wrote *Macroeconomics* (with Rüdiger Dornbusch and Richard Startz), which had nine editions (1978, 1981, 1984, 1987, 1990, 1994, 1998, 2001, 2004) and *Economics* (with Dornbusch and David Begg), which had the same number of editions (1983, 1987, 1991, 1994, 1997, 2000, 2002, 2005, 2008). The other two textbook authors of that generation were Richard Schmalensee, who cowrote the second edition of Fischer's *Economics* (1988) and *An Introduction to Applied Macroeconomics* (1973) with MIT colleague Edwin Kuh, and Robert Merton, who wrote or cowrote several textbooks in financial economics. However, in the latter case, those textbooks were published during Merton's time away from MIT (1988–2010).

13. His two textbooks were published in the 1990s and in coauthorship: *Capital Markets: Institutions and Instruments* (with Frank Fabozzi: 1991, 1996, 2003, 2009); and *Foundations of Financial Markets and Institutions* (with Fabozzi and Michael Ferri: 1994, 1997, 2002, 2009).

14. For a detailed analysis of these networks between the older and the younger generations, especially on the supervisory and mentoring roles, see Duarte, this volume, and Svorenčík, this volume.

Then there are faculty members who were not trained at MIT but joined the department in the 1960s and 1970s. This group included Lester Thurow (Harvard, 1964; MIT, 1968 on); Michael Piore (Harvard, 1966; MIT, 1966 on); Duncan Foley (Yale, 1966; MIT, 1966–79); Franklin Fisher (Harvard, 1960; MIT, 1960 on); Myron Scholes (Chicago, 1969; MIT, 1968–73); Daniel McFadden (Minnesota, 1962; MIT, 1978–91); Rüdiger Dornbusch (Chicago, 1971; MIT, 1975–2002); Robert Engle (Cornell, 1969; MIT, 1969–75); and Eric Maskin (Harvard, 1976; MIT, 1977–85). A few of them became authors of well-known textbooks, notably Dornbusch, who joined forces with Fischer for the nine editions of their textbook. Then there are those economists who published textbooks after leaving MIT to join other academic institutions, such as Maskin and Myron Scholes.

The case of Dornbusch and Fischer is interesting in several ways. First, their textbook represents a generation of texts that to a large extent replaced Samuelson's *Economics*. It indicates that MIT had an important contender in the textbook market that could sustain the reputation of the institute in this regard and that would convey a message that continued to include some important aspects of the *Samuelsonian* synthesis and of a certain degree of Keynesianism (especially in the macroeconomic parts), even at a time when this was under attack by certain parts of the discipline. In the preface to the first edition of *Macroeconomics* (1978), the authors claim that their approach is the result of a synthesis; that despite the differences between Keynesians and monetarists, there were "substantial areas of agreement"; and that the claim that macroeconomics was a battleground was "seriously misleading," and they preferred to avoid the areas of disagreement and to discuss instead the substantive matters. This would be reiterated nine years later in the preface to the fourth edition, where they claim to take an eclectic view on macroeconomics.

Second, not unlike Samuelson's text, their textbook had a reputation for being rather technical, especially when compared with others. This is recognized in the preface of the first edition and continues to be noted in subsequent editions, although over time it comes to seem less the case. In fact, in one analysis of *Macroeconomics*, they are criticized for being too technical and for introducing a degree of complexity that could create problems for some students (Policano 1985). This is an aspect that jibed with the reputation of MIT among economists and with the reputation of MIT economists within MIT.

Third, their text is also characterized with a clearly mainstream view, without much attention paid to different schools of thought in economics. This has multiple interpretations and explanatory factors, including the publishers' motivation to aim at the largest chunk of the market. However, it is tempting to interpret this as reflecting the culture of the department and its aims of playing a central position in the life of the discipline.

With the exceptions of Fischer and Dornbusch, the generation of MIT economists of the 1960s–70s had less involvement with the production of textbooks. It is nevertheless interesting that one of the few members of that generation who emphasized the importance of good teaching and the availability of faculty at MIT was Fischer (2005, 265). This view is corroborated by Duncan Foley's recollections (see his interview in Colander, Holt, and Rosser 2006, 191–92): "One great thing about MIT was that they were so student oriented and interested in making sure that people would come through the department with what they needed to play leading roles in the discipline." Moreover, compared with other elite departments, Foley emphasized the importance at MIT of discussions about curricular development and research methodology. Thus, although this generation was clearly geared toward reputation building through research achievements, pedagogical concerns were still very relevant for the life of the department and for the success of its programs, showing a certain degree of continuity with its early days.

MIT Economists as Authors of Textbooks—a Contemporary Overview

To complete this analysis I present a quantitative overview of textbooks authored by a sample of economists related to MIT.[15] Initial selection included 1,168 authors, although the final selection presents data for only 743. From these 743 I have identified 105 economists who had some kind of relationship with MIT: either they had studied for a degree (bachelor's, master's, or PhD) there, or they were members of the faculty at the time of the selection of the sample (2003). I then analyzed the CVs of these 105 economists to identify the books or monographs they published (I excluded conference proceedings and policy reports). The total output of books they wrote was then classified into textbooks or other books. Both categories

15. The sample was based on Mark Blaug and Howard R. Vane's *Who's Who in Economics* (2003), which includes the economists most cited in ISI (Institute for Scientific Information) publications during 1990–2000. Because of this criteria, authors such as Samuelson and Modigliani are excluded. I have decided not to complete the sample for the purpose of consistency of the sample, and since this will be complementary with the analysis presented in the previous sections.

were also classified with regard to the main topic (following the *JEL* classification). Since the sample included economists who were trained at MIT but pursued their career elsewhere and others who taught at MIT but were not trained there, I tried to analyze these groups separately for each of the criterion used.

I identified 39 authors of textbooks who either studied for their PhD in economics at MIT and/or taught in the department during their career. The largest group (30) consists of those who were trained there but moved elsewhere. This is hardly surprising, since the department (like any other) has a limited capacity to employ those trained within it. To these should be added 9 faculty members who published textbooks (5 of whom trained at MIT). That seems to be a significant number and sufficient to confirm the reputation of the economics department, especially in more recent decades. Moreover, this also indicates that the department played an important role in training a large group of future academics who became important and respected scholars in their fields, regardless of the institution in which they developed their career. I then analyzed the number of textbooks published by those economists decade by decade (table 1). The number of new textbooks published by authors related to MIT was rather small in the 1960s; it started to grow in the 1970s, continued to grow in the 1980s, and peaked in the 1990s, but it seems it will have declined in the first decade of the twenty-first century.

I also analyzed the data on the publication of new editions of existing textbooks. These were absent in the 1960s and 1970s but grew rapidly from the 1980s onward, building on a growing stock of texts but also on the growing reputation of MIT economists. In fact, new editions are a good indication of the commercial and academic success of the previous editions, since neither publishers nor authors would spend additional time and resources on them if they were unsuccessful. Moreover, new editions are also a way to undercut the secondhand market, which is also relevant only in those cases in which a textbook is widely used.

I tried to analyze the data with regard not only to the date of publication but also in combination with the date of PhD completion, to identify which authors and generations of MIT economists were more predominant in this respect. From the data presented in table 1 we can see that the greatest number of textbooks were written by authors who completed their PhDs in the 1970s, followed by those graduating in the 1960s, in the 1980s, and finally in the 1990s. This confirms that it takes some time to become an author of a textbook. Moreover, it seems that the great expansion in the

Table 1 Number of Textbooks by Economists Linked to MIT, by Date of Publication and of Graduation

	Date of Publication												
	1960s or before		1970s		1980s		1990s		2000s		2010s		Total
Author's date of PhD	1st Ed	Other Ed	1st Ed	Other Eds	1st Ed	Other Eds	1st Ed	Other Eds	1st Ed	Other Eds	1st Ed	Other Eds	by Date of PhD
1960s or before	2	0	5	0	4	12	8	15	1	22	0	4	20/53
1970s	0	0	5	0	11	13	12	43	5	55	1	18	34/129
1980s	0	0	0	0	1	0	11	6	4	24	0	7	16/37
1990s	0	0	0	0	0	0	0	1	2	2	0	1	2/4
Total by date of publication	2	0	10	0	16	25	31	65	12	103	1	30	72/223

Note: The sample consists of thirty-nine economists who wrote textbooks and who either studied for their PhD in economics at MIT and/or taught in the department during their career; it was constructed in consultation with Blaug and Vane 2003. As an example of what the table shows, in the 1980s sixteen new textbooks were written by the economists in my sample; of those sixteen, four were written by economists who earned their PhDs in the 1960s or before.

1980s and 1990s has made it more difficult for those coming afterward to get into the textbook market, which has been captured by new editions of existing textbooks.

Then I analyzed the data by looking at the fields of specialization (according to *JEL* codes) of the textbooks published by my sample of MIT economists. Here I looked only at the first editions of the textbooks, since subsequent editions did not change that aspect, and the number of subsequent editions was far less relevant for this matter. According to the data presented in table 2, we can say that the dominant topics of textbooks written by academics related to MIT are macro and money, micro, general economics and teaching, and mathematics and quantitative methods. There are some topics about which no textbooks have been written, including history of economics, economic history, labor and population economics, and industrial economics—not surprising, since they are specialized fields in which MIT has not traditionally been strong (such as history of economics and labor) or in which it has lost some preeminence in recent years (as in the case of economic history; see Temin, this volume).

There are also a few differences between the fields of the textbooks written by those who were trained and taught at MIT with those who were trained there and then left, or who taught there but were not trained there. The main difference seems to be that the first group has concentrated on macro and monetary textbooks to a far larger degree than the other two groups; although they have not written as many macro and monetary textbooks as members of the second group, the number they have written, five, represents almost half of the eleven textbooks the group has written, confirming the reputation of the department in those topics. In the case of those who were trained at MIT but moved away, there is an even division between macro and micro topics. This group of MIT economists is also the one that presents greater diversity in terms of textbook topics, suggesting some differences in the profiles of specialization and reputation between those economists who remained attached to MIT and those who left.

Finally, I tried to distinguish between textbooks for undergraduate students and those for graduate students. I also included a category for intermediate levels. In my analysis, presented in table 3, I also looked at only the first edition of a given textbook, since the level (introductory, intermediate, advanced) of the textbook did not change in subsequent editions and would tend to distort the sample toward the largest group. Thus the data were classified by the date of the textbook's first edition. According to the data in table 3, roughly half of the textbooks were aimed at undergraduate

Table 2 First Editions of Textbooks by Economists Linked to MIT, by *JEL* Code

	JEL Code	Textbooks	PhD and Faculty at MIT	Only PhD at MIT	MIT Faculty but Not Trained at MIT
Macroeconomics and Monetary Economics	E	18	5	12	1
Microeconomics	D	15	1	12	2
General Economics and Teaching	A	10	2	7	1
Mathematical and Quantitative Methods	C	10	2	5	3
Financial Economics	G	5	0	4	1
International Economics	F	4	0	4	0
Economic Systems	P	3	0	3	0
Public Economics	H	2	0	2	0
Law and Economics	K	2	0	2	0
Urban and Regional	R	1	0	1	0
Business Administration	M	1	1	0	0
Development and Growth	O	1	0	0	1
HET and Methodology	B	0	0	0	0
Health, Education, and Welfare	I	0	0	0	0
Labor and Demographic Economics	J	0	0	0	0
Industrial Economics	L	0	0	0	0
Economic History	N	0	0	0	0
Agricultural and Environmental Economics	Q	0	0	0	0
Miscellaneous Categories	Y	0	0	0	0
Other Special Topics	Z	0	0	0	0
Nonclassified	X	0	0	0	0
	Total	72	11	52	9

Note: The sample consists of thirty-nine economists who wrote textbooks and who either studied for their PhD in economics at MIT and/or taught in the department during their career; it was constructed in consultation with Blaug and Vane 2003.

Table 3 Distribution of Textbooks by Economists Linked to MIT, by Their Level and Decade of Publication of the First Edition

Level/Decade	Total	1960s or Earlier	1970s	1980s	1990s	2000s
Undergraduate (introductory)	30	0	2	10	12	6
Intermediate	24	1	6	3	12	2
Graduate	18	1	1	3	8	5
Total	72	2	9	16	32	13

Note: The sample consists of thirty-nine economists who wrote textbooks and who either studied for their PhD in economics at MIT and/or taught in the department during their career; it was constructed in consultation with Blaug and Vane 2003.

students. If we add the share of intermediate textbooks, then it is clear that the college level represents almost three-quarters of the whole output of textbooks by our sample of MIT economists. For the graduate level, although it represents a smaller share, the absolute number is still significant and becomes increasingly relevant, especially in the 1990s and 2000s.

The balance between undergraduate and graduate textbooks deserves a few additional remarks. To a certain extent, the recent quantitative pre-eminence of undergraduate and intermediate textbooks may not be a major surprise given that enrollments are much larger at that level, making it the largest and most attractive share of the textbook market for publishers and authors (from a financial viewpoint). However, undergraduate textbooks are normally regarded as less significant for the development and dissemination of scientific ideas, and some would expect that they are less visible in this case, given the preeminence of MIT's graduate program in economics. The results show that MIT economists have recently come to play a major role in training economists at the undergraduate level.

Although less significant from a quantitative point of view, the graduate share is still high and relevant given the greater intellectual prestige associated with it (and increased at the end of the period under analysis). Moreover, these graduate textbooks are even more influential because of their role in shaping younger generations of economists' views about economics and the possibility that many of those students became junior academics after completing their doctorates. This is even more significant, since, as I have shown above, the majority of textbooks have concentrated on microeconomics and macroeconomics, contributing to shaping the views of many future academics, who may go on to reproduce those views among future students. Their role as authors of textbooks has further amplified MIT economists' impact in economics over the past decades.

Concluding Remarks

Over the past half-century MIT economists have had significant involvement with the production of textbooks, although the factors contributing to that engagement seem to have evolved. Whereas in the department's early years, the production and popularity of a textbook was seen as fitting the strong teaching mission of MIT (and of its economics department in particular), with the growing legitimization and reputation of research purposes, those earlier teaching purposes have become less relevant. In the latter part of the twentieth century, textbooks again became an important dimension of the department's activity, though this corresponded much less to an internally led motivation and more to a disciplinary recognition of the prestige of the economics department. This is also supported by the growing share of graduate textbooks vis-à-vis undergraduate ones.

The analysis of textbooks also presents some interesting aspects that corroborate the portrait presented by other analyses of MIT economics (including several of the articles in this volume). Moreover, some of the best-known cases of textbooks associated with MIT economists display some commonalities that led to a certain perception about the type of economics developed and taught at MIT and about the department's position among other economics departments. One aspect worth underlining is the emphasis on technicality, reflecting and promoting the department's reputation for taking a technical approach to economics that started with Paul Samuelson and continues today (and which was also relevant bearing in mind the internal position and perceptions about the role and type of economics within MIT). Another is the emphasis on the discipline's core areas, especially economic theory and policy, which corresponds to the department's ambition to shape the views of future generations of economists, both at the undergraduate and at the graduate levels. Finally, and related to those two previous aspects, several major textbooks produced by leading faculty members of the economics department state their explicit attempt to adopt a synthetic view about economics that tries to combine what they regarded as one-dimensional or more polarizing views of economics and, especially, macroeconomics. This more synthetic view was not innocent and placed the department symbolically as a mainstream, balanced, and central point in a divided and contentious discipline. This position was sustained by an aura of technicality that was often portrayed as less ideologically driven and more scientifically oriented (and superior).

Although the research presented here is exploratory, I believe that these are interesting insights for the analysis of MIT and its role in economics during the second half of the twentieth century. The focus on teaching and teaching-related publications such as textbooks provides additional elements for analyzing the role of economics at MIT and the role of economists associated with MIT in the development of modern economics, especially by looking at how academic activity is shaped by the surrounding institutional fabric. As this article has tried to suggest, the analysis of textbooks, of educational practices, and of the institutional context of economics departments is a rich topic in the history of economics that deserves to be more fully explored.

References

Altbach, P., G. Kelly, H. Petrie, and L. Weis, eds. 1991. *Textbooks in American Society—Politics, Policy, and Pedagogy.* Albany: State University of New York Press.

Apple, M. W., and L. K. Christian-Smith, eds. 1991. *The Politics of the Textbook.* London: Routledge.

Bhagwati, J., and R. S. Eckaus, eds. 1973. *Development and Planning: Essays in Honour of Paul Rosenstein-Rodan.* Cambridge, Mass.: MIT Press.

Blaug, Mark. 2003. "The Formalist Revolution in Economics in the 1950s." *Journal of the History of Economic Thought* 25 (2): 145–56.

Blaug, M., and H. R. Vane. 2003. *Who's Who in Economics.* 4th ed. Cheltenham: Elgar.

Chevalier, Judith, and Austan Goolsbee. 2009. "Are Durable Goods Consumers Forward-Looking? Evidence from College Textbooks." *Quarterly Journal of Economics* 124 (4): 1853–84.

Clawson, Rosalyn. 2002. "Poor People, Black Faces: The Portrayal of Poverty in Economics Textbooks." *Journal of Black Studies* 32 (3): 352–61.

Colander, D., R. Holt, and J. Barkley Rosser, eds. 2006. *The Changing Face of Economics: Conversations with Cutting Edge Economists.* Ann Arbor: University of Michigan Press.

Coser, Lewis A., Charles Kadushin, and Walter W. Powell. 1985. *Books—the Culture and Commerce of Publishing.* Chicago: University of Chicago Press.

Domar, E. 1957. *Essays in the Theory of Economic Growth.* New York: Oxford University Press.

Dornbusch, R., and S. Fischer. 1978. *Macroeconomics.* New York: McGraw-Hill.

Eckaus, R. S., and P. Rosenstein-Rodan, eds. 1973. *Analysis of Development Problems: Studies of the Chilean Economy.* Amsterdam: North-Holland.

Etzkowitz, Henry. 2002. *MIT and the Rise of the Entrepreneurial Science*. London: Routledge.

Fischer, Stanley. 2005. "An Interview with Stanley Fischer (by Olivier Blanchard)." *Macroeconomics Dynamics* 9:244–62.

Fischer, S., and R. Dornbusch. 1983. *Economics*. New York: McGraw-Hill.

Foley, D. 2006. Interview with Duncan Foley. In *The Changing Face of Economics: Conversations with Cutting Edge Economists*, edited by D. Colander, R. Holt, and J. Barkley Rosser, 183–213. Ann Arbor: University of Michigan Press.

Fourcade, Marion. 2009. *Economists and Societies: Discipline and Profession in the United States, Britain, and France, 1890s to 1990s*. Princeton, N.J.: Princeton University Press.

Freeland, Richard M. 1992. *Academia's Golden Age: Universities in Massachusetts, 1945–1970*. New York: Oxford University Press.

Freeman, R. 1928. *Economics for Canadians*. Toronto: Sir I. Pitman & Sons.

Freeman, R., and F. Armstrong. 1938. *The Economic Process*. [Boston]: Massachusetts Institute of Technology.

Geiger, Roger L. 1986. *To Advance Knowledge: The Growth of American Research Universities, 1900–1940*. New York: Oxford University Press.

———. 1993. *Research and Relevant Knowledge: American Research Universities since World War II*. New York: Oxford University Press.

Kaiser, D. 2005a. *Drawing Theories Apart: The Dispersion of Feynman Diagrams in Postwar Physics*. Chicago: University of Chicago Press.

———, ed. 2005b. *Pedagogy and the Practice of Science: Historical and Contemporary Perspectives*. Cambridge, Mass.: MIT Press.

———, ed. 2010. *Becoming MIT: Moments of Decision*. Cambridge, Mass.: MIT Press.

Kalmi, P. 2007. "The Disappearance of Cooperatives from Economics Textbooks." *Cambridge Journal of Economics* 31:625–47.

Kerr, C., C. Myers, J. Dunlop, and F. Harbison. 1960. *Industrialism and Industrial Man: The Problems of Labor and Management in Economic Growth*. New York: Oxford University Press.

Killian, James E., Jr. 1985. *The Education of a College President: A Memoir*. Cambridge, Mass.: MIT Press.

Kindleberger, Charles P. 1953. *International Economics*. Homewood, Ill.: R. D. Irwin.

———. 1958. *Economic Development*. New York: McGraw-Hill.

———. 1978. *Manias, Panics, and Crashes: A History of Financial Crises*. New York: Basic Books.

———. 1991. *The Life of an Economist*. Cambridge, Mass.: Basil Blackwell.

———. 1992. "My Working Philosophy." In *Eminent Economists: Their Life Philosophies*, edited by M. Szenberg, 167–79. Cambridge: Cambridge University Press.

Kornblith, G. J., and C. Lasser. 2005. "'The Truth, the Whole Truth, and Nothing but the Truth': Writing, Producing, and Using College-Level American History Textbooks." *Journal of American History* 91 (4): 1380–82.

Kuh, Edwin, and Richard L. Schmalensee. 1973. *An Introduction to Applied Macroeconomics*. Amsterdam: North-Holland/Elsevier.

Kuhn, T. 2012. *The Structure of Scientific Revolutions*. 50th anniversary ed. Chicago: University of Chicago Press.
Meyer, J., and E. Schofer. (2006) 2009. "The University in Europe and the World: Twentieth Century Expansion." In *World Society: The Writings of John W. Meyer*, edited by G. Krücken and G. S. Drori, 355–69. Oxford: Oxford University Press.
Modigliani, F. 2001. *The Adventures of an Economist*. New York: Texere Publishing.
Modigliani, F., and F. Fabozzi. 1991. *Capital Markets: Institutions and Instruments*. Englewood Cliffs, N.J.: Prentice-Hall International.
Modigliani, F., F. Fabozzi, and M. Ferri. 1994. *Foundations of Financial Markets and Institutions*. Englewood Cliffs, N.J.: Prentice-Hall International.
Myers, C., and F. Harbison. 1964. *Education, Manpower, and Economic Growth: Strategies of Human Resource Development*. New York: McGraw-Hill.
Myers, C., and P. Pigors. 1947. *Personnel Administration: A Point of View and a Method*. New York: McGraw-Hill.
——. 1952. *Readings in Personnel Administration*. New York: McGraw-Hill.
Policano, A. J. 1985. "The Current State of Macroeconomics: A View from the Textbooks." *Journal of Monetary Economics* 15:389–97.
Rostow, W. W. 1952. *The Process of Economic Growth*. Oxford: Clarendon Press.
——. 1960. *The Stages of Economic Growth: A Non-Communist Manifesto*. Cambridge: Cambridge University Press.
Samuelson, P. 1948. *Economics*. New York: McGraw-Hill.
——. 1985. "Modes of Thought in Economics and Biology." *American Economic Review: AEA Papers and Proceedings* 75 (2): 166–72.
——. 1997. "Credo of a Lucky Textbook Author." *Journal of Economic Perspectives* 11 (2): 153–60.
——. 2004. "An Interview with Paul Samuelson (by William A. Barnett)." *Macroeconomics Dynamics* 8:519–42.
Samuelson, P., R. Bishop, and J. Coleman. 1952. *Readings in Economics*. New York: McGraw-Hill.
Samuelson, P., and W. Nordhaus. 1989. *Macroeconomics*. New York: McGraw-Hill.
——. 1989. *Microeconomics*. New York: McGraw-Hill.
Shultz, G. P., and J. Coleman. 1953. *Labor Problems: Cases and Readings*. New York: McGraw-Hill.
Solow, Robert. 1965. Review of Gary Becker's *Human Capital*. *Journal of Political Economy* 73 (5): 552–53.
——. 1970. *Growth Theory: An Exposition*. Oxford: Clarendon Press.
Stratton, Julius, and Loretta Mannix. 2005. *Mind and Hand: The Birth of MIT*. Cambridge, Mass.: MIT Press.
Swedberg, Richard. 1990. *Economics and Sociology: Redefining Their Boundaries; Conversations with Economists and Sociologists*. Princeton, N.J.: Princeton University Press.
Thelin, J. R. 2004. *A History of American Higher Education*. Baltimore: Johns Hopkins University Press.
Thompson, J. B. 2005. *Books in the Digital Age*. Cambridge: Polity.

Trow, Martin. 2010. *Twentieth-Century Higher Education: Elite to Mass to Universal*. Edited by Michael Burrage. Baltimore: Johns Hopkins University Press.

Vicedo, Marga. 2012a. "Playing the Game: Psychology Textbooks Speak Out about Love." *Isis* 103 (1): 111–25.

———. 2012b. "The Secret Lives of Textbooks." *Isis* 103 (1): 83–87.

Warwick, Andrew. 2003. *Masters of Theory: Cambridge and the Rise of Mathematical Physics*. Chicago: University of Chicago Press.

Part 3
Distinctiveness

MIT and Money

Perry Mehrling

A Study of Industrial Fluctuation (1915) . . . was written in good part when [Dennis] Robertson was but twenty-two years of age and in the third year of his economic study! Such precocity is hard to match. It reminds one again of the incredible ability of talented youth to master in a season all that the past has established, and then to push the flag forward another furlong.
—Paul A. Samuelson, "D. H. Robertson (1890–1963)" (1963)

Money at MIT was always fundamentally about monetary policy and so could not really get started until after the 1951 Treasury-Fed Accord allowed the Federal Reserve System to shift away from its wartime policy of pegging Treasury rates to support the government bond market (Hetzel and Leach 2001). And even then, the Keynesian priors of the founders of the MIT economics department for a long time downgraded the importance of monetary policy relative to fiscal policy, and hence also of monetary theory relative to the theory of public finance.

Neither of these background facts particularly differentiated MIT from many other institutions in the immediate postwar period, with the crucial

Correspondence may be addressed to Perry Mehrling, Barnard College, Columbia University, 3009 Broadway, New York, NY 10027; e-mail: pmehrlin@barnard.edu. I would like to thank all the participants at the *HOPE* conference for helpful suggestions and stimulating discussion, and in addition Robert Solow, Roger E. Backhouse, Goncalo Fonseca, Duncan Foley, and E. Roy Weintraub for thoughtful and searching comments on early drafts.

History of Political Economy 46 (annual suppl.) DOI 10.1215/00182702-2716163

exception of the University of Chicago, which early on positioned itself as the center of anti-Keynesian reaction, organized under the banner of Milton Friedman's "monetarism." This exception, however, proved vitally important for the development of MIT. Indeed, one thing that would eventually differentiate MIT from other institutions on the subject of money was its deliberate decision to position itself as the center of antimonetarist reaction. Money at MIT was always about monetary policy, but it was also always about countering monetarism.

Thus, at Chicago, even before the 1951 accord made monetary policy possible, Friedman (1946) had already mounted a sustained attack on Oskar Lange's crypto-Keynesian *Price Flexibility and Employment* (1944) and had already put forth his own alternative in "A Monetary and Fiscal Framework for Economic Stability" (Friedman 1948), which can be read as a reformulation of Henry Simons's 1934 manifesto "A Positive Program for Laissez Faire." Subsequently, the students in Friedman's famous Workshop on Money and Banking produced *Studies in the Quantity Theory of Money* (Friedman 1956), and Friedman's essay for that collection, "The Quantity Theory of Money: A Restatement," was the analytical foundation for his subsequent manifesto, *A Program for Monetary Stability* (1959). The empirical foundation of the monetarist edifice, *A Monetary History of the United States* (Friedman and Schwartz 1963), followed soon after. In the field of money, Chicago got a very big jump on MIT.

The central figure in MIT's response to the Chicago initiative was clearly Franco Modigliani, who joined MIT in 1962 after visiting for a year in 1960. But the choice of Modigliani as MIT's champion was very much a consequence of the economic department's prior conception of how one ought to think about money as a matter of pure economic theory, which is to say that it was very much a consequence of Paul Samuelson's views on the matter. I start therefore with Samuelson.

Don Patinkin (1983, 163–65), writing retrospectively for Samuelson's Festschrift, traced the evolution of Samuelson's treatment of monetary policy, and of the quantity equation, through all editions of his best-selling textbook, *Economics* (for the backstory of *Economics*, see Giraud, this volume). In general he tells a story of Samuelson's increasing appreciation of both, starting with monetary policy, which comes into its own in the fourth and fifth editions (1958, 1961), and continuing with the monetarist practice of using the quantity equation as the preferred framework for thinking about macroeconomic issues, which gets respectful notice in the eighth edition (1970) and after. The evolution of Samuelson's textbook treatment follows the profession, of course, but it also reflects the evolution of Samuelson's own personal views. Samuelson started professional life, it is important to appreciate, with a nonmonetary view of the cycle as driven by the interaction of real investment and consumption in the multiplier-accelerator model (Samuelson 1939). But he concluded, as we shall see, with the view that monetary disequilibrium is of the essence for departures from long-run equilibrium.

Throughout that evolution, one constant was Samuelson's practice of viewing monetary matters through the lens of neoclassical price theory; for him, it was all a matter of money demand and supply. Money demand was just a special case of the general theory of consumer demand, and money supply was a decision variable of the monetary authority. This approach to monetary theory he shared with most of the profession, notably including Patinkin, so much so that it has often been hard for historians of this period even to recognize the shared perspective as a specific approach, rather than just logic or science. My coinage of the term "Monetary Walrasianism" (Mehrling 1998, 2002a, 2010), and my insistence on tracing the roots of the approach to the early work of Jacob Marschak (1934, 1938) as well as John R. Hicks's more familiar "Suggestion for Simplifying the Theory of Money" (1935), has drawn critical attention to this surprising unanimity. Although Samuelson left the formal development of this approach largely to others (most importantly James Tobin and Franco Modigliani), he quite definitely endorsed it. Even more, for Samuelson, Monetary Walrasianism provided the crucial link between value theory and macroeconomic modeling, a link that could be depended on to persist (so he hoped) even as the postwar world evolved toward more flexible prices, in globally integrated and developed private capital markets.

Just so, James Tobin (1983, 197), following after Patinkin in the 1983 Festschrift, states firmly: "Paul Samuelson's greatest contribution to macroeconomics was the neoclassical synthesis, of which he was the principal architect. This *Weltanschauung* reconciled the classical and Keynesian strands of his thinking and that of many of his contemporaries." "Classical" in this context means Léon Walras and neoclassical price theory, as in Samuelson 1947. "Keynesian" means Alvin Hansen and the aggregative multiplier-accelerator model, as in Samuelson 1939. Classical is about long-run equilibrium, while Keynesian is about short-run disequilibrium caused by "adjustment costs and lags, market imperfections, and discrepancies of information and expectations" (Tobin 1983, 198). Wearing his classical hat, Samuelson was concerned about efficient allocation;

wearing his Keynesian hat, he was concerned about aggregate income stabilization.

But, notwithstanding Tobin, Frank Hahn (1983, 51) writes in the same Festschrift that "Samuelson, like all his contemporaries, and indeed most of his successors, never seems to have found it necessary to provide a link between his general equilibrium (value) theory and his macroeconomic modeling." Fair enough, perhaps, from the viewpoint of pure theory, since "the pure Arrow-Debreu model predicts that there is no money and that there is no Stock Exchange" (32; see also Hahn 1965). Samuelson himself, however, seems to have felt that a more informal link was sufficient for his purposes, and it is that informal link that also apparently satisfied Tobin and others.

The most complete account of that link that Samuelson himself ([1967] 1972, 557) ever offered can be found in his purely verbal account "Money, Interest Rates, and Economic Activity: Their Interrelationship in a Market Economy," which emphasizes "dynamic modifications of the crude classical system," in particular "dynamic assumptions . . . about the creation of money growth as a result of mines, banks, or governments." (The "market imperfections, and discrepancies of information and expectations" emphasized by Tobin are, in Samuelson's own account, not so fundamental to the neoclassical synthesis, though clearly important for specific policy applications.) As a consequence, the money rate of interest can and does deviate from the rate of profit, with consequences for investment spending and hence real activity. More generally, Samuelson insists, "once we introduce systematically into a post-Keynesian system treatment of stocks of assets, monetary and real, and take into account fluctuating levels of real unemployment, there remain no inconsistencies between the classical system and the Keynesian system. The synthesis of common content emerges with an eclectic position on the interplay of real and monetary factors in determining the structure and levels of interest rates" (559).

This emphasis on stocks of assets, and the consequent disequilibrium dynamics of adjustment, is the core of Samuelson's mature vision of the neoclassical synthesis and also the connection to finance in his thinking, because introducing asset stocks means also introducing asset prices. For Samuelson in 1967, monetary disequilibrium inevitably involves asset price disequilibrium in the form of deviation of the level of market prices from their fundamental values, hence inefficiency. As he said years later, "Modern markets show considerable *micro* efficiency [but also] considerable *macro* inefficiency, in the sense of long waves in the time series of aggregate indexes of security prices below and above various definitions of fundamental values" (quoted in Jung and Shiller 2005, 221). In his mature formulation it is these disequilibrium asset price fluctuations that drive the investment fluctuations that kick-start the multiplier-accelerator mechanism that produces aggregate instability.

Paul A. Samuelson

Paul Samuelson (1968, 3) began his career as a mathematical economist, which at that time meant being a "specialist in value theory," and it is this starting point that shaped his conception of monetary economics. Although his 1941 Harvard dissertation, "Foundations of Analytical Economics," had little to say about money, Samuelson (1968, 4) claimed retrospectively to have had "a correct vision of the proper version" of neoclassical monetary theory as early as 1937, by which date he had already drafted the bulk of the dissertation. (Note that such dating of the dissertation would put Samuelson, born in 1915, in the running to match the precocity of Robertson.) The essentials of that 1937 vision he published ten years later in a few pages added to the revised version of his dissertation, *Foundations of Economic Analysis* (Samuelson 1947, 117–24). Given the importance of Samuelson in shaping the MIT economics department, and the importance of these few pages for understanding Samuelson's own conception of money, our investigation must begin here.

If he had the correct vision in 1937, why did he not include it in his dissertation? Thirty years later, Samuelson (1968, 4) offered an explanation for why he waited: "Frankly, I was repelled by the abstract level at which Oskar Lange, Hicks, and others carried on their discussion of Say's Law, staying at the level of equation counting and homogeneity reckoning, without entering into the concrete character of the models." Pushed by Don Patinkin to elaborate, he added that he had chosen not to involve himself in the "then-popular game of reconciling 'loanable funds' and 'liquidity preference' theories of interest determination," a debate that built on the analytical framework of Hicks's 1939 *Value and Capital* and culminated in Lange's *Price Flexibility and Employment* (1944). Specifically, writes Samuelson (1972, 288), "I never felt that indifference curve analysis of the triad, money, goods, and bonds, had the fruitfulness of such analysis of tea, salt, and apples."

And yet, in the 1947 sketch, it was exactly indifference curve analysis that Samuelson (1968, 4) did offer, and it was exactly this 1947 analysis that he retrospectively characterized as the "nub of the matter." Simply put, in 1947 Samuelson approached monetary economics as nothing more than an extension of consumer demand theory. His starting point was the observation that "money yields a real service" in facilitating transactions, in which respect it is much like other commodities that enter the neoclassical utility function. Money is different only because its real service depends on its value, and that means we have to include prices as well as quantities as arguments in the neoclassical utility function. That done, however, all we have to do is to maximize utility subject to a budget constraint and out drops the demand for money (I is income, r is an exogenous rate of interest, and p_m is the price of money):

$$M = M(p_1, \ldots, p_n, p_m, I, r). \text{ (Samuelson 1947, 121)}$$

Repelled in 1937 but ready to commit to print in 1947, what changed Samuelson's mind? As he says, not *Value and Capital* (Hicks 1939), notwithstanding his respectful nod in the preface to his 1941 thesis to "Professor Hicks' long-awaited treatise," whose "similarity in point of view has been reassuring." Instead, we perhaps find the clue in Samuelson's (1947, 121) citation of Jacob Marschak's 1943 "Money Illusion and Demand Analysis," an empirical paper that concludes with these words: "A reduction of money incomes is likely to have a somewhat stronger effect on the real expenditure on meat than would a proportionate rise in the price of meat, accompanied by a proportionate rise in the price of other foods and/or in other living costs" (48). In other words, the simple dichotomy between nominal and real that is such a characteristic feature of classical monetary theory seems not to be a feature of the real world. Samuelson took the lesson that the classical equation of exchange, $MV = PY$, presents an overly simplified view of the role of money, and that modern neoclassical methods might be able to add something.

Marschak's empirical finding seems to have emboldened Samuelson not only to publish but also (unlike Hicks and Lange) to leave Keynes entirely aside and to proceed instead solely from Walras. Thus in 1947 Samuelson blithely abstracts from dynamical considerations and expectations, risk and uncertainty, and hence also liquidity preference and speculative demand. He considers the Hicks-Keynes notion of a possible monetary theory of interest, but only to reject it in favor of the marginal productivity of capital theory of interest. And he also considers the Hicks-Keynes notion of liquidity preference as the origin of the tendency for the term structure of interest rates to be positively sloped (122–24), but rejects that too on the grounds that the supposed empirical regularity is a mere historical anomaly and hence nothing that needs to be explained. In 1947 Samuelson's monetary theory is self-consciously neoclassical, which is to say pre-Keynesian. He merely sets himself the task of translating the best of neoclassical monetary thought into mathematics.

In doing so Samuelson was following, perhaps unconsciously, in the footsteps of Dennis Robertson, whose *Money* (1922) Samuelson (1963, 519) remembers as his "earliest introduction" to the subject. In the preface to that book, Robertson explicitly states his intention to "treat the theory of money as a special case of the general theory of value," and that of course is exactly what Samuelson was doing in 1947. Like Robertson, Samuelson embraced the foundational insight of the quantity *theory* of money that money is that special thing which, if its quantity were doubled along with all prices, would leave real quantities unchanged for the simple reason that such doubling would leave unchanged the real service that money can provide. Unlike Robertson, Samuelson rejected the quantity *equation* as a useful analytical starting point for understanding the consequences of actual changes in the money supply. In 1947 he offered an alternative analytical starting point based in neoclassical price theory that abstracted from dynamics and uncertainty because he thought he did not need them. In his mind, he was establishing the frictionless surface result; adding in the frictions was for someone else, a problem of engineering, not of science.

Here enters Friedman. From Samuelson's point of view, most of the claims of Friedman's monetarism must have seemed to be more about engineering than about science, as for example Friedman's claim about the superiority of monetary policy over fiscal policy, and his claim about the superiority of a constant money growth rule over a more activist countercyclical interest rate policy. After all, on the scientific fundamentals of the theory of money, there was no real difference between Samuelson and Friedman. Instead, the big scientific difference at stake seemed to be about the optimality of laissez-faire, so it was here that Samuelson (1958) chose to deploy his efforts, starting with his celebrated overlapping generations model in "An Exact Consumption-Loan Model of Interest with or without the Social Contrivance of Money." The paper was never intended to provide theoretical foundations for monetary theory, and certainly not to replace the foundations Samuelson had laid in 1947. (The paper does not even cite that earlier work but instead takes off from Samuelson's "Pure Theory of Public Expenditure" [1954].) Patinkin (1983, 160–62) quite correctly reviews negatively the cottage industry that missed Samuelson's point, and so attempted to build monetary theory on these purported alternative foundations.

In the 1958 paper, by contrast to the 1947 one, money does not enter directly into the utility function or serve as a medium of exchange. Rather, money is a store of wealth in which the working generation accumulates its saving for retirement. In the model, money is the only store of wealth (by assumption), and without it there is no way for the competitive market to achieve the social optimum. Under the special assumptions that Samuelson makes, the social optimum is achieved when the rate of interest on consumption-loans is exactly equal to the rate of population growth. Thus, in the special case when the population is stationary, money that bears zero nominal interest can help achieve the optimum. But it can help also in the case when population is growing or shrinking so long as prices fall or rise at a rate sufficient to set the real rate of interest equal to the rate of population growth. Contrary to monetarist presumption, price stability is not necessarily a feature of the social optimum.

Observe that this 1958 argument implicitly accepts, presumably just for the sake of argument, the simplistic quantity equation that Samuelson rejects in 1947 and that Friedman resuscitates in his 1956 "Restatement." But, to repeat, that is because Samuelson in 1958 was not mainly trying to make a contribution to the theory of money. Rather, his central point was that competitive markets cannot always be depended on to achieve the social optimum. The social contrivance of money is one possible solution, but there are others. A social security system, for example, that taxes the current working generation and transfers the proceeds to the current retired generation could also achieve the social optimum. More generally, the challenge facing economists is to devise "social collusions," "self-imposed fiats," and other "social contrivances" to achieve the social optimum. Fiat money, used as a store of value, is only one such possible social contrivance.

So much for the scientific claims of monetarism, but what about the engineering claims? Robertson had followed up *Money* with a manual for central bankers, *Banking Policy and the Price Level* (1926), that Samuelson (1963, 518) found "almost unreadable." Clearly someone else would have to be recruited to engage the engineering claims of monetarism. What about Franco Modigliani? Because MIT was basically an engineering school, it was important for the economics department to have someone representing the engineering side of economics (for a deeper exploration of the importance of this engineering dimension, see Halsmayer, this volume). Even more, because the policy success of the Keynesian agenda in the outside world was so important for elevating the scientific status of Keynesian economics, it was important to have someone serving as the public face of MIT's views on money for the next generation. Modigliani would fill both the inside and the outside roles.

Modigliani and Monetarism

On the scientific fundamentals, regarding both the theory of money and the nonoptimality of laissez-faire, Modigliani agreed entirely with Samuelson. Himself a student of Marschak at the New School in New York, Modigliani (2001, 19) was a Monetary Walrasian born and bred. Even more, his 1944 paper "Liquidity Preference and the Theory of Interest and Money," part of his PhD dissertation, advanced a specifically monetary interpretation of Keynes that would become the analytical frame through which he viewed macroeconomics for the rest of his life (cf. Modigliani 2001, 20–44). Following Hicks (1937) more than Keynes himself, Modigliani always viewed the problem of economic stabilization largely as a matter of adjusting the supply of money to the quantity that would be demanded at full employment. Thus, like Friedman and the monetarists, he emphasized monetary policy over fiscal policy, but, unlike Friedman and the monetarists, he also emphasized active intervention over a constant money growth rule. "In other words, unemployment is caused by a lack of money. And since money is determined by the central bank, this is caused by an improper monetary policy" (Modigliani 2001, 39).

In 1944 Modigliani's emphasis on monetary intervention placed him in diametric opposition to the more radical Keynesians, such as Abba Lerner (1943), whose "functional finance" urged a policy of deficit spending to achieve full employment, without regard for the consequence in mounting government debt (Modigliani 2001, 43–44). In Modigliani's view, by contrast, fiscal policy came into its own only when monetary policy lost its traction, which is to say under conditions of a liquidity trap, such as during the Great Depression. In normal times, monetary policy had plenty of traction simply because of the downward stickiness of prices and wages; changes in the nominal money supply produced changes also in the real money supply, hence in the rate of interest, real output, and employment. To be sure, once full employment was reached, continued monetary expansion would have no real effect, since prices and wages would rise to neutralize the effect of any increase in the nominal money supply. But below full employment, the real effect was significant. Monetary policy *could* stabilize output and employment, and therefore monetary policy *should* stabilize output and employment.

Having adopted this intellectual framework, Modigliani organized his subsequent work to elaborate the underlying mechanisms. Interestingly, it was not money demand and supply that initially occupied him but the links with real expenditure, and it was these investigations that would be recognized in the 1985 Nobel award (Kouri 1986). Thus the life cycle hypothesis arose from an investigation of the determinants of consumption spending and saving, while the Modigliani-Miller theorem arose from an investigation of the determinants of business investment spending. On money, it was Tobin (1956, 1958) at Yale who initially took the lead for the Keynesians, not Modigliani. Only after Modigliani (1963) joined MIT did he turn his attention seriously to the monetary transmission mechanism in "The Monetary Mechanism and Its Interaction with Real Phenomena" and also to direct confrontation with Friedman and monetarism (Ando and Modigliani 1965, 1969; Modigliani 1964, 1977, [1977] 1986).

Not only MIT but eventually the entire Federal Reserve System had its hopes riding on Modigliani when, in 1964, he took on supervisory responsibility for development of what was then known as the FMP (Fed-MIT-Penn) model, the first large-scale econometric model of the United States (Modigliani 1971a, 1975). In subsequent years, a generation of graduate students found employment and dissertation topics, and so launched their careers, by working on that model (see, e.g., Modigliani and Sutch 1966, 1969; Modigliani, Rasche, and Cooper 1970). (For the larger story of how graduate teaching spread the MIT gospel, see Svorenčík, this volume.) The way the model worked, monetary policy set the short-term rate of interest, which then got translated into a long-term rate by a term structure equation (preferred habitat version) and a risky rate through an equity pricing equation. These capital market rates then entered the expenditure equations in the "real" sector of the model. Modigliani (1975) provides a simplified graphical representation, which is reproduced below as figure 1.

As a forecasting model, the initial FMP was a disappointment; financial innovation and institutional change meant that the estimated equations were not stable. As Pentti Kouri (1986, 318) states, "The criticism of Lucas [1976] and the rational expectations school applies as much to the MIT model as to all other large-scale models." But as a concrete crystallization of postwar central bank ambition, it carried the day. The importance of

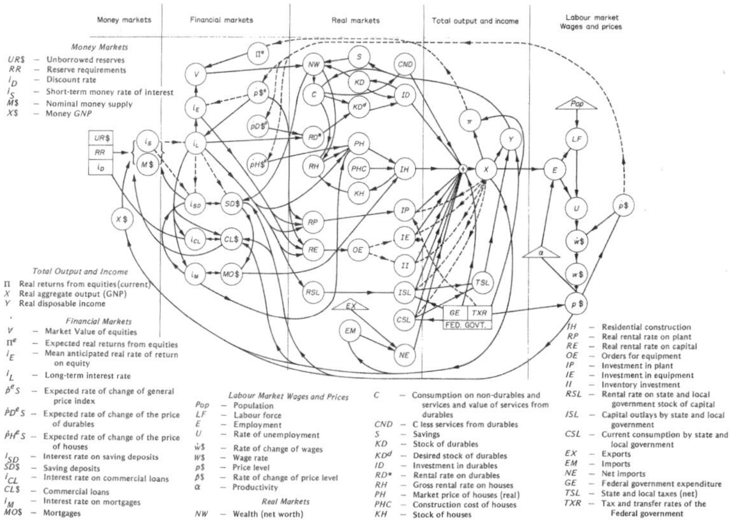

Figure 1 Modigliani's (1975) graphical representation of the FMP (Fed-MIT-Penn) econometric model

central banks as contributors to macroeconomic stabilization became the new orthodoxy, and it was Modigliani (1971b) who got that ball rolling. In the event, the criticism of Tobin and William Brainard (1968) proved decisive, and the alternative framework suggested by Tobin (1969) provided the starting point for the next generation of econometric modeling (Fromm and Klein 1975).

Samuelson Redux

Until 1965 the MIT economics department was two departments in one, the original industrial relations department that had been established as a service department for the MIT engineers, and a newly emerging scientific economics department that had been growing slowly around the personage of Paul Samuelson. In 1965 the industrial relations faculty moved into the Sloan School of Business, while a new crop of the best and brightest junior faculty that could be found was added to the economics department: Duncan Foley from Yale, Miguel Sidrauski from Chicago, and Michael Piore from Harvard (Piore 2013, 21; Cherrier, this volume).

The plan was for MIT to be the place where the scientific debate of the next generation would take place, get resolved, and then be transmitted to the world through successive graduating classes of newly minted PhDs. During the Kennedy administration, when MIT's Bob Solow joined Yale's James Tobin on the Council of Economic Advisers, the ascendance of Keynesian policy activism was established, and the MIT department emerged as a proud center of scientific support for that policy consensus. But neither policy nor science stands still, and so neither could MIT. Debate would therefore proceed, albeit under the watchful eye of the old heads—in 1965 Samuelson turned fifty—so ensuring that the hard-won Keynesian wisdom of the past would be bolstered, not overturned.

Unfortunately for the plan, all was not well with the scientific foundations of Monetary Walrasianism, notwithstanding the tacit agreement by both monetarists and Keynesians to continue building on those foundations. The difficulty was something called the Hahn problem, pointed out by Frank Hahn in a short paper "On Some Problems of Proving the Existence of Equilibrium in a Monetary Economy" (1965). Hahn's target was Don Patinkin's magnum opus *Money, Interest, and Prices* ([1956] 1965), not Samuelson's *Foundations* sketch, but the force of the criticism applied to both equally. Simply put, adding money balances to the utility function does not provide the foundations for monetary theory that one might think it does, because there is no guarantee that equilibrium exists (unless other auxiliary assumptions are made as well), and even when it does, there will always also exist an equilibrium in which the price of money is zero, so that zero real balances are held.

In plain terms, money is inessential in Walrasian equilibrium. The problem is not, as is often asserted, that Walrasian equilibrium is a model of a barter economy without money. Quite the contrary, it is more accurate to say that Walrasian equilibrium is about a world in which the monetary mechanism is so efficient that the velocity of money is infinite, so that a vanishingly small amount of money is able to do all the work that is needed to facilitate transactions. Obviously that is not the world we live in, so one response to Hahn was simply to abandon the search for a foundational model and attend instead to practical models; that is essentially what Modigliani was doing. But the question of analytical foundations remained.

Samuelson's paper "What Classical and Neoclassical Monetary Theory Really Was" (1968) can be read as his attempt to sketch a possible road forward that would, by embracing dynamical considerations, provide a more adequate response to Hahn. It was only a sketch, but it was a tremendously influential sketch for the generation of students, and junior faculty, who were passing through MIT. Footnote 4 of the paper in effect passes the torch to the younger generation: "My colleague, Professor Miguel Sidrauski, has independently arrived at such a dynamic formulation" (7). Samuelson is sketching an outline of the direction he hopes and expects the young tyros to follow.

The 1968 paper came to be known colloquially as Samuelson's "jackass" paper on account of its opening rhetorical gambit about a farmer in search of a lost animal who asks himself, "If I were a jackass, where would I have gone?" Samuelson identifies his own younger self as the jackass lost in classical monetary theory, while his current self looks back and reflects on where he had gone astray and how he had managed to find his way to the correct neoclassical monetary theory. Speaking mathematically, his mistake had been simply to append the quantity equation to a system of real supply and demand equations, rather than to integrate money more deeply into the analysis by taking explicit account of its real services in one of the real demand equations.

It was in reading Keynes, so Samuelson reflects, that he managed to find his way. No doubt. But the reference to Marschak (1943) hints at a further influence, perhaps a mediating influence. Indeed, the intellectual journey that Samuelson recalls for his young self is very much the intellectual journey that Marschak himself had followed, just a few years earlier, and in print.

In *Econometrica* Marschak (1934, 196) published the following system of equations:

$$q_i = \sigma_i\left(\frac{p_i}{w}\right) = \delta_i\left(p_1, p_2 \ldots w \cdot e\right),$$
$$\textstyle\sum_i p_i q_i = w \cdot e = MV,$$
$$P = \lambda\left(p_1 \ldots p_n, q_1 \ldots q_n\right).$$

The first of these is more or less exactly the set of equations that Samuelson (1968, 3–4) reconstructs as the mistaken version of the classical system, that is, a set of supply σ and demand δ equations for each good i (that Samuelson labels A'), with a quantity equation appended to determine the absolute level of prices (that Samuelson labels B').

Then, in 1938, Marschak published "Money and the Theory of Assets," which puts money in the utility function along with other assets, and proposes the following first-order conditions (x and y are moments of the statistical distribution of asset a and asset b, and p and q are their market prices):

$$\frac{p}{q} = \frac{U_x \dfrac{dx}{da} + U_y \dfrac{dy}{da} + \dots}{U_x \dfrac{dx}{db} + U_y \dfrac{dy}{db} + \dots}.$$

This is more or less exactly the condition that Samuelson (1968, 9, equation AIII) sets forth as the mathematical essence of the correct version of the neoclassical system.

In 1968 Samuelson makes clear that for him, at the most foundational level, the neoclassical synthesis is not about price stickiness (notwithstanding Modigliani) but more fundamentally about integrating dynamical considerations. By contrast to 1947, in 1968 Samuelson adds capital, labor, and land to the simple Walrasian exchange schema, and focuses attention on the steady state, which he thinks of as the end result of dynamic convergence. In that steady state the marginal productivity of capital determines the rate of interest (no longer exogenous), and the convenience yield on money is equalized to that rate of interest. As in 1947, there is no equation of exchange in the model, but nonetheless the model is homogeneous in the sense that doubling money and all prices (including asset prices) leaves real allocations unchanged. Notwithstanding this homogeneity, he concludes, "Correct neoclassical theory does not lead to the narrow anti-Keynesian view of those Chicago economists who allege that velocity of circulation is not a function of interest rates" (Samuelson 1968, 11).

A new claim in 1968, disarmingly introduced as nothing more than a digression, is that the steady-state equilibrium with money is suboptimal, since money is "a free good from society's point of view," and hence the social optimum is achieved only when money demand is satiated:

$$\partial U/\partial M = 0 \text{ instead of } r \times (\text{positive constant}) > 0$$

Says Samuelson (1968, 10; see also 1969): "Evidently we have here an instance of a lack of optimality of laissez-faire; there is a kind of fictitious internal diseconomy from holding more cash balances, as things look to the individual. Yet if all were made to hold larger cash balances, which they turned over more slowly, the resulting lowering of absolute price would end up making everybody better off." This new claim would almost immediately be countered by Milton Friedman in his famous essay "The Optimum Quantity of Money" (1969), with its audacious proposal for achieving the social optimum simply by engineering a steady deflation at the rate of interest. So far as I have been able to determine, Samuelson never responded to Friedman's sally, leaving that task to others such as Hahn (1971), although he did respond to other critics (Samuelson 1969).

As for the larger challenge, Foley and Sidrauski (1971) soon produced *Monetary and Fiscal Policy in a Growing Economy* as a "revision and reconstruction of macroeconomic theory." This work, more than anything else, represents the high point of the MIT approach to monetary theory, integrating statics and dynamics, goods markets and asset markets, fiscal policy and monetary policy. But for all its many virtues, it simply sidestepped the looming foundational issues, leaving them for later. "Indeed, we still lack in 1972 a really adequate theoretical structure that encompasses the foundations of a money economy. On to the drawing boards!" (Samuelson 1972, 292).

But the necessary foundational undershoring never happened. Instead the 1970s saw not only the rise of Friedman's monetarism but also the beginnings of the new classical revolution, rational expectations, and ultimately real business cycle theory (Lucas 1972; Sargent 1976; Sargent and Wallace 1975).

Losing Control

Always in the history of monetary economics there is debate between those who start from state-issued fiat money and those who start from privately issued bank credit money. In the United States, the former starting point has typically dominated academic circles, while the latter starting point has typically dominated practical banking, including central banking, starting with the debate over the founding of the Federal Reserve (Mehrling 2002b). At MIT, both Samuelson and Modigliani belonged to the first camp (as also did Friedman at Chicago), which meant conceptualizing money as a kind of paper gold, an asset that is no one's liability, issued by the state through its proxy the central bank. Since there is no cost to producing it, the basic policy question is how the state should best manipulate the quantity it produces to maximize social benefit. Samuelson characteristically asked that question in the context of a steady-state intertemporal equilibrium, while Modigliani asked it in the context of a short-run unemployment equilibrium, but for both men the unit of analysis was the nation-state, and for both men the social optimum referenced the citizens of that nation-state.

From an international standpoint, however, state-issued fiat money is a promise to pay international reserves, much the same as bank money is a promise to pay national currency, which is to say that it is a promise to pay gold under a gold standard, sterling under a sterling standard, or dollars under a dollar standard. Under the fixed exchange rate system established at Bretton Woods, the promise to pay was more or less explicitly the obligation of each national central bank to settle its official balance of payments in dollars, at the agreed rate of exchange. Nondollar currencies were thus clearly forms of credit. For our purposes, this institutional arrangement is important because it opened the door to the alternative tradition of monetary analysis that starts from bank credit.

At MIT, the keeper of this alternative tradition was Charles Kindleberger. Recruited to MIT in 1948, and only five years older than Samuelson, he was a generation older intellectually with a lifetime's worth of wartime adventure behind him (Kindleberger 1991; see also Meardon, this volume). An unreconstructed student of the indigenous American institutionalist tradition of monetary economics (see Mehrling 1997), Kindleberger had an international perspective informed by his experience with prewar monetary instability, which experience he had explored in his Columbia dissertation, "International Short-Term Capital Movements" (1937). For him, dollars were not a fiat currency issued by the state to its citizens but rather the short-term liability of the United States to the rest of the world. As world currency markets recovered in the aftermath of war, the United States was operating like a bank, providing liquidity to the world by borrowing short and lending long (Kindleberger, Despres, and Salant 1966).

A second source of dissent from the dominant academic view came from the emerging field of finance, which arose in concert with the postwar recovery of private capital markets domestically. Financial assets are forms of credit, promises to pay money at some point in the future. But they also have a current market price at which they are shiftable into current money. And some assets, for example, short-term money market assets, have prices that are sufficiently stable that the assets serve as good substitutes for bank deposits. From this point of view, not only bank liabilities but also all high-quality, short-term debts are forms of money, even if not formally means of payment. As private credit markets recovered, this institutional fact opened a second door to the alternative tradition of monetary analysis.

At MIT, the keeper of this second alternative tradition was Fischer Black (Mehrling 2005). Recruited to MIT from the University of Chicago in 1975 on the strength of his contributions to the pricing of financial derivatives (as

Black and Scholes 1973), Black always viewed macroeconomics as the biggest unsolved problem of finance. Lacking any formal education in finance or economics, he was introduced to the capital asset pricing model by his friend and colleague Jack Treynor, and used that model for the rest of his life as the intellectual framework for understanding the world around him. For him, dollars were not fiat currency issued by the nation-state but rather the short-term liabilities of financial intermediaries who stand between investors who want to hold less risk than the risky market portfolio (which they achieve by holding some of their wealth in bank deposits) and investors who want to hold more risk than the risky market portfolio (which they achieve by borrowing from the banking system to leverage their positions). This vision of a possible future world Black (1970) published as "Banking and Interest Rates in a World without Money," and then spent his life working to make that possibility an actuality.

Strange bedfellows, Charles Kindleberger and Fischer Black, but each one in his own way sensed a crucial dimension of the gathering forces that would sweep away the rigidities of the Bretton Woods apparatus put in place in the closing days of World War II, and replace it with a new world of financial globalization under a dollar standard that would rival the era of financial globalization under the sterling standard of the late nineteenth century. The intellectual edifice built by Samuelson and Modigliani was about a world passing away, even while Samuelson and Modigliani remained at the helm and continued to defend that edifice. Within MIT, Kindleberger adapted by refashioning himself as an economic historian before retiring in 1976 to write his best seller *Manias, Panics, and Crashes* (1978). Black bided his time until the financial revolution was sufficiently far advanced to have room for him, whereupon he left MIT for Goldman Sachs in 1984.

Kindleberger and Black both saw the future because they both understood a dimension of money that was simply left out of the standard models, both Keynesian and monetarist. They saw a common future, but they saw it from opposite sides. For Black, the important thing was the way that financial innovation was breaking down existing outdated institutions of national supervision, regulation, and management. For Kindleberger, the important thing was the way that globalization was challenging economists to develop new institutions for supranational supervision, regulation, and management. Both were right. The collapse of Bretton Woods was a vindication of Black, and the subsequent poor economic performance of the flexible exchange system was a vindication of Kindleberger.

Meanwhile, the task of incorporating the Kindleberger-Black perspective on money into the standard corpus of economic theory remains to be done. Echoing Samuelson, it could be said that we still lack a really adequate theoretical structure that encompasses the foundations of a money economy. Monetary Walrasianism, in both its Keynesian and its monetarist variants, has had its run. Perhaps it is now time to try something else. "On to the drawing boards!"

References

Ando, Albert K., and Franco Modigliani. 1965. "The Relative Stability of Monetary Velocity and the Investment Multiplier." *American Economic Review* 55 (September): 693–728.

———. 1969. "Econometric Analysis of Stabilization Policies." *American Economic Review* 59 (2): 296–314.

Black, Fischer. 1970. "Banking and Interest Rates in a World without Money: The Effects of Uncontrolled Banking." *Journal of Bank Research* 1 (Autumn): 8–20.

Black, Fischer, and Myron Scholes. 1973. "The Pricing of Options and Corporate Liabilities." *Journal of Political Economy* 81 (3): 637–54.

Brown, E. Cary, and Robert M. Solow. 1983. *Paul Samuelson and Modern Economic Theory*. New York: McGraw-Hill.

Foley, Duncan, and Miguel Sidrauski. 1971. *Monetary and Fiscal Policy in a Growing Economy*. New York: Macmillan.

Friedman, Milton. 1946. "Lange on Price Flexibility and Employment: A Methodological Criticism." *American Economic Review* 36 (4): 613–31.

———. 1948. "A Monetary and Fiscal Framework for Economic Stability." *American Economic Review* 38 (3): 245–64.

———, ed. 1956. *Studies in the Quantity Theory of Money*. Chicago: University of Chicago Press.

———. 1959. *A Program for Monetary Stability*. New York: Fordham University Press.

———. 1969. *The Optimum Quantity of Money, and Other Essays*. Chicago: Aldine.

Friedman, Milton, and Anna Jacobson Schwartz. 1963. *A Monetary History of the United States, 1867–1960*. Princeton, N.J.: Princeton University Press.

Fromm, Gary, and Lawrence R. Klein, eds. 1975. *The Brookings Model: Perspective and Recent Developments*. Amsterdam: North-Holland.

Hahn, Frank. 1965. "On Some Problems of Proving the Existence of Equilibrium in a Monetary Economy." In *The Theory of Interest Rates*, edited by F. H. Hahn and F. P. R. Brechling, 126–35. London: Macmillan.

———. 1971. "Professor Friedman's Views on Money." *Economica* 38 (February): 61–80.

———. 1983. "On General Equilibrium and Stability." In Brown and Solow 1983, 31–55.

Hetzel, Robert L., and Ralph F. Leach. 2001. "The Treasury-Fed Accord: A New Narrative Account." *Economic Quarterly, Federal Reserve Bank of Richmond* 87 (1): 33–55.
Hicks, John R. 1935. "A Suggestion for Simplifying the Theory of Money." *Economica* 2 (5): 1–19.
———. 1937. "Mr. Keynes and the 'Classics': A Suggested Interpretation." *Econometrica* 5 (2): 147–59.
———. 1939. *Value and Capital: An Inquiry into Some Fundamental Principles of Economic Theory*. Oxford: Clarendon Press.
Jung, Jeeman, and Robert J. Shiller. 2005. "Samuelson's Dictum and the Stock Market." *Economic Inquiry* 43 (2): 221–28.
Kindleberger, Charles P. 1937. *International Short-Term Capital Movements*. New York: Columbia University Press.
———. 1978. *Manias, Panics, and Crashes: A History of Financial Crises*. New York: Basic Books.
———. 1991. *The Life of an Economist: An Autobiography*. Cambridge, Mass.: Basil Blackwell.
Kindleberger, Charles P., Emile Despres, and Walter S. Salant. 1966. "The Dollar and World Liquidity—a Minority View." *Economist* 218 (6389). Reprinted in Kindleberger 1981, 42–52.
Kouri, Pentti J. K. 1986. "Franco Modigliani's Contributions to Economics." *Scandinavian Journal of Economics* 88 (2): 311–34.
Lange, Oskar. 1944. *Price Flexibility and Employment*. Bloomington, Ind.: Principia.
Lerner, Abba. 1943. "Functional Finance and the Federal Debt." *Social Research* 10 (1): 38–51.
Lucas, Robert E., Jr. 1972. "Expectations and the Neutrality of Money." *Journal of Economic Theory* 4 (2): 103–24.
———. 1976. "Econometric Policy Evaluation: A Critique." *Carnegie-Rochester Conference Series on Public Policy* 1 (1): 19–46.
Marschak, Jacob. 1934. "The Meeting of the Econometric Society in Leyden, September–October 1933." *Econometrica* 2 (2): 187–203.
———. 1938. "Money and the Theory of Assets." *Econometrica* 6 (4): 311–25.
———. 1943. "Money Illusion and Demand Analysis." *Review of Economic Statistics* 25 (1): 40–48.
Mehrling, Perry. 1997. *The Money Interest and the Public Interest: American Monetary Thought, 1920–1970*. Cambridge, Mass.: Harvard University Press.
———. 1998. "The Money Muddle: The Transformation of American Monetary Thought, 1920–1970." In *From Interwar Pluralism to Postwar Neoclassicism*, edited by Mary S. Morgan and Malcolm Rutherford. *History of Political Economy* 30 (supplement): 293–306.
———. 2002a. "Don Patinkin and the Origins of Postwar Monetary Orthodoxy." *European Journal of the History of Economic Thought* 9 (2): 161–85.
———. 2002b. "Economists and the Fed: Beginnings." *Journal of Economic Perspectives* 16 (4): 207–18.

——. 2005. *Fischer Black and the Revolutionary Idea of Finance*. Hoboken, N.J.: John Wiley.
——. 2010. "A Tale of Two Cities." *History of Political Economy* 42 (2): 201–19.
Modigliani, Franco. 1944. "Liquidity Preference and the Theory of Interest and Money." *Econometrica* 12 (1): 45–88.
——. 1963. "The Monetary Mechanism and Its Interaction with Real Phenomena." *Review of Economics and Statistics* 45 (1, pt. 2, suppl.): 79–107.
——. 1964. "Some Empirical Tests of Monetary Management and of Rules versus Discretion." *Journal of Political Economy* 72 (June): 211–45.
——. 1971a. "Monetary Policy and Consumption: Linkages via Interest Rate and Wealth Effects in the FMP Model." In *Consumer Spending and Monetary Policy: The Linkages*, 9–84. Conference Series No. 5 (June). Federal Reserve Bank of Boston.
——. 1971b. "Some Proposals for a Reform of the Discount Window." In *Reappraisal of the Federal Reserve Discount Mechanism* 2 (December): 58–76. Board of Governors of the Federal Reserve System.
——. 1975. "Channels of Monetary Policy in the Federal Reserve-MIT-University of Pennsylvania Econometric Model of the United States." In *Modelling the Economy*, edited by George A. Renton, 240–67. London: Heinemann Educational Books.
——. 1977. "The Monetarist Controversy or, Should We Forsake Stabilization Policies?" *American Economic Review* 67 (2): 1–19.
——. (1977) 1986. *The Debate over Stabilization Policy*. Raffaele Mattioli Lectures. Cambridge: Cambridge University Press.
——. 2001. *Adventures of an Economist*. London: Texere.
Modigliani, Franco, and Albert K. Ando. 1965. "The Relative Stability of Monetary Velocity and the Investment Multiplier." *American Economic Review* 55 (September): 693–728.
——. 1966. "Econometric Analysis of Stabilization Policies." *American Economic Review* 59 (2): 296–314.
Modigliani, Franco, Robert Rasche, and J. Phillip Cooper. 1970. "Central Bank Policy, the Money Supply, and the Short-Term Rate of Interest." *Journal of Money, Credit, and Banking* 2 (2): 171–223.
Modigliani, Franco, and Richard Sutch. 1966. "Innovations in Interest Rate Policy." *American Economic Review* 56 (2): 178–97.
——. 1969. "The Term Structure of Interest Rates: A Re-examination of the Evidence." *Journal of Money, Credit, and Banking* 1 (1): 112–20.
Patinkin, Don. (1956) 1965. *Money, Interest, and Prices*. 2nd ed. New York: Harper and Row.
——. 1983. "Monetary Economics." In Brown and Solow 1983, 157–67.
Piore, Michael J. 2013. "Keynes and Marx, Duncan, and Me." In *Social Fairness and Economics: Economic Essays in the Spirit of Duncan Foley*, edited by Lance Taylor, Armon Rezai, and Thomas Michl, 21–30. New York: Routledge.
Robertson, Dennis H. 1922. *Money*. New York: Harcourt, Brace.

——. 1926. *Banking Policy and the Price Level: An Essay in the Theory of the Trade Cycle*. London: P. S. King.

Samuelson, Paul A. 1939. "Interactions between the Multiplier Analysis and the Principle of Acceleration." *Review of Economics and Statistics* 21 (2): 75–78.

——. 1947. *Foundations of Economic Analysis*. Cambridge, Mass.: Harvard University Press.

——. 1954. "Pure Theory of Public Expenditure." *Review of Economics and Statistics* 36 (November): 387–89.

——. 1958. "An Exact Consumption-Loan Model of Interest with or without the Social Contrivance of Money." *Journal of Political Economy* 66 (6): 467–82.

——. 1963. "D. H. Robertson (1890–1963)." *Quarterly Journal of Economics* 77 (4): 517–36.

——. (1967) 1972. "Money, Interest Rates, and Economic Activity: Their Interrelationship in a Market Economy." In *Proceedings of a Symposium on Money, Interest Rates, and Economic Activity*. New York: American Bankers Association. Reprinted in vol. 3 of *The Collected Scientific Papers of Paul A. Samuelson*, edited by Robert C. Merton, 550–70. Cambridge, Mass.: MIT Press.

——. 1968. "What Classical and Neoclassical Monetary Theory Really Was." *Canadian Journal of Economics* 1 (1): 1–15.

——. 1969. "Nonoptimality of Money Holding under Laissez Faire." *Canadian Journal of Economics* 2 (2): 303–8.

——. 1972. "Samuelson on the Neoclassical Dichotomy: A Reply." *Canadian Journal of Economics* 5 (2): 283–92.

Sargent, Thomas J. 1976. "A Classical Macroeconomic Model for the United States." *Journal of Political Economy* 84 (2): 207–37.

Sargent, Thomas J., and Neil Wallace. 1975. "'Rational' Expectations, the Optimal Monetary Instrument, and the Optimal Money Supply Rule." *Journal of Political Economy* 83 (2): 241–54.

Simons, Henry. (1934) 1948. "A Positive Program for Laissez Faire." In *Economic Policy for a Free Society*. Chicago: University of Chicago Press.

Tobin, James. 1956. "The Interest Elasticity of Transactions Demand for Cash." *Review of Economics and Statistics* 38 (3): 241–47.

——. 1958. "Liquidity Preference as Behavior towards Risk." *Review of Economic Studies* 25 (2): 65–86.

——. 1969. "A General Equilibrium Approach to Monetary Theory." *Journal of Money, Credit, and Banking* 1 (1): 15–29.

——. 1983. "Macroeconomics and Fiscal Policy." In Brown and Solow 1983, 189–201.

Tobin, James, and William C. Brainard. 1968. "Pitfalls in Financial Model Building." *American Economic Review* 58 (2): 99–122.

In the Kingdom of Solovia: The Rise of Growth Economics at MIT, 1956–70

Mauro Boianovsky and Kevin D. Hoover

1. Growthmanship

In the early 1960s the Massachusetts Institute of Technology (MIT) was the native land of the "growthmen." Its leading light, Paul Samuelson (1948a), had published a pathbreaking undergraduate textbook, *Economics: An Introductory Analysis*. The book was striking partly because it gave pride of place to the analysis of national income and outlined the vision of the "mixed economy" in which Keynesian demand management would secure full employment and the price system operating under the usual neoclassical analysis would govern allocation (Pearce and Hoover 1995). (By the third edition this stance had gained a name: "the neoclassical synthesis" [Samuelson 1955, vi].) The focus was on the short run—avoiding a replay of the Great Depression and combating the anticipated postwar slump loomed large in Samuelson's vision. He paid no attention

Correspondence may be addressed to Mauro Boianovsky, Department of Economics, Universidade de Brasilia, Brasilia DF, 70910-900, Brazil (e-mail: mboianovsky@gmail.com), and to Kevin D. Hoover, Department of Economics, Duke University, Box 90097, Durham, NC 27708-0097 (e-mail: kd.hoover@duke.edu). We thank Edwin Burmeister, Peter Diamond, Pedro Garcia Duarte, Geoffrey Harcourt, William Nordhaus, Eytan Sheshinski, Robert Solow, and participants at the conferences "MIT and the Transformation of American Economics" (Duke University, April 26–28, 2013) and the UK HET Conference (University of Sheffield, September 4–6, 2013), and at seminars at the University of Salento (Lecce), UFRGS (Porto Alegre), and UnB (Brasilia) for helpful comments on an earlier draft, and Matthew Panhans for efficient research assistance. Mauro Boianovsky gratefully acknowledges a research grant from CNPq (Brazilian Research Council).

History of Political Economy 46 (annual suppl.) DOI 10.1215/00182702-2716172

to economic growth per se. In the sixth edition of *Economics*, Samuelson (1964, vi) added a "new chapter on the *theory* of growth." Samuelson had become a growthman.

Richard Nixon coined "growthmanship" in the bitterly contested presidential election of 1960. No less a Cold Warrior than Nixon, John F. Kennedy had previously harped on the (later discredited) "missile gap" with the Soviet Union. And putting Vice President Nixon on the defensive with regard to the economic stewardship of the Eisenhower administration, he saw an economic gap as well: Western Europe and, especially, the Soviet Union appeared to have grown economically far faster than United States (Solow [1962] 1964, 101). Nixon used "growthman" to criticize Kennedy's single-mindedness in allowing growth to dominate the political debate (Tobin 1964; Arndt 1978, chap. 5; Collins 2000, chap. 1).

Growthmanship was originally informed by policy concerns, rather than formal economic theory (Collins 2000, chap. 1). Walt Rostow, a colleague of Samuelson's at MIT, became a national security adviser in the Kennedy administration. But Rostow was an economic historian, not a theorist. His book *The Stages of Growth: A Non-Communist Manifesto* (1960) influenced the formulation of American security policy (Lodewijks 1991). Yet, as its subtitle suggests, the practical concern of winning the Cold War dominated formal economic analysis. Samuelson (1964, 723) himself acknowledged the Soviet challenge and criticized the belief—presumably based on the notion of diminishing returns—that the Soviet Union's rate of growth would have to slow down as its economy approached American levels of economic development as "wishful thinking" and "rightwing determinism." It was characteristic, however, of Samuelson and MIT at this period to emphasize the utility of economic analysis for policy. Indeed, what perhaps most distinguished *Economics* from earlier textbooks was the way in which even an elementary exposition was informed by formal analysis. In the sixth edition, Samuelson drew on the work on growth theory of his younger colleague Robert Solow (1956)—an indication that growthmanship was taking an analytical turn. Solow ([1962] 1964, 101–3), who also worked in the Kennedy administration, had happily adopted Nixon's term of abuse: he was a "growthman," and "growthmanship has become respectable."

The MIT economists were thus growthmen in two senses: in seeing growth as an absolutely central policy imperative and in seeing the theory of growth as a focus for economic research. The first fed the second. Evsey Domar (1957, 14–15), a growth economist and expert on the economy of the Soviet Union, captured the policy imperative: economic growth was the "fashion of the day" because, when "an aggressive part of the world is strongly and quite successfully committed to rapid growth, the other can disregard this objective only if it is tired of its own existence as a society." Growth theory itself was a substantive field in economics, at least since the late 1940s. What the MIT growthmen added was a distinctive style of analysis that made it easier to address the dominant policy concerns in tractable formal models. Solow's (1956) model was the perfect exemplar of the MIT style. It provided the central framework for the subsequent developments in growth theory and secured MIT as the center of the universe in the golden age of growth theory in the 1960s. To Eytan Sheshinski (1990, 41), an MIT graduate student from 1963 to 1966, the "Solovian equipment" was a "natural monopoly with a non-duplicable resource" operating in high gear throughout the decade. Both the centrality of Solow's growth model and the policy imperative are captured nicely in the opening of Edmund Phelps's "A Fable for Growthmen":

> Once upon a time the Kingdom of Solovia was gripped by a great debate. "This is a growing economy but it can grow faster," many argued. "Sustainable growth is best," came the reply, "and that can come only from natural forces."
>
> A few called the debate growthmanship. But most thought it would be healthy if it led to a better understanding of Solovian growth. So the King appointed a task force to learn the facts of Solovian economic life. (Phelps 1961, 638)

2. Founding the Kingdom

Various historians have documented the development of growth theory in the 1950s (e.g., Boianovsky and Hoover 2009a; Halsmayer and Hoover 2013; and Halsmayer, this volume). Solow (1956) and the Australian economist Trevor Swan (1956) each developed independently what is essentially the same model, now often referred to as the *neoclassical growth model* (Dimand and Spencer 2009). The single-sector neoclassical growth model appears to be an elegant theoretical exercise in which aggregate economic growth is characterized by a single first-order differential equation. But Solow's version arose from empirical and pedagogical concerns.[1]

1. The remainder of this section is informed by, and complements, Halsmayer, this volume.

Solow, who was the student of Wassily Leontief at Harvard, had worked on the empirical implementation of Leontief's input-output analysis, constructing large multisectoral tables for the United States. In the early 1950s Solow, who had taken up a post at MIT, worked with Samuelson to analyze the theory of dynamic input-output analysis. This work was tied closely to work on activity analysis and linear von Neumann growth models, some of which informed Dorfman, Samuelson, and Solow's *Linear Programing and Economic Analysis* (1958). While much of this work was theoretical, it was empirically motivated and supported partly under defense contracts.

Solow's (1956) model grew out this work. He regarded its core to be a "collapsed production function" that helped him to characterize and explore the causal dynamics of the aggregate economy in a transparent way for his MIT engineering students. Solow regarded the model as a tool—a drastic simplification of the complexities that he had explored with Leontief and Samuelson, but not a denial of them, and not a turning away from empirical motivations. He used the model to teach craftsmanship to provide a basis for "reconnaissance exercises" to understand what factors really matter for how the economy behaves. An early exercise—not in fact by Solow himself but by Swan (1956), his codiscoverer of the neoclassical growth model—was a surprise: the rate of growth in the neoclassical growth model is independent of the rate of investment (or savings).

Solow's model arrived at a propitious moment for growth economics. He offered three reasons to account for the turn to growth economics after the mid-1950s: (1) the political attention given to the problem of the economic development of preindustrial areas; (2) the intellectual pursuit of extending Keynesian macroeconomics into the long run, initiated by Roy Harrod and Domar; and, tongue in cheek, (3) the feeling that "short-run macroeconomic theory is pretty well in hand . . . all that is left is the trivial job of filling in the empty boxes" (Solow [1962] 1964, 101–3; and letter from Solow to Hoover, July 8, 2013). The neoclassical model proved to be the principal tool in the analytical turn to growth and the workhorse of growth research, not only in MIT's economics department but around the world.

3. Development Economics and the Cold War

At the time of the publication of Solow's neoclassical growth model, MIT was already deeply engaged with growth as a front in the Cold War. Beyond the direct worry about the United States being eclipsed by the East Bloc—1956 was also the year that Nikita Khrushchev declared to the West, "We will bury you!"—the first world of the Western democracies competed with the second world of the communist states for the allegiance of the third world of newly independent and developing countries. A central question was, which economic system would lift the third world out of poverty? Understanding growth was the key to development economics. Rostow had joined MIT as part of the newly created Center for International Studies (CENIS) in 1951. He was joined two years later by the economist Paul Rosenstein-Rodan. The work at CENIS was not mathematical. Rostow and Rosenstein-Rodan understood the growth process to be complex and viewed developing countries as facing special hurdles that impeded any spontaneous convergence to Western standards of living. In an influential article, Rostow (1956) introduced the idea of a "take-off into self-sustained growth" (see also Rostow 1960). In a similar vein, Rosenstein-Rodan (1943) had already argued that poor economies with large agricultural sectors could be moved to a path of sustained growth only through a deliberate massive investment in industrial capital—a "Big Push."

The economists at CENIS were skeptical of the value of formal economic models as guides to development. Rosenstein-Rodan's (1961) essay (originally a CENIS working paper in 1957) did not cite Solow or any other growth theorist directly but, nonetheless, offered a sustained criticism of neoclassical growth theory. Growth models built on production functions that display constant returns to scale were deemed "completely unrealistic," since they implied "no economies of scale or of agglomeration, no entrepreneurship, no phenomenon of minimum quantum or threshold" (Rosenstein-Rodan 1961, 60). Rosenstein-Rodan based his theory of the Big Push on the assumption of indivisibilities in the production functions—particularly in the form of social overhead capital—which generated increasing returns to scale and external economies. The rate of return in each industry, he believed, is influenced by demand from complementary ones, opening up the possibility of coordination failures in which the economy becomes trapped in a low-level equilibrium. The Big Push—a policy intervention that created a coordinated quantum of investment in different sectors—aimed at internalizing the external economies to establish *balanced growth*. (See also the work of his MIT colleague Charles Kindleberger [(1958) 1965, chap. 9].)

International trade, Rosenstein-Rodan (1961, 63–65) believed, could reduce, but not eliminate, the size of the required quantum of investment.

Here he directly challenged the relevance of Samuelson's (1948b) well-known factor-price equalization theorem: historical experience did not support its implication that wages and rates of return would converge among different countries. Nonetheless, he quoted approvingly Samuelson's (1948b) own suggestion that different production functions and technology in each country caused the observed divergences. The differences in technology were not, in Samuelson's view, a matter of the relative scarcity of knowledge, which he considered a "crypto-explanation": knowledge "is *not* an input such that the more you use of it, the less there is left" (181).

Similarly, Rosenstein-Rodan (1961) challenged another prediction of trade theory: abundant manpower should result in low wages, which should attract capital from abroad, driving up wages and income. However, "lower wages in underdeveloped countries did not attract enough capital to reduce the inequality in factor rewards nor did international trade fully achieve this effect" (66). Orthodox theory had neglected external economies, in the sense that the deficiency of social overhead capital caused "diseconomies on capital account which more than outweighed any economies on wage account" (66).[2]

The difference between the economists of the economics department and those of CENIS were less about the aims of policy or even the underlying causes of underdevelopment per se than about the appropriate methodology for addressing the messy, complex problem of underdevelopment and the relevance of highly simplified theoretical models—differences brought into clear relief in September 1960 at a conference of the International Economic Association held at Konstanz in West Germany to examine Rostow's (1956, 1960) economics of take-off into sustained growth (Rostow 1963). Solow's assessment in the final session of the conference (Rostow 1963, 468–74) illustrates the difficult dialogue between economic historians and growth theorists. Solow taxed Rostow with failing to establish an "orderly relation between economic theory and economic history," which should start with a clear distinction between initial conditions, laws of behavior and parameters. Rostow (1963, xiii–xxvi; see also 1984, 235–37) accepted the challenge: in his after-conference "introduction and epilogue," he tried to give the concept of take-off some added precision. He maintained, nonetheless, that economic theory was a "world of

2. Thirty years later, Robert Lucas (1988, 15–17) would mount a similar criticism of the neoclassical theory of trade and growth.

problems of simplicity," unable to function in the "world of organized complexity" of economic growth (Rostow 1963, xxiv).

Solow, of course, dissented—not because he challenged the notion of take-off, but because he believed that surrendering to the complex details of the growth process was to give up too soon on understanding the causal essence of the problem. He had already suggested a way for the neoclassical growth model to generate multiple equilibria and explain a poverty trap (Solow 1956, 90–91). In the basic model, the steady state is achieved at a unique capital-labor ratio (r) where the need for capital to outfit a growing workforce at that ratio (*capital widening*) exactly equals savings (or investment). In an extension of the basic model, Solow considers what happens if the rate of population growth depends on per capita income, which is itself a function of the capital-labor ratio. Population decreases for very low levels of income; it begins to increase for higher levels of income; and declines for still higher levels. Because of the variable rate of population growth, the needs for capital widening will match the available savings (or investment) at two different capital-labor ratios. Solow shows that the larger of these (r_2) is unstable, in the sense that, if the initial ratio is less than r_2, the economy will tend to return to the lower steady state at r_1, and if it is greater than r_2, the economy will move to a non-steady-state growth path in which the capital-labor ratio increases (*capital deepening*). But the lower ratio corresponds to a low per capita income. The stability of this low steady state marks it out as a poverty trap. If, on the other hand, a Big Push (to use Rosenstein-Rodan's but not Solow's term) could drive the economy above r_2, then the instability would carry the economy toward rising capital-labor ratios with rising per capita incomes—a take-off to a path of self-sustained growth. Solow remarks:

> The interesting thing about this case is that it shows how, *in the total absence of indivisibilities or of increasing returns*, a situation may still arise in which small-scale capital accumulation only leads back to stagnation but a major burst of investment can lift the system into a self-generating expansion of income and capital per head. (91; emphasis added)

Despite being published in 1956, Solow's version of the Big Push reads as if he were reacting to Rosenstein-Rodan's 1957 CENIS essay (published in 1961). Looking back, Solow, in a letter to one of the present authors (Hoover) dated August 11, 2013, denies that he was familiar with Rosenstein-Rodan's earlier essay (1943), but suggests the idea of poverty traps was already well known in the mid-1950s.[3]

Solow's (1956) account of poverty traps illustrates a methodological strategy: keep the models simple, yet adapt them to the demands of the real world. Solow's remark about "other possibilities" illustrates that he regarded his analysis as a "reconnaissance exercise" and a demonstration of the capacities of his model qua tool of analysis. He did not see his models as competing with the work of the historians or development economists, but as clarifying the causal mechanisms that lay behind the facts that they documented. Those facts included the differences in income levels and growth rates between developed and underdeveloped countries. Confirming Nicholas Kaldor's (1961, 178–79) sixth "stylised fact" of economic growth, Samuelson (1964, 757) observed that "in contrast to the narrowing of income differentials within the advanced nations, the divergence between advanced and underdeveloped countries is probably now widening rather than narrowing."

What lay behind the differences between developed and developing countries? To the extent that development economists employed a formal model of growth, it was the Harrod-Domar model, which was interpreted as a neoclassical growth model with a production function with technologically fixed proportions (fixed coefficients) between capital and labor (Harrod 1939, 1948; Domar 1946).[4] The Harrod-Domar model appeared to suit the problems of development, since it readily explained situations in which labor was in excess supply and capital was a binding constraint. It connected growth rates in both the short and the long runs to increases in investment rates and opened up the possibility of a self-sustaining growth

3. On the occasion of the conferring of the degree of Doctor of Humane Letters to Rosenstein-Rodan in 1982, Solow recalled that it was not easy for the relatively small MIT Department of Economics in the 1950s to absorb CENIS, with its large number of senior scholars in one specialized field. Rosenstein-Rodan was a key figure in the process, because he "saw himself and wanted others to see him as someone in the main stream of economics, and not as the practitioner of some rather different art . . . to be measured against different standards" ("Address by Professor Robert Solow on the occasion of the conferring of the degree of Doctor of Humane Letters to P.N. Rosenstein-Rodan," December 3, 1982, Robert M. Solow Papers, David M. Rubenstein Rare Book and Manuscript Library, Duke University, box 59).

4. Verena Halsmayer and Kevin D. Hoover (2013) show that the interpretation of Harrod's model either as a growth model or as embodying a fixed-proportions production function (or, indeed, any production function) is untrue to Harrod's purpose or presentation. It remains true, however, that Harrod was widely interpreted in this way and that his analysis was typically assimilated to Domar's.

path from the massive underutilization of a poverty trap to full employment at a high "natural rate" of growth (see, e.g., Boianovsky 2010).

Some of the very features that recommend the Harrod-Domar model to development economists were the direct target of Solow's (1956) paper. In particular, the same mechanism that offered the possibility of self-sustained growth for an impoverished country seemed to suggest the fragility of steady-state growth paths, predicting that developed economies would be susceptible to self-reinforcing collapse. Solow attributed this property to the assumption of a fixed-proportions production function. In reality, he believed, the mix of factors of production responded to price signals, and a flexible-proportions production function (such as the Cobb-Douglas or constant-elasticity of substitution [CES] production functions) would not suffer from the instability problem (see Halsmayer and Hoover 2013). Domar, who had been recruited to MIT in 1958, recanted his growth models of the 1940s and endorsed Solow's approach, with its "less rigid production function" (Domar 1957, 7–8).

By the mid-1960s Samuelson (1964, 760) argued that development economists had no unified theory differing from the dominant growth model, but that they did add to it some "special features." The Solow model predicted that, given some parameters (savings and fertility rates), economies move to their steady states. Because of diminishing returns, countries with lower capital-labor ratios would have a high rate of return to capital. Hence, controlling for savings rates, poorer countries would tend to go faster and converge. But clearly, poorer countries were not converging very rapidly, if at all, toward developing countries' per capita incomes. Samuelson argued that for the "poor countries there must be added the important additional concepts of 'external economies,' 'social overhead capital,' and 'increasing returns'" (752). Neoclassical diminishing returns and constant returns to scale should be replaced in "dynamic economic development" by "*increasing* returns," which "can make it possible for the dramatic spurts and acceleration to occur in economic development" (761–62).[5] Samuelson associated those discontinuities in the development process with Rostow's take-off and, especially, with Rosen-

5. Samuelson, however, did not formalize the argument. After the matter was tackled by "new growth theory," he recalled that "the problem with increasing scale returns is that after you have said the first things about it, it is deucedly hard to find interesting second and third themes to develop. Most pretty modern mathematics lacks elegant applications to the combinatorial swamp that nonconvexity irreducibly entails. My conscience was long bothered by our guild's neglect of a subject on the ground that it is so hard to tackle" (Samuelson 2001, 499).

stein-Rodan's Big Push—a view that focused on multiple equilibria rather than on convergence to steady states.

Thus there was substantial agreement with CENIS on the goals of policy. But in contrast to Rostow and Rosenstein-Rodan's skepticism about the theory, Solow advocated the flexible adaptation of simple, formal models to different aspects of the development problem. He recognized that the actual substantive application of economic analysis to development would have to move beyond the reconnaissance stage, and that was difficult work. As a consequence, formal growth economics and economic development would fracture into distinct fields.

On the one hand, the fracture was a typical division of labor: the development of methods belonged to growth economics; the applications to policy problems belonged to development. On the other hand, Solow's reconnaissance exercises had already begun to show that the special assumptions needed to fit the neoclassical growth model to developed and developing economies would be different, so that growth economics and development economics were also distinguished by their domain of application.

Seen this way, the debate in the late 1950s and early 1960s over the realism and relevance of the neoclassical growth model gave way to the systematic adaptation of it to the needs of development economics. At the Konstanz conference, Solow complained that no mention had been made of Arthur Lewis's (1954) concept of dual economies in which underemployment in the traditional low-productivity sectors results in an infinitely elastic supply of labor at an exogenous real wage rate (Rostow 1963, 472). By the end of our period, economists in both the economics department and CENIS were following through on Solow's preferred strategy: Stephen Marglin (1967) and Sukhamoy Chakravarty (1969), both at CENIS, and Avinash Dixit (1968a, 1968b, 1973) in the department deployed optimal control theory to investigate the choice of techniques and growth paths in economies with a surplus of labor (Burmeister and Dobell 1970, 408–9). Samuelson's preface to Chakravarty (1969) illustrates the mutually beneficial trade between growth and development economics at MIT.

4. Setting the Agenda

Formal modeling of economic growth at MIT was never an abstract enterprise, but was always motivated by underlying policy concerns, a respect for empirical results, and a goal of providing illuminating and relevant tools. But the models were artifacts in their own right, subject to their own constraints and imperatives (see Halsmayer, this volume). Much of the 1960s was devoted to the formal elaboration of the models, but based on an agenda set in the second half of the 1950s.

In the short, final section of his article on the "policy implications" of his growth model, Solow (1956, 93) cited Samuelson in support of the view that the rate of growth should be one of the targets of macroeconomic policy. Samuelson ([1956] 1969, 73) claimed that "with proper fiscal and monetary policies, our economy can have full employment and whatever rate of capital formation and growth it wants"—a position that he viewed as an element of the "neoclassical synthesis" (Samuelson 1961, 807). One fault of the Harrod-Domar model, in Samuelson's view, was that, by regarding technology as fixed, it suggested that economic policy would be helpless to deepen capital and raise per capita income, once surplus labor had been absorbed, and that, once fully employed, society must "accept the growth rate that fate metes out to it" (Samuelson 1961, 809n1; see also 1964, 788). Samuelson (1961, 809n1) argues that it is "misleading to think [as implied by the Harrod-Domar model] that growth is fatalistically determined by some simple formula involving the saving and capital-output ratios." That formula allows a warranted rate of growth that exceeds the natural rate of growth of population and, therefore, cannot last long:

> If deepening of capital were impossible, so that the capital-output ratio could never be increased, fiscal policy would have to be set fatalistically at so expansionary a level as to bring down the percentage of income saved to the level set by the rate of population growth and the capital-output ratio. Society would have to accept passively this fate-given growth rate (plus what technical change will itself bring). (Samuelson 1961, 809n1)

Here Samuelson appears to argue that it is the neoclassical growth model with its flexible capital-output ratio, rather than the Harrod-Domar model, that offers hope for growth-promoting macroeconomic policy. He viewed the Kennedy administration's investment tax credit of 1962 as an application of that conception (Samuelson 1964, 787).

In retrospect, Samuelson appears to have muddled different issues. A flexible-proportions production function does permit capital deepening not available in the Harrod-Domar model. But the neoclassical model, unlike the Harrod-Domar model, builds in the convergence of the warranted rate of growth, given by savings and production technology, to a steady-state natural rate of growth, given by population and the rate of technical progress. At this point, Samuelson's optimism about growth policy seems not to have fully taken on board two challenges exposed by the neoclassical growth model itself.

The first was the "stunning result" (Stiglitz 1990, 52) that the rate of growth in the neoclassical growth model is independent of the rate of savings. In his own paper, the codiscoverer of the neoclassical growth model, Swan (1956, 337–38), had already noted what was only implicit in Solow's analysis: increases in investment (or savings) rates can boost the rate of growth initially and deepen capital, but diminishing returns to factors of production imply that the increased rate of growth plays itself out when the extra output is just sufficient to cover the needs of capital widening.[6] At that point, the economy is returned to the same steady-state growth rate, though at a higher capital-output ratio. A few years later, James Meade ([1961] 1962, 42–45, 110–13) further elaborated what was regarded as a "most paradoxical conclusion." Still, the point took a while to sink in.

Swan (1956, 338–39) remarked that the "anti-accumulation" implications of the neoclassical growth model could be mitigated if the rate of technological progress depended on capital accumulation. Investment could generate external economies, which would render the social yield of capital higher than its private value and bring about increasing returns to scale. Moreover, the rate of population growth might not be independent of the rate of accumulation, which was the "distinctively classical answer." Solow (1956) had already made a related point in his discussion of the poverty trap (see section 3).

The second challenge to Samuelson's optimism about growth-promoting policy was framed by Solow's brief, but influential, foray into empirical research. Using the constant-returns-to-scale production function that formed the heart of the neoclassical growth model, Solow (1957) developed an accounting framework that attributed definite fractions of US economic growth between 1909 and 1949 to the different factors of production. He interpreted the unattributed share of growth as technical progress. The result was deeply surprising to those who saw growth as driven principally by capital accumulation: the growth in technical progress accounted for the lion's share of overall growth in US gross national product. The challenge to the neoclassical growth model was simply that technical progress had hitherto been taken to be an exogenous factor, and an

6. Swan visited MIT in 1958.

exogenous factor does not amount to a substantive explanation. The lack of explanatory force was highlighted by the common practice of referring to technical progress measured this way as a "residual."[7]

Solow (1960) suggested a modification to the neoclassical growth model that he hoped would simultaneously address both challenges. In Solow's 1957 paper, technical progress is *disembodied*—that is, it adds to output merely through the passage of time, as if it did not have to be physically incorporated into the means of production. Solow (1960, 90) sought to relax the assumption that "the pace of investment has no influence on the rate at which technique improves." He allowed the rate of *technological knowledge* progress in this disembodied manner, but modeled it as adding to *productive capacity* only to the degree that it was embodied in new capital goods. The productivity of any particular piece of capital would depend, therefore, on its *vintage*. Faster investment would raise the rate of growth in the economy by accelerating the incorporation of new knowledge into the capital stock, answering the first challenge. And the residual would be—at least partly—explained as an endogenous response to investment rates. Of course, the underlying rate of improvement in technical know-how itself remained unexplained.

Samuelson and Solow were both optimistic about the "new view" of investment (Phelps 1962).[8] Based on his idea of vintage capital, Solow (1962) constructed econometric estimates of the rates of investment necessary to accelerate American economic growth in the following decade. His vintage-capital model and these estimates were used to provide the benchmark for the chapter on growth in the 1962 *Economic Report* of the Council of Economic Advisers, which Solow drafted in his capacity as a staff economist (see Solow 2000).

Optimism that this "new view" of investment would meet the two challenges exposed by the neoclassical growth model was soon dashed. Phelps (1962), who visited MIT in 1962–63, demonstrated that in a vintage-capi-

7. The practice of referring to the component of the measured growth rate of output per capita unaccounted for by capital deepening as the "residual" may be due to Domar (1961, 709). Kindleberger ([1958] 1965, 150) ascribed to Rosenstein-Rodan the notion that the "residual growth" is the result of external economies of scale. Later, in the literature on real business cycle models, the "residual" becomes the "Solow residual" (see Hartley, Hoover, and Salyer 1997, 1998).

8. Samuelson (1964, 737) suggested as much in his observation that "innovations can be introduced faster in a society which is performing *net* investment in addition to the gross investment . . . the society which gets to try out more new things will run that much ahead of the one which does little or no saving."

tal model, a once-and-for-all change in the saving ratio cannot permanently alter the age distribution of capital. Thus it can accelerate the rate of growth in the transition between steady states in the vintage model, which might make a substantial difference over a ten- or twenty-year period, but the steady rate is still determined by the rates of growth of population and of the underlying (exogenous) technical knowledge (Solow [1962] 1964, 108; 1970, 55). Solow ([1968] 1969, 94–97) concluded from cross-section and historical evidence that "fast-growing countries are high-investment countries," despite the theoretical irrelevance of the investment ratio for the determination of long-run growth.

5. All the King's Men

The two challenges were unmet. But they set a twofold agenda for research into formal growth models in the Kingdom of Solovia in the 1960s. One focus would be optimal growth, which had three aspects: (1) the optimal capital-labor ratio; (2) whether it was susceptible to policy intervention—as it was not in the earlier neoclassical models—the optimal growth rate; and (3) the optimal rate of transition between steady states. The second (and not completely independent) focus was to explain or endogenize technical progress.

Rather than Solow and Samuelson, it was MIT graduate students, most supervised by Solow, who implemented the research agenda.[9] MIT also served as a beacon for growth economics, attracting important visitors and new faculty. Karl Shell, a Stanford PhD who had worked with Kenneth Arrow and Hiro Uzawa (on optimal growth), joined the MIT department in 1964 (and remained until 1968). He recalls that

> the MIT pyramid was inverted. At times I was the sole member below full rank. . . . Since the senior faculty was so busy (in Washington and in those capital debates with Cambridge, England), the graduate students had a lot of time for me. (Shell 2001, 708)

Shell recounts a two-way relationship in which students were the sources of ideas, as well as the targets of instruction.

9. Solow supervised the doctoral dissertations on growth of Ronald Findlay (1960), Peter Diamond (1963), Eytan Sheshinski (1966), Joseph Stiglitz (1966), George Akerlof (1966), William Nordhaus (1967b), and Avinash Dixit (1968a). Samuelson supervised David Levhari (1964) and Edwin Burmeister (1965).

5.1. Optimal Growth

How should we evaluate economic policy in a growth model? What could it mean to target optimal growth? As we have seen, the versions of the neoclassical growth model available around 1960 provided no lever for the *rate* of economic growth in the long run. Policy—to the degree that it could influence the rate of investment, savings, or population growth–could influence capital deepening. The question of optimal growth in the long run could, therefore, be turned into a question not about the rate of growth but about the best capital-labor ratio. Phelps (1961) proposed the "golden rule of growth." Taking consumption per capita as the desideratum, Phelps showed that it was maximized when the capital-labor ratio was set to a point such that the rate of profit (identified with the marginal product of capital or the real rate of interest) equaled the natural rate of growth (i.e., the sum of the rates of growth of population and technical progress). The academic year 1962–63 was a "golden year for Golden-Rulers at MIT"; Christian von Weizsäcker, Christopher Bliss, and others "proved all kinds of theorems" in Economics 14.123 (Advanced Economic Theory)—the course taught jointly by Solow and Phelps (Samuelson 1965a, 487n).[10]

The normative target of Phelps's golden-rule analysis, maximum consumption per capita, is straightforward but not economically natural. In a world with capital, there is a trade-off between consumption today and consumption tomorrow over which different preferences are possible. As was soon appreciated, it is most naturally an intertemporal utility maximization problem (e.g., Pearce 1962, 1093). This problem had been solved—though not in the context of a growth model—in Frank Ramsey's (1928) work on optimal saving. Ramsey's paper was well known to Samuelson, Solow, and others at MIT (see Duarte 2009, 170, 172).

Intertemporal utility maximization in a growth model was technically challenging. The translation from the Russian of the book on optimal control by L. S. Pontryagin and his associates in 1962 immediately changed the landscape of growth economics—not only at MIT but elsewhere (Wulwick 1995, 418–21). Edwin Burmeister (2009, 38), a student in Economics

10. From Samuelson's (1964, 748) perspective, the golden rule was a special case of John von Neumann's theorem that a self-reproducing, linear economy has a maximum balanced-growth path, or *turnpike*. If short-run policy could move the economy to the turnpike, it could grow optimally toward some target, at which point short-run policy could move the distribution of production and income to a desired configuration (Dorfman, Samuelson, and Solow 1958, 329–34).

14.123, recalled that the subject of the lecture on December 12, 1962, was optimality problems in capital theory:

> We were shown how to use the Maximum Principle of Pontryagin to solve the famous Ramsey problem of optimal saving over time. In this lecture we covered essentially everything that is contained in the famous David Cass paper that was not published until July 1965!

At Stanford, Uzawa and his students David Cass and Karl Shell quickly incorporated Pontryagin's methods into their own work on the theory of optimal growth. A volume edited by Shell (1967a) demonstrated the application of Pontryagin's technique to a variety of issues in the theory of optimal economic growth. Once Shell joined the MIT faculty, he organized a seminar on optimal economic growth in the 1965–66 academic year, which included several presentations by MIT students. Reactions to Shell's conference volume, however, were mixed. Frank Hahn (1968, 561) complained that the enthusiasm for the new technique often led to neglecting the economics of the models: "Very little is said by any of the authors about the choice of the maximand. Indeed there is something of an unseemly haste to get down to the Hamiltonian."[11]

Samuelson's original vision of applying the neoclassical synthesis to growth models had invoked macroeconomic policy, but the literature on optimal growth focused in the main on the appropriate rates of investment—often with the artificial but convenient invocation of a central planner. The MIT economists Duncan Foley and Miguel Sidrauski (1970, 1971) turned back to the original problem by constructing a growth model in which consumption and investment goods were produced in distinct sectors and in which the effects of alternative fiscal and monetary policies on the non-steady-state growth path of flow and stock variables could be investigated. To achieve the optimal growth paths for consumption and investment while maintaining stable consumer prices, fiscal and monetary policies must induce the capital goods sector to produce investment goods at

11. Hahn was one of the participants at another conference (and monthlong workshop) on optimal growth, led by Arrow in Stanford in July 1965 (see Kenneth J. Arrow Papers, David M. Rubenstein Rare Book and Manuscript Library, Duke University, box 28; McKenzie 1999). Conference participants also included Lionel McKenzie, Roy Radner, Tjalling Koopmans, James Mirrlees, Uzawa, and Sheshinski (the only one from MIT), among others. Sheshinski presented a joint paper (with Burmeister) about reswitching. David Warsh (2006, 155–56) reports that optimal growth papers by some young MIT scholars were coldly received at the conference. Apparently, those papers were not included in the Stanford conference program, and were later discussed at the MIT 1965–66 seminar run by Shell.

the optimal rate. The framework presupposes policies operating through private markets, as in the neoclassical synthesis, rather than through a central planner, as in the most common understanding of Ramsey's (1928) original framework for analyzing optimal savings.[12]

5.2. Technical Progress

The focus of research on optimal growth turned out to be on optimal level of the capital-output ratio, and did nothing to advance normative guidance with respect to the rate of steady-state growth. The second item on the MIT agenda, while mainly aiming to open the black box of exogenous technical progress, also offered hope of connecting the rate of growth with economic policy and, so, vindicating Samuelson's initial optimism about the scope of economic policy.

The idea of disembodied technical progress was not a natural one; it found its way into Solow's (1957) paper only as a strategy for measuring as a residual an economic characteristic that was otherwise hard to observe.[13] The idea that technical progress was an economically explicable element of the growth process, of course, went back to the very first chapter of *The Wealth of Nations*, and it found a powerful modern expression in Joseph Schumpeter's ([1911] 1934, 1942) analysis of capitalist development, with its emphasis on "creative destruction." Both Solow and Samuelson had been students of Schumpeter at Harvard. Samuelson credited Schumpeter as an important influence. Solow—perhaps because he first encountered Schumpeter some ten years after Samuelson, at which point Schumpeter's interests were no longer primarily theoretical—was less favorably impressed. In a comment on Samuelson's papers with Schumpeterian themes, Solow (1983, 185) recalled that "Schumpeter was a teacher of mine, too . . . but he either meant less to me or I lack adequate intellectual piety." Samuelson (1964, 742) suggested that Solow's growth model vindicated Schumpeter's argument that innovations were the engine of growth, yet he did not attempt to use Schumpeter's notion of creative destruction to model the pace of technological progress.

12. Whether Ramsey intended the single utility function of an immortal individual in his model to refer to a central planner or to a "representative agent" in the private economy is disputed among historians; see Duarte 2012, 126–30; see also Duarte 2009. An alternative demographic structure (to both Solow's and Ramsey's models) was put forward by Samuelson's (1958) overlapping generations model, later extended to growth economics by Peter Diamond (1965). That was not part of Diamond's 1963 thesis; it was written when he was teaching public finance at Berkeley in 1964. In 1966 Solow recruited Diamond to MIT.

13. It is an old strategy; see Hoover and Dowell 2002 and Duarte and Hoover 2012.

While biased technical progress was an old topic, technical change itself had not been modeled formally. Work at MIT began with visitors—Weizsäcker (1962–63) and Charles Kennedy (May 1964)—who prompted Samuelson to address the notion of *induced* factor bias in invention in some detail.

Samuelson (1965b, 1966) incorporated Kennedy's (1964) *invention-possibility frontier* into a neoclassical growth model. The invention-possibility curve represented a trade-off faced by entrepreneurs between capital-augmenting and labor-augmenting technical progress. He showed that, if the elasticity of substitution is less than one, there exists a stable balanced-growth path characterized by labor-augmenting (i.e., Harrod-neutral) technical progress and constant relative factor shares in output. Samuelson found the results compelling enough that he added a note to the seventh edition of *Economics*, claiming that the theory of induced technical progress met the challenge of explaining all the basic trends of capitalism, including increasing capital-labor ratio and increasing real wages, as well as the near constancy of the capital-output ratio and interest rates (Samuelson 1967, 721n17; see also 1966, 447–48).

Once again, the work of elaboration fell mainly to the younger generation and followed three interrelated streams: (1) the role of publicly supported research and development; (2) the role of "learning by doing"; and (3) the role of privately motivated research and development.

William Nordhaus (1967a, 1967b; 1969b, chap. 6) contributed to the first stream, addressing the role of government in promoting technical progress. Following Uzawa (1965), he assumed that central planners can allocate a fraction of the labor force to research or education and, thereby, push out the invention-possibility curve, which in turn determines the rate of technical progress. A central planner can choose the rate of capital accumulation and the rate and direction of technical progress to maximize present discounted value of consumption per capita. Having solved the central planner's problem, Nordhaus (1967a, 64–65; 1969b, 111–13) asked whether the results would carry over to a competitive market economy, only to conclude that "competition will break down." The problem was that by Euler's theorem, if technical progress resulted in increasing returns to scale, then output would fall short of factor shares in a competitive market in which all factors are paid their marginal products.

The theme of the December 1965 meetings of the American Economic Association (AEA) was "knowledge, production and innovation." At the invitation of AEA president Fritz Machlup, Solow arranged a session that included a paper by Shell (1966) outlining a new model of endogenous technical change based on the assumption that knowledge is a government-funded, pure public good (Solow to Machlup, Solow Papers, box 58). Shell (1966, 63) adopted Arrow's (1962b) view of knowledge as characterized by "inappropriability" and "indivisibility": while it may be costly to produce a new idea, "knowledge can be used by many economic units without altering its character," with but a "small cost of transmission in comparison to the cost of production" (see also Meade 1968, chap. 9; Nordhaus 1969a, 18–19). Aside from the well-known problem of public goods, that the private sector would not receive sufficient incentive to support the socially optimal quantity of technological knowledge, the model shares the characteristic of Nordhaus's model that increasing returns are incompatible with perfect competition, so that technical progress would not be compensated in the market, apparently bolstering the case for government intervention (Shell 1966, 64).

Shell's model also contained a theoretical surprise: almost every point in technology/capital-output-ratio space is unstable; the only exception was a narrow locus of points, the *saddle path*. By and large, Shell's result was unwelcome—the instability was an instance of the same property that Solow (1956) had rejected as implausible and counterempirical in the Harrod-Domar model. Citing M. Maruyama's (1960) characterization of social systems as fundamentally *morphogenic* as opposed to *morphostatic*, Shell (1966, 65) embraced the result, arguing that, while global stability was an "interesting property," it should not be considered "essential" for a growth model. Shell's (1967b, 79) model predicted that, whereas rich countries tend to grow at increasing rates, poor countries tend to decay and might need a Big Push (see also Neher 1971, 199–205). Ironically, Solow's and the economics department's methodology of simple models, to which Rostow had objected at the Konstanz conference, provided yet another rationale for the substantive policies of CENIS.

Focus on the second stream originated in the work of David Levhari (1964, 1966a, 1966b) and Sheshinski (1966, 1967a, 1967b), who approached technical progress not from the perspective of research and development but from Arrow's (1962a) notion of *learning by doing*. Based on, among other things, empirical evidence that productivity in the airframe industry increased regularly with the number of airframes produced, Arrow had suggested, more generally, that technological progress was an increasing function of cumulative gross investment—an unintended, though welcome, by-product of production.

If learning by doing were pervasive, then the economy as a whole would display increasing returns to scale. In contrast to typical cases, these increasing returns would be compatible with perfect competition, because the private marginal productivity of capital is less than its social marginal productivity—learning provides a positive externality uncompensated by the market. Since it did not threaten perfect competition, learning by doing was easy to slot into the neoclassical growth model (see Solow 1967, 38–41).

Levhari's and Sheshinski's models, like Arrow's (1962a) model, generated the surprising result that the rate of output growth is proportional to the rate of population growth. The mechanism is that increasing population stimulates output, which in turn stimulates technical progress (the more doing, the more learning). But diminishing returns to past investment implies that the rate of technical progress must converge to a unique rate compatible with a steady-state growth path, in the same way that capital per head must converge to a unique steady-state rate in an ordinary growth model with diminishing returns to capital. A higher population growth rate that raises the rate of technical progress acts like a higher savings rate that raises capital per head. If population growth stops, then the steady-state rate of output growth falls to zero—with labor input not growing, neither does capital, so that technical progress itself stops.

Solow discussed Arrow's model in detail in Economics 14.123 (Advanced Economic Theory) in 1962 (Burmeister 1962). He extended the model to the "linear" case in which there are no diminishing returns to accumulated production experience—a case that Arrow (1962a, 159) had mentioned but not explored. Burmeister (1962) records in his class notes: "now the savings rate determines the rate of growth." Solow made little of the linear case, which played no part in his survey of production theory (Solow 1967), but it proved to be a touchstone for the "new growth theory" thirty years later (Solow 1997).

While key work on technical progress came out of Stanford (Arrow) and later Chicago (where Uzawa had relocated from Stanford), MIT students remained important players. Shell (2001, 709) recalls: "One summer . . . Hiro [Uzawa] borrowed a dozen students, taking them to Chicago." Although, Shell continues, "friendships and rivalries were strengthened in the Chicago heat," Uzawa wrote to Lionel McKenzie, "I am afraid [the Chicago 1965] seminar might not have had any particular impact upon the students who visited from MIT" (undated memo from Uzawa to McKenzie, Solow Papers, box 58). Underwriting this assessment, Uzawa observed, "I have been enjoying my association with the group of MIT students. We have been working on a couple of projects on economic growth, although none of us have come up with anything concrete" (Uzawa to Solow, June 18, 1965, Solow Papers, box 61). But still, he was "particularly impressed by Joe Stiglitz."

Stiglitz's paper titled "Towards an Endogenous Theory of Technological Change" was presented during his academic year visiting Cambridge University (1965–66) (Stiglitz to Solow, November 2, 1965, Solow Papers, box 60). But the paper did not form part of Stiglitz's doctoral dissertation and was never published.

Shell's (1966, 68) remark in the conclusion to his AEA conference paper characterizes the third stream of research on technical progress—privately motivated research and development:

> The recent contribution of Kennedy warns us that additions to technical knowledge should not be thought of as increasing efficiency in any specified way. That is, the "bias of technical progress," whether in a stylized [competitive] economy or in a planned economy, should be a subject for economic decision.

Nordhaus (1969a), who had already addressed other aspects of technical progress in his doctoral dissertation in 1967, was the first MIT economist to take up the Kennedy-Shell challenge. Nordhaus focused on the role of an inventor, who has a monopoly over his invention for a limited period of time (a patent). The "crucial" and "questionable" assumption of the model is the relationship between the inventive input and the rate of technical change (Nordhaus 1969a, 21). The rate of growth of technology was modeled as directly related under diminishing returns to the number of inventions and inversely related to the level of technology. Through an analogous mechanism to the one by which the rate of population growth limits the rate of technical progress, the rate of output growth in Nordhaus's model limits the rate of invention. The incompatibility between a competitive market and increasing returns to scale is resolved because "information is temporarily monopolized" through patents (24). When Nordhaus presented his paper at the AEA meetings in December 1968, one discussant pointed to a cognitive dissonance: such concepts as a long-run balanced-growth path and a termination of the inventive process because of the end of population growth "do not really belong to [Nordhaus's] Schumpeterian world" (Domar 1969, 44). The other discussant defended the notion of a stable production function for technology (Stiglitz 1969, 46), which had also been attacked earlier in the session by Arrow (1969, 34).

6. The Ebb Tide of MIT Growth Theory

For the fifteen years after Solow and Swan introduced the neoclassical growth model, growth economics was a dominant field, and the MIT economics department was its beating heart. E. Roy Weintraub (1991) has described the process through which a field comes to be defined and delimited as *stabilization*. Growth economics provides a perfect case study. From the 1930s until the advent of the neoclassical growth model in 1956, growth economics had been exploratory in character, mixing various analytical strategies and substantive concerns in a heterogeneous brew. By the early 1950s development economists had begun to adopt the Harrod-Domar model as a standard approach. The neoclassical growth model challenged the analytical framework of the Harrod-Domar model, while Solow's (1957) empirical investigation based on the neoclassical growth model challenged the widespread understanding that economic growth was principally the result of investment in physical capital. The next fifteen years can be thought of as a contest between frameworks (e.g., neoclassical vs. Harrod-Domar, and neoclassical vs. Cambridge, UK; see Backhouse, this volume, "The Other Cambridge") and a process of delimiting the range of applications for different approaches. This is well illustrated by the interests and approaches of the MIT economics department and CENIS. Stabilization was, in part, a (not perfectly complete) division of labor between the methodological contribution of the department (simple, precise, formal models) and the substantive, empirical interests of the development economists and, in part, a definition of domains, with development economics and the growth economics of the already developed countries coming to be defined as distinct and separable problems.

The process of stabilization throws up some characteristic markers. Already by the mid-1960s, Hahn and R. C. O. Matthews (1964) had published a famous and influential survey article—which, in fact, was issued as part of a hardcover book as well. At the same time, neoclassical growth economics became sufficiently intellectually secure that it was incorporated into Samuelson's undergraduate textbook. By the end of the 1960s, a canon had been established: in 1968–69 Solow's (1970) Radcliffe Lectures at the University of Warwick offered a consolidated account of the state of growth economics.[14] Anthologies of important articles on growth began to be published (Stiglitz and Uzawa 1969; Sen 1970). And the

14. Solow's Radcliffe Lectures follow very closely a set of lectures that he developed for his MIT course (Solow 1966).

appearance of the first graduate textbook (by two MIT PhDs), Burmeister and Dobell's *Mathematical Theories of Economic Growth* (1970), began to standardize instruction for the next generation (see also Wan 1971 [Wan was an MIT PhD] and Teixeira, this volume). Growth economics had never been an exclusively MIT project, but many of these stabilizing activities were centered at MIT, and MIT students and affiliates rapidly filled the ranks of economics departments around the world.

The future looked bright. Solow's foreword to Burmeister and Dobell's (1970, viii–ix) graduate textbook suggested that growth theorists faced a busy agenda of important problems. Yet, in retrospect, the end of the 1960s marked the high tide of growth economics. Just as the field appeared to stabilize, it also began to ebb as a preeminent research program. Why?

First, the political climate had changed radically. The Cold War and growthmanship of 1960 had yielded to the first Earth Day and environmentalism of 1970. The publication of the Club of Rome's report *The Limits to Growth*—the product of a research group in MIT's Sloan School of Management—exemplified the shift in mood (Meadows et al. 1972; see also Arndt 1978 and Collins 2000). Growth was increasingly viewed not as the optimistic project of "lifting all boats" but as a threat to life itself.[15]

A second reason for the ebbing of growth economics was the business cycle. Macroeconomic management in the Kennedy and Johnson administrations appeared to be a success. The business cycle expansion that started in 1961 proved to be the longest in US history up to that time. Economists began to ask, "Is the business cycle obsolete?" (Bronfenbrenner 1969). Such questions are leading indicators of a crash: the boom ended in December 1969. The commodity price boom, the first oil crisis of 1973, Nixon's price controls, and the perceived failure of "Keynesian" macroeconometric models to account for the stagflation of the early 1970s moved short-run macroeconomic analysis to the fore. In the sixth edition of *Economics*, Samuelson (1964, 722) had added the sentence,

15. The economics department did not simply capitulate to its colleagues in the Sloan School. Drawing on his well-developed expertise in the characteristics of the kind of multi-equation linear models that informed the *Limits to Growth*, Solow (1973) argued that the crash states that it predicted were built into its modeling assumptions independently of the empirical facts of the world and that it ignored basic economics: as resources became scarcer, their prices would rise, leading both to economies in use and to substitution into alternative factors of production. Solow's criticisms of the Harrod-Domar model found a new target. Nordhaus and Tobin (1972) and Samuelson (1976, 814–17) similarly rejected the doomsday scenarios and reaffirmed the possibility of continued growth. Nordhaus's shift into natural resources economics and climate change was a reflection that externalities are an important phenomenon, but whereas his earlier work on technical progress was on positive externalities, the later was on negative externalities (e-mail from Nordhaus to Boianovsky, May 18, 2013).

"The key word in most economic discussions these days is 'growth.'" In the ninth edition, he not only dropped the sentence but suggested that a short course could omit the chapter on growth altogether (Samuelson 1973, 731).

A third reason for the ebbing of growth economics was frustration that its early promise—precise formal models that would illuminate policy—had not been redeemed. Research strategies ran up against a variety of intellectual barriers. For example:

- For all its supposed importance and for all the effort put into modeling it, Solow (1970, 76) concluded that "very little is known about the exact connection between research expenditure and actual technological progress." Indeed, endogenous growth models put forward by Shell, Nordhaus, Levhari, and Sheshinski at MIT in the 1960s were largely invisible in the renditions of growth economics offered by Solow (1970) and Burmeister and Dobell (1970).
- One of the supposedly great advantages of the neoclassical growth model over the Harrod-Domar model was that it displayed a stable steady-state growth path. Thus, when saddle-point instability was first discovered it was thought to be "potentially fatal" to the whole theory (Dixit 1990, 6).
- Referring to the development of endogenous growth models, Stiglitz (1990, 55) recalled the "stumbling blocks" related to nonconvexities in the production function: "We knew how to construct models that 'worked,' but we felt uneasy making special assumptions" to guarantee the existence of a steady state. Sheshinski wrote that "we already knew in 1965 that a production function linear in capital leads to endogenous growth rate. But this was unattractive because of the knife-edge properties (lack of stability)" (e-mail from Sheshinski to Boianovsky, March 3, 2013). Nonconvexities are incompatible with perfect competition, but there were no aggregative models of imperfect competition available in the 1960s (cf. Nordhaus 1969b, 113).[16]

Finally, and related to the third reason, a point is reached in the history of any field when—for some time, at least—its progress slows markedly. Hahn and Matthews (1964, 890) had detected the signs early:

16. Solow (1956, 71–72) considered the possibility that the marginal product is bounded away from zero (and labor, therefore, is not essential for production). In this case, similarly to the so-called *AK* growth models of the 1990s, the long-run rate of growth becomes endogenous in respect to savings behavior. Such a "pathological" possibility was discussed by Burmeister and Dobell (1970, 33–34), but dismissed as empirically implausible.

> While not disparaging the insights that have been gained, we feel that in these areas the point of diminishing returns may have been reached. Nothing is easier than to ring the changes on more and more complicated models, without bringing in any really new ideas and without bringing the theory any nearer to casting light on the causes of the wealth of nations. The problems posed may well have intellectual fascination. But it is essentially a frivolous occupation to take a chain with links of very uneven strength and devote one's energies to strengthening and polishing the links that are already relatively strong.

Six years later, Solow (1970, 105) still argued that the effort was "not a game." Yet by 1978 he had thrown in the towel, noting the "definite signs that [growth theory] is just about played out. . . . Growth theory is now an unpromising pond for an enterprising theorist to fish in" (quoted in Solow 1991, 393).

The early 1970s did not prove to be the end of growth economics at MIT or elsewhere. Work continued on growth theory, albeit at a lower level. Development economists and specialists in productivity and technology continued to advance empirical studies. But for the time being, growth economics was no longer the field in which stellar reputations were forged. Yet intellectual tides are like natural tides: they flow as well as ebb. Growth theory revived in the mid-1980s in the work of Paul Romer (1986) and Robert Lucas (1988), as well as many others. They addressed many of the same issues that had animated the growthmen of the 1960s, but the center of growth economics was no longer the banks of the Charles River but the shores of Lake Michigan.

References

Akerlof, G. 1966. "Wages and Capital." PhD thesis, MIT.

Arndt, H. W. 1978. *The Rise and Fall of Economic Growth*. Melbourne: Longman Cheshire.

Arrow, K. 1962a. "The Economic Implications of Learning by Doing." *Review of Economic Studies* 29:155–73.

———. 1962b. "Economic Welfare and the Allocation of Resources for Invention." In *The Rate and Direction of Inventive Activity: Economic and Social Factors*, 609–25. Princeton, N.J.: Princeton University Press for NBER.

———. 1969. "Classificatory Notes on the Production and Transmission of Technological Knowledge." *American Economic Review* 59:29–35.

Boianovsky, M. 2010. "A View from the Tropics: Celso Furtado and the Theory of Economic Development in the 1950s." *History of Political Economy* 42:221–66.

Boianovsky, M., and K. D. Hoover. 2009a. "The Neoclassical Growth Model and Twentieth-Century Economics." In Boianovsky and Hoover 2009b, 1–23.
———, eds. 2009b. *Robert Solow and the Development of Growth Economics*. Supplemental issue to vol. 41 of *History of Political Economy*. Durham, N.C.: Duke University Press.
Bronfenbrenner, M., ed. 1969. *Is the Business Cycle Obsolete?* New York: Wiley.
Burmeister, E. 1962. Lecture notes, Solow's Advanced Economic Theory 14.123. Edwin Burmeister Papers, Economists' Papers Project, David M. Rubenstein Rare Book and Manuscript Library, Duke University.
———. 1965. "Stability and Causality in Two-Sector Models of Economic Growth." PhD thesis, MIT.
———. 2009. "Reflections." In Boianovsky and Hoover 2009b, 35–43.
Burmeister, E., and A. R. Dobell. 1970. *Mathematical Theories of Economic Growth*. London: Macmillan.
Chakravarty, S. 1969. *Capital and Development Planning*. Cambridge, Mass.: MIT Press.
Collins, R. M. 2000. *More: The Politics of Economic Growth in Postwar America*. New York: Oxford University Press.
Diamond, P. 1963. "Essays on Optimal Economic Growth." PhD thesis, MIT.
———. 1965. "National Debt in a Neoclassical Growth Model." *American Economic Review* 55:1126–50.
———, ed. 1990. *Growth/Productivity/Unemployment: Essays to Celebrate Bob Solow's Birthday*. Cambridge, Mass.: MIT Press.
Dimand, R. W., and B. J. Spencer. 2009. "Trevor Swan and the Neoclassical Growth Model." In Boianovsky and Hoover 2009b, 107–26.
Dixit, A. 1968a. "Development Planning in a Dual Economy." PhD thesis, MIT.
———. 1968b. "Optimal Development in the Labour-Surplus Economy." *Review of Economic Studies* 35:23–34.
———. 1973. "Models of Dual Economies." In Mirrlees and Stern 1973, 325–52.
———. 1990. "Growth Theory after Thirty Years." In Diamond 1990, 4–22.
Domar, Evsey D. 1946. "Capital Expansion, Rate of Growth, and Employment." *Econometrica* 14 (2): 137–47.
———. 1957. *Essays in the Theory of Economic Growth*. New York: Oxford University Press.
———. 1961. "On the Measurement of Technological Change." *Economic Journal* 71:709–29.
———. 1969. "Discussion." *American Economic Review* 59:44–46.
Dorfman, R., P. Samuelson, and R. Solow. 1958. *Linear Programming and Economic Analysis*. New York: McGraw-Hill.
Duarte, P. G. 2009. "The Growing of Ramsey's Growth Model." In *Robert Solow and the Development of Growth Economics*, edited by Mauro Boianovsky and Kevin D. Hoover. *History of Political Economy* 41 (supplement): 161–81.
———. 2012. "Beyond Samuelson's Chapter on Ramsey." *History of Economic Ideas* 18:121–59.

Duarte, P. G., and K. D. Hoover. 2012. "Observing Shocks." In *Observing the Economy: Historical Perspectives*, edited by Harro Maas and Mary S. Morgan. *History of Political Economy* 44 (supplement): 226–49.

Findlay, R. 1960. "Essays on Some Theoretical Aspects of Economic Growth." PhD thesis, MIT.

Foley, D. K., and M. Sidrauski. 1970. "Portfolio Choice, Investment, and Growth." *American Economic Review* 60:44–63.

———. 1971. *Monetary and Fiscal Policy in a Growing Economy*. New York: Macmillan.

Hahn, F. H. 1968. Review of Shell 1967a. *American Economic Review* 58:561–65.

Hahn, F. H., and R. C. O. Matthews. 1964. "The Theory of Economic Growth: A Survey." *Economic Journal* 74:779–902.

Halsmayer, V., and K. D. Hoover. 2013. "Solow's Harrod: Transforming Cyclical Dynamics into a Model of Long-Run Growth." Working Paper 2013-02, Center for the History of Political Economy at Duke University.

Harrod, Roy F. 1939. "An Essay in Dynamic Theory." *Economic Journal* 49:14–33.

———. 1948. *Towards a Dynamic Economics*. London: Macmillan.

Hartley, J. E., K. D. Hoover, and K. D. Salyer. 1997. "The Limits of Business Cycle Research: Assessing the Real-Business-Cycle Model." *Oxford Review of Economic Policy* 13:34–54.

———. 1998. "The Limits of Business Cycle Research." In *Real Business Cycles: A Reader*, edited by J. E. Hartley, K. D. Hoover, and K. D. Salyer, 3–42. London: Routledge.

Hoover, K. D., and M. E. Dowell. 2002. "Measuring Causes: Episodes in the Quantitative Assessment of the Value of Money." In *The Age of Economic Measurement*, edited by Judy L. Klein and Mary S. Morgan. *History of Political Economy* 33 (supplement): 137–61.

Kaldor, N. 1961. "Capital Accumulation and Economic Growth." In *The Theory of Capital*, edited by F. Lutz, 177–222. London: Macmillan.

Kennedy, C. 1964. "Induced Bias in Innovation and the Theory of Distribution." *Economic Journal* 74:541–47.

Kindleberger, C. (1958) 1965. *Economic Development*. 2nd ed. New York: McGraw-Hill.

Levhari, D. 1964. "Essays on Optimal Economic Growth." PhD thesis, MIT.

———. 1966a. "Extensions of Arrow's Learning by Doing." *Review of Economic Studies* 33:117–31.

———. 1966b. "Further Implications of Learning by Doing." *Review of Economic Studies* 33:31–38.

Lewis, A. 1954. "Economic Development with Unlimited Supplies of Labour." *Manchester School* 22:139–91.

Lodewijks, J. 1991. "Rostow, Developing Economies, and National Security Policy." In *Economics and National Security: A History of Their Interaction*, edited by C. D. Goodwin. *History of Political Economy* 23 (supplement): 285–310.

Lucas, R. E., Jr. 1988. "On the Mechanics of Economic Development." *Journal of Monetary Economics* 22:3–42.

Marglin, S. 1967. "The Rate of Interest and the Value of Capital with Unlimited Supplies of Labour." In Shell 1967a, 141–63.

Maruyama, M. 1960. "Morphogenesis and Morphostasis." *Methodos* 12:251–96.

McKenzie, L. 1999. "The First Conferences on the Theory of Economic Growth." Working Paper 459, Rochester Center for Economic Research.

Meade, J. (1961) 1962. *A Neo-classical Theory of Economic Growth*. 2nd ed. London: Unwin.

———. 1968. *The Growing Economy*. London: Allen and Unwin.

Meadows, D. H., D. L. Meadows, J. Randers, and W. W. Behrens. 1972. *The Limits to Growth*. New York: Universe.

Mirrlees, J., and N. Stern, eds. 1973. *Models of Economic Growth*. New York: Wiley.

Neher, P. 1971. *Economic Growth and Development: A Mathematical Introduction*. New York: John Wiley and Sons.

Nordhaus, W. D. 1967a. "The Optimal Rate and Direction of Technical Change." In Shell 1967a, 53–66.

———. 1967b. "A Theory of Endogenous Technological Change." PhD thesis, MIT.

———. 1969a. "An Economic Theory of Technical Change." *American Economic Review* 59:18–28.

———. 1969b. *Invention, Growth, and Welfare*. Cambridge, Mass.: MIT Press.

Nordhaus, W. D., and J. Tobin. 1972. "Is Growth Obsolete?" In *Economic Growth*, vol. 5 of *Economic Research: Retrospect and Prospect*, 1–80. New York: NBER.

Pearce, I. F. 1962. "The End of the Golden Age in Solovia: A Further Fable for Growthmen Hoping to Be 'One Up' on Oiko." *American Economic Review* 52 (5): 1088–97.

Pearce, K. A., and K. D. Hoover. 1995. "After the Revolution: Paul Samuelson and the Textbook Keynesian Model." In *New Perspectives on Keynes*, edited by A. F. Cottrell and M. S. Lawlor. *History of Political Economy* 27 (supplement): 183–216.

Phelps, E. S. 1961. "The Golden Rule of Accumulation: A Fable for Growthmen." *American Economic Review* 51:638–43.

———. 1962. "The New View of Investment: A Neoclassical Analysis." *Quarterly Journal of Economics* 78:548–67.

Pontryagin, J. S., et al. 1962. *The Mathematical Theory of Optimal Processes*. Translated by K. W. Trirogoff. New York: International Publishers.

Ramsey, F. P. 1928. "A Mathematical Theory of Saving." *Economic Journal* 38:543–59.

Romer, P. M. 1986. "Increasing Returns and Long-Run Growth." *Journal of Political Economy* 94:1002–37.

Rosenstein-Rodan, P. 1943. "Problems of Industrialization of Eastern and Southeastern Europe." *Economic Journal* 53:202–11.

———. 1957. "Notes on the Theory of the 'Big Push.'" Center for International Studies, MIT.

———. 1961. "Notes on the Theory of the 'Big Push.'" In *Economic Development of Latin America*, edited by H. S. Ellis and H. C. Wallich, 57–67. London: Macmillan.

Rostow, W. W. 1956. "The Take-off into Self-Sustained Growth." *Economic Journal* 66:25–48.

———. 1960. *The Stages of Economic Growth: A Non-Communist Manifesto*. Cambridge: Cambridge University Press.

———, ed. 1963. *The Economics of Take-off into Sustained Growth*. London: Macmillan.

———. 1984. "Development: The Political Economy of the Marshallian Long-Period." In *Pioneers in Development*, ed. G. M. Meier and D. Seers, 229–61. New York: Oxford University Press.

Samuelson, P. A. 1948a. *Economics: An Introductory Analysis*. New York: McGraw-Hill.

———. 1948b. "International Trade and Equalisation of Factor Prices." *Economic Journal* 58:163–84.

———. 1955. *Economics: An Introductory Analysis*. 3rd ed. New York: McGraw-Hill.

———. (1956) 1969. "Public Responsibility for Growth and Stability." In *The Goal of Economic Growth*, edited by E. S. Phelps, 70–73. 2nd ed. New York: Norton.

———. 1958. "An Exact Consumption-Loan Model with or without the Social Contrivance of Money." *Journal of Political Economy* 66:467–82.

———. 1961. *Economics: An Introductory Analysis*. 5th ed. New York: McGraw-Hill.

———. 1964. *Economics: An Introductory Analysis*. 6th ed. New York: McGraw-Hill.

———. 1965a. "A Catenary Turnpike Theorem involving Consumption and the Golden Rule." *American Economic Review* 55:486–96.

———. 1965b. "A Theory of Induced Innovations along Kennedy-Weizsäcker Lines." *Review of Economics and Statistics* 47:343–56.

———. 1966. "Rejoinder: Agreements, Disagreements, Doubts, and the Case of Induced Harrod-Neutral Technical Change." *Review of Economics and Statistics* 48:444–48.

———. 1967. *Economics: An Introductory Analysis*. 7th ed. New York: McGraw-Hill.

———. 1973. *Economics*. 9th ed. New York: McGraw-Hill.

———. 1976. *Economics*. 10th ed. New York: McGraw-Hill.

———. 2001. "Sparks and Grit from the Anvil of Growth." In *Frontiers of Development Economics*, edited by G. Meier and J. Stiglitz, 492–505. New York: Oxford University Press.

Schumpeter, J. A. (1911) 1934. *The Theory of Economic Development: An Inquiry into Profits, Capital, Credit, Interest, and the Business Cycle*. Cambridge, Mass.: Harvard University Press.

———. 1942. *Capitalism, Socialism, and Democracy*. New York: Harper and Brothers.

Sen, A. K. 1970. *Growth Economics: Selected Readings*. London: Penguin.

Shell, K. 1966. "Toward a Theory of Inventive Activity and Capital Accumulation." *American Economic Review* 56:62–68.

———, ed. 1967a. *Essays on the Theory of Optimal Economic Growth*. Cambridge, Mass.: MIT Press.

———. 1967b. "A Model of Inventive Activity and Capital Accumulation." In Shell 1967a, 67–85.

———. 2001. "An Interview with Karl Shell [by Stephen E. Spear and Randall Wright]." *Macroeconomic Dynamics* 5 (5): 701–41.

Sheshinski, E. 1966. "Essays on the Theory of Production and Technical Progress." PhD thesis, MIT.
———. 1967a. "Optimal Accumulation with Learning by Doing." In Shell 1967a, 31–52.
———. 1967b. "Tests of the 'Learning by Doing' Hypothesis." *Review of Economics and Statistics* 49:568–78.
———. 1990. "Comments: Fixed Costs in Investment Theory." In Diamond 1990, 41–49.
Solow, R. M. 1956. "A Contribution to the Theory of Economic Growth." *Quarterly Journal of Economics* 70:65–94.
———. 1957. "Technical Change and the Aggregate Production Function." *Review of Economics and Statistics* 39:748–62.
———. 1960. "Investment and Technical Progress." In *Mathematical Methods in the Social Sciences 1959*, edited by K. J. Arrow and S. Karbin, 89–104. Stanford, Calif.: Stanford University Press.
———. 1962. "Technical Progress, Capital Formation, and Economic Growth." *American Economic Review* 52:76–86.
———. (1962) 1964. "Economic Growth." In *Economic Growth: An American Problem*, edited P. M. Gutmann, 101–15. Englewood Cliffs, N.J.: Prentice-Hall.
———. 1966. "Lectures on Growth Theory." Typed manuscript. Robert M. Solow Papers, Economists' Papers Project, David M. Rubenstein Rare Book and Manuscript Library, Duke University.
———. 1967. "Some Recent Developments in the Theory of Production." In *The Theory and Empirical Analysis of Production*, edited by M. Brown, 25–50. New York: NBER.
———. (1968) 1969. "Fixed Investment and Economic Growth." In *The Goal of Economic Growth*, edited by E. S. Phelps, 90–105. New York: Norton.
———. 1970. *Growth Theory—an Exposition*. New York: Oxford University Press.
———. 1973. "Is the End of the World at Hand?" *Challenge* 16:39–50.
———. 1983. "Modern Capital Theory." In *Paul Samuelson and Modern Economic Theory*, edited by E. C. Brown and R. M. Solow, 169–87. New York: McGraw-Hill.
———. 1991. "Growth Theory." In *Companion to Contemporary Economic Thought*, edited by D. Greenaway, M. Bleaney, and I. Stewart, 393–415. London: Routledge.
———. 1997. *Learning from "Learning by Doing": Lessons for Economic Growth*. Stanford, Calif.: Stanford University Press.
———. 2000. "The Kennedy Council and the Long Run." In *Economic Events, Ideas, and Policies: The 1960s and after*, edited by G. L. Perry and J. Tobin, 111–13. Washington, D.C.: Brookings Institution.
Stiglitz, J. 1966. "Studies in the Theory of Economic Growth and Income Distribution." PhD thesis, MIT.
———. 1969. "Discussion." *American Economic Review* 59:46–49.
———. 1990. "Comments: Some Retrospective Views on Growth Theory." In Diamond 1990, 50–68.

Stiglitz, J., and H. Uzawa, eds. 1969. *Readings in the Modern Theory of Economic Growth*. Cambridge, Mass.: MIT Press.

Swan, T. W. 1956. "Economic Growth and Capital Accumulation." *Economic Record* 32:334–61.

Tobin, J. 1964. "Economic Growth as an Objective of Government Policy." *American Economic Review* 54:1–20.

Uzawa, H. 1965. "Optimum Technical Change in an Aggregative Model of Economic Growth." *International Economic Review* 6:18–31.

Wan, H. Y., Jr. 1971. *Economic Growth*. New York: Harcourt Brace Jovanovich.

Warsh, D. 2006. *Knowledge and the Wealth of Nations: A Story of Economic Discovery*. New York: Norton.

Weintraub, E. R. 1991. *Stabilizing Dynamics: Constructing Economic Knowledge*. Cambridge: Cambridge University Press.

Wulwick, N. J. 1995. "The Hamiltonian Formalism and Optimal Growth Theory." In *Measurement, Quantification, and Economic Analysis: Numeracy in Economics*, ed. by I. Rima, 406–35. London: Routledge.

From Exploratory Modeling to Technical Expertise: Solow's Growth Model as a Multipurpose Design

Verena Halsmayer

On January 10, 1954, the journalist and author Godfrey Blunden sent a letter to Harold Isaacs, a member of the Department of Political Science at MIT, asking for help on a novel he planned to write:

> The novel . . . is about some New York and Connecticut people, among them a mathematician. I have got involved in the notion that in a highly mechanised society the "pure" mathematician is pretty much under pressure from the physicists, economists and statisticians to produce new theorems which may be of practical use in the applied fields. . . . I am thinking of a theorem, or a calculus, as fundamental to the analysis of our social economy as the Archimedian geometry was to the great builders, the infinitesimal calculus to the age of motion, the theory of

Correspondence may be addressed to Verena Halsmayer, DK The Sciences in Context, Maria-Theresien-Straße 3/27, 1090 Vienna, Austria; e-mail: verena.halsmayer@univie.ac.at. For his many helpful suggestions and motivating advice, I want to thank Marcel Boumans. I am especially grateful to Robert Solow for granting me an interview and commenting on a previous draft of this article. I gratefully acknowledge the suggestions I received from Mary S. Morgan as well as from the participants at the *HOPE* conference "MIT and the Transformation of American Economics," especially those from Roger E. Backhouse, Edwin Burmeister, Kevin D. Hoover, Harro Maas, and E. Roy Weintraub. The research for this article was conducted during my stay at Duke's Center for the History of Political Economy, where I profited from discussions with faculty and fellows. For their professional support during my work on the Solow Papers, I am thankful to the archivists at the David M. Rubenstein Rare Book and Manuscript Library, Duke University.

History of Political Economy 46 (annual suppl.) DOI 10.1215/00182702-2716181

> relativity to the atomic physicists. Which is the same thing as saying that a mathematician may (or may fail) to answer some deep need in his society. . . . I just want to see how they do it. In other words I want to have a look at the kind of thing my man might be expected to turn out.[1]

Isaacs forwarded Blunden's letter to Robert M. Solow, a colleague in the economics department. Solow thought himself the right person to answer Blunden's question, since "the area where economic theory, mathematics, and statistics run together is exactly my line of work." Contrary to Blunden's suggestion, Solow did not emphasize the great advantages of "pure mathematics" in economics but instead pointed out the difficulties that arise when formulating "complicated economic systems in mathematical terms":

> What holds up the analysis is not any gaps in mathematical knowledge. . . . Nor is it the lack of large-scale computing machinery. The bottleneck is that the functions and relationships that make up a theoretical model have to be given some empirical form and content. Information of this kind has to come from observation and statistical calculation. But it takes a year to get a year's figures on consumption and investment and inventories and so forth. And it takes many years' figures before any statistical sense can be made: the irregular, non-systematic element in economic life is far from trivial. And by the time the years have passed, the quantities and relations one is trying to estimate will probably have changed in some substantial but unknown way. The mathematics that appears in modern economic theory is by no means elementary; but it seems unlikely that any purely mathematical discovery would set economics on its ear.[2]

According to Solow, mathematical knowledge was indeed useful for economic analysis in a "highly mechanised society," but the crucial aspect of economic research was the empirical content given to a mathematical model. However, as Solow knew from his own experience, empirical research was tedious, time- and cost-intensive. At the time of writing the letter, he was engaged in research on dynamic programming and linear modeling. Only two years later Solow published "a simple model" in his

1. Blunden to Isaacs, January 10, 1954, box 53, file B: 7 of 7, Robert M. Solow Papers, David M. Rubenstein Rare Book and Manuscript Library, Duke University. Unless otherwise indicated, all archival material cited is taken from the Solow Papers.

2. Solow to Blunden, January 26, 1954, box 53, file B: 7 of 7.

"Contribution to the Theory of Economic Growth." This model was not the first to show a balanced growth path not entirely dependent on capital accumulation. Neither was his empirical model published in 1957 the first to claim that productivity growth in the United States had come from the contribution of a residual (see Crafts 2009, 200). Instead, what set Solow's model apart from earlier contributions was the form of the object he created: a simple, clean, and tractable, yet fully articulated and empirically usable, artifact.[3] It became the standard growth model of neoclassical macroeconomics, an "engine of research" that was easy to use, adopt, extend, and apply in a variety of different projects (see Boianovsky and Hoover, this volume).[4]

My aim in the present article is to understand what made constructing and using such a model plausible, and what this way of doing economics might have signified. Combining concrete policy-oriented modeling strategies of World War II with what was received as traditional neoclassical theory, Solow's model developed as a "design" that came to serve multiple purposes. In what follows I focus on the various uses that Solow's design model was put to, the associated modeling practices, and the respective professional identity of the economist as—what Solow called in retrospect—an "engineer in the design sense."[5]

Godfrey Blunden never finished his novel. Had he done so, he might have told the story of the postwar development of a specific way of doing economics, one that combined simple mathematical models with econometrics, but was less complex, and less laborious, than large-scale empirical research. A way of doing economics that created small and tractable

3. The same year, Trevor Swan published a very similar model. When eventually getting to know Swan's work, Solow was intrigued: "I must tell you that I can't remember when I've enjoyed a piece of economics so much. It was sheer pleasure" (Solow to Swan, April 1, 1957, box 60, file S: 2 of 7). However, priority is not at issue in the present article; Swan's work was not part of Solow's background. The fact that the model was initially coined "the Solow model" is itself a question of crediting that is, in turn, linked to MIT's becoming one of the centers of economics in the second half of the twentieth century.

4. Solow, interview with author, May 3, 2011. My analysis builds on recent literature on economic modeling as a practice, and the notion of economic models as quasi-material objects: Morgan 2012, Boumans 2005, and Morrison and Morgan 1999. On the social construction of economic models, see Breslau and Yonay 1999; on the somewhat related notion of (techno)scientific objects, see Nordmann 2011 and Bensaude-Vincent et al. 2011; on material models, see Chadarevian and Hopwood 2004.

5. Historicizing and contextualizing Solow's modeling practice will provide a complementary account to the existing literature on growth theory. On the theoretical development of growth economics, see for instance the contributions in Boianovsky and Hoover 2009; Harcourt 2006, chap. 7; and Sen 1970.

artifacts that were easy to investigate, to extend, and to apply, yet embodied high hopes of producing useful and practical knowledge for economic governance.

1. The "Collapsed Production Function"

We might, when we look at economic modeling as a research practice that consists in the construction of artifacts, through tracking the components of a specific model, get a grip on the specificities of the model as well as on the context out of which it developed. The "collapsed production function" was a major component of Solow's 1956 model. In 1948 and 1949, while a graduate student in economics at Harvard, Solow worked at the Harvard Economic Research Project (HERP), calculating the first set of capital coefficients for input-output models.[6] In the late 1940s input-output research at HERP was directed at investigating the feasibility of wartime mobilization plans.[7] To that end, Wassily Leontief and his assistants produced large input-output tables of five hundred economic sectors that were meant to "visualize" the national economy as a system of industries mutually interrelated via their "capital structure." The data stemmed from what Leontief (1953, 14) described as "direct empirical information": in addition to corporation and government agency reports, papers in trade journals, and engineering handbooks, HERP gathered data from production officials, design engineers, technicians, and other experts.[8] Turned into matrix form, the input-output tables enabled the formulation of linear equations systems of so-called technical production functions with linear technologies. These were understood to provide a "more realistic" account of production than the smooth differentiable production function of "traditional neoclassical theory" (see Mirowski 1989, chap. 6; Boumans 2012, 8; Backhouse 2012b, 42).[9]

6. See Solow 1987 as well as Leontief 1953, vii. The HERP had been established on grounds of the collaboration between the US Bureau of Labor Statistics with Leontief and his input-output analysis and was financed by the Air Force–funded interagency project SCOOP (see Kohli 2001, 205).

7. Preliminary Report of the Final Progress Report 1950, Leontief Papers, HUG 4517.5, box 8, folder: Progress Reports, Wassily Leontief Papers, Faculty Archives, Collections of the Harvard University Archives.

8. For an insider's account of how research at the HERP was done, see Carter 2012.

9. The label *traditional theory* referred to the received theory of production from the 1930s, consisting basically of Gustav Cassel's version of the Walrasian system. Solow, for instance, mentioned Schneider 1934 as one of the most commonly used textbooks at the time (Solow, interview with author, May 3, 2011).

This concern with observing and measuring was abandoned at the Cowles Commission's Activity Analysis Conference of 1949. At the same time that Solow calculated capital coefficients at HERP, Tjalling C. Koopmans, recently appointed research director of the Cowles Commission, organized a conference, financed by the RAND Corporation, that brought together over fifty participants from different fields.[10] The conference aspired to show the "unity of [the participants'] major lines of thought" in what was considered the fundamental problem of "normative economics: the best allocation of limited means toward desired ends" (Koopmans 1951, 1). Linear programming techniques had recently been developed in wartime research to work out efficient ways to achieve specified objectives. The major aim of the conference participants was now to investigate how far these techniques might shed new light on traditional economic theory. The production of a whole economy was looked at as an "efficient combination of activities" (Koopmans 1951, 33) in the form of a system of linear equations where commodities are transformed into each other at constant returns to scale.

There was a certain tension at the conference: on the one hand, if one approach was dominant, it was Leontief's input-output analysis. On the other hand, Leontief's most prominent concern, namely, how to gather and deal with data to give "a description of the capital structure of the economy,"[11] was almost absent (see Backhouse 2012b, 29–34). Since HERP's capital coefficients were taken to be given by engineers and therefore would not change, they entered input-output analysis as fixed. The participants of the Activity Analysis Conference considered the fixed coefficient form too narrow an assumption, thereby brushing aside the issue of measurement. Paul Samuelson (1951, 142–43), for instance, redefined the fixed coefficients as equilibrium positions: "*All desirable substitutions have already been made by the competitive market*, and no variation in the

10. William Thomas (this volume) also provides a short account of the conference and shows how economists selectively used OR's decision models to model economic dynamics. Till Düppe and E. Roy Weintraub (2014) focus on the emergence of a new community of mathematical economists that took mathematical values of rigor and axiomatization for granted while disengaging with the intellectual values that had shaped economics departments before World War II. Backhouse (2012b) puts Paul Samuelson's relation to the conference in the center and shows that he had been working on the relationship between linear models and smooth, differentiable production function models since he started at RAND in 1949. On operations research, see also Judy L. Klein's work, for instance Klein 2001, and Erickson et al. 2013.

11. Preliminary Report of the Final Progress Report 1950, HUG 4517.5, box 8, folder: Progress Reports, Leontief Papers.

composition of final output or in the total quantity of labor will give rise to price change or substitution." In his substitution theorem Samuelson interpreted HERP's coefficients as the solution to a system of substitutable production functions, as a social optimum independent of the market—changes in final output or the total quantity of labor would not give rise to "price change or substitution." Samuelson identified that optimum with the equilibrium of neoclassical production theory: the relative equilibrium prices are identical to the "shadow prices" or "efficiency prices," that is, the dual variables of linear programming as given via the input coefficient matrix. In this way, the model became possible to integrate with traditional neoclassical theory (see Backhouse 2012b, 18–19; Akhabbar 2006), paving the way for Solow's growth model.

In 1951 Solow received an invitation from Charles J. Hitch to spend some time at the RAND Corporation to work on "problems connected with dynamics of input/output models."[12] Solow had been recruited to MIT the year before and, in close cooperation with Samuelson, had started to investigate "optimization over time in Leontief and other dynamic input-output models," including the stability of growth systems and "optimal capital programming over time."[13] Linear systems showed efficiently working production in which equilibrium was divorced from market activities. With the duality theorems of linear programming, this equilibrium was interpreted as an outcome of competitive market processes, but lacked any price, interest, and wage dynamics. Solow's (1953–54, 79) "economic intuition" said that this was "all wrong." Consequently, he aimed to develop an appropriate price theory for dynamic input-output systems.

While "simplifying" a dynamic input-output system to teach to his students at MIT, he came up with the idea of a "one-commodity-world" (75). HERP's input-output models were already based on the concept of dividing industries into several subindustries "such that the achieved detailed

12. Herr to Solow, April 25, 1951, box 59, file: Rand Corporation, 2 of 3. Solow had received almost all his professional training at Harvard with the exception of one year he spent at Columbia University, since "it was impossible to obtain anything beyond an elementary education in mathematical statistics at Harvard" (Application for a NSF senior postdoctoral fellowship October 10, 1962, box 58, file N: 1 of 2). With the financial support of a Social Science Research Council Pre-Doctoral Fellowship, he attended courses by Abraham Wald, Jacob Wolfowitz, and T. W. Anderson in mathematical statistics while working on his dissertation on income distribution. Solow's advisers were Leontief and Guy Orcutt, both of whom dealt with detailed empirical schemes.

13. Solow to Friedman, October 25, 1954, box 55, file F: 3 of 3.

information of sub-industries could then be 'collapsed' into a single aggregate industry so as to reduce the amount of necessary computations."[14] Similarly, Solow collapsed various capital inputs in a single index, resulting in the "collapsed production function" that showed output as a function of inputs of labor and "capital-in-general." Unlike HERP's input-output tables, this production function was not about "visualizing" the capital structure of a national economy; unlike the heterogeneous capital-goods models that Samuelson and Solow worked on at the time, it was not supposed to provide a normative solution for capital programming (see Backhouse, this volume, "The Other Cambridge").[15] The structural matrix of HERP had been transformed and redefined into an entirely different object, a handy device for integrating the price-wage-interest dynamics—the "causal dynamics"—into what Solow already called his "neoclassical model."

2. Solow's 1956 Growth Model

In 1956 the *Quarterly Journal of Economics* published "A Contribution to the Theory of Economic Growth." In the spirit of the unification endeavors of the Cowles Commission's Activity Analysis Conference, which put forth the formal similarities between linear programming models and "traditional economic theory," Solow (1953–54, 74) had identified a "strong analogy" between "Leontief's and Mr. Harrod's system." Building on this analogy, he now presented his own aggregative model as "a model of long-run growth which accepts all the Harrod-Domar assumptions except that of fixed proportions" (Solow 1956, 66). The "Harrod-Domar model" was one of the dominant research sites in the immediate postwar era—"countless craftsmen" had made it the "most over-worked tool in economics."[16] By dropping the assumption that production takes place under conditions of fixed proportions, which Solow claimed to have found

14. Preliminary Report of the Final Progress Report 1950.

15. Samuelson and Solow (1956) extended Ramsey's growth model to the case of numerous consumers and heterogeneous capital goods. As a by-product of their dynamic programming work, the authors showed that the necessary condition for optimality over time was identical in the cases of one capital good and many capital goods, thus arguing for a heuristic use of a homogeneous capital substance. See Wulwick 1990, 20–34; Sent 1998, 40. On the development of Dorfman, Samuelson, and Solow 1958, see Backhouse 2012a.

16. Tobin to Solow, March 19, 1959, box 61, file T: 2 of 2.

in both Leontief's and Harrod's work, he aimed at repudiating the so-called knife-edge of the "Harrod-Domar line of thought."[17]

The collapsed production function showed a model economy producing a single commodity (Y) with constant returns to scale and smooth substitution between capital and labor. It was embedded in the model with the following assumptions: there is a constant savings rate (s) so that savings $S = sY$; there is "no scarce nonaugmentable resource like land"; prices and wages are fully flexible; there is constant full employment of factors of production; and *ex ante* is always equal to *ex post* investment. In the model world of perfect foresight and perfect competition, the "fundamental equation" shows its equilibrium mechanism: $\dot{r} = sF(r, 1) - nr$ (Solow 1956, 69). The change of the capital-labor ratio r equals the difference of two terms. The first term indicates the amount of investment (equal to saving) in the model economy, while the second term indicates the amount of investment needed to maintain the workforce (expanding at rate n) at the same capital-labor ratio, so that the difference between them (i.e., the amount of capital surplus to requirement) indicates the rate at which the capital-labor ratio changes. Solow then demonstrated the stability of the equilibrium value r^* by showing how the capital-labor ratio changes over time when $r \neq r^*$: "Whatever the initial value of the capital-labor ratio, the system will develop *toward* a state of balanced growth at the natural rate" (70).

The closed form of the model made graphic representation straightforward. Drawing different shapes for the productivity curve, Solow demonstrated that this stability would apply only when production took place under the "usual neoclassical conditions" of variable proportions and constant returns to scale; "[the] system can adjust to any given rate of growth of the labor force, and eventually approach a state of steady proportional expansion" (73). He backed up his conclusion with the analytical treatment of three different cases: the Harrod-Domar case (exhibiting fixed proportions and therefore the "knife-edge" property), the Cobb-Douglas function (where the natural rate of growth equals the warranted rate as a consequence of demand-supply adjustments), and the whole family of

17. Alternately, Solow referred to "the Harrod-Domar line of thought" and "Harrod's model." Interestingly, what Solow associated with Harrod bore hardly any resemblance to Harrod's own work, but drew instead on the Harrod-Domar literature that developed only after the war. For the reception of Harrod's work in the context of the Harrod-Domar literature, see Hagemann 2009; for its reception as a model of growth, see Besomi 2001. For an interpretation of Solow's reading of Harrod's work, see Halsmayer and Hoover 2013.

constant-returns-to-scale production functions (differing from the Cobb-Douglas case in that production is possible with only one factor).

After constructing the model and investigating its properties, Solow extended his analysis by introducing small changes ceteris paribus to see whether the model economy with Cobb-Douglas production would still find its way to the stable equilibrium path (86). One of these "experiments," as Solow called them, was to introduce technological change by letting it float "down from the outside" (Solow [1959] 1960, 90). The collapsed production function was supplemented by a separate term $A(t)$ accounting for changes of technology: $F = A(t)\,F(K, L)$ (Solow 1956, 85).[18]

The key characteristic of Solow's working object was simplicity: "A good model makes the right strategic simplifications. In fact, a really good model is one that generates a lot of understanding from focusing on a very small number of causal arrows" (92). The choice of strategic simplification lies in the hands of the modeler, and unlike HERP's input-output models, Solow's target was not production but growth. Hence he defended the assumption of homogeneous capital, but was critical of his use of perfect foresight.[19] By pointing out the strong assumptions of the absence of risk and uncertainty, a fixed average propensity to save, and no monetary complications, he made clear that he was dealing with a "model economy" (78): his aim was to present not a "credible theory of investment" but a simple, tractable, and manipulable model of long-run equilibrium growth. To support his "experiments," Solow constructed a model that would ensure the existence of an equilibrium. As he argued in a discussion with Leontief: "The real point at issue is the consistency of a model: if it will not guarantee the existence of an equilibrium solution, what confidence can we have in its other promises?"[20]

18. Other "experiments" encompassed the formulation of supply of labor as a function of the real wage rate and time, letting the rate of saving depend on the yield of capital, adding a personal income tax, and assuming variable population growth. Only in the last case does the model economy need a major burst of investment instead of small-scale capital accumulation; none of these changes leads the system to a "stationary state" (Solow 1956, 85–91).

19. The concern with perfect foresight fit well with Solow's preoccupation with dynamic programming. As he stated two years before publishing "Contribution to the Theory of Economic Growth": "This is always a hard assumption to swallow. . . . The logic of this result is that in an equilibrium system with perfect foresight the future is implicit in the present, a seed literally is its own future stream of net outputs of fruit, and must be worth the present value of its own future" (Solow 1953–54, 76–77). See also Backhouse, this volume, "The Other Cambridge."

20. Solow to Leontief, January 27, 1954, box 57, file L: 2 of 2.

3. The Model as a Working Object and the Economist as a Modeler

Solow's growth model was a simple, clean, and transparent world, created to demonstrate not the phenomenological but the mathematical possibility of a stable long-run equilibrium, and to investigate what factors would determine this growth path. It was the simplicity of Solow's model that differentiated it from HERP's input-output tables and from the linear equation systems of activity analysis, both of which required a large amount of data and the requisite computing capacities. Solow himself called the practice of constructing and manipulating a simple model a "pen-and-pencil operation," a rather inexpensive way of doing economics compared with the empirical work done by large research groups.[21]

Retrospectively, Solow (1988, 308) described modeling as a trial-and-error process, a sort of "tinkering with the theory of economic growth." As Mary S. Morgan (2012, 25) points out, model building is not driven by a mechanical process, and involves not only the relevant articulated scientific knowledge but also the modeler's craft-based, tacit knowledge as well as her "intuitive, imaginative, and creative qualities." Modeling is both a craft and an art, or as Solow put it: "What model building probably isn't, is a science, in the sense that I doubt that you can reduce model building to a model of model building."[22] Hence, in the first place, Solow's model served as a "working object."[23] Following Morgan (2012), the construction and manipulation of models constitute processes of building up and using new worlds, processes that prompt new concepts and new ways of reasoning, and thereby afford opportunities for surprise. Interacting with the material of the model, the modeler-economist might develop new ideas: even though Solow had shaped the aggregate production function to fit the requirements of a simple model, the model was still a new kind of object, and Solow did not know the results of his manipulations in advance. He even claimed he was surprised that the model's steady-state rate of growth was independent of the savings rate: "I thought it was a

21. Solow to Nicholson, November 13, 1969, box 58, file N: 1 of 2. Solow retrospectively puts these two kinds of models in opposition: "Either you can work it out mathematically or, and of course this was less true when I started in the 1950s, you can do computation, which you couldn't do then, so there was a bigger premium on simplicity in the 1950s and 60s than there is now" (Solow, interview with author, May 3, 2011).

22. Solow, interview with author, May 3, 2011.

23. Lorraine Daston and Peter Galison (1992, 85) define the working objects of science as "not yet concepts, much less conjectures or theories; they are the materials from which concepts are formed and to which they are applied." See also Morgan 2012, 387–89.

real shocker. It is not what I expected at all" (quoted in Snowdon and Vane 1999, 275).

With modeling becoming the dominant research practice of economists, the attributes associated with economics as a science changed. The English economist J. R. Sargent's talk "Are American Economists Better?," delivered to the Political Economy Club at Nuffield College, is an expression of the epistemic virtues of the ideal new modeling economist.[24] Sargent compared US American economics with English economics, characterizing the former as "more scientific, exploratory, more professional, more serious, and borne out by the higher degree of specialisation."[25] He complemented this characterization with an account of the personal qualities he saw in American economists. Among these he emphasized the craft aspect of a modeling enterprise, the—indeed truly "American"—quality of an "exploratory spirit," which could "in no way be better felt than by reading consecutively Robert Solow's 'Contribution to the Theory of Economic Growth' and Mrs. Robinson's 'Accumulation of Capital.'" Putting aside the all-too-common dismissal of Joan V. Robinson and her work, it is striking that, for Sargent, what made Solow's work special was an ability associated with the skills of the modeler as a craftsperson: "No American economist ever thinks; he uses his analytical tools to arrive at meaningful theorems."[26] Solow would distinguish himself precisely not by following mathematical rules but by "being careless," by experimenting with ideas and by departing "from the standards of rigour":[27] "What is important is that the willingness to innovate exists. The experiment may fail, or it may succeed; but something may be gained, and nothing will be lost, by trying."[28]

4. The Model as an Instrument of Measurement

In an extensive chapter titled "Qualifications," Solow emphasized that policy conclusions should not be directly drawn from his model. By

24. November 12, 1960, box 60, file S: 1 of 7. Eventually, the talk was published in Sargent 1963. The year after, Sargent founded the Department of Economics at the University of Warwick, modeled after the kind of "American economics" he had investigated in his talk. The department was supposed to "use, and train its students to use the critical mathematical tools needed for analysis of complex economic issues" (Muthoo 2004). On the spread of what Sargent called "American economics," see also section 7.

25. Sargent talk, November 12, 1960, box 60, file S: 1 of 7, p. 6.

26. Sargent talk, 3.

27. Sargent talk, 5.

28. Sargent talk, 4.

assuming perfect foresight, he had swept aside all kinds of Keynesian rigidities:

> Everything above is the neoclassical side of the coin. Most especially it is full employment economics—in the dual aspect of equilibrium condition and frictionless, competitive, causal system. . . . It is not my contention that these problems [of Keynesian income analysis] don't exist, nor that they are of no significance in the long run. (Solow 1956, 91)

The point of Solow's article was not "to discuss the bearing of the previous highly abstract analysis on the practical problems of economic stabilization." It was instead supposed to serve as "a theoretical counterpart" to the "practical possibilities" of maintaining full employment (93). While the model had initially developed as a by-product of dynamic programming endeavors, and had served as a working object, it proved to be useful for still another purpose. When reacting to Robinson's (1953–54) early critique of the use of a homogeneous capital substance, Solow defended the collapsed production function on pragmatic grounds: it would be "useful," since it enabled the measurement of and in the same units (Solow 1955–56, 103).

In 1957 Solow applied his growth model to time-series data as an instrument of measurement.[29] He estimated the long-term rates of technical change by using the collapsed production function as a simple factor-share device. Written in "intensive form," each point of the production function associated a level of capital-labor ratio with a level of labor productivity (i.e., the output-labor ratio). The state of technology $A(t)$—usually referred to as "total factor productivity"—was identified as an exogenous factor. Thus changes in $A(t)$ shift the production function. This kind of empirical work was not supposed to provide a test of Solow's 1956 model, the aggregate production function, or of marginal productivity. Rather, it was a way to interpret given time-series data, assuming that they were generated from an aggregate production function and that the competitive marginal-product-relations applied (see Weintraub 1988, 367):[30] if the observed factor shares were exactly constant, Solow's (1974, 121) approach would "yield an exact Cobb-Douglas and tuck everything else into the shift factor."[31] While

29. On economic models as instruments of measurement, see Morgan 2001, Boumans 2005, and Maas and Morgan 2012.

30. As Boumans (2005, 121) explicates: "Confronting a model with phenomenological facts rather means comparing this instrument with another instrument that generated these facts."

31. Although Solow talks about Cobb-Douglas in this quote, in his 1957 article he does not assume a Cobb-Douglas production function but merely any function with constant returns to scale.

Robinson had contested the theoretical compatibility and logical consistency of Solow's model, Solow presented it as a *useful* instrument for measuring "technological change," enabling the estimation of "a single production function for society," as Samuelson (1962, 193) eventually called it.

5. The Model as a Prototype

Like Sargent, Solow emphasized the "exploratory spirit" of his artisanal engagement as a "reconnaissance exercise":

> I am trying to express an attitude towards the building of very simple models. I don't think that models like this lead directly to prescription for policy or even to detailed diagnosis. . . . They are more like reconnaissance exercises. If you want to know what it's like out there, it's all right to send two or three fellows in sneakers to find out the lay of the land and whether it will support human life. If it turns out to be worth settling, then that requires an altogether bigger operation. The job of building usable larger-scale econometric models on the basis of whatever analytical insights come from simple models is much more difficult and less glamorous. (Solow 1970, 105)

Here, Solow alluded to the function of his model as a prototype: the simple model was a closed, clean, and transparent world that could be manipulated and investigated. The simplicity of the model enables the modeler-economist to enter a new, unexplored, world. If the simple model proved productive, it would provide a basis for building more complex econometric models. In retrospect, Solow would describe his pen-and-pencil operation as an engineering enterprise, not in the sense of engineering the macroeconomy, but as "engineering in the design sense." Economists as "engineers in the design sense" do not design the economy—they design a model economy, which serves not only as a working object and instrument for measurement but also as a kind of prototype for more complex measuring rods.[32]

The image of the design model as a prototype is found in several places in the contemporary literature. Oskar Morgenstern (1954, 499–500), for instance, explicated how simple models—"with proper abstractions and simplifications"—are used to investigate "the general properties of a

32. Solow, interview with author, May 3, 2011. Of course, Solow's retrospective use of the term *engineering* might be motivated by contemporary issues, for example, to make a counterpoint to the "engineering" notion of Robert E. Lucas. Nevertheless, "engineering in the design sense" provides a terminology that nicely captures what I believe to be a specific characteristic of Solow's modeling practice in the 1950s.

system by its manipulation on the basis of a theory of the system." As an example from another field, Morgenstern mentioned the model of an airplane. Instead of computing the breaking point or determining it with a real plane, a model of an airplane is "put into a wind-tunnel and is exposed to stresses until it breaks" (501). Such experiments could be carried out repeatedly with all kinds of variations in the smaller model. Correspondingly, the major asset of small models is their simplicity, because, if they are more complicated, they "lose their didactic value of visualizing economic interdependencies" (504).

Similarly, Solow (1956) developed three cases with three different production functions—the Harrod-Domar case, the Cobb-Douglas case, and the set of constant-returns-to-scale production functions. To see what effects specific changes (introduction of technological change, a personal income tax, variable population growth, etc.) would have on the dynamic model economy, Solow used the case of the Cobb-Douglas production function: "Generality leads to complications, and instead I turn . . . to the tractable Cobb-Douglas function" (86). In his empirical application, Solow (1957) used a general constant-returns-to-scale production function. The Harrod-Domar case was presented as exhibiting a design flaw: the constant capital coefficient led to the "knife-edge," in which any step away from the warranted rate of growth led to collision with a full employment ceiling or to mass unemployment and depression. Therefore, neither the Harrod-Domar case nor the "Leontief production function" was seen as a suitable component of a design for larger-scale econometric models.

In the second edition of *The Keynesian Revolution*, Lawrence Klein argued for a similar view of simple models as design tools for more complex ones. He presented the Keynesian model of income determination (with the three pillars of the propensity to save, the marginal efficiency of capital schedule, and the liquidity-preference function) as a "pedagogical model" that had "teaching attributes," but provided "only a crude framework for thinking and illustrating main ideas" (Klein 1968, 193).[33] Klein noted that "intelligent discussion cannot be carried on unless this system is expanded to include fifteen to twenty or even more equations. In current econometric model construction, I am working with some macro-systems that have more than 100 equations" (223). The very simplicity that made a model intelligible restricted its usefulness for dealing with complex data. To "explain the determination of output, employment, wage rate, price

33. I deal with Solow's model as a "teaching object" in the next section.

level, interest rate, and other variables," it had to be extended in a number of directions (212–13). The Klein-Goldberger model (1955) and the Brookings model are just two of many macroeconometric models constructed in the 1960s (see Nerlove 1966; Bodkin, Klein, and Marwah 1991). Solow devised his simple model to provide a design for more complex constructions, among them dynamic input-output models, on which he had worked with Samuelson in the 1950s; later, it became some kind of prototype for multisectoral models such as Johansen 1960. Eventually, despite disagreeing with this line of research, Solow (1957) provided the design for a vast literature on growth and development accounting, measuring changes in total factor productivity (see Snowdon and Vane 1999, 277).[34]

As Philip Mirowski (1989, 328) and Esther-Mirjam Sent (1998, 57) have both pointed out in slightly different contexts, engineers do, in their applications, deal with the particularities of the specific material even when working with the absence of frictions in theory. Equally, it is questionable whether the use of Solow's model as a prototypal design for larger-scale econometric models permits any kind of recalcitrance of the data. Solow's statement that "everything is tucked into Cobb-Douglas" holds for the long line of growth accounting exercises. Among others, Leontief (1983, 104) criticized the estimation of production functions as "methodological devices that [are] employ[ed] to avoid or cut short the use of concrete factual information."

6. The Model as a Teaching Object

Both Morgenstern and Klein emphasized the didactic and pedagogical role of simple design models. Solow pointed to the connection between his way of modeling and his teaching at MIT: "Remember that engineering is an academic subject, I lived my whole professional life in an engineering school, that's what MIT is, and so the notion that one of the functions of a professor of engineering is not necessarily to build a bridge but to design a bridge . . . came perfectly natural to us at MIT."[35] After being involved in national planning and defense on an unprecedented scale during World War II, MIT aimed to return to its alleged primary mission: the

34. Tiago Mata and Francisco Louçã (2009) show how "Solow's growth residual" developed a life of its own, being given to multiple uses—rhetorical, symbolic, and instrumental. On the history of the residual before Solow's publication, see for instance Griliches 1995 and Crafts 2009.

35. Solow, interview with author, May 3, 2011. See Cherrier, this volume.

professional education "of imaginative and creative leadership" (*Report of the Committee* 1949, 4–5). To this end, the humanities and social sciences should form a unified academic community with engineering, science, architecture, and planning in order to launch "a coöperative attack on vitally important problems and a good educational unit for the development of leaders for a technological world" (46). Economics was thus considered an important part of a strong professional education not only for economists but for businesspeople and engineers alike.

One of the economists recruited to meet the increased teaching needs in the social sciences was Robert Solow (see Cherrier, this volume). In making dynamic economic issues intelligible to his engineering students, Solow had formulated the collapsed production function, the essential component of his design model. He used his simple model as a teaching device. One concern about the use of design models as teaching objects was that students and teachers too often stuck with these simple models: they were "too taken with technique and theory," and did not care enough "about the practical meaning" of what they were doing.[36] In this respect, Robert Dorfman complained to Solow about "our profession and the way it is set up to force the tremendous talents and energies of young men into made work and artificial tasks."[37]

Building simple, transparent, and exploratory design models, and conducting econometric applications with a focus on clear-cut definitions and closed systems, became the "proper" way of doing economics and was associated with MIT from the 1960s on. MIT's students—whether destined to become modeler-economists themselves, experts in government, or informed businesspersons—learned the craft: they were trained to reason with simple models and to perceive economics as a "modeling science." As a teacher, Solow wrote shoals of letters of recommendations to help place the newly educated modeler-economists in academe, government, business, the military, and so forth. He himself emphasized the "line of terrific graduate students that spread the technique."[38] For Solow, edu-

36. Solow to Hunter, October 26, 1955, box 55, file H: 2 of 3.

37. Dorfman to Solow, January 14, 1966, box 53, file D: 2 of 4. Robinson (1953–54, 81) also pondered the pedagogical problems of simple models: "The dominance in neoclassical economic teaching of the concept of a production function . . . has had an enervating effect upon the development of the subject, for by concentrating upon the question of the proportions of factors it had distracted attention from the more difficult but more rewarding questions of the influences governing the supplies of the factors and the causes and consequences of technical change."

38. Solow, interview with author, May 3, 2011.

cating future teachers was the main way in which the "model building philosophy, and not only the model building philosophy, but the utility of building small, understandable, relatively transparent models, not to mimic or model the whole economy," spread.[39]

7. The "Engineer in the Design Sense" as a Technical Expert

Solow's design model was used for various purposes: as a working object, it served as a clean and transparent world for investigating long-run equilibrium growth; as an instrument of measurement, it was applied to time-series data; as a teaching object, it helped "spreading the technique." Used as what I have tentatively called a "prototype," the design model was supposed to feed into larger-scale econometric models, and it was these models that lent legitimacy to the modeler-economist as a technical expert.

In a review of the Activity Analysis conference volume, Solow (1952, 427) stated that "[Koopmans's] theorem is of immense significance for welfare economics, and for the possibility of a decentralized mechanism of economic planning." Input-output modeling and linear programming were "technical economics" proper about, as Leontief (1965, 46) later described it, the "effective application of mathematical methods to the operational solution of many practical economic problems." While input-output analysis models and linear programming provided tools for directly solving "practical economic problems," such as the feasibility of production plans or the efficient allocation and utilization of economic resources on the level of a plant, an industry, or the entire economy, Solow's design model did not extend to direct application to economic problems, and the question of how the characteristics of the small, well-working design would apply to the kinds of phenomena that economic policymakers were interested in was addressed by Solow as a matter of interpretation, involving further resources, that is, different kinds of knowledge.[40] However, the "usable larger-scale macroeconometric models" that were supposed to be built on the basis of the insights gained from the design model were indeed intended as technologies for giving policy advice. With their help, modeler-economists would be able to give clear answers to "what-happens-if

39. Solow, interview with author, May 3, 2011. See also Svorenčík, this volume.

40. Solow, interview with author, May 3, 2011. See also Samuelson 1962 on the "surrogate production function."

questions" of economic governance (see Maas, this volume; Giraud, this volume; Morgan 2003; and Porter 2006).

One of the bureaucratic bodies demanding the expertise of technical economists was the Council of Economic Advisers. With the end of the Korean War and the advent of the Eisenhower administration, Washington had not only reverted to a less activist policy stance but also brought the influence of economists connected with the now-shunned "planning" to a minimum. This changed during the 1950s, as economists established themselves as technical experts and a new way of macroeconomic "planning with the market" developed (see Balisciano 1998; Goodwin 1998). With the Kennedy administration, economists had "revived their influence at the top" and were now again in a position "to influence policy from its start":

> Things are different now. Just count. Paul Samuelson and Dick Musgrave and countless others have been advising Kennedy since summer. Paul was offered the chairmanship of the Council of Economic Advisers and turned it down. It went instead to Walter Heller. . . . Jim Tobin will be a member of the Council of Economic Advisers and he is as good an economist as we have. Bob Roosa is undersecretary of Treasury. Speaking of RAND, Charlie Hitch . . . has just been appointed Assistant Secretary of Defense.[41]

A few months after writing this letter, Solow himself joined the Council of Economic Advisers, chaired by Walter Heller. The kind of technical expertise that Solow and others provided came with left-liberal Keynesian views. Planning to dampen cycles, to create economic growth, low inflation, and low unemployment, was a rather neutral concept; it was seen as an organizational necessity rather than a political option (see Düppe and Weintraub 2014 with regard to Koopmans; and Mirowski 2006). As Solow noted in the early 1960s:

> Nowadays it has become clear that economic planning is a matter of degree, not a matter of Manchester liberalism on one side and Big Brother on the other. The government has an important guiding role even in capitalist countries, and the degree of centralization varies widely among socialist countries. . . . Instead of a full dress theory of economic planning, what makes more sense now is plain economic

41. Solow to Sargent, January 5, 1961, box 60, file S: 1 of 7.

analysis and discussion of general principles, which will no doubt apply differently in different institutional contexts.[42]

In a way, Solow's design model embodied the utopian idea that in the long run there would be "another, better, world" that was possible to reach through the appropriate macroeconomic planning (Toye 2009, 222; see also Assous 2013 on Solow's work on medium-run dynamics). However, Solow's design circulated widely, and grew autonomous from its immediate enabling conditions. It eventually became a symbol for the view that "there was nothing wrong with capitalism," and Solow was to regret having unleashed "a standing temptation to sound like Dr. Pangloss" on behalf of the economics profession (Solow 1988, 309; see Mata and Louçã 2009 and Toye 2009).

References

Akhabbar, Amanar. 2006. "Leontief and Samuelson on the Non-Substitution Theorem: Some Methodological Remarks." Paper presented at the Intermediate Input-Output Conference, International Input-Output Association and Pan Pacific Association of Input-Output Studies, Sendai, Japan, July 26–28.

Assous, Michaël. 2013. "Solow's Struggle with Medium-Run Macroeconomics: 1956–1995." Working Paper 2013-17, Center for the History of Political Economy at Duke University.

Backhouse, Roger E. 2012a. "Linear Programming and Economic Analysis: The Collaboration between Samuelson, Dorfman and Solow, 1949–1958." Version 1, September.

———. 2012b. "Paul Samuelson, RAND and the Cowles Commission Activity Analysis Conference, 1947–1949." Version 2, October.

Balisciano, Márcia L. 1998. "Hope for America: American Notions of Economic Planning between Pluralism and Neoclassicism, 1930–1950." In *From Interwar Pluralism to Postwar Neoclassicism*, edited by Mary S. Morgan and Malcolm Rutherford. *History of Political Economy* 30 (supplement): 153–78.

Bensaude-Vincent, Bernadette, Sacha Loeve, Alfred Nordmann, and Astrid Schwarz. 2011. "Matters of Interest: The Objects of Research in Science and Technoscience." *Journal for General Philosophy of Science* 42:365–83.

Besomi, Daniele. 2001. "Harrod's Dynamics and the Theory of Growth: The Story of a Mistaken Attribution." *Cambridge Journal of Economics* 25 (1): 79–96.

Bodkin, Ronald G., Lawrence R. Klein, and Kanta Marwah. 1991. *A History of Macroeconometric Model-Building*. Brookfield, Vt.: Elgar.

42. Manuscript Review Dobb "Economic Growth and Planning," box 54, file D: 4 of 4. The review was eventually published in Solow 1962.

Boianovsky, Mauro, and Kevin D. Hoover, eds. 2009. *Robert Solow and the Development of Growth Economics*. Supplemental issue to vol. 41 of *History of Political Economy*. Durham, N.C.: Duke University Press.

Boumans, Marcel. 2005. *How Economists Model the World into Numbers*. New York: Routledge.

———. 2012. "Logical Positivism and Leontief." Working paper, University of Amsterdam.

Breslau, Daniel, and Yuval Yonay. 1999. "Beyond Metaphor: Mathematical Models in Economics as Empirical Research." *Science in Context* 12:317–32.

Carter, Anne P. 2012. "Leontief's 'Stuff': An Archeology of Input-Output Material." *Oeconomia* 1 (1): 51–59.

Chadarevian, Soraya de, and Nick Hopwood, eds. 2004. *Models: The Third Dimension of Science*. Stanford, Calif.: Stanford University Press.

Crafts, Nicholas. 2009. "Solow and Growth Accounting: A Perspective from Quantitative Economic History." In *Robert Solow and the Development of Growth Economics*, edited by Mauro Boianovsky and Kevin D. Hoover. *History of Political Economy* 41 (supplement): 200–220.

Daston, Lorraine, and Peter Galison. 1992. "The Image of Objectivity." "Seeing Science," special issue, *Representations* 40 (Autumn): 81–128.

Dorfman, Robert, Paul Samuelson, and Robert Solow. 1958. *Linear Programming and Economic Analysis*. New York: McGraw-Hill.

Düppe, Till, and E. Roy Weintraub. 2014. "Siting the New Economic Science: The Cowles Commission's Activity Analysis Conference of June 1949." *Science in Context* 27 (3).

Erickson, Paul, Judy L. Klein, Lorraine Daston, Rebecca Lemov, Thomas Strum, and Michael D. Gordin. 2013. *How Reason Almost Lost Its Mind: The Strange Career of Cold War Rationality*. Chicago: University of Chicago Press.

Goodwin, Craufurd. 1998. "The Patrons of Economics in a Time of Transformation." In *From Interwar Pluralism to Postwar Neoclassicism*, edited by Mary S. Morgan and Malcolm Rutherford. *History of Political Economy* 30 (supplement): 53–81.

Griliches, Zvi. 1995. "The Discovery of the Residual: An Historical Note." National Bureau of Economic Research Working Paper 5348.

Hagemann, Harald. 2009. "Solow's 1956 Contribution in the Context of the Harrod-Domar Model." In *Robert Solow and the Development of Growth Economics*, edited by Mauro Boianovsky and Kevin D. Hoover. *History of Political Economy* 41 (supplement): 67–87.

Halsmayer, Verena, and Kevin D. Hoover. 2013. "Solow's Harrod: Transforming Cyclical Dynamics into a Model of Long-Run Growth." Working Paper 2013-02, Center for the History of Political Economy at Duke University.

Harcourt, Geoffrey C. 2006. *The Structure of Post-Keynesian Economics: The Core Contributions of the Pioneers*. Cambridge: Cambridge University Press.

Johansen, Leif. 1960. *A Multi-sectoral Study of Economic Growth*. Amsterdam: North-Holland.

Klein, Judy L. 2001. "Reflections from the Age of Economic Measurement." In *The Age of Economic Measurement*, edited by Judy L. Klein and Mary S. Morgan. *History of Political Economy* 33 (supplement): 111–36.

Klein, Lawrence R. 1968. *The Keynesian Revolution*. 2nd ed. London: Macmillan.

Kohli, Martin C. 2001. "Leontief and the U.S. Bureau of Labor Statistics, 1941–1954: Developing a Framework for Measurement." In *The Age of Economic Measurement*, edited by Judy L. Klein and Mary S. Morgan. *History of Political Economy* 30 (supplement): 190–212.

Koopmans, Tjalling C., ed. 1951. *Activity Analysis of Production and Allocation*. Cowles Commission Monograph 13. New York: John Wiley and Sons.

Leontief, Wassily. 1953. *The Structure of the American Economy*. Oxford: Oxford University Press.

———. 1965. "An Institute for Technical Economics." *Bulletin of the Atomic Scientists*, September, 46.

———. 1983. "Academic Economics." *Science*, July 9, 104–7.

Maas, Harro, and Mary S. Morgan. 2012. "Observation and Observing in Economics." In *Observing the Economy: Historical Perspectives*, edited by Harro Maas and Mary S. Morgan. *History of Political Economy* 44 (supplement): 1–24.

Mata, Tiago, and Francisco Louçã. 2009. "The Solow Residual as a Black Box: Attempts at Integrating Business Cycle and Growth Theories." In *Robert Solow and the Development of Growth Economics*, edited by Mauro Boianovsky and Kevin D. Hoover. *History of Political Economy* 41 (supplement): 334–55.

Mirowski, Philip. 1989. *More Heat Than Light: Economics as Social Physics, Physics as Nature's Economics*. Cambridge: Cambridge University Press.

———. 2006. "Twelve Theses concerning the History of Postwar Neoclassical Price Theory." In *Agreement on Demand: Consumer Theory in the Twentieth Century*, edited by Philip Mirowski and D. Wade Hands. *History of Political Economy* 38 (supplement): 343–79.

Morgan, Mary S. 2001. "Making Measuring Instruments." In *The Age of Economic Measurement*, edited by Judy L. Klein and Mary S. Morgan. *History of Political Economy* 33 (supplement): 235–51.

———. 2003. "Economics." In *The Cambridge History of Science*, edited by Theodore M. Porter and Dorothy Ross, 275–305. Cambridge: Cambridge University Press.

———. 2012. *The World in the Model: How Economists Work and Think*. Cambridge: Cambridge University Press.

Morgenstern, Oskar. 1954. "Experiment and Large Scale Computation in Economics." In *Economic Activity Analysis*, edited by Oskar Morgenstern, 484–549. New York: Wiley.

Morrison, Margaret, and Mary S. Morgan, eds. 1999. *Models as Mediators: Perspectives on Natural and Social Science*. Cambridge: Cambridge University Press.

Muthoo, Abhinay. 2004. "Warwick Economics: Approaching Fifty." www2.warwick.ac.uk/fac/soc/ economics/about/history/ (17.10.2013).

Nerlove, Marc. 1966. "A Tabular Survey of Macro-Econometric Models. " *International Economic Review* 7 (2): 127–75.

Nordmann, Alfred. 2011. "Im Blickwinkel der Technik: Neue Verhältnisse von Wissenschaftstheorie und Wissenschaftsgeschichte." *Berichte zur Wissenschaftsgeschichte* 35:200–216.

Porter, Theodore M. 2006. "Speaking Precision to Power: The Modern Political Role of Social Science." *Social Research* 73 (4): 1273–94.

Report of the Committee on Educational Survey to the Faculty of the Massachusetts Institute of Technology. 1949. libraries.mit.edu/archives/mithistory/pdf/lewis.pdf.

Robinson, Joan V. 1953–54. "The Production Function and the Theory of Capital." *Review of Economic Studies* 21 (2): 81–106.

Samuelson, Paul. 1951. "Abstract of a Theorem Concerning Substitutability in Open Leontief Models." In *Activity Analysis of Production and Allocation*, edited by Tjalling Koopmans, 142–46. New York: John Wiley and Sons.

———. 1962. "Parable and Realism in Capital Theory: The Surrogate Production Function." *Review of Economic Studies* 29 (3): 193–206.

Samuelson, Paul A., and Robert Solow. 1956. "A Complete Capital Model involving Heterogeneous Capital Goods." *Quarterly Journal of Economics* 70 (4): 537–62.

Sargent, J. R. 1963. "Are American Economists Better?" *Oxford Economic Papers* 18 (1): 1–7.

Schneider, Erich. 1934. *Theorie der Produktion*. Vienna: Springer.

Sen, Amartya K. 1970. *Growth Economics: Selected Readings*. Harmondsworth: Penguin Books.

Sent, Esther-Mirjam. 1998. "Engineering Dynamic Economics." In *New Economics and Its History*, edited by John B. Davis. *History of Political Economy* 29 (supplement): 41–62.

Snowdon, Brian, and Howard R. Vane. 1999. *Conversations with Leading Economists: Interpreting Modern Macroeconomics*. Cheltenham: Elgar.

Solow, Robert M. 1952. "Review Koopmans Activity Analysis of Production and Allocation." *American Economic Review* 42 (3): 424–29.

———. 1953–54. "A Note on the Price Level and Interest Rate in a Growth Model." *Review of Economic Studies* 21 (1): 74–79.

———. 1955–56. "The Production Function and the Theory of Capital." *Review of Economic Studies* 23 (2): 101–8.

———. 1956. "A Contribution to the Theory of Economic Growth." *Quarterly Journal of Economics* 70 (1): 65–94.

———. 1957. "Technical Change and the Aggregate Production Function." *Review of Economics and Statistics* 39 (3): 312–20.

———. (1959) 1960. "Investment and Technical Progress." In *Mathematical Methods in the Social Sciences*, edited by Kenneth Arrow, Samuel Karlin, and Patrick Suppes, 89–105. Stanford: Stanford University Press.

———. 1962. "Some Problems of the Theory and Practice of Economic Planning," review of *An Essay on Economic Growth and Planning*, by Maurice Dobb. *Economic Development and Cultural Change* 10 (2): 216–22.

———. 1970. *Growth Theory*. Oxford: Clarendon Press.

——. 1974. "Law of Production and Laws of Algebra: The Humbug Production Function: A Comment." *Review of Economics and Statistics* 56 (1): 121.

——. 1987. "Autobiography." nobelprize.org/nobel_prizes/economic-sciences/laureates/1987/solow-bio.html.

——. 1988. "Growth Theory and After." *American Economic Review* 78 (3): 307–17.

Swan, Trevor W. 1956. "Economic Growth and Capital Accumulation." *Economic Record* 32 (63): 334–61.

Toye, John. 2009. "Solow in the Tropics." In *Robert Solow and the Development of Growth Economics*, edited by Mauro Boianovsky and Kevin D. Hoover. *History of Political Economy* 41 (supplement): 221–40.

Weintraub, E. Roy. 1988. "Commentary on Learning Economic Method from the Invention of Vintage Models by Bert Hamminga." In *Post-Popperian Methodology of Economics: Recovering Practice*, edited by Neil De Marchi, 355–73. Boston: Kluwer Academic Publishers.

Wulwick, Nancy. 1990. "The Mathematics of Economic Growth." Working Paper 38, Jerome Levy Institute.

MIT and the Other Cambridge

Roger E. Backhouse

1. Preliminaries

In 1953 Joan Robinson, at the University of Cambridge, in England, published a challenge to what she chose to call the neoclassical theory of production. She claimed that it did not make sense to use a production function of the form $Q = f(L, K)$,[1] in which the rate of interest or profit (the two terms are used interchangeably) was assumed to equal the marginal product of capital, $\partial Q/\partial K$, for it confused two distinct concepts of capital. The variable K could not represent simultaneously the physical stock of capital goods and the value of capital from which the rate of profit was calculated. A related critique was then offered by Piero Sraffa (1960). In place of the marginal productivity theory of income distribution, Robinson and her Cambridge colleagues, Nicholas Kaldor and Luigi Pasinetti, argued for what they called a "Keynesian" theory of distribution in which

Correspondence may be addressed to Roger E. Backhouse, University of Birmingham, Edgbaston, Birmingham B15 2TT, UK; e-mail: reb@bhouse.org.uk. This article is part of a project, supported by a Major Research Fellowship from the Leverhulme Trust, to write an intellectual biography of Paul Samuelson. I am grateful to Tony Brewer, Geoffrey Harcourt, Steven Medema, Neri Salvadori, Bertram Schefold, Anthony Waterman, and participants at the 2013 *HOPE* conference for comments on an earlier draft. Material from the Paul A. Samuelson Papers, David M. Rubenstein Rare Book and Manuscript Library, Duke University, is cited as PASP box n (folder name). Material from the Robert M. Solow Papers, David M. Rubenstein Rare Book and Manuscript Library, Duke University, is cited as RMSP box n (folder name).

1. Solow's C has been changed to the more commonly used K.

History of Political Economy 46 (annual suppl.) DOI 10.1215/00182702-2716190

the rate of profit was determined by the rate of capital accumulation and the propensities to save out of wages and profits. This challenge was taken up by the MIT economists Robert Solow and Paul Samuelson, who claimed that her objections were unfounded. The resulting controversy, which continued for more than a decade, came to be known as the "two Cambridges" controversy because the main participants, including a host of younger scholars, including many graduate students, were based at MIT and the other Cambridge.

The classic account of this debate is *Some Cambridge Controversies in the Theory of Capital* (Harcourt 1972), an expanded version of an article in the widely read *Journal of Economic Literature* (Harcourt 1969). This book, presenting the controversy as a boxing match involving two camps, is written from the Cambridge perspective, according to which there was an ideological divide.[2] In criticizing marginal productivity theory, Robinson, Sraffa, and their followers saw themselves as pointing out that income distribution was not simply a by-product of the pricing system but was the result of class conflict rooted in the structures of capitalism, including the institution of private property and the existence of entrepreneurial and wage-earning classes (Harcourt 1972, 2). Because the capital controversy was believed to concern the very foundations of capitalism, it served as a crucial factor in the emergence of a distinct "Post Keynesian" identity (see Hamouda and Harcourt 1988). As Tiago Mata (2004) has pointed out, Harcourt's survey played a role in that process by constructing a history of how the controversy looked from the Cambridge end.

In contrast with Harcourt's survey, the present article seeks to establish how the arguments of Robinson, Kaldor, Sraffa, and their followers looked from the perspective of MIT. It is clear why the debate was important to Robinson—it was the foundation for her left-wing Keynesianism, very different from the centrist, "neoclassical synthesis" Keynesianism of Samuelson and Solow—but why did the latter become so involved in the controversy given that their arguments with Milton Friedman's Chicago were more important for economic policy? The article argues that Samuelson's and Solow's interest in capital theory has to be explained in terms of their interest in the techniques that Robinson was using. She developed her arguments about capital theory using a class of linear models that they thought they understood and for the analysis of which they had developed the relevant techniques. Robinson's arguments did represent a challenge to

2. Henceforth "Cambridge" is used to denote the University of Cambridge, UK.

the way they thought about the economy, but less because they thought in terms of continuously differentiable aggregate production functions than because it raised questions about the relation between such models and the discrete technologies used in linear programming, analyzed in "Market Mechanisms and Maximization" (Samuelson 1966a), circulated as a series of RAND discussion papers in 1949 and 1953,[3] and *Linear Programming and Economic Analysis* (Dorfman, Samuelson, and Solow 1958).

The article also points to a less-known but significant outcome of the controversy—the pathbreaking article by Solow and Joseph Stiglitz (1968) that marked the beginning of a long period when MIT was associated with various forms of "disequilibrium" macroeconomics and the "new Keynesian" macroeconomics (see Backhouse and Boianovsky 2013). This ushered in a new phase in MIT economics, in which Samuelson and Solow played a smaller role in relation to a younger generation (e.g., Peter Diamond, Stiglitz, George Akerlof, Robert Gordon, John Taylor, Stanley Fischer, Alan Blinder, Olivier Blanchard, Michael Woodford, and Gregory Mankiw), though many of these had been supervised by Solow, who remained active in the field. With this transition, the relationship between the two Cambridges changed significantly.[4]

Interactions between MIT and the other Cambridge would have been very different had there not been close links between the two institutions and had the other Cambridge not been home to many who took a "neoclassical" position on capital theory. These links went back to 1948 when Samuelson, on his first sabbatical from MIT, visited Cambridge, meeting Joan and Austin Robinson, Piero Sraffa, Richard Kahn, Richard Stone, and Dennis Robertson, with whom he formed lasting friendships. On his return home, he sought to develop connections between the two institutions, writing to Sraffa, "I should like to return evil for good. Can we rob you of any of your bright young men for a limited time?"[5] Samuelson returned to Cambridge in 1952, and Solow, after his arrival at MIT in 1950, also built strong links with Cambridge economists, including Harry Johnson (whom he had known when they were graduate students at Harvard, and who taught at Cambridge from 1948 to 1956) and Frank Hahn, whose

3. The editor, Stiglitz, cites these as having been circulated in March and June 1949, but omits mention of an addendum not circulated till 1953.

4. There were also significant changes at Cambridge, but these are beyond the scope of a paper focused on MIT.

5. P. A. Samuelson to Piero Sraffa, December 16, 1948, PASP box 70 (Sraffa). The question mark has been added.

PhD had been supervised by Kaldor at the London School of Economics, who visited MIT in 1956–57, and who was at Cambridge from 1960 to 1967 and from 1972 onward. Hahn and Solow arranged for graduate students and young faculty members from one Cambridge to spend part of their time at the other. The list included Peter Diamond, Christopher Bliss, Tony Atkinson, Joseph Stiglitz, and James Mirrlees. Samuelson and Solow were repeatedly encouraging their Cambridge counterparts to visit MIT or to stop over en route to other destinations in the United States.

In focusing on relations between MIT and Cambridge, the article is picking out one of many links in a transatlantic group of economists that had developed close friendships and collaborations. Though dealing with only one of MIT's many connections with other groups of economists, it serves as a reminder that MIT's identity was as much the result of interactions with other places as the outcome of developments within MIT itself.

2. The Meaning of Capital, 1948–66

Harcourt (1972, 11) dates the two-Cambridges controversy to Robinson's article "The Production Function and the Theory of Capital" (1953). However, Samuelson has recalled that their first exchange on the theory of capital might have been the previous year, when he attended the "secret seminar" in Cambridge (Turner 1989, 267n23). Unfortunately, the details of their exchange on that occasion are not recorded. Solow's first reaction to Robinson's paper came in a letter, dated August 26, 1953, to Harry Johnson. Solow wrote that he had been struggling with her paper, because he thought it was related to a problem on which he and Samuelson had been working. However, he found it impenetrable, and he could not understand a word of it.[6] This elicited a long explanation from Johnson, who noted that the paper was causing confusion in Cambridge as well.[7] He opined that "the point is quite simple once the usual Joan-isms and the signs of mental breakdown have been eliminated, as they have been, we hope, in the version coming out in the Review [of Economic Studies] in February." Robinson's innovation lay not in identifying a new problem, for the dependence on the measured capital stock on the rate of interest was well-known: it was in supplying a solution through "the pedagogically-useful device of discrete techniques," which Johnson explained using a

6. R. M. Solow to Harry G. Johnson, August 26, 1953, RMSP box 65 (H-J).
7. H. G. Johnson to Robert M. Solow, August 31, 1953, RMSP box 65 (H-J).

one-commodity "corn" economy. What made the paper complicated was that she refused to regard it as a dynamic problem, insisting on expressing it in terms of comparative statics, and it was mixed in with arguments related to her generalization of John Maynard Keynes's *General Theory* about the impossibility of an economy with a falling rate of interest to adjust smoothly to capital accumulation. Johnson's explanation seemed to help, for Solow responded, a month later, by saying that "I think I see what Mrs. Robinson is driving at."[8] He explained that he did not mind the political propaganda, but was "a little put off by the withering attacks on what may be neo-classical stinking fish in England, but bears no visible relation to any doctrine taught on this side of the Atlantic." This exchange shows the importance of Johnson, not usually associated with this controversy, as a liaison between two different ways of thinking.

The correspondence makes it clear that the problem intrigued Solow because Robinson seemed to be making arguments about issues that Samuelson and Solow believed that they understood because it related directly to their recent work. However, it was difficult to understand because several issues were involved. One was aggregation, where the conditions for rigorous aggregation were known to be very restrictive: Samuelson and Solow were, after all, students of Wassily Leontief (1947), who had shown that the conditions for aggregation of production functions were very strict. Another concerned the relationship between models with finite numbers of techniques (input-output or linear-programming models) and ones with continuous substitution between inputs.

Robinson used examples involving three or four distinct techniques because she did not have the mathematics needed to work with large numbers of techniques, and as a result it was easy to get the impression that some of the effects she was finding were the result of having a finite number of techniques. In contrast, Samuelson and Solow used such models because they were potentially computable. The problem of the relationship of "linear-programming" models to models with smooth substitution was one on which Samuelson had been working since he started working at RAND in December 1948. He had explored this problem in several RAND discussion papers, one of which had been the opening paper in a major conference on linear programming that proved immensely important for the community of American mathematical economists (reported in Koopmans 1951; see Düppe and Weintraub 2014). Samuelson, whose main concern was with the comparative statics properties of maximum

8. R. M. Solow to Harry G. Johnson, September 28, 1953, RMSP box 65 (H-J).

points, had shown that working with discrete numbers of techniques, though it necessitated using different mathematical techniques, did not cause any problems for the underlying economic theory. He and Solow were, therefore, puzzled by Robinson's claims that she was raising problems that were fatal for neoclassical theory. Furthermore, they were working on models with arbitrary numbers of commodities, in which aggregation over capital goods was not required, having published a joint paper (Solow and Samuelson 1953) in which outputs of n goods were functions of n inputs; in this paper they postulated differentiable production functions, but there was no aggregation over commodities. This meant that they failed to recognize themselves in Robinson's picture of neoclassical economics.

The disagreement became public in the mid-1950s, when Solow (1955) published a response to Robinson's article. He took the point of her article to be proposing a specific, somewhat old-fashioned, way to measure capital in terms of labor units plus interest payments, *not* to be arguing that capital could not be measured. Like Johnson,[9] he understood Robinson to be turning to linear-programming models to solve the well-known problem that the quantity of capital depended on the rate of interest. He challenged this and an alternative approach to capital measurement offered by David Champernowne (1953), by questioning whether it was necessary to have a concept of "capital-in-general" at all (Solow 1955, 101). In explaining the reasons that capital could not rigorously be aggregated, he used production functions of the form $Q = f(L, K)$,[10] an idea that he linked to the Cambridge philosopher and mathematician Frank Ramsey, but he was confident that his results would hold for the case of discrete activities. Noting that "everyone who invents linear programming these days seems to be charmed by it," Solow (1955, 108) averred that using linear-programming technologies solved nothing, for "only in very special cases will it be possible to define a consistent measure of capital-in-general." Contrary to common perceptions, Solow was arguing *against* measuring the aggregate capital stock. His argument became even stronger if one took account of "the intertwining of past, present and future": there was, he contended, something foolish about a theory of capital built on the assumption of perfect foresight" (102).[11] Robinson (1955), however, believed that Solow

9. H. G. Johnson to Robert M. Solow, August 31, 1953, RMSP box 65 (H-J).

10. Solow's C has been changed to the more commonly used K.

11. These were criticisms that Cambridge economists liked to make of neoclassical theory, but Solow was using them to defend his own work against Robinson.

had missed the point, because he had not considered how capital goods were produced.

For Samuelson and Solow, their alternative to the model of production that Robinson (1956) proposed in *The Accumulation of Capital* was not the "Solow-Swan model" (independently derived by Solow and Trevor Swan [1956]) but more general models with heterogeneous capital goods. Solow (1956, 1957) made it clear that the one-sector growth model was never intended as more than a useful heuristic device for analyzing aggregate data. Because they accepted that capital goods were heterogeneous, they were, in the mid-1950s, working on models involving many capital goods (Samuelson and Solow 1956; Dorfman, Samuelson, and Solow 1958), from which they concluded:

> Even though there is no such thing as a single abstract capital substance that transmutes itself from one machine form to another like a restless reincarnating soul, the rigorous investigation of a heterogeneous capital-goods model shows that over extended periods of time an economic society can in a perfectly straightforward way reconstruct the composition of its diverse capital goods so that there may remain great heuristic value in the simpler J. B. Clark-Ramsey models of abstract capital substance. (Samuelson and Solow 1956, 537–38)

Thus when their debate with Robinson continued in correspondence, Samuelson claimed that his work with Solow showed how any number of heterogeneous capital goods could be handled, sending Kahn (more likely to understand it than Robinson) a copy of *Linear Programming and Economic Analysis*.[12] Robinson's reply was that they were still missing her point: "You and Solow are a case of None so deaf as he who will not hear—so I shan't make myself hoarse shouting at you."[13] Despite this threat to ignore them, their exchanges heated up, in print and in correspondence, with over one hundred letters being exchanged, expressing increasing exasperation with each other, and with the three protagonists being joined by mostly younger colleagues on both sides. In the course of this, Samuelson (1962) sought to show that a Ramsey production function could serve as a surrogate for a more rigorous model; Solow (1963) tried to finesse Robinson's problem by switching to a model of intertemporal choice, in which investment could be measured simply in terms of oppor-

12. P. A. Samuelson to Joan Robinson, February 3, 1958, PASP box 63 (Robinson, Joan [1]).

13. J. Robinson to Paul A. Samuelson, January 22, 1958, PASP box 63 (Robinson, Joan [1]).

tunity cost (a sum of consumption goods); David Levhari (1965), an MIT student, tried to use a nonsubstitution theorem proved by Samuelson to show that reswitching—the phenomenon where, as the rate of interest falls, technique α is replaced by technique β, which is then replaced by α—could not take place. Unfortunately, all these defenses failed in that they turned out to rely on particular assumptions: that the capital-labor ratio used to produce all commodities was the same.[14]

The denouement is widely considered to have come in 1966 when, in summing up a symposium on "paradoxes in capital theory," involving papers by, among others, two economists with recent Cambridge doctorates (Pasinetti and Pierangelo Garegnani) and three with recent MIT doctorates (Levhari, Edwin Burmeister, and Eytan Sheshinski), Samuelson (1966b, 582–83) conceded that the position he and Solow had been defending was wrong.

> Lower interest rates may bring lower steady-state consumption and lower capital/output ratios, and the transition to such lower interest rate can involve denial of diminishing returns and entail reverse capital deepening in which current consumption is augmented rather than sacrificed.
>
> There often turns out to be no unambiguous way of characterizing different processes as more "capital-intensive," more "mechanized," more "roundabout," except in the ex post tautological sense of being adopted at a lower interest rate and involving a higher real wage. Such a tautological labeling is shown, in the case of reswitching, to lead to inconsistent ranking between pairs of unchanged technologies, depending upon which interest rate happens to prevail in the market.
>
> If all this causes headaches for those nostalgic for the old time parables of neoclassical writing, we must remind ourselves that scholars are not born to live an easy existence. We must respect, and appraise, the facts of life.

This statement by Samuelson marked MIT's recognition of Robinson's technical point, but, to the frustration of their critics, Samuelson and Solow did not stop using aggregate production functions. The reason was that they had never considered Ramsey production functions any more than a useful heuristic device that was almost essential in doing empirical

14. This paragraph summarizes a very long and torturous debate; readers should consult other surveys for the details.

work, where it was necessary to work with aggregate data. The "Solow-Swan model" abstracted from heterogeneity of capital in the same way that it abstracted from problems of unemployment, money, and finance. It is significant that, aside from a footnote in which he discussed aggregation over firms, not commodities (Solow 1956, 79n7), the phrase "aggregate production function" is used only in the context of data analysis (Solow 1957, 317). The fact that Solow had himself "thrown up still further obstacles" (312) meant that, as far as he and Samuelson were concerned, the problem Robinson identified was simply one of *many* problems surrounding the Ramsey production function.

One reason that Samuelson and Solow believed that the revaluation of the capital stock caused by changes in the rate of interest was not the most important of these problems is that they were concerned, throughout, with dynamics. Neither Robinson, whose capital theory involved steady-state comparisons, nor Sraffa, whose model abstracted altogether from time, offered any formal dynamic model of capital accumulation, whereas Samuelson and Solow insisted on using properly dynamic models that were not necessarily on steady-state growth paths.[15] As Solow wrote to Hahn,

> The Harrod-Domar legacy of paying attention only to equilibrium paths is by now an obstacle. All these ad hoc stability statements about what happens off such a path are useless without an explicit causal dynamics. But if we had the latter, then the equilibrium paths would appear as certain special motions and one could deal with them directly.[16]

This was exactly the approach taken by Dorfman, Samuelson, and Solow (1958, 329), who concluded that there was nothing special about balanced-growth paths: "General balanced growth is not even intertemporally efficient, let alone somehow special among efficient paths." Efficiency required balanced growth with capital goods in the optimal (von Neumann) proportions.[17] So, from this perspective, the significance of the "Solow model" was that it was a model in which, for all its simplifications, the dynamics were fully specified in that it gave a formal account of what would happen when the economy was not experiencing steady-state growth.

15. Sraffa's book cannot be discussed in detail here. To economists immersed in Leontief models and the von Neumann growth model, Sraffa's model looked familiar.

16. R. M. Solow to Frank H. Hahn, March 23, 1959, RMSP box 55 (E-H).

17. These are the intensities with which different processes are used found in von Neumann 1945.

Part of the problem with the capital theory debate was that so many issues were intertwined. Robinson turned out to be raising an issue whose significance Samuelson and Solow had not understood, but in explaining it, she introduced many complications that distracted attention from the central problem. Samuelson and Solow believed that they possessed the mathematical techniques necessary to analyze the problems she was identifying, but, even so, they found it necessary to abstract from problems she thought important.

3. Two Views of Distribution, 1958–68

If Robinson's critique were accepted, it was necessary to find an alternative theory of distribution. Inspired by the "widow's cruse" theory found in Keynes's *Treatise on Money* (1930), and the work of the Polish economist Michał Kalecki, several Cambridge economists tried to develop a "Keynesian" theory in which the rate of profit was determined by aggregate demand. Such a theory had been developed by Hahn (1972) in the PhD dissertation he wrote under Kaldor's supervision and submitted to the London School of Economics in 1948. However, the version that attracted interest was Kaldor's "Alternative Theories of Distribution" (1955). Here, Kaldor viewed the theories of David Ricardo and Karl Marx and "neoclassical" theories involving marginal productivity and monopoly power, before offering the Keynesian theory that he supported. The basic idea is that if there was a reverse-L-shaped aggregate supply curve, rises in aggregate demand would produce rises in output (the Keynesian multiplier) up to the kink (full capacity); after that point rises in demand would cause prices to rise relative to wages. If, as Kaldor believed was the case, the propensity to save out of profits (s_p) was higher than the propensity to save out of wages, this process would raise savings, choking off the rise in demand. In the simplest case, where workers consumed all their income, equilibrium implied that $I = s_p P$ (where I is investment and P is profits). Dividing both sides by the capital stock, K, yields a relationship between the rate of profit and the growth rate of the capital stock, $r = g/s_p$. The ideological significance of this equation was that its distribution was, as for Ricardo and Marx, the outcome of an asymmetric relationship between capitalists and workers.

On September 4–11, 1958, the International Economic Association held a conference on the island of Corfu, on the theory of capital, at which Cambridge was represented by Sraffa, Kaldor, and Austin Robinson, and

MIT by Samuelson, Solow, and Evsey Domar (Champernowne, also present, had moved from Cambridge to Oxford). Immediately afterward, Solow wrote to Hahn, "Nicky [Kaldor] and I had an eight-day battle royal, in the course of which I came to have considerable respect and even a certain affection for him."[18] The cause of this battle was the growth model that Kaldor had constructed around his Keynesian theory of income distribution.

One reason for their disagreement was that Kaldor, who had been familiar with capital measurement problems since the 1930s, chose not to work with an aggregate production function but with what he termed a "technical progress function" in which the rate of growth of output was a function of the growth rate of the capital stock, as shown in figure 1. If, as Kaldor believed was the case, this was nonlinear, it could not be integrated to obtain an aggregate production function, for output would depend not just on the capital stock but on the time path over which it had been accumulated. However, to solve his growth model, Kaldor worked with a linear technical progress function. As Solow explained to him, not only could a linear technical progress function be integrated, it was equivalent to a Cobb-Douglas production function.

That was not the only reason for disquiet over Kaldor's model. His Keynesian distribution theory required full employment, but he also wanted Keynesian unemployment to be possible, so he sought to reconcile the two with a theory of demand that involved elements of monopoly (Kaldor 1961, 195–203). In Solow's view, "Nicky's model simply will not stand up under scrutiny. When it is not self-contradictory it is more or less completely arbitrary."[19] In the next few years, the theory provoked considerable debate.

Shortly afterward, Kaldor, assisted by Mirrlees, who was to become a frequent visitor to MIT (Kaldor and Mirrlees 1962), provided a more rigorous model based on improved assumptions about technology but adopting the same assumptions about saving and investment. Kaldor's theory of distribution was challenged by Pasinetti (1962) on the grounds that it was wrong to specify propensities to save out of profits and wages. If workers saved, they would receive a share of profits, undermining the sociological basis for assuming different propensities to save out of these two types of income. Remarkably, Pasinetti showed that, if capitalists and

18. R. M. Solow to Frank H. Hahn, September 30, 1958, RMSP box 55 (E-H).
19. R. M. Solow to Frank H. Hahn, March 23, 1959, RMSP box 55 (E-H).

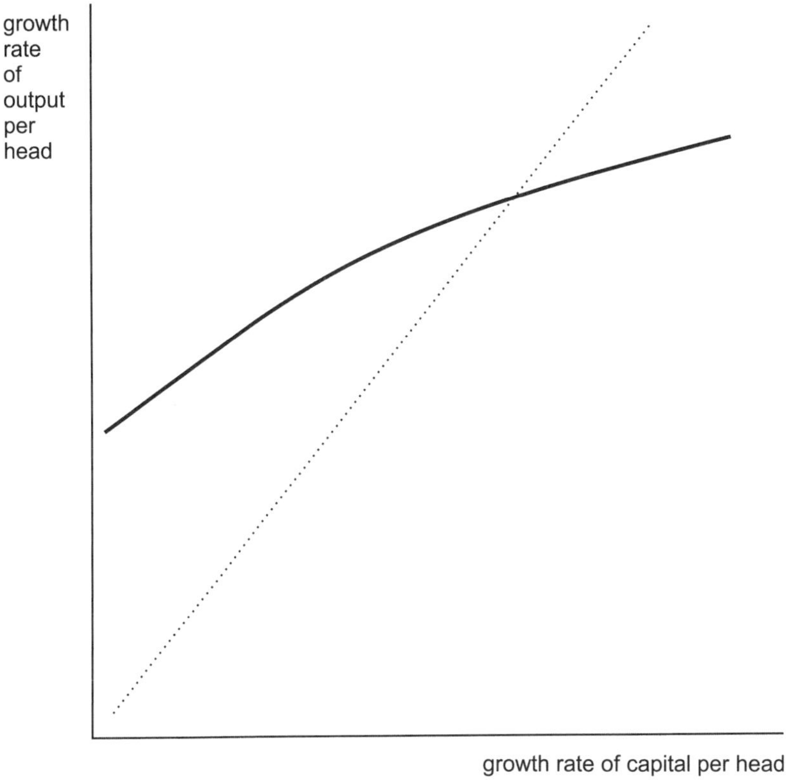

Figure 1 Kaldor's technical progress function. Drawn by author, based on a figure Kaldor uses in virtually all of his papers on growth

workers had different savings propensities, allowing for the fact that workers earned interest (profits) on their savings simplified the model. Even if workers saved, the rate of profit would depend only on the capitalists' propensity to save and the rate of capital accumulation. This was taken up by Samuelson and Franco Modigliani, who had by then moved to MIT (Samuelson and Modigliani 1966), who pointed out not only that Pasinetti's result required that the workers' propensity to save was sufficiently small but also that there was a dual case where profits depended solely on the workers' propensity to save. In contrast to Kaldor and his colleagues, Samuelson and Modigliani saw Kaldorian and marginal productivity theories not as alternatives but as parts of a more complicated theory.

The relation between marginal productivity theory and what he called the "Cambridge" wage (output minus profits determined according to the Kaldor formula) was taken up by Joseph Stiglitz in the year that he spent at Cambridge, receiving supervision from Hahn as well as advice from Solow by mail.[20] He produced a draft, involving imperfect competition and Kaldorian savings propensities, putting them together with a standard model of production involving a production function. Solow pointed out that adding differential savings propensities was entirely consistent with traditional Keynesian theory: "If savings are sensitive to the distribution of income, fine. If there are other variables, like wealth, in the saving function, fine. The theory doesn't mind."[21] In short, there was no reason why the Kaldorian theory should be seen as an alternative to traditional theory.

What makes this development significant is that through looking for ways in which the "Cambridge wage" might differ from the full-employment marginal product of labor, Stiglitz began to develop a theory of macroeconomic disequilibrium. Solow encouraged him, argued that there was great potential in using imperfect competition in macroeconomics, but saying that Stiglitz needed to work it out with more care, paying greater attention to the dynamics describing out-of-equilibrium behavior. In his reply, Stiglitz, referring to the effects of lags in consumption and production, asked Solow, "Does all of this boil down to what assumptions we make about adjustment mechanisms and speeds?"[22] Solow agreed with this, though he emphasized that a wide variety of outcomes was possible.[23] He continued:

> The hard problem is to formulate a good theory of what micro-behavior corresponds to a macroeconomic deficiency of effective demand; the problem is to reconcile the assumption that aggregate output is limited by effective demand with the worm's-eye view that any single approximately-competitive firm whose price exceeds marginal cost can apparently increase its profits by hiring more labor (even with a slight increase in the real wage) and selling more. It doesn't surprise an old Keynesian like me that except in a singular case there should be either unemployment or inflation.

20. He was also appointed a supervisor from the other side of the Cambridge faculty, and had discussions with Robinson.

21. R. M. Solow to Joseph E. Stiglitz, September 28, 1965, RMSP box 60 (R-S).

22. J. E. Stiglitz to Robert M. Solow, October 3, 1965, RMSP box 60 (R-S).

23. R. M. Solow to Joseph E. Stiglitz, October 14, 1965, RMSP box 60 (R-S).

In an undated "note on the marginal productivity wage and the Keynesian wage at full employment," Stiglitz took up these points, exploring assumptions about wage and price dynamics and using a labor demand curve that was kinked at full employment, to reach the conclusion:

> The point again is clear: if there is unemployment in an economy with profit maximization and a competitive labor market, but in which adjustments do not occur instantaneously, whether the real wage will eventually be zero, equal to the marginal product, or somewhere in between depends on the adjustment mechanism assumed. We have explored two quite striking cases; one in which depending on the relative speeds of adjustment, the real wage is either zero or equal to the marginal product of labor, (in the competitive case), and the other in which the real wage [is] determined completely by initial conditions.[24]

Starting with the problems posed by the capital controversy, Stiglitz, guided by Solow (and presumably in consultation with Hahn), developed an approach to macroeconomics that they modestly described as "a slightly novel theory of the determination of aggregate output and employment in the short run" (Solow and Stiglitz 1968, 537).[25]

4. Countering the New Classical Macroeconomics after 1970

Research into the constellation of growth, capital, and income-distribution theory framed by the two-Cambridges controversy did not lose momentum till well into the 1970s. Solow's *Growth Theory* (1970) was widely read, and textbooks appeared throughout the decade, by the MIT students Henry Wan (1971), Burmeister and A. Rodney Dobell (1970), while those committed to the "classical" approach inspired by Sraffa, whose *Production of Commodities by Means of Commodities* (1960) offered a theory of value that could be combined with the Keynesian theory of distribution to provide a theory that dispensed altogether with marginal analysis, continued their criticisms of neoclassical theory. The definitive summary of the issues in the controversy, at least from the neoclassical side, was arguably

24. J. E. Stiglitz, 1965, A note on the marginal productivity wage and the Keynesian wage at full employment, RMSP box 60 (R-S), last page.

25. Here the focus is on Stiglitz. The episode is discussed in relation to the development of Solow's thinking by Michaël Assous (2013). This literature is discussed in detail in Backhouse and Boianovsky 2013.

Capital Theory and the Distribution of Income (1975), in which Christopher Bliss, a Cambridge student who had spent 1963–64 at MIT, framed the issues in terms of a rigorously formulated intertemporal general equilibrium model, resolving the apparent paradox of reswitching by expanding the set of steady states to include ones in which rates of profit were not constant, and distinguishing clearly the problems of dynamic investment processes from comparisons of steady states. However, the momentum was lost: not only were problems now understood, but it was clear, at least to most economists, that the theory had little light to shed on the problems of stagflation that erupted after 1973–74. Indeed, the most dramatic productivity shock for a generation provided renewed scope for using Solow's aggregative model and the associated notion of total factor productivity to work out why productivity had fallen so far: the need for a practical way to measure contributions to productivity growth trumped concerns with the conceptual precision.

However, although the problem that had motivated Stiglitz to start working on the disequilibrium macroeconomics no longer resonated, the type of modeling that he and Solow had developed was perceived to have traction, even though their paper received less attention than works by other economists. The importance of adjustment speeds for macroeconomic equilibrium came to be associated not with Solow and Stiglitz but with Axel Leijonhufvud (1968), who had got to the idea by reexamining the foundations of Keynesian economics. The idea of a macroeconomic equilibrium with rationing, a dimension of Solow and Stiglitz's more complex model, came to be associated with Robert Barro and Herschel Grossman (1971), who discussed explicitly the microfoundations that Solow and Stiglitz had thought too obvious to need explicit statement. Though this literature came, in retrospect, to be equated with "fixed-price" models, it was seen by some as essential to explain stagflation, for it strained credibility to suggest that markets were in equilibrium during the 1970s (see Backhouse and Boianovsky 2013).

One reason that interest in capital theory declined was the emergence in the 1970s and 1980s of new theoretical challenges to the Keynesianism associated above all with Samuelson, Solow, and Modigliani, and their Yale colleague James Tobin. In challenging Keynesian policy prescriptions, the new classical macroeconomists (led by Robert Lucas, Thomas Sargent, Robert Barro, Fynn Kydland, and Edward Prescott) raised new theoretical issues. Rational expectations not only challenged the foundations of Keynesian policy analysis but also posed serious conceptual problems for econometricians, prompting a reconsideration of the relationship between macroeconomic theory and econometric modeling. The argument that models must assume consistent rational behavior on the part of economic agents (an assumption that not even Milton Friedman had been willing to make) and that markets must be modeled as being in equilibrium meant that Keynesian macroeconomics had to be defended in new ways.

Standing against this trend, Solow continued to teach disequilibrium macroeconomics, the central ideas of which went back to Stiglitz's time at Cambridge, and he trained many of those who were instrumental in forging a macroeconomics that reconciled the analytical innovations of Lucas with the Keynesian observation that markets might not work as efficiently as in the Lucasian world. Economists linked to MIT, including Stiglitz, Peter Diamond, and Michael Woodford, showed that asymmetric information, imperfect competition, and search theory could generate results sharply at variance with models of perfect competition.

However, even if MIT economists were generally lined up against the new classical/real business cycle view of the world, these developments were never associated with MIT in the same way that the neoclassical stance on capital theory had been. Though the number of high-profile "new Keynesians" coming out of MIT was high, too many economists from Columbia,[26] Princeton, Harvard, and Berkeley were involved, not to mention a very significant group of French economists, for this to be possible. If Robinson's debates with Samuelson and Solow had been central to the capital-theory phase of the MIT-Cambridge relationship, the close relationship between Hahn and Solow was central to the new phase. Not only did Cambridge graduate students come over to MIT, and vice versa, but Hahn and Solow embarked on a long project to counter the new classical macroeconomics, culminating in their jointly authored book, *A Critical Essay on Modern Macroeconomic Theory* (1995).

5. Conclusions

The capital controversy was important for the group of Cambridge economists challenging Samuelson and Solow, for it helped establish the identity of those who came to identify themselves as "post-Keynesian" (Mata 2004).[27] They increasingly developed a Keynesianism that was politically and conceptually very different from the Keynesian orthodoxy in which

26. The influence of Edmund Phelps pervaded this literature.

27. The term *Post Keynesian* had also been used more literally in the early 1950s to describe work that came after Keynes, contributing to the Keynesianism that was later challenged by those appropriating the term in the 1970s.

Samuelson and Solow were significant players. For around twenty years, "Cambridge" came to be identified with this group, centered on Robinson, Sraffa, and Pasinetti, despite the presence at Cambridge of many influential Keynesians whose intellectual commitments were closer to those of their counterparts at MIT.

However, whereas their Cambridge counterparts might focus on the political element, the MIT economists were motivated much more by technical issues. Samuelson (1962, 193), in a paper dedicated to Robinson on the occasion of her "memorable" visit to MIT, explained that the "MIT school" was often seen to involve the use of the tools of "modern linear and more general programming" to analyze growth in models with heterogeneous capital goods. Because of the methods she chose to use, Robinson engaged directly with the linear models with which Samuelson and Solow hoped to operationalize general equilibrium theory. Neither the passion with which Samuelson and Solow engaged with the arguments of Robinson and her colleagues, nor the way in which they argued, can be understood apart from their prior work on linear programming and multisector modeling. *Linear Programming and Economic Analysis* and the papers that led up to it were important because they analyzed precisely the techniques that Robinson used to make her case about the measurement of capital. However, though this book contained the first published formulation of the theorems about efficient capital accumulation that Samuelson and Solow considered their main contribution to the theory of growth, it was not mentioned in the best-known account of the controversy (Harcourt 1972).[28]

A further reason for their engagement concerned the relationship between different types of model. Taking Solow as exemplifying the MIT school, Samuelson (1962, 193) opined that

> one might almost say that there are two Solows—the orthodox priest of the MIT school and the busman on a holiday who operates brilliantly and without inhibitions in the rough-and-ready realm of empirical heuristics. Just as red wine and white wine are both good, so are both Solows of vintage quality. But if I were forced to choose between red and white wine, I for one would reveal a preference for the red.

The important characteristic Samuelson identified here was the simultaneous use of two different types of model, the choice being made accord-

28. Harcourt did rectify this neglect in other work.

ing to the problem in hand. Robinson appeared to be challenging the crucial result, demonstrated by Samuelson in the 1940s, that lay beneath this modeling strategy: that though the mathematics of linear inequalities might look very different from the differential calculus traditionally used by economists, they were consistent with each other.

The controversy between the two Cambridges eventually came to be seen by MIT economists (and most of the economics profession) as a waste of time. Samuelson and Solow become increasingly frustrated by Robinson's repetition of what they saw as the same points, and they published replies to her work out of a sense of duty. They found Kaldor's models completely unconvincing. However, the controversy had an important spin-off: the development of disequilibrium theory, which Solow continued to teach to generations of MIT graduate students whose work was a significant input into what became the "new Neoclassical synthesis" codified by Woodford (2003).

The story of MIT's relationship with Cambridge is one of the passing of the generation associated with the Keynesian revolution. On the Cambridge side, the end of the controversy was connected to the departure of Robinson, Kaldor, Sraffa, and Kahn, all of whom had done their main work in the 1920s and 1930s, and for whom Samuelson, in particular, had immense respect.[29] On the MIT side, though Samuelson and Solow remained active, a younger generation became more important. After Hahn's appointment as a professor at Cambridge and with the rise of monetarism and the new classical macroeconomics, strongly opposed by both Hahn and Solow, the dominant strand of MIT-Cambridge interaction became one of cooperation against Chicago and Minnesota rather than competition with each other.

References

Assous, M. 2013. "Solow's Struggle with Medium-Run Macroeconomics: 1956–1995." Working Paper 2013-17, Center for the History of Political Economy at Duke University.

Backhouse, R. E., and M. Boianovsky. 2013. *Transforming Modern Macroeconomics: Searching for Disequilibrium Microfoundations, 1956–2003*. Cambridge: Cambridge University Press.

Barro, R. J., and H. I. Grossman. 1971. "A General Disequilibrium Model of Income and Employment." *American Economic Review* 61 (1): 82–93.

29. Solow never understood Samuelson's enthusiasm for Sraffa's work.

Bliss, C. J. 1975. *Capital Theory and the Distribution of Income*. Amsterdam: North-Holland.

Burmeister, E., and A. R. Dobell. 1970. *Mathematical Theories of Economic Growth*. London: Macmillan.

Champernowne, D. G. 1953. "The Production Function and the Theory of Capital: A Comment." *Review of Economic Studies* 21 (2): 112–35.

Dorfman, R., P. A. Samuelson, and R. M. Solow. 1958. *Linear Programming and Economic Analysis*. New York: McGraw Hill.

Düppe, T., and E. R. Weintraub. 2014. "Siting the New Economic Science: The Cowles Commission's Activity Analysis Conference of June 1949." *Science in Context* 27 (3).

Hahn, F. 1972. *The Share of Wages in the National Income: An Enquiry into the Theory of Distribution*. London: Weidenfeld and Nicolson.

Hahn, F. H., and R. M. Solow. 1995. *A Critical Essay on Modern Macroeconomic Theory*. Cambridge, Mass.: MIT Press.

Hamouda, O. F., and G. C. Harcourt. 1988. "Post Keynesianism: From Criticism to Coherence?" *Bulletin of Economic Research* 40 (1): 1–33.

Harcourt, G. C. 1969. "Some Cambridge Controversies in the Theory of Capital." *Journal of Economic Literature* 7 (2): 369–405.

———. 1972. *Some Cambridge Controversies in the Theory of Capital*. Cambridge: Cambridge University Press.

Kaldor, N. 1955. "Alternative Theories of Distribution." *Review of Economic Studies* 23 (2): 83–100.

———. 1961. "Capital Accumulation and Economic Growth." In *The Theory of Capital: Proceedings of a Conference Held by the International Economic Association,* edited by D. C. Hague and L. A. Lutz, 177–222. London: Macmillan.

Kaldor, N., and J. A. Mirrlees. 1962. "A New Model of Economic Growth." *Review of Economic Studies* 29 (3): 174–92.

Keynes, J. M. 1930. *A Treatise on Money*. 2 vols. London: Macmillan.

Koopmans, T. C. 1951. *Activity Analysis of Production and Allocation: Proceedings of a Conference*. New York: Wiley.

Leijonhufvud, A. 1968. *On Keynesian Economics and the Economics of Keynes*. Oxford: Oxford University Press.

Leontief, W. 1947. "Introduction to a Theory of the Internal Structure of Functional Relationships." *Econometrica* 15 (4): 361–73.

Levhari, D. 1965. "A Nonsubstitution Theorem and Switching of Techniques." *Quarterly Journal of Economics* 79 (1): 98–105.

Mata, T. 2004. "Constructing Identity: The Post Keynesians and the Capital Controversies." *Journal of the History of Economic Thought* 26 (2): 241.

Pasinetti, L. L. 1962. "Rate of Profit and Income Distribution in Relation to the Rate of Economic Growth." *Review of Economic Studies* 29 (4): 267.

Robinson, J. 1953. "The Production Function and the Theory of Capital." *Review of Economic Studies* 21 (2): 81–106.

———. 1955. “The Production Function and the Theory of Capital—a Reply.” *Review of Economic Studies* 23 (3): 247.
———. 1956. *The Accumulation of Capital*. London: Macmillan.
Samuelson, P. A. 1962. “Parable and Realism in Capital Theory: The Surrogate Production Function.” *Review of Economic Studies* 29 (3): 193–206.
———. 1966a. “Market Mechanisms and Maximization.” In *The Collected Scientific Papers of Paul A. Samuelson*, edited by J. E. Stiglitz, 425–92. Cambridge, Mass.: MIT Press.
———. 1966b. “A Summing Up.” *Quarterly Journal of Economics* 80 (4): 568–83.
Samuelson, P. A., and F. Modigliani. 1966. “The Pasinetti Paradox in Neoclassical and More General Models.” *Review of Economic Studies* 33 (4): 269–301.
Samuelson, P. A., and R. M. Solow. 1956. “A Complete Capital Model Involving Heterogeneous Capital Goods.” *Quarterly Journal of Economics* 70 (4): 537–62.
Solow, R. M. 1955. “The Production Function and the Theory of Capital.” *Review of Economic Studies* 23 (2): 101–8.
———. 1956. “A Contribution to the Theory of Economic Growth.” *Quarterly Journal of Economics* 70 (1): 65–94.
———. 1957. Technical Change and the Aggregate Production Function. *Review of Economics and Statistics* 39 (3): 312–20.
———. 1963. *Capital Theory and the Rate of Return*. Amsterdam: North-Holland.
———. 1970. *Growth Theory: An Exposition*. Oxford: Oxford University Press.
Solow, R. M., and P. A. Samuelson. 1953. “Balanced Growth under Constant Return to Scale. *Econometrica* 21 (3): 412–24.
Solow, R. M., and J. E. Stiglitz. 1968. “Output, Employment, and Wages in the Short Run.” *Quarterly Journal of Economics* 82 (4): 537–60.
Sraffa, P. 1960. *Production of Commodities by Means of Commodities: Prelude to a Critique of Economic Theory*. Cambridge: Cambridge University Press.
Swan, T. W. 1956. “Economic Growth and Capital Accumulation.” *Economic Record* 32 (2): 334–61.
Turner, M. S. 1989. *Joan Robinson and the Americans*. Illustrated ed. Armonk, N.Y.: M. E. Sharpe.
von Neumann, J. 1945. “A Model of General Economic Equilibrium.” *Review of Economic Studies* 13 (1): 1–9.
Wan, H. Y. 1971. *Economic Growth*. Illustrated ed. New York: Harcourt Brace Jovanovich.
Woodford, M. 2003. *Interest and Prices*. Princeton, N.J.: Princeton University Press.

Making Things Technical: Samuelson at MIT

Harro Maas

> Going to MIT turned out to be the best thing that could have happened to me and for my lifetime productivity. That is why I never left for Chicago, Harvard, or numerous other prestigious research centers. I always had the best of two worlds: Solow, Modigliani, Kindleberger et al. at MIT with marvelous graduate students and research facilities. At the same time close contact with Widener Library, Schumpeter, Leontief, Haberler, Hansen, Musgrave, and Arrow.
> —Paul Samuelson to Wolfgang Stolper, March 11, 2002

In 1961, at the age of forty-six, Paul Samuelson delivered his presidential address to the American Economic Association (AEA) on economists and the history of ideas. Samuelson promised not to discuss "technical economics" but to concentrate on the political and ideological importance attributed to economists in the public sphere. Yet it quickly became clear that Samuelson's address actually was a tribute to those econo-

Correspondence may be addressed to Harro Maas, Utrecht School of Economics, Kriekenpitplein 21-22, 3584 EC Utrecht, The Netherlands; e-mail: h.b.j.b.maas@uu.nl. I would like to thank Roger E. Backhouse for generous help at various stages of this essay, E. Roy Weintraub, Tiago Mata, the participants at the 2013 *HOPE* conference, and the referees of this journal for encouragement and comments. A special word of thanks goes to the librarians of the David M. Rubenstein Rare Book and Manuscript Library at Duke University for their great help. Sources from the Paul A. Samuelson Papers, David M. Rubenstein Rare Book and Manuscript Library, Duke University, are referred to as PASP box, folder, item, or PASP box, item, if folder and item are the same.

History of Political Economy 46 (annual suppl.) DOI 10.1215/00182702-2716199

mists who, outside the "limelight," had brought rigor and precision to the discipline.

Samuelson clearly identified with this analytical lineage that had helped turn economics into a mathematical, modeling science in which analytical precision outweighed ideological impact.[1] He referred to his own modeling work on "welfare economics and factor-prize equalization; turnpike theorems and osculating envelopes; nonsubstitutability relations in Minkowski-Ricardo-Leontief-Metzler matrices of Mosak-Hicks type, or balanced-budget multipliers under conditions of balanced uncertainty in locally impacted topological spaces and molar equivalences" (Samuelson 1962, 1).

Thus emphasizing technicality might obscure Samuelson's more important message that the technical economist, in the postwar era, had brought rigor and precision to economic policy. Economics freed from ideology enabled the economist to, in Theodore M. Porter's phrase, "speak precision to power."[2] Indeed, a technical analysis could well lead to conclusions that ran against the popular or political current. That, at root, was the meaning of Samuelson's famous (or notorious) closing words of his address that economists, at the end of the day, were interested only "in our own applause." Technicality implied impartiality and detachment. Samuelson thus exemplifies for economics the general move of science in the postwar era to define itself as technical (Porter 2009), a move that fit well with the teaching and research profile that MIT developed in the postwar era.

This essay examines the history of this stance. My aim is to show how Samuelson from the 1940s defined his own role as an economist as a technical expert. I connect this theme with Samuelson's decision to stay at MIT, despite tempting offers from Chicago and Harvard, with his consultancy work for the National Resources Planning Board (NRPB), and with his defense of his textbook as a technical introduction to then come back to Theodore W. Schultz, who at least twice—in 1947 and again in 1949—offered Samuelson a position at Chicago. Halfway through the 1950s this strategy of defining economics as technical had transformed the MIT economics department into one of the centers of economics academe, with Samuelson as its nucleus. Paradoxically, Samuelson's emphasis on technical expertise made him an economist whom everyone, from whatever political denomination or layer of society, could and did turn to for advice. It moved him from the shadows into the limelight.

1. Samuelson mentions his "astonishment" when Schumpeter singled out three French economists out of the four he considered still relevant for this lineage: Quesnay, Cournot, Walras.

2. See Porter 2006.

The Promise of an Institute

On November 15, 1949, Paul Samuelson wrote a long letter to Theodore W. Schultz, chairman of the economics department at Chicago, declining the latest offer for a full professorship and explaining his decision to stay at MIT.[3] In retrospect, in a letter of condolence to Schultz's son Paul of March 4, 1998, Samuelson reminisced about Schultz's perseverance in recruiting him to Chicago, which, at one moment, "almost" made him accept the Chicago chair.[4] That moment was in March 1947, when after refusing Chicago's "flattering offer," Samuelson came to regret his decision and then, "without telling anyone in the department," called Schultz to accept "the Chicago job." When his colleagues at MIT recognized Samuelson's "acute uneasiness of mind," they suggested that he take leave for a "quiet weekend to think the matter through" with his wife, Marion.[5]

That weekend James Rhyme Killian, at the time vice president of MIT, came over for lunch to talk things over. After reconsidering the situation, Samuelson found it "very easy to arrive at" his final decision "to stay at M.I.T."[6] An increase in his salary to a level that matched the Chicago offer may have helped, along with MIT's decision just a week earlier to raise his rank to a full professorship, but from the records it is clear that these considerations were not decisive.[7] Samuelson was especially appreciative of Killian's firm determination to support Samuelson's research "in every possible way." What did this promise mean in practice?

The Cowles Commission's Interest in Samuelson

Schultz began his campaign to win Samuelson for Chicago early in 1946, to the shock and dismay of important faculty members like Milton Fried-

3. PASP box 68, Schultz, Samuelson to Schultz, November 15, 1949.

4. PASP box 68, T. W. Schultz, Samuelson to T. Paul Schultz, March 4, 1998.

5. PASP box 68, T. W. Schultz, Samuelson to Schultz, March 11, 1947. Earlier, Samuelson had rejected an offer at a salary of $8,500 (PASP box 68, Schultz, Schultz to Samuelson, February 17, 1949, and Samuelson to Schultz, February 28, 1947). Schultz also suggested suitable housing. Roy Blough, one of Chicago's institutionalists, praised Chicago as a family place and Schultz for showing "real leadership as a departmental chairman" (PASP box 17, Blough, Blough to Samuelson, February 4, 1947).

6. PASP box 53, MIT correspondence 1940–2007, Samuelson to Killian, March 11, 1947.

7. PASP box 53, MIT correspondence 1940–2007, Killian to Samuelson, March 3, 1947; Killian to Samuelson, March 10, 1947. The Chicago offer was matched in violation of the "standing policy" not to do so. Killian emphasized that in this case MIT decided to give a clear message of support to Samuelson's "own program and the general program here in Economics and to do everything possible to insure that this program be as strong as we can make it."

man, Frank Knight, and others.[8] Schultz possibly acted in consultation with the Cowles Commission, which had prodded Samuelson to accept a job offer, if made. On March 20, 1946, Jacob Marschak wrote to Samuelson that he would soon receive an invitation for a "customary visit" with the administration and the department. Marschak went to great lengths to explain the meaning of such a visit, which might not be clear to outsiders, and perhaps was not clear to insiders either.

Marschak clearly wrote on the assumption that the economics department was about to make Samuelson an offer. It was "usually agreed" that a visit to the department did not "commit" the department or the administration, while it was also unlikely that the administration would act against the department's recommendation. Marschak did not leave his own hopes and expectations in doubt: "I so hope you will be able to come, and that the visit will bring positive results," meaning that Samuelson would "consider accepting a position here, if offered."[9] If Samuelson accepted, it would bring him back to the city where he spent an important part of his youth and to the university department where he studied as an undergraduate.

Samuelson visited Chicago April 16–18, shortly after receiving the invitation. Immediately after his return to Cambridge, Samuelson expressed his gratitude about the warm welcome and intense conversations with the members of the department, with Schultz himself, and with Maynard Hutchins and Robert Redfield, chancellor of the university and dean of the Division of Social Sciences, respectively. Then there was silence. If an offer was made, it was only by the end of November that the archival records show Schultz explicitly mentioning "the genuine long run interest" in having Samuelson in the economics department, hopefully by the "beginning of next fall."[10] In this intermediate period, tensions within the department must have grown to a boiling point, but Schultz, backed by a faculty vote forced by Paul Douglas, went ahead despite fierce opposition. Friedman of course feared his plan of bringing in George Stigler from Columbia would fall to pieces, and the department would be lost to the Keynesians.[11]

8. Hammond and Hammond (2006, 4, 46, letter of Friedman to Stigler, November 27, 1946). I thank Roy Weintraub for bringing this source to my attention.

9. PASP box 68, Schultz, Marschak to Samuelson, March 20, 1946.

10. PASP box 68, Schultz, Schultz to Samuelson, November 25, 1946.

11. On November 27, 1946, Friedman wrote to Stigler: "We don't know yet the end of the story, but whatever it is, I am very much afraid we're lost. The Keynesians have the votes & mean to use them. Knight is bitter & says he will withdraw from active participation in the dep't. Mints, Gregg [Lewis HM] & I are very low about it. Brown [University] or Hopkins may be pretty good after all" (quoted in Hammond and Hammond 2006, 46). In this same letter Friedman discussed Douglas's role in the matter.

Samuelson sent Schultz a telegram stating that he was willing to discuss things at the January meeting of the AEA in Atlantic City.[12]

Following on this correspondence and in close consultation with Marschak, Tjalling Koopmans explained to Samuelson how much Chicago needed him.[13] Samuelson combined interests in a "sharper mathematical formulation of economic theory" with an interest in the "sharper formulation of statistical procedures" for testing. These interests in rigor and precision combined with Samuelson's strong Keynesian profile: an interest in macroeconomics and an interest in the practical and pressing question of how to reach a full employment economy, a clear reference to Samuelson's consultancy work for the NRPB during the war. Such interests Koopmans found underdeveloped, if not altogether wanting, in the Chicago economics department, which was either way an understatement. "Of all theoretical economists," Samuelson would be most receptive to the Cowles Commission's adaptation of statistical methods to "real economic problems" and to its urge to have economic theorists engage with measuring and testing their theories.[14]

Koopmans rightly considered Samuelson one of the prominent Keynesians in the immediate aftermath of the war, but Samuelson emphasized rigor and precision in theory rather than in the testing of the Keynesian stance. This does not mean that Samuelson was uninterested in statistics. But separating the modeling from the statistics enabled Samuelson to separate his defense of the technical apparatus of Keynesian analysis from the concomitant political profile of a market interventionist. This does not mean that Samuelson's own political profile was absent or unimportant (as witnessed from the unease in the Chicago faculty), but it was concealed behind technicality. After ideology all too visibly had eclipsed reason before and during the war, who could be against rigor and precision in arguments and facts? Put otherwise: emphasizing the operational significance of economic theory was for Samuelson another way to defend its ideological neutrality.

12. PASP box 68, Schultz, Samuelson to Schultz, January 18, 1947.

13. The rapid sequence of Schultz's and Koopmans's correspondence almost reads as a coup against powerful economists within the department, such as Milton Friedman and Frank Knight, who were highly critical of the Cowles Commission and its methods. This may well have added fuel to the much-discussed uneasy relation between the economics department and the Cowles Commission.

14. PASP box 45, Koopmans, Koopmans to Samuelson, December 17, 1946.

Weaving the Social Sciences into the MIT Curriculum

For a then still young associate professor, the offer of a full professorship in one of the leading economics departments must have been extremely tempting. Samuelson left Harvard for MIT in 1941, exchanging an offer on the level of a teaching assistant for that of an assistant professor.[15] For much of the war Samuelson had been involved in projects outside the economics department; at the NRPB and at MIT's Radiation Laboratory. As argued by Roger E. Backhouse (this volume, "Samuelson's Move"), E. B. Wilson's advice played an important role in Samuelson's decision to change a prestigious Ivy League university for an unassuming economics department in a technical university that had only recently significantly increased its visibility because of the war.

Shortly after the war, MIT began reconsidering its place in the US research and educational landscape, and this was especially important for the place of the social sciences, including economics, in the curriculum.[16] From its inception, MIT had combined professional training in the sciences with courses in the social sciences and the humanities at the bachelor's level, mimicking in an engineering context the educational profile of a liberal arts school. The committee investigating the curriculum considered that the new demands posed by the aftermath of the war asked for more, and more serious, training in the social sciences, as well as more training in science fundamentals.[17] With this emphasis on the social sciences, MIT followed the general trend in postwar social science education and research that saw a veritable explosion in growth until the beginning of the 1970s (Solovey 2012).

The response of the administration to these challenges was principled as well as pragmatic. Published in 1949 after a full two years of investigation, the committee report recommended an expansion of the role of the social sciences in the curriculum by building on its current strengths. The School of Humanities and Social Science should become a full-fledged school, on a par with the technical schools, where not only undergraduate

15. This episode is extensively treated in Roger Backhouse's ("Samuelson's Move") and Roy Weintraub's ("MIT's Openness") contributions to this volume.

16. See Cherrier, this volume.

17. On this report, see also Cherrier, this volume; Weintraub, this volume, introduction; and Giraud, this volume.

and graduate teaching should be given at a competitive level with neighboring institutes and universities but also research should aspire to be competitive with research elsewhere. This of course would imply serious investments.

Cleary the institute had already committed itself to such investments. Killian's delicate maneuvering with Samuelson fit the committee's recommendation to strengthen the research profile of the social sciences by building on the quality that was already there. Even if we do not know exactly what Killian promised to Samuelson, appointments over the ensuing years confirm Killian's retrospective account that MIT's economics department was built around Samuelson by hiring such promising economists as Robert M. Solow, Franco Modigliani, and Charles P. Kindleberger, "who found satisfaction in being members of a team that included Samuelson" (Killian 1985, 201). Killian most likely promised Samuelson to build a team from which he could benefit, without being responsible for daily affairs.

Thus the enfolding policy at MIT promised Samuelson a congenial intellectual research environment that would secure his role as a premium researcher who was guaranteed the freedom to follow his research interests free from institutional constraints. In the years that follow, Samuelson moved around. The prestigious Guggenheim fellowship brought him to Britain in the fall of 1948. The department enabled Samuelson to extend short research trips to RAND in Palo Alto, California, over several months. Samuelson's engagements with RAND led to his contribution to the Activity Analysis Conference that was organized by Koopmans in Chicago. By bringing in an interdisciplinary group of scholars from mathematics and economics, as Till Düppe and E. Roy Weintraub argue (forthcoming), this conference enabled mathematics to bring rigor to economics, and economics to innovate applied mathematics.[18]

Samuelson thanked Killian for the "highly satisfactory provisions for leave of absence" arranged by Killian and Ralph Freeman that "could not be better." If we look at the management of daily affairs in the economics department, Samuelson was, as Beatrice Cherrier (this volume) shows, remarkably absent. But that does not mean he was absent intellectually. The period in which Schultz tried to bring Samuelson to Chicago was crucial for the institutional profiling of the economics department within MIT and consequential for Samuelson's ultimate decision to stay at MIT.

18. On Samuelson's role in this conference, see Backhouse 2012.

To better understand the parallels between the self-image of MIT and Samuelson's intellectual pathway, I will now turn to Samuelson's years as a nonresident consultant to the National Resources Planning Board (NRPB) during the war years. These years make visible how Samuelson translated his profile of a mathematical economic theorist into the domain of empirical and policy research, broadening himself out, as E. B. Wilson suggested, to applied work (Backhouse, this volume, "Samuelson's Move"). As I show, Samuelson's consultancy work put him in a position to organize applied economic research, situating himself in the center intellectually without being administratively responsible. This consulting role of research to politics became an essential part of MIT's self-assessment after the war.[19]

Modeling Scenarios

Early in 1947 Samuelson wrote to Schultz that one of his reasons for staying at MIT was his "feeling" that an academic position on the East Coast was not "limited by the University of Chicago form of professional contact" and could give him more opportunities in "outside consulting activities." For a "potentially 'narrow' theoretical economist" like himself, such activities had a value that went far beyond their "pecuniary return."[20] Even though Samuelson in the next sentence downplayed these consulting activities as a "very minor point," their consequences were not.

Samuelson indicated that his consultancy work helped convert an abstract, modeling approach to theory to a format that could be used to generate empirically informed scenarios for policy purposes. Consultancy work taught Samuelson to see models as a site for policy exploration and as a technology for policy advice, characteristics that would become markers of the MIT economists' approach to modeling (Halsmayer, this volume). Thus his consulting work for the NRPB enabled Samuelson to become an expert who stayed in the shadows, to let the model speak to its

19. See part 1, chapter 4, and part 3 of the *Report of the Committee on Educational Survey* (1949). On the general importance of consultancy for the economics discipline in the postwar period, see Fourcade 2009.

20. PASP box 68, Schultz, Samuelson to Schultz, January 13, 1947. Samuelson's remark echoes the suggestion of E. B. Wilson to Samuelson that his move to MIT might offer "a chance to broaden yourself out on certain types of application," apart from Wilson's hope that such a move might in fact strengthen both departments. See Backhouse, this volume, "Samuelson's Move."

audience. While Samuelson got a taste of consultancy work during the war years, MIT enabled him to maintain and expand his consultancy network and to use the inflow of information for his theoretical work.

Before he became involved in consultancy work, Samuelson had developed a generic modeling strategy. He outlined different scenarios and indicated ranges of inferences that could be drawn from models encapsulating assumptions that were not too far off the economists' intuitions, sometimes producing highly unexpected results. A good example is his 1939 article on the multiplier-accelerator mechanism that outlined qualitative scenarios showing the different types of interactions for different parameter values of the propensities to consume and invest. This modeling approach showed (policy) possibilities in logical space: the generic characteristics of a problem that was in need of specification in the concrete.[21]

Becoming a Technical Expert

Samuelson had started his consultancy work for the NRPB in exactly this vein. At Alvin Hansen's request, Samuelson had agreed to work on how to "plan" for full employment after the war.[22] Hansen had his doubts about the section within the NRPB, which had "hurriedly" produced a report that, he was sure, could improve greatly from Samuelson's criticism. At the beginning of August 1941, Samuelson started his activities in Thomas Blaisdell's Full Employment Stabilization Section, which was responsible for reporting on business trends, science activities, and economics and government (Clawson 1981, 50). This section fell under Oscar L. Altman's responsibilities. The contract was for fifteen days a month of consulting work at a maximum.[23]

In a meeting chaired by Hansen, Samuelson's project was described as "making varying assumptions about income distribution under a stalemate economy, high consumption economy, a redistributed income economy, and a full employment economy," mimicking in an applied setting the format of

21. For a recent discussion of generic versus specific modeling strategies, see Morgan 2012. See also Maas 2014.

22. PASP box 55, NRPB, Hansen to Samuelson, July 10, 1941. Thomas Blaisdell confirmed the invitation in a letter of July 23, 1941. For different notions of planning in that period, see Balisciano 1998.

23. PASP box 55, NRPB, approval of contract by L. A. Moyer, executive office of the president, August 11, 1941.

scenario analyses he had explored in his 1939 Keynes-Hansen model. Samuelson could handle the small-scale simulation on this model very well by himself, but to bring the NRPB project to a successful end, he needed a team of collaborators. Though not formally responsible for personnel, Samuelson made suggestions whom to hire for what part of the job. This figure of standing in the shadows while leaving responsibility to others is exemplary for how Samuelson defined his own detached position of the economic academic. It impersonalized the results of his work, while everyone knew he had an important hand in it. It was exactly because of this combination of detachment and know-how that his advice became much asked for.

Samuelson started at the NRPB at the beginning of August 1941 and quickly became much more involved in its activities than could have been inferred from Hansen's initial request.[24] In part, this was because the war effort itself would soon draw many economists and statisticians to the military and state agencies that called on their skills and advice. Reflecting on his Washington years, Samuelson wrote that by 1943 the "*center of population* (in the sense of Gini) of the American economics profession" was to be found "somewhere between 10th and 11th Avenues, near Pennsylvania Avenue, N.W."[25]

Setting up a Team by Remote Control

Samuelson traveled back and forth on the night train from Cambridge to Washington on a fortnightly basis, mostly sleeping over with friends during his nights in Washington. By "remote control" he had to "build up and maintain" a research staff, a team, of which possible candidates now and then were "pirated away" during his trips back and forth to Washington. On the positive side, living in Cambridge also meant being outside the cabal of daily administrative affairs and having at hand economics and statistics journals that even a small-town state college would have, but that were absent in Washington.[26]

24. Samuelson was appointed August 7, 1941 (PASP box 55, NRPB, L. A. Moyer, executive director and chief examiner of the United States Civil Service Commission, to Samuelson, August 11, 1941).

25. PASP box 152, Post-war planning as seen by a retired post-war planner, 1940s, undated and unfinished typescript speech.

26. PASP box 152, Post-war planning as seen by a retired post-war planner, 1940s, undated and unfinished typescript speech.

Following on his comment on Hansen's "masterly" memorandum *Post-Defense Full Employment*, Samuelson made suggestions for the composition of his team. His group was not going to collect data first-hand but would seek, analyze, and interpret data sets often painstakingly collected by others.[27] Samuelson therefore emphasized the "urgent need for personnel" with sufficient imagination to "formulate the right questions and enough ingenuity to dig out the answers." He needed economist-statisticians who had mastered "high powered theoretical and statistical tools." As a minimum staff, he considered two economists, one to keep contact with the other units, and two assistant economists, and for computing and secretarial assistance he expected to draw on the general pool available at the NRPB.[28]

In consultation with Samuelson, a list of scholars was made that the study unit might recruit from. Some of them Samuelson knew from his Harvard years. Thus, in an undated list, we find James Tobin, whom he had taught as a teaching assistant, Abram Bergson, and Sidney Alexander, all cosigners of the petition that asked Joseph Schumpeter to stay at Harvard,[29] and Dudley Dillard, Walt Rostow, Avron Douglis, and Martin Bronfenbrenner, the latter two from his undergraduate years in Chicago. They were listed with their current affiliation and most important skills. Samuelson sent letters to a selection of them and, though his section was formally headed by Oscar L. Altman, also held interviews.[30] Some, such as Rutledge Vining, had to decline Samuelson's offer because work at the NRPB could not be combined with obligations at their home university.[31] Avron Douglis, an economist with strong mathematical interests, declined because he was on the draft, but made suggestions for other names. Samuelson was

27. Especially by Kuznets at the NBER.

28. PASP box 135, Getting to an economy of post-war full employment, 1940s. Memorandum by Samuelson of August 25, 1941, on a Research Unit to Study Implications of Full Employment Economy. In a memorandum by Samuelson of October 3, 1941, the number of staff to be hired had grown to nine economists in grades P-1 to P-5, two statistical clerks at CAF-4, and three stenographers. This second memorandum is mentioned in a letter from Altman to Blaisdell of December 11, 1941, in PASP box 55, National Resources Planning Board (NRPB).

29. When Samuelson was offered only a teaching assistantship at Harvard, Schumpeter threatened to resign. For details, see Backhouse, this volume, "Samuelson's Move."

30. Samuelson sent letters to Abram Bergson, W. W. Rostow, F. L. Kidner, H. Gregg Lewis, Mr. Alfred Neal, David Durand, Rutledge Vining, M. F. Millikan, and Ray Jastrum (PASP box 55, NRPB, letters of August 23, 1941).

31. PASP box 55, NRPB, Vining to Samuelson, September 21, 1941.

Table 1 List of Institutes and Persons with Whom the Section "Full Employment after the War" Had Been in Contact

Agency	Person
Department of Commerce	Arthur Upgren
	H. W. Bissell Jr.
Department of Labor	D. H. Davenport
	Dal Hitchcock
	J. M. G. Pierson
	Wassily Leontief
Department of Agriculture, Bureau of Agricultural Economics	Roy Kimmel
	Oris Wells
	Mrs. H. F. Goldsmith
Office of Price Administration	Hildegarde Kneeland
Securities and Exchange Commission	H. W. Goldsmith
Federal Reserve Board	A. H. Hansen
	A. B. Hersey
	Harvey Perloff
Bureau of the Budget	Gerhard Colm
Board of Economic Warfare	Louis Beam

Source: PASP box 55, NRPB, memorandum from Altman to Blaisdell on the status of Studies of War-Time Planning for Consumer Demand and Continuing Full Employment.

also approached by economists who had heard "through the grapevine" that he was looking for personnel for his full-employment postwartime study.[32] Thus, setting up an empirical study, of the evaluative kind he envisaged, put Samuelson in the position to estimate not only the work to be done but also the qualities of those to do it. Not in charge formally, he nevertheless functioned as the intellectual and institutional organizer.

Samuelson's arm reached into the (semi-)governmental institutes the study group was in contact with. The files contain the following list of persons and institutions consulted in an early stage of the project (see table 1). By remote control, Samuelson's consultancy work thus gave him access to the inner offices of almost every government agency of importance.[33]

32. PASP box 55, NRPB, John W. Seybold to Samuelson, September 24, 1941.

33. PASP box 55, NRPB, memorandum from Altman to Blaisdell on the status of Studies of War-Time Planning for Consumer Demand and Continuing Full Employment.

Without Government Intervention: Unemployment Ahead

Various versions of the report appeared in 1942. The study would stand at the center of Samuelson's failed forecast of an economic depression after the war, which he published in his *New Republic* article "Unemployment Ahead" for September 18, 1944.[34] "Studies in Wartime Planning for Continuing Full Employment" was a mix of description and analysis. It described the state of the economy in the run-up to the war and its most likely state after the ending of the war. It made an extensive comparison with the demobilization and return to a peacetime economy after World War I, outlining differences with that period and ending with policy suggestions.

The report was sent out for "technical criticism and comment" and received specific criticism and suggestions from NRPB economists and other government agencies, but also from academics and businesspersons. Among the academics were Jacob Marschak, then still at the New School; Paul Sweezy, from Harvard; and George Stigler, then at the University of Minnesota. Stuart Chase, whose 1932 book had been foundational for President Franklin D. Roosevelt's New Deal, went "entirely overboard" on the interim report, receiving it with "whoops of joy" and considering it a "swell job."[35]

The report was clear in its Keynesian message.[36] It could not be expected that market forces by themselves would transform the economy from a war- to a peacetime economy, and so government intervention in the economy would be necessary to sustain full employment after the war. But this was not just a Keynesian message. The sheer magnitude of the demobilization made it highly unlikely, by any estimate, that markets would be able to absorb all by themselves the increase in labor supply that ran in the millions. On any theoretical account, government action would be necessary.

This sense of urgency for government action was also clear in the two offspring of this study that more explicitly carried Samuelson's signature, a separate NRPB brochure on the demobilization after World War I, and Samuelson's contribution to Seymour Harris's edited volume *Postwar Economic Problems* (1943). The first study, prepared under the direction

34. The second version lists Altman, in charge of the unit, and Samuelson, as consultant, first, and then in two separate sections, the list of collaborators.

35. PASP box 55, NRPB, memorandum of Bernard Jacobs to Herbert Goodwin, December 14, 194, General Criticism, p. 1.

36. For a more extensive analysis of this report, see Backhouse 2012.

of Samuelson and Everett Hagen, who would become a professor of economics and political science at MIT's Center for International Studies in the 1950s, looked at how returning soldiers were reintegrated into the American economy after the end of World War I.

Relying on Simon Kuznets's estimates of US National Income Accounts, the study investigated the course of events in and after the demobilization after World War I, especially the causes of and possible relations between the postwar boom and successive depression. Samuelson and Hagen's descriptive analysis revealed that what in the public image had been remembered as a healthy upswing followed by an unfortunate downturn had rather been the result of the unplanned, unstable, but fortunate circumstances of high government expenditures that could not be lowered immediately, a substantially increased export-demand from a war worn-out Europe, and the fading from the public memory of an economic depression after the return to the United States of millions of soldiers in 1918.

The lack of a public memory of the brief depression of 1918 was also due to the lack of appropriate statistics. At the time, there had been no plan on how to accommodate the returning soldiers in the economy, and the initial course of events had been sheer luck rather than foresight. But the collapse of the economy halfway through the 1920s could have been avoided had appropriate actions been taken. This report was published in 1943, and its message to Washington policymakers was perceived in the Keynes-Hansen line that was prominent among economic consultants in the Washington arena.

Precision Is in the Arguments, Not in the Forecasts

Samuelson's contribution to Seymour Harris's volume *Postwar Economic Problems* was a combination of this assessment of the economic course of events after the Great War with a graphical exposition of John Maynard Keynes's multiplier analysis (the Keynesian cross), without which, according to a note added by Harris, one could not "understand the problem of unemployment and its relation to savings and a rising standard of living" (Samuelson 1943, 27). Samuelson's explanation of the diagram loosely used stylized facts about the business cycle to show the effects of shifts in the consumption function and thus the effects of different policies.

Within the economics profession Harris's *Postwar Economic Problems* was considered a partisan collection of contributions that "for the majority of the writers" was a "manifesto of a very definite credo of the shape of things to come." This creed was stated forcefully by Alvin Hansen and subscribed to by the "majority of the writers" (Weidenhammer 1943, 664). However, Samuelson presented his Keynesian message not as a policy creed but as a technical assessment.

Samuelson made it clear that he saw his task as an economist to "weigh the strategic factors and considerations" that speak in favor of or against specific assessments of the current and future economic conditions of the United States and to give a survey of possible strategies of response. Samuelson did not consider it his task to be partisan for one particular line of economic policy, or to compromise between opposite policy positions, but to step back, or better, "step aside," and offer an analytical perspective from which to choose. Also, Harris's note to the article made clear Samuelson's contribution was pitched as technical, not political (Samuelson 1943, 27n).

Samuelson carefully explained that a difference should be made between policy prescriptions that were considered Keynesian and the applications of a "technique of analysis" that could be considered Keynesian, but that was neutral in principle in its policy prescriptions (31). On this second notion of Keynesianism that Samuelson himself adhered to, one could investigate different "hypotheses" that could well conflict in their policy prescriptions, but it was an empirical question which of these hypotheses was true as a matter of fact.

Samuelson cautioned especially against the "better informed observers" and "experts" who were "taking the pulse of public opinion" and were running "ahead of the business community" in seeing "clear signs" of a "postwar boom of some duration." Whatever "hidden" or "unknown" facts such optimists might be in the possession of, given the state of data collection and forecasting powers, "precision in forecasting is simply out of the question." It would be shortsighted to follow "those who are optimistic concerning the prospects for a spontaneous postwar boom of some duration based upon private demand alone" (46). Such a boom would occur only "if we are lucky." Expertise had to be based on assessing the available evidence, but precision was not in the forecast but in the weighing of the range of possibilities in the light of uncertain evidence.[37]

37. In response to Samuelson's *New Republic* forecast, Everett Hagen reproached him for not having distinguished "between an estimate of the single most probable course of events and the contingencies against which policy measures should be adopted" (PASP 36, Hagen, Hagen to Samuelson, November 20, 1944). In answer, Samuelson apologized if his articles would have done "any harm" (PASP 36, Hagen, Samuelson to Hagen, November 28, 1944).

Thus Samuelson was led to conclude that "statistically, theoretically, and institutionally," it was better to be on the safe side. The "bitter experience" of the Great Depression, "if not of the last century and a half," had shown that "there is no invisible hand guaranteeing that we shall always be lucky." It was highly unlikely, though not impossible, that the sheer luck of the boom after World War I would be repeated, but at least policy-makers would do well to prevent a repetition of the unplanned handling of the subsequent slump.

Thus Samuelson used the technical and theoretical apparatus at his disposal to step back and to weigh the outstanding evidence, carving out possible strategies of response. To a large extent, Samuelson had created and systematized this apparatus in his Harvard thesis, in what was to become *Foundations*. This apparatus enabled him to act as a technician, not as a judge or advocate. In contrast with the advocate or judge, the technician analyzes and weighs, but leaves the decision elsewhere. Samuelson's choice for this last role embodies a transformation in the role of the academic economist that sits well with the rise of scientism and a technical definition of the role of (economic) science in the United States in and after the Second World War (Furner 1975; Fourcade 2009; Hands 2007; Porter 2009).

In a note, Samuelson (1943, 36n1) implicitly subscribed to the Keynes-Hansen creed, but explicitly he was reluctant to participate in outspoken political projects and preferred to be the technical expert in the shadows. His reactions to Harris's appeals for partisanship are exemplary. I do not know whether Samuelson followed Harris's "command" to be "present at the Hayek seminar" of April 6, 1945, that I venture was devoted to Friedrich Hayek's *Road to Serfdom*.[38] But he declined Hansen and Harris's request to contribute to a discussion on the thirty-hour workweek because he had "no specific expertise" on that topic.[39] He was willing to contribute to Harris's Harvard Economic Handbook series, even though by then the writing of *Economics* was limiting his availability and might also make his contribution ill-timed.[40] He gave rather technical comments on Harris's political response to Albert G. Hart's criticism of using economic blueprints for policy purposes.[41] He declined Harris's invitation

38. PASP box 37, Seymour E. Harris, Harris to Samuelson, March 23, 1945.

39. PASP box 37, Seymour E. Harris, Samuelson to Hansen and Harris, May 9, 1945.

40. PASP box 37, Seymour E. Harris, Samuelson to Harris, April 27, 1946.

41. PASP box 37, Seymour E. Harris, Samuelson to Harris, February 27, 1946. Harris responded to Hart's "model-builders and Fiscal Policy," published in the *American Economic Review* for September 1945, pages 531–58. The phrase *model-builders* misleadingly might be

of September 1947 to contribute to *An Economic Program for Liberal America*, though Samuelson's decision may well have been influenced by the row over his textbook that by then was unfolding at full strength (Giraud, this volume).[42] On a planned reply from Hansen on a "Chicago outburst" on monetary policy, Samuelson considered it a "mistake" to react, but continued to suggest changes in Hansen's draft answer that made reasons for criticism "technical" and so not in need to be argued at length in the popular press.[43] There is no question Samuelson was annoyed by all-too-enthusiastic libertarian initiatives at Chicago and Virginia, but even in a rare outburst of anger against Friedman (who was a "bloody nuisance"), Samuelson's concern was that it took so much scholarly effort to correct his "provocative stands," efforts that could have been used more productively than for "sterile debate."[44]

Stepping Aside to Become the Middle of the Road

We find this same attitude in Samuelson's comportment over the row that evolved over his own and Lorie Tarshis's economic textbooks after the war (Giraud, this volume). When Killian asked Samuelson if something more positive and productive could be made from the tensions around the textbook, Samuelson referred to the experience of the Committee for Economic Development, which consisted of "top-notch business executives," and suggested as a "constructive step in the general direction of mutual understanding" to use the Sloan program, and various other "get-togethers and conferences" as something MIT might do to move in the same direction.[45]

Samuelson attached a fragment of the review of *Economics* for the *American Economic Review* by Albert G. Hart, whom he considered, just like himself, a "distinguished middle-of-the-road" economist.[46] After the war both Hart and Schultz had become active in the Committee for Eco-

read as referring to mathematical modeling, whereas Hart is criticizing economic blueprints that put high confidence in government action to steer the economy.

42. PASP box 37, Seymour E. Harris, Samuelson to Harris, September 19, 1947.

43. PASP box 37, Seymour E. Harris, Samuelson to Harris, February 4, 1948.

44. PASP box 36, Alvin Hansen, Samuelson to Hansen, January 18, 1966.

45. PASP box 45, Killian, Samuelson to Killian, August 30, 1950 (in reply to Killian's letter of August 29, 1950).

46. PASP box 45, Killian, Samuelson to Killian, August 30, 1950 (in reply to Killian's letter of August 29, 1950).

nomic Development that had as its motto "neither left nor right, but responsible" (Burnett 2011, 389–90). Hart praised Samuelson's "systematic effort to find points of contact between different points of view," which made the book "congenial to teachers and students over a wide range to the right and left of Samuelson's own political position" (Hart 1948, 912).

In "Testing Time for Prophets," a short article for the *Economic Digest* in April 1954 on the assessment of the present condition of the American economy, and how to respond to it, Samuelson wrote that if Arthur Burns's (and the Eisenhower administration's) "wager about the brevity and the mildness of the recession proved correct," he "earned his grey hairs and is deserving the highest congratulations." But Samuelson's (1954, 147) own "misgivings" were, first, that he lacked the courage of making policy decisions himself, and second, that if he had to err, he "preferred to be wrong on the expansionary rather than the contractionary side."

> It is on this vital point, and only in this, that I perceive any partisan difference between the Republicans and the Democrats: rightly or wrongly the former show greater concern for the fixed-income widow and *rentier*, the latter for the non-seniority negro worker in Detroit who is last to be hired and first to be laid-off.

It is not difficult to see Samuelson's own personal predilection for the Democrat position, but it is clear that even here, Samuelson does not judge or advocate ("rightly or wrongly"). It was not up to the economist but to the voters to decide on such matters: "On this vital clash of interests, the professional economist must step aside and the voters must decide" (147). "Stepping aside" precisely indicates the role of the technical expert, who cedes his place to those who should judge—the voters and politicians.

Institutional Backing

I think it had not escaped Schultz's notice that Samuelson defined his own economic role as technical, much as Schultz had perceived his own role at Iowa State College. But there was an important difference with Samuelson's stance. Before moving to Chicago, Schultz had been the director of Iowa State's important agricultural economics study group. Like Samuelson, Schultz and his colleagues, such as Mary Jean Bowman and Arthur G. Hart, emphasized innovative quantitative analysis—on economics as a technique. In contrast with Samuelson, at Iowa State the emphasis was on statistical analysis, not on a modeling approach that sketched alternative scenarios to its audience. Samuelson's scenario analysis secured his independence; Schultz's statistics did not do so at Iowa State College.

In the notorious oleomargarine controversy that erupted in 1943, the empirical analysis of Schultz and his colleagues became a bone of contention. In his recent analysis of this episode, Paul Burnett (2011, 375) writes that "quantitative work, unlike naked lobbying, could at least appear to have a transparency that brought it above narrow parochial interests." But the unequivocal conclusions that Schultz and his colleagues drew from their data, that price regulations of agricultural produce had been counterproductive, left no space for alternative policies. When partisan farming interests broke out over their work, Iowa State College's president Charles E. Friley did not back their stated intention to deliver an objective quantitative, statistical analysis.

Samuelson was heavily backed by the MIT administration and reciprocated by committing to MIT. Schultz, in contrast, felt that Friley lacked the stamina to support him and his collaborators in their scientific independence and expertise against the interests of state farming organizations. This made Schultz lose all confidence in the administration and to accept Chicago's open offer for a chair that had been made in early 1941, taking Margaret Reid, Hart, and Oswald H. Brownlee with him (Burnett 2011, 389; see also Burnett 2010).

From the records, it is unclear if there was any interaction between Schultz and Samuelson during the war, even though it is unlikely they never met or corresponded in that period, the more so since Oscar Altman suggested Hart as his replacement when Altman enlisted for military service in 1942. On that occasion Hart preferred not to move to Washington to better function as an independent voice against Washington's policy proposals, and made the suggestion to move some of the statistical work from the NRPB to Iowa State College, a suggestion that Altman asked Blaisdell to consider carefully.[47] Significantly, Hart, whom Samuelson considered a middle-of-the-road economist like himself, declined his own job offer at Chicago to move to Columbia instead.

When Schultz tried to enlist Samuelson for Chicago, Samuelson was in the middle of writing his textbook. While it was not difficult to identify its Keynesian policy agenda, Samuelson's response to criticism stressed the technicalities of new theories and methods, and in this was

47. As this correspondence is among Samuelson's papers, Samuelson at least was kept abreast of these movements.

fully backed by MIT (Giraud, this volume). Not being at Chicago or Harvard, by any standards the premium economics institutes in the country, but at an institute that defined its mission as consulting enabled Samuelson, the political liberal, to define his own role as the detached technician to better pronounce on the state of the economy and on the government's policy options.

When Harvard in 1954 tried to piggyback on the prestige created by making good on its "biggest recruiting blunder in the history of social science,"[48] it had missed its chance. MIT's president James Rhyme Killian wrote "how delighted" he was about Samuelson's decision "in regard to the neighboring institution" and added his hope that Samuelson would "know how fully you have our enthusiastic support in your work here at the Institute."[49] McGeorge Bundy, dean of arts and sciences at Harvard, somewhat belatedly wrote that however disappointed he was about Samuelson's decision, he was at least glad that Harvard would have Samuelson and the "excellence" of the MIT community in its proximity.[50]

Taking stock in his reply to Killian, Samuelson acknowledged that MIT had become one of the best economics departments in the country, which made its competition with "the older established departments . . . sorely felt."[51] By then Samuelson was littering academic journals with his papers and figured prominently on committees and in public outlets in which he was taking the pulse of the current state of the US economy and laying out possible lines of response. He wrote one after another letters of recommendation and actively promoted the careers of scholars he considered good for the profession. The newly hired staff contributed of its own to the prestige of the department. Men of business sent their data to Samuelson in hopes that he would report back on the results of the analysis, or they dropped by for a talk over lunch. Being technical enabled Samuelson to stand in the

48. PASP box 45, Kindleberger. Quoted from Kindleberger's alphabet presented on the occasion of Samuelson's retirement from MIT in 1985: "H stands for Harvard Graduate Department of Economics and the biggest recruiting blunder in the history of social science; and for the History of Economic Thought: poor old Smith, Ricardo, Mill, Marx, Jevons et al never knew what Hit them."

49. PASP box 45, Killian, James R. (president), 1944–1954, letter from Killian to Samuelson, December 20, 1954.

50. PASP box 12, General correspondence B 1939–1954, McGeorge Bundy to Samuelson, December 13, 1954. Samuelson declined the offer in a letter to Bundy of December 3, 1954, in PASP box 12, General correspondence B 1939–1954.

51. PASP box 45, Killian, James R. (president), 1944–1954, Samuelson to Killian, December 22, 1954.

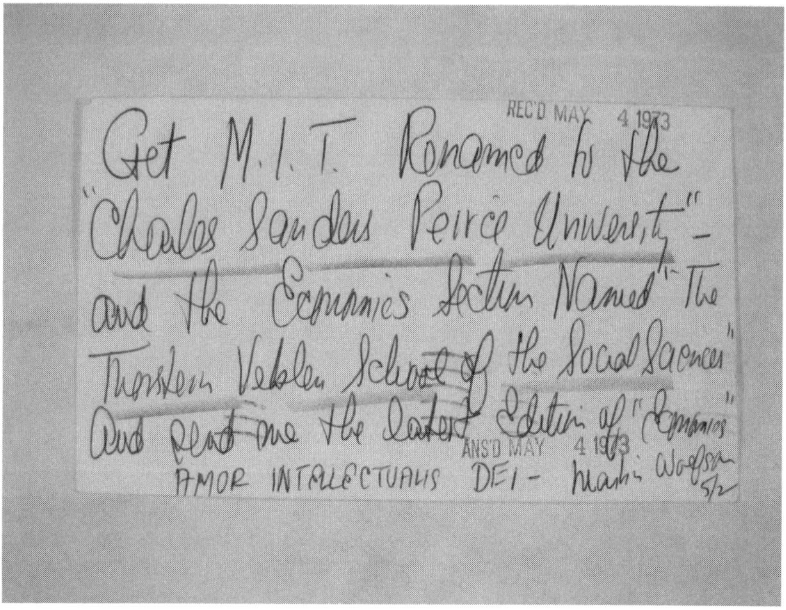

Figure 1 "Get M.I.T. Renamed to the 'Charles Sanders Peirce University'—and the Economics Section Named 'the Thorstein Veblen School of the Social Sciences' And send me the latest Edition of 'Economics' AMOR INTELLECTUALIS DEI—Martin Wolfson 5/2." Card of Martin Wolfson to Paul Samuelson, received May 4, 1973, PASP box 77, Martin Wolfson, Brooklyn, 1947–1984.

shadows yet define the center of the economics profession. Halfway through the fifties Samuelson had become the inescapable expert and the economics department at MIT a world center of economics expertise.

Situating Technicality

Not all agreed with economics becoming technical. From 1947 Samuelson had been in irregular correspondence with a Brooklyn Jew and economics schoolteacher named Martin Wolfson. Samuelson clearly had been charmed by Wolfson's aphorisms, complaints about the state of economics, and requests for free copies of his books. But in later years "old Wolfson" was getting "uppity."[52] In 1972 Wolfson lambasted "the people who choose

52. PASP box 77, Martin Wolfson, Brooklyn, Martin Wolfson to Samuelson, received October 30, 1972, and undated.

the Nobel Prize Winners in Economics" and angrily complained that economics had become a "technology, A Techne" and MIT "too mechanical, too technical, too technological," and summoned Samuelson to change the name of MIT to Charles Sanders Peirce University and to name the economics department after Thorstein Veblen (see figure 1).

One can of course dismiss such postcards from minor figures, though it speaks for Samuelson that he never did so. There was a mild irony in Wolfson's command. If there ever was an economist who trusted technicians, it was Veblen. "Veblen's experts," as Theodore Porter (2009, 305) notes, "were hired experts who could serve capitalists as well as communists." But Veblen's technicians were engineers, knowledgeable about nature's principles. In the postwar era, economists themselves had become engineers who carved out, with "neutral, self-effacing objectivity" (305), the logical space of economic policy. Naming the economics department after Veblen would have marked that shift.[53]

References

Backhouse, Roger. 2012. "Paul Samuelson, RAND, and the Cowles Commission Activity Analysis Conference, 1947–1949." Mimeo, version 2.

Balisciano, Marcia L. 1998. "Hope for America: American Notions of Economic Planning between Pluralism and Neoclassicism, 1930–1950." In *From Interwar Pluralism to Postwar Neoclassicism*, edited by Mary S. Morgan and Malcolm Rutherford. *History of Political Economy* 30 (supplement): 153–78.

Burnett, Paul. 2010. "The Price Is Not Right: Theodore W. Schultz, Policy Planning, and Agricultural Economics in the Cold-War United States." In *Building Chicago Economics: New Perspectives on the History of America's Most Powerful Economics Program*, edited by Robert Van Horn, Philip Mirowski, and Thomas A. Stapleford, 67–93. New York: Cambridge University Press.

———. 2011. "Academic Freedom or Political Maneuvers: Theodore W. Schultz and the Oleomargarine Controversy Revisited." *Agricultural History* 85 (3): 373–97.

Clawson, Marion. 1981. *New Deal Planning: The National Resources Planning Board*. Baltimore: Johns Hopkins University Press.

Düppe, Till, and E. Roy Weintraub. Forthcoming. "Siting the New Economic Science: The Cowles Commission's Activity Analysis Conference of June 1949." *Science in Context* 27 (3).

Fourcade, Marion. 2009. *Economists and Societies: Discipline and Profession in the United States, Britain, and France, 1890s to 1990s*. Princeton, N.J.: Princeton University Press.

Furner, Mary O. 1975. *Advocacy and Objectivity: A Crisis in the Professionalization of Social Science, 1865–1905*. Lexington: University Press of Kentucky.

53. On the twentieth-century economist as an engineer, see Morgan 2003.

Hammond, Daniel J., and Claire H. Hammond, eds. 2006. *Making Chicago Price Theory: Friedman-Stigler Correspondence, 1945–1957.* New York: Routledge.

Hands, D. Wade. 2007. "A Tale of Two Mainstreams: Economics and Philosophy of Natural Science in the Mid-Twentieth Century." *Journal of the History of Economic Thought* 29 (1): 1–13.

Hart, Albert G. 1945. "'Model-Building' and Fiscal Policy." *American Economic Review* 35 (4): 531–58.

———. 1948. "Economics: An Introductory Analysis." *American Economic Review* 38 (5): 910–15.

Killian, James R., Jr. 1985. *Education of a College President: A Memoir.* Cambridge, Mass.: MIT Press.

Maas, Harro. 2014. *Economic Methodology: A Historical Introduction*. London: Routledge.

Morgan, Mary S. 2003. "Economics." In *The Modern Social Sciences*, edited by Theodore M. Porter and Dorothy Ross, 275–305. Vol. 7 of *The Cambridge History of Science*. Cambridge: Cambridge University Press.

———. 2012. *The World in the Model: How Economists Work and Think*. Cambridge: Cambridge University Press.

Porter, Theodore M. 2006. "Speaking Precision to Power: The Modern Political Role of Social Science." *Social Research: An International Quarterly* 73 (4): 1273–94.

———. 2009. "How Science Became Technical." *Isis* 100:292–309.

Report of the Committee on Educational Survey to the Faculty of the Massachusetts Institute of Technology. 1949. Cambridge, Mass.: MIT Press.

Samuelson, Paul A. 1943. "Full Employment after the War." In *Postwar Economic Problems*, ed. Seymour E. Harris, 27–53. New York: McGraw-Hill.

———. 1954. "Testing Time for Prophets." *Economic Digest* 7 (4): 145–48. Reprint from the *Financial Times*, February 25, 1954.

———. 1962. "Economists and the History of Ideas." *American Economic Review* 52 (1): 1–18.

Solovey, Mark. 2012. *Cold War Social Science: Knowledge Production, Liberal Democracy, and Human Nature*. Basingstoke: Palgrave Macmillan.

Weidenhammer, Robert M. 1943. Review of *Postwar Economic Problems*, by Seymour Harris. *American Economic Review* 33 (3): 664–68.

Decisions and Dynamics: Postwar Theoretical Problems and the MIT Style of Economics

William Thomas

Several of the articles in this volume discuss the development of a peculiar MIT style of economics, which complemented MIT's heavy concentration in engineering. However, characterizations of this style remain vague. It is certainly associated with the arrival of Paul Samuelson at MIT after World War II, and the mathematical rigor he applied to economic reasoning. Among all the students of economics in America, MIT's engineering students were clearly unusually capable of comprehending its technicalities. Beyond formalization, the MIT style also connotes a policy-oriented practicality, which stands in contrast with other, more abstract varieties of formalized neoclassical economics, particularly contemporaneous work surrounding general equilibrium theory.[1] In this volume, Verena Halsmayer elucidates this aspect of the MIT style for the case of Robert Solow's dynamic theory of growth and his conceptualization of it as analogous to "engineering in the design sense."

Correspondence may be addressed to gwilliamthomas@gmail.com. This article was written with the support of a Junior Research Fellowship from Imperial College London. Archival work was conducted at the Institute Archives and Special Collections of the Massachusetts Institute of Technology. I would like to thank MIT's archival staff, and particularly Nora Murphy, for their great help. I would like to thank Roger E. Backhouse, Beatrice Cherrier, E. Roy Weintraub, and other participants of the 2013 *HOPE* conference for their very helpful comments, and Till Düppe, Judy L. Klein, and Mark Eisner for illuminating conversations.

1. On general equilibrium theory and this more abstract style, see Düppe and Weintraub 2014.

History of Political Economy 46 (annual suppl.) DOI 10.1215/00182702-2716208

In this article, I propose to develop further insights into what aspects of MIT economics should and should not be strongly associated with the MIT milieu. I compare some intellectual problems in post–World War II economics, including at MIT, with similar intellectual problems in other fields that were gaining a foothold at MIT at that time: cybernetics, industrial dynamics, and operations research (OR). This comparison, in turn, allows us to determine what aspects of MIT economics had strong affinities with those other fields at MIT, and what aspects can be more appropriately linked to conversations taking place in and around the economics profession at large. Although this article cannot do justice to either MIT economics or the wide variety of intellectual currents running through the postwar period, I highlight the prevalence of certain key issues. First, at MIT and elsewhere, there existed a strong interest in the relationship between local decision making and observable macro-scale phenomena (e.g., factory production cycles, business cycles, and the apparent rationality of market mechanisms).[2] Second, theoreticians across fields were increasingly interested in the prospect that many emergent phenomena could be properly understood only when analyzed as dynamic processes. To an extent, the prevalence of these issues across fields was merely thematic similarity. However, there were also more concrete connections worthy of serious attention. Here I stress the strong attention paid in this period to the economic and managerial problem of inventory control, and to the mathematical method of linear programming (LP).

The general conclusion that I offer is that there were clear affinities between the agenda-setting work of Samuelson and Solow and other activities at MIT. However, I further argue that these affinities were in some ways superficial, and that, at a deeper substantive and methodological level, MIT economists' work was clearly more indebted to conversations taking place elsewhere in and around the economics profession. This article thus corroborates and elaborates upon Mary Morgan's (2012) recent discussion of the way that formal models have been used by economists to clarify the meanings of particular economic concepts and to explore their logical implications. More particularly, this article also concludes that, through this shared conception of modeling, methodological bridges did develop between economics, OR, and management studies at MIT during

2. The relationship between market functions and individual decision making was later given the convenient label "microfoundations."

the 1950s. However, I stress that this disciplinary alignment was probably not a product of their shared institutional context. Rather, MIT was merely well positioned to borrow it, in large part, from other places, in particular the Graduate School of Industrial Administration (GSIA) at the Carnegie Institute of Technology (Carnegie Tech).

Institutional Context: MIT in World War II and After

MIT's deep connections to what President Dwight Eisenhower called the military-industrial complex are well surveyed. Following on the success of the wartime Radiation Laboratory, which was run by contract with the government under the ad hoc wartime Office of Scientific Research and Development (OSRD), MIT maintained and expanded its contracting work. The Rad Lab was replaced directly by the Research Laboratory for Electronics (RLE). The RLE was led for a time by the physicist and Rad Lab researcher Julius Stratton, who in 1949 became MIT's provost, and later vice president, chancellor, and in 1959, its president. Another wartime laboratory, the aeronautical engineer Charles Draper's Instrumentation Laboratory, likewise expanded, and was fairly typical of other MIT-affiliated "Route 128" institutions. The most prominent such institution, the Lincoln Laboratory, developed out of the electrical engineer and servomechanism expert Jay Forrester's work on the Whirlwind I digital computer, and the Semi-Automated Ground Environment (SAGE) continental defense system that the Whirlwind project begot (Leslie 1993; Redmond and Smith 2000).

MIT also had numerous connections to the network of policy analysis organizations responsible for aiding the integration of technologies into practical use. Part of the wartime success of radar derived from the efforts of the US Navy's Operations Research Group, led by the MIT physicist Philip Morse (1977; Tidman 1984); "expert consultants," including Stratton, who were dispatched to the field by an office working directly under the secretary of war, led by the MIT electrical engineer Edward Bowles (Collins 2002); and a "British Branch" of the Rad Lab. By 1944 recognition of the importance of this sort of liaison work led to the creation in the OSRD of an Office of Field Services, which was led by MIT's then president Karl Compton (Thiesmeyer and Burchard 1947). Given the depth of its involvement in these developments, it is unsurprising that MIT remained interested in OR and related initiatives after the war. In 1946 it agreed to administer the US Navy's postwar successor to the ORG, the Operations Evaluation Group (Tidman 1984), and began to experiment in a pedagogy of OR in 1948, leading to the establishment of an Institute Committee on OR in 1952, which became MIT's OR Center several years later (Morse 1977; Thomas 2012). The committee and center were led by Morse, who was also a major player in the drive to develop a new OR profession after World War II. He was named first president of the Operations Research Society of America (ORSA) in 1952.

In the late 1950s the GM magnate Alfred Sloan agreed to donate over $5 million toward the creation of a new School of Industrial Management (SIM) at MIT. MIT administrators immediately began speculating as to how MIT's strengths in science and technology could inform the work of the new school. One early idea concerned drawing on the field of "automatic control." That term would have connoted work in servo and electrical engineering, particularly Forrester's, as well the MIT mathematician Norbert Wiener's foundational theoretical work in what he called "cybernetics," which was gaining a diverse circle of adherents (Heims 1991). Quickly, though, attention turned instead to the idea of making a civilianized field of OR central to SIM's work (MIT Office of the President Records, 1930–1959 [AC 4], box 202, folder 1, Institute Archives and Special Collections, MIT Libraries). This idea also foundered once an early investigation of OR, ordered by SIM's dean and led by an accounting professor, concluded that it was unclear what exactly OR's proponents had to offer to business, and thus that the subject could not form the basis of the school's identity (Thomas 2012). As Beatrice Cherrier points out in this volume, SIM did quickly forge links with the economics department. However, the existence of these links did not stop MIT's administrators (spurred partly by the aforementioned Bowles, then serving as a "consulting professor") from hiring Forrester away from the Lincoln Laboratory in 1956 in another attempt to lend a special MIT imprint to work at SIM (Thomas and Williams 2009). While Forrester's work did gain significant notoriety, it did not become the dominant face of SIM.

Individual Decisions, Emergent Phenomena, and System Management

By the late 1930s economists had begun to develop theories to handle phenomena that were "dynamic" in character, particularly business cycles and long-term growth. In the aftermath of the Great Depression, and in the wake of John Maynard Keynes's major works, there was also a perceived need to relate these phenomena with how individuals make personally beneficial choices. Such theories were, of course, intended to augment intellectual understanding. But, because the phenomena described were undesired products of locally rational behaviors, the theories also implied that higher-level government intervention was required to remedy economic ills. Thus these theories were expected to have prescriptive implications, wherein understanding of the underlying nature of particular economic phenomena could indicate what countervailing policies were and were not apt to function as effective remedies.

The rudiments of such a dynamic theory were posited in 1939 by the Oxford economist Roy Harrod (1939), who proposed a model in which Keynesian multipliers exacerbated an economy's deviations from a certain "warranted" growth rate, a model later termed the "knife edge." At the same time, models of business cycles were developed, which drew analogies with steadily oscillating physical systems, wherein economic displacements are lagged in time by forces of adjustment, which is what drives the cycle. Such dynamic questions were taken up with some enthusiasm at Harvard in this period, particularly by Lloyd Metzler (1941), but also by Alvin Hansen (1941) and, indeed, by Paul Samuelson (1939, 1941) while he was still at the Harvard Society of Fellows. Several years later Evsey Domar (1946) formulated an equivalent to Harrod's growth theory while studying for his PhD at Harvard.

It was not obvious in the immediate postwar years how dynamic phenomena could be effectively prevented, counteracted, or damped. The theoretical apparatuses of feedback and control from servo engineering offered one possible way forward. Servo theory had been extremely important during World War II in a number of applications, but especially in the design of improved "fire control" mechanisms for directing antiaircraft guns and other such semi-automated weapons. Wiener had been employed to design such devices during the war for the OSRD, but had been more interested in the generalizable theoretical aspects of the problem than in pressing technical issues. Consequently, his services were not long retained (Mindell 2002). However, in the postwar period Wiener's wartime work became the basis of his program of cybernetics. Named after the Greek word for "steersman," the subject promised to aid those seeking to intervene in systems to determine what effects various actions were apt to have on systemwide behavior, and it drew adherents who saw applications across a wide variety of sciences (Heims 1991). Richard Goodwin

(1951, 465–66),[3] another Harvard economist, took up the cybernetic analogy in a chapter he wrote for Hansen's *Business Cycles and National Income*. In it he depicted the then recently founded Council of Economic Advisers as analogous to an "error-detecting device," which "reports on the deviation between desired course and actual course." The Congress, he supposed, "amplifies this signal into some large-scale input of the creation or destruction of purchasing power." He did not suppose that economists could divine any hard and fast rules for advisers to follow, and credited the Keynesian theoretical program for refraining from declaring any.

On a more local level, individual firms' inventories were beginning to come under scrutiny both as a crucial factor driving wider economic cycles—business cycles were often referred to as "inventory cycles"[4]—and as an important problem facing individual managers. After World War II the US military services developed a strong interest in the problem of inventory management. A new initiative in inventory studies was sponsored by the Office of Naval Research. Part of that initiative was a bibliographical research project undertaken by Louise Haack of George Washington University and Thomson Whitin of Princeton University's economics department. Whitin's work was published in 1953 as *The Theory of Inventory Management*. In it, he explained that in Keynes's *Treatise on Money* (1930), inventories had been treated in terms of "liquid capital," denoting surplus stocks, and "working capital," denoting goods in production, transport, or being held as a hedge against interruptions of service. Whitin (1953, 115), however, preferred the taxonomy of other authors, who distinguished between "planned" and "unplanned" inventories. He felt that the formulation "would be extremely useful" for understanding how business cycles related to decisions made based on managers' expectations. Yet, he admitted, "to estimate the volume of planned and unplanned inventories . . . is no simple matter because of the lack of any objective standard for indicating what plans have been."

As Whitin was completing his book, theories of rational inventory planning and control were, in fact, already under development. There were several branches of inventory theory. One, developed by Herbert Simon (1952) at Carnegie Tech's newly established GSIA, treated inventory control as a problem in the control of a dynamic system. His approach

3. Goodwin was soon to leave for Cambridge University.

4. For his part, Samuelson felt that the role of inventories in driving business cycles was overstated, a point he made clear in his second 1962 Wicksell Lecture (Samuelson [1962] 1972).

employed servo theory to develop decision rules for managers, which would determine, analogously to a low pass filter, when fluctuations in sales, measured over time, would be absorbed by inventories, and when they should be taken to represent long-term shifts necessitating increased factory orders. Simon's project, like Whitin's bibliographic project, was sponsored by the ONR, and was part of the general mission of the GSIA to develop a new approach to managerial training (Fourcade and Khurana 2011). And, as Judy Klein (2012) and Antonella Rancan (2013) have discussed in some detail, this program in managerial studies was unified with studies in economic theory by an overarching theoretical concern with how economic decisions are made under conditions of uncertainty.

Several years after the GSIA began to formulate its particular approach to economics and management training, MIT's SIM hired the electrical engineer Jay Forrester to craft his own novel approach to management. As previously noted, Forrester had made his career in servo engineering before turning to digital computation. After his move to SIM, he combined these experiences by using digital computers to simulate the complexes of unintended feedback phenomena that arose, as a matter of course, from the systemic relations between various decisions made at lower levels of an organization's management. Like Keynesian theorists, Forrester recognized that pathological phenomena required the informed intervention of high-level managers. He believed his simulations could help managers expand and revise their own prior understanding of the behaviors of the systems they managed, and so craft more effective interventions. He also hoped these same managers would use simulations to help them develop decision rules for lower-tier managers, which would suppress pathological phenomena without the need for ad hoc intervention (Thomas and Williams 2009). His paradigmatic example of such a system was a supply chain consisting of factories and warehouse inventories serving a sales force. In this chain, delays in responses to shifts in demand amplify inventory depletions and compensatory shifts in production. Managers could use simulations to decide on what changes in system structure (e.g., eliminating an extraneous link in the supply chain) or in inventory replenishment policy would suppress such amplifications (Forrester 1958). This concern with time lags clearly resembled the concerns addressed by business cycle theorists and management theorists like Simon some years earlier. However, Forrester was keen to differentiate his simulations from prior work. To him, economists worked "backward," attempting to discern root causes of observed phenomena, which could realistically be explained only in terms of the ad hoc confluence of many causes within a holistic system that was likely much more complex than a simple supply chain. Meanwhile, management theory and OR tended to focus on the rationality of a particular decision, when, in his view, the worth of a decision could be considered only in chorus with all other decisions made within an integrated system (Forrester 1961, 3–4, 8–9, 53–55).

While Forrester managed to construct a lasting niche for himself at SIM, his vision did not become an integral part of SIM's institutional identity. We might ascribe Forrester's failure to his insistence on the insularity and peculiar virtues of his work when it was so clearly linked to other strands of thought. We might also point to Forrester's later insistence on scaling up his renamed "system dynamics" project into the realms of "urban dynamics" and "world dynamics," even though this divorced his simulations from the more-or-less concrete realities his original industrial dynamics simulations described. However, another more subtle explanation might involve the fact that Forrester's simulations followed largely, if tacitly, in the Keynesian tradition of exploring the unintended pathological consequences of locally rational decisions. Yet Keynesian economists, unlike Forrester, did not regard it as constantly essential to trace such phenomena to their microfoundations. Many postwar economic theorists were, of course, interested in interrelating local-level decisions with macro-level phenomena. However, their models were less focused on emergent pathologies in markets and managerial systems than on trying to discern how it is that markets work at all. Thus, their focus was on how locally rational decisions produce market behaviors, which, themselves, are apparently rational.

Optimization Models and Descriptions of Market Rationality

Historians of economics are presently paying serious attention to the intimately interrelated histories of LP, game theory, and neoclassical economics in the immediate postwar era. Philip Mirowski (2002), in his early foray into this territory, argued that OR models, created to optimize the design and functioning of military systems, were quickly and unselfconsciously exported into Walrasian market models, where they established an influential paradigm of treating market agents as calculating machines. Mirowski is right to highlight the historical importance of connections between OR and economics. However, because he does not delve deeply into the actual theories developed by operations researchers and economists, and because he insinuates more than demonstrates how theorists conceived of their tasks and their tools, his presentation fails to satisfy. Other historians (Akhabbar 2006; Backhouse 2012a, 2012b; Düppe and Weintraub 2014) have begun to develop stronger pictures of economists' interest in LP. In particular, where Mirowski concentrates almost exclusively on equilibrium models, these more recent contributions acknowledge the importance of connections between LP and the Harvard economist Wassily Leontief's input-output models of national economic structures.

The original developer of LP, the mathematician George Dantzig (1963, 2002), consistently acknowledged that his formulation of linear programming, while he was attempting to automate US Air Force scheduling (i.e., "programming") processes, was inspired by Leontief's models. Once he established that programs could be represented as a set of linear equations and inequalities, he used his mathematical knowledge of convex sets to develop the "simplex algorithm." In many cases, provided that the linear program was formulated appropriately, the algorithm could prescribe an optimally rational solution to the problem. Dantzig's method quickly proved extremely versatile, where different sets of constraints applied to a program could represent a wide array of possible problems. In the "diet problem," for instance, a combination of foods must be selected to satisfy nutrition requirements at a minimal price. Typically, in an LP problem, these most basic constraints did not place strong limits on the number of possible solutions to the problem. In fact, for the nascent professional OR community eagerly adopting the method, its whole value resided in its ability to render problems accepting extremely large numbers of feasible solutions tractable to practical, machine-aided computation.

Once Dantzig formulated his simplex algorithm, it was perhaps natural to turn LP back on the economic model that inspired it. Initially, Leontief had developed his model as a way to represent, and possibly organize, the production and consumption relations between the different sectors of a national economy. By integrating input-output models with LP, such static models could, in principle, be made dynamic. This prospect was first aired at the Cowles Commission's 1949 "Activity Analysis of Production and Allocation" conference (Koopmans 1951).[5] Papers

5. Among the other attendees of the conference were Armen Alchian, Domar (then affiliated with the US Army's Operations Research Office), Lloyd Metzler (then at Chicago), and Thomson Whitin. In spite of the growing work on the conference, the full range of interests at play has yet to be fully worked out.

relating LP to Leontief's model were given by the conference's convener Tjalling Koopmans, Harlan Smith, Nicholas Georgescu-Roegen, Kenneth Arrow, Samuelson, and Simon. Simon (1951), for instance, used the model to develop a more finely tuned conceptualization of "technological change" in economic models. For his part, Samuelson (1951) deployed a tightly constrained LP model to logically demonstrate that when substitution was allowed between production factors in a market where the only primary production factor is labor, changes in the labor market, such as an increase in the total quantity of laborers, would not actually result in changes in prices or substitution between production factors. Koopmans, Arrow, and Georgescu-Roegen proposed related proofs.[6]

At that very early stage of the application of LP (and the related area of game theory) to economic analysis, it was not yet clear what sorts of applications would be deemed valuable, and what sorts had to be deemed specious. One logical, if ambitious, path of development would have been to treat LP economic models in the same fashion as LP models in OR, so that all possible inputs and outputs in an economy constituted feasible solutions to a vast linear program, which market mechanisms served to optimize (Düppe and Weintraub 2014). This possibility certainly enticed Koopmans. It also partially motivated Arrow and Gerard Debreu's foundational proof that, in a perfectly competitive economy represented as a Walrasian auction, and formulated mathematically as an n-person game, a point of general equilibrium was guaranteed to exist. They considered this model "a reasonably accurate description of reality, at least for certain purposes" (Arrow and Debreu 1954, 265). Others, though, were unconvinced that such open-ended models were genuinely useful. For instance, Charles Hitch (1950), the head of the economics department at the RAND Corporation, acknowledged that the design of defense budgets could, in principle, be expressed as a linear program, and that adding a game theoretical element could even allow the program to be solved in view of prospective Soviet budgets. Yet he doubted that such a formulation could ever aid in the formulation of actual defense budgets.

Hitch appears to have shared his viewpoint toward LP with Samuelson. As Backhouse (2012b) relates, not long after Samuelson arrived at MIT, Hitch attempted to recruit him to RAND. Failing in this, Hitch encouraged Samuelson to work on LP in collaboration with RAND. And, indeed,

6. For further discussion of Leontief's and Samuelson's views on the Leontief model, and particularly their views of the criteria rendering a theory "operational," see Akhabbar 2006.

Samuelson seems to have been initially enthusiastic about LP. In one memorandum that he wrote for RAND, he speculated that the empirical observation of market mechanisms could provide new tools for people working on LP as an optimization technique. This notion came to naught. It did, however, lead to Samuelson undertaking a slow-moving project to write a book on the application of LP to economic analysis, which eventually enveloped Solow as well as Robert Dorfman, an economist and OR theorist at Harvard. *Linear Programming and Economic Analysis* (Dorfman, Samuelson, and Solow 1958) finally appeared almost a decade after it was begun (Backhouse 2012a).

Although Dorfman, Samuelson, and Solow discussed general equilibrium models in their book, they clearly felt that LP models were primarily useful in tightly constrained situations where linear programs described economic actors' rational actions, *and* where such actions were not adequately accounted for by a prior theory. Thus, Samuelson's nonsubstitution proof expanded on the utility of Leontief's formulation, because it created a dynamic model in which actors' substitutions of production factors would have been captured if the incentives created by the posited changes in the market had called for them. Similarly, as Halsmayer (this volume) shows, Solow's theory of growth likewise used a highly constrained linear model—assuming an economy with only one commodity—because the depiction of substitutions between labor and capital in that model were sufficient to preclude the knife-edge phenomenon found in the Harrod-Domar growth model, which implicitly disallowed such substitutions (Solow 1956). Samuelson's and Solow's lack of interest in using LP in less constrained ways no doubt owed to their sense that its inaccuracies in describing economic actors' actual thought processes would compound if an LP model were made too general. As they wrote in their chapter on firm behavior in *Linear Programming and Economic Analysis*, for "most purposes of economic analysis," it was sufficient to simply presume that industrial managers' decisions concerning their production functions *were* solved. *How* they were solved was less important. Samuelson and Solow explicitly reckoned that it was "usually not done by formulating the production function mathematically and finding its optimum by the methods of the differential calculus. More plausibly, they supposed, "the solution process is one of trial and error or survival of the fittest" (Dorfman, Samuelson, and Solow 1958, 130). The notion of such a solution could be considered meaningful only within the context of a tightly constrained model.

This brief rumination on the adequacy of LP to describe economic actors' thought processes reflected more general conversations taking place at that time about what role rational decisions should play in economic theory. Before the war, Samuelson (1938) articulated the doctrine that economic actors' actions should be considered rational by definition, in that their desires could be defined to be whatever ends those actors seemed to rationally pursue. In the early postwar period, he termed this the theory of "revealed preferences" (Samuelson 1948; Wong 1978). If Samuelson was ambivalent to actors' actual rationality, a somewhat stronger position was articulated in 1950 by the UCLA economist Armen Alchian (1950), who suggested that, instead of simply presuming that "profit maximization" behavior generated market phenomena, the existential pressures of the "economic system" could be regarded as an "adoptive mechanism," akin to natural selection, "which chooses among exploratory actions generated by the adaptive pursuit of 'success' or 'profits.'" This, as I have shown, was the position taken toward LP in *Linear Programming and Economic Analysis*. Still another approach was Simon's concept of "bounded rationality," which sought to develop models of how decision makers actually made decisions in ways that yielded results that were satisfying to decision makers, rather than in some sense optimal (Augier 2000; Sent 2000; Klaes and Sent 2005; Crowther-Heyck 2005). Later, some of Simon's colleagues at Carnegie Tech, notably John Muth and Robert Lucas, developed models embodying the much more stringent assumption that economic actors made deeply reasoned decisions based on their "rational expectations" (Klein 2012; Rancan 2013).

These foundational problems about the status of rationality in theoretical models also went beyond considerations of whether and when OR-type optimization models should be incorporated into economic theories. OR theoreticians likewise had to cope with the problem of whether their models clearly described (and therefore prescribed) the most rational decision possible, whether they described some suboptimal decision measured against some as-yet-unarticulated optimal decision, or, indeed, whether they satisfactorily described the rationality already implicit within seasoned decision makers' intuitive choices. These concerns dated back to World War II and were widely appreciated by economists and statisticians. They were, notably, at the heart of the formulation of the statistical technique of sequential analysis developed by Allen Wallis, Milton Friedman, and especially Abraham Wald, who articulated for the first time the intuitive calculations made by supervisors of quality-control tests when they decided to truncate tests early based on data obtained during the test (Klein 2000). The attempt to capture such *meta-rational* calculations, as we might call rational calculations external to existing models, was the major intellectual driver behind the explosion of postwar interest in statistical decision theory.

We may surmise that the development of an academic body of OR theory was driven by economists and statisticians rather than by proponents of a new professional OR field. Such was clearly the case in inventory theory, which, like LP, became integrated into the canon of OR techniques during the 1950s. I have already discussed Herbert Simon's early contribution to inventory studies. Another seminal contribution was formulated by Arrow and former Cowles Commission director Jacob Marschak, who sought to define optimal decision rules for inventory replenishment, given a stochastic distribution of demand, to minimize storage and depletion costs (Arrow, Harris, and Marschak 1951). Their formulation, employing Markov branching processes, no doubt exceeded the intuitive calculations of most inventory managers' decisions. Indeed, it exceeded their own calculative ability, necessitating collaboration with RAND mathematician Theodore Harris (Arrow 2002). Most inventory decisions would not require the numerical precision that these mathematics supplied, but that was not necessarily the point of the exercise. As Arrow (1957) later argued in a lecture titled "Decision Theory and Operations Research," the act of modeling decisions could itself be productively conceived of as a dynamic process. In this process a theoretical formulation's real worth was not in its explicit solution but in its ability to reveal its own inadequacies compared with future formulations. When and how one *stopped* modeling was dependent on the modeler's assessment of how well the model's purpose was fulfilled.

Clearly, then, the standards by which theoreticians viewed a model as adequate or inadequate—whether in economics, OR, or some other field—went well beyond any underlying beliefs they might have harbored about whether actual decision-making actors are or are not rational. Rather, the crucial issue seems to have revolved around the sorts of questions theoreticians sought to answer using models, and whether, in any given instance, their heuristic of model building dictated that idealized models needed to be de-idealized to capture real market behaviors, or whether rudimentary models had to be improved to encompass additional rational behavior. Sometimes differences in approaches could lead to different visions of reality. For example, postwar business cycle theorists were content to view business cycles as pathological consequences of locally rational behaviors. Later, "real" business cycle theory, founded on assumptions of rational expectations, would depict business cycles as the necessary consequence of intentional economic restructuring. Other times, however, differences merely entailed different philosophical conceptualizations of the same problem. For example, Arrow (2004) has evaluated (and tentatively rejected) the suggestion that Simon's models of bounded rationality can be regarded as modeling optimally rational behaviors, if only the concept of rationality were differently construed to encompass those considerations dictating why it was preferable to satisfice rather than seek optimal solutions.

OR vis-à-vis Management and Economics at MIT

By tracing continuities in approaches to modeling, it is possible to gain a better sense of the flow of ideas through the rich intellectual ferment of the postwar world. For discussing the importance of the MIT milieu to the style of economics done at MIT, we may note that the rather deep connections between OR and economics, and the abstruse ruminations on the epistemological status of models of rational decision making to be found in the work of people like Arrow and Simon, were initially absent at MIT. Although MIT was one of the first institutions to develop OR as an academic discipline, and although MIT's proponents of the subject were certainly interested in subjects like inventory theory and LP, their interest in those subjects was vocally pragmatic. For them, these were merely techniques to be applied in a direct, prescriptive, and judicious manner, and were thus not to be unnecessarily refined or overtheorized. Thus the instructors of one of the earliest courses in OR at MIT were careful to warn students that, when using mathematical techniques, a "crude solution" to a "real problem" was preferable to "a precise solution to an unjustified idealization of the problem." They suggested that a student who had difficulty coming to terms with such pragmatic uses of mathematical techniques would "probably not become an effective O/R man" (Thomas 2012, 110). MIT's lead proponent of OR, Philip Morse (1955), encouraged a similarly unadventurous attitude toward formalism in his capacity as an early leader of the Operations Research Society of America.

Over in the economics department, Samuelson and Solow fostered their own sort of pragmatism, which nevertheless made substantially more room for theoretical reflection. They were, accordingly, also rather less interested in numerical applications of mathematics than MIT's OR proponents. And, for their part, the OR proponents—who were nearly all scientists, engineers, and mathematicians—seem not to have paid substantial mind to the MIT economists' theoretical proclivities. When they formed MIT's Committee on OR in 1952, they naturally recognized a potential for collaboration with the economics department and the new School of Industrial Management, but worried that graduate students in those areas would not typically "have the necessary Mathematics background" to do OR, though they allowed "a few would." For those few, they reckoned, "a concentration on the Operations Research aspect would not be difficult." The trouble "was not a matter of finding a thesis problem specifically in Operations Research, but of looking for Operations Research aspects in the various theses that were being carried on." On this meager foundation, bridges were built into SIM and the economics department. Tom Hill, the accounting professor whose report prevented OR from becoming part of SIM, nevertheless signed up to become a member of the OR committee. Solow joined the committee from its second meeting. Thomson Whitin, author of *The Theory of Inventory Management*, likewise joined once he left the Princeton economics department for SIM in 1953 (Philip M. Morse Papers [MC 75], box 2, Committee on OR Minutes, Institute Archives and Special Collections, MIT Libraries).

Through the OR committee, MIT's OR proponents, economists, and SIM faculty soon grew closer. In 1954 Hill communicated to SIM's dean that it might now be desirable to take a stronger interest in technical subjects such as "autocorrelation, linear programming, game theory, and other such areas pertinent to industrial activity," and might supplement OR by assisting in "the reduction of theory to practice" (Thomas 2012, 117–18). Around that same time, some economics students began to undertake work through the OR committee (Philip M. Morse Papers [MC 75], box 2, Committee on OR Minutes, Institute Archives and Special Collections, MIT Libraries). Michel Balinski, for instance, received his bachelor's degree in mathematics at Williams College. After receiving a master's degree in MIT's economics department in cooperation with the OR committee, he moved on to Princeton to do a PhD in mathematics, where he wrote a thesis on the mathematics of convex sets underlying linear programming (Balinski 1959). He soon became an authority in mathematical programming before, in his later career, moving on to voting theory. Harvey Wagner was a doctoral student studying under Solow, but also worked as a research assistant to Whitin. In 1956 Whitin recruited Wagner to help write an appendix to a new edition of *The Theory of Inventory Management*, which addressed the substantial body of theoretical work that had already developed on the subject since its original publication (Wagner 2004). Wagner completed his PhD thesis on inventory management and made his career in OR and MS. He wrote a major textbook in the field, for which he won ORSA's Lanchester Prize in 1969.

As figures such as Solow and Whitin bridged the originally strong methodological divide between OR and economics, work at SIM and the MIT OR Center increasingly began to reflect an arrangement that had been developing since about 1950 beyond MIT. This arrangement involved the creation of a large, diverse, but nevertheless well-integrated body of theory, in which models of decision and resource allocation could be developed for their own sake, *or* become components of descriptive models of the economy, *or* be applied prescriptively to real management and engineering problems. This arrangement had been pioneered at places such as Carnegie Tech, where some individuals, such as William Cooper (2002) and Abraham Charnes, focused on practical applications of tools, but also mixed freely with more academically inclined scholars such as Herbert Simon and Franco Modigliani. This flexible approach to theory was absorbed into SIM and the MIT OR community through figures like Whitin and, at least through Solow, into the economics department as well. We might suppose it to have been well established at MIT by the time Modigliani made his move from Carnegie Tech to SIM in 1960.

Conclusion

It is clear that Paul Samuelson and Robert Solow shared an interest with colleagues in other departments at MIT in how individual-level decisions related to system-level behavior, in the functioning of dynamic systems, and in the use of linear programming. These shared interests strongly suggest that the MIT milieu was unusually conducive to the study of such problems. That said, when attention is turned to the actual strategies of theorizing, it is evident that Samuelson's and Solow's emphasis on using models heuristically to clarify concepts and arguments had stronger links to conversations taking place elsewhere within the ambit of economics. At MIT, economics never forged strong links with either Norbert Wiener's cybernetics or Jay Forrester's industrial dynamics. Both those fields treated dynamic phenomena very differently from economics. If we seek the origins of the dynamic style of Keynesian economics adopted by Samuelson and Solow, we should look closely at their connections with figures at nearby Harvard, particularly Wassily Leontief, Lloyd Metzler, Alvin Hansen, Evsey Domar, and Richard Goodwin. Meanwhile, insofar as MIT adopted a disciplinary arrangement wherein the theoretical apparatuses of OR and economics were tightly intertwined, this arrangement appears to have been imported from places such as Carnegie Tech and from individuals such as Kenneth Arrow and Charles Hitch. In the future, it may prove more fruitful to draw connections between economics at MIT and economics elsewhere, as Roger Backhouse does in this volume, than it would be to define further the peculiarities of an MIT style of economics.

References

Akhabbar, Amanar. 2006. "Leontief and Samuelson on the Non-Substitution Theorem: Some Methodological Remarks." Paper presented at the International Input-Output Association and Pan-Pacific Association of Input-Output Studies, Intermediate Input-Output Conference, Sendai, Japan, July 26–28.

Alchian, Armen A. 1950. "Uncertainty, Evolution, and Economic Theory." *Journal of Political Economy* 58 (3): 211–21.

Arrow, Kenneth J. 1957. "Decision Theory and Operations Research." *Operations Research* 5 (3): 765–74.

———. 2002. "The Genesis of 'Optimal Inventory Policy.'" *Operations Research* 50 (1): 1–2.

———. 2004. "Is Bounded Rationality Unboundedly Rational? Some Ruminations." In *Models of a Man: Essays in Memory of Herbert A. Simon*, edited by Mie Augier and James G. March, 47–56. Cambridge, Mass.: MIT Press.

Arrow, Kenneth J., and Gerard Debreu. 1954. "Existence of an Equilibrium for a Competitive Economy." *Econometrica* 22 (3): 265–90.

Arrow, Kenneth J., Theodore E. Harris, and Jacob Marschak. 1951. "Optimal Inventory Policy." *Econometrica* 19 (3): 250–72.

Augier, Mie. 2000. "Models of Herbert A. Simon." *Perspectives on Science* 8 (4): 407–43.

Backhouse, Roger E. 2012a. "Linear Programming and Economic Analysis: The Collaboration between Samuelson, Dorfman, and Solow, 1949–1958." Unpublished draft.

———. 2012b. "Paul Samuelson, RAND, and the Cowles Commission Activity Analysis Conference, 1947–1949." Unpublished draft.

Balinski, Michel. 1959. "An Algorithm for Finding All Vertices of Convex Polyhedral Sets." PhD diss., Princeton University.

Collins, Martin J. 2002. *Cold War Laboratory: RAND, the Air Force, and the American State, 1945–1950*. Washington, D.C.: Smithsonian Institution Press.

Cooper, W. W. 2002. "Abraham Charnes and W. W. Cooper (et al.): A Brief History in a Long Collaboration in Developing Industrial Uses of Linear Programming." *Operations Research* 50 (1): 35–41.

Crowther-Heyck, Hunter. 2005. *Herbert A. Simon: The Bounds of Reason in Modern America*. Baltimore: Johns Hopkins University Press.

Dantzig, George B. 1963. *Linear Programming and Extensions*. Princeton, N.J.: Princeton University Press.

——. 2002. "Linear Programming." *Operations Research* 50 (1): 42–47.

Domar, Evsey D. 1946. "Capital Expansion, Rate of Growth, and Employment." *Econometrica* 14 (2): 137–47.

Dorfman, Robert, Paul A. Samuelson, and Robert M. Solow. 1958. *Linear Programming and Economic Analysis*. New York: McGraw-Hill.

Düppe, Till, and E. Roy Weintraub. 2014. *Finding Equilibrium: Arrow, Debreu, McKenzie, and the Problem of Scientific Credit*. Princeton, N.J.: Princeton University Press.

Forrester, Jay W. 1958. "Industrial Dynamics: A Major Breakthrough for Decision Makers." *Harvard Business Review* 36 (4): 37–66.

——. 1961. *Industrial Dynamics*. Cambridge, Mass.: MIT Press.

Fourcade, Marion, and Rakesh Khurana. 2011. "From Social Control to Financial Economics: The Linked Ecologies of Economics and Business in Twentieth-Century America." Working Paper 11–071, Harvard Business School.

Goodwin, Richard M. 1951. "Econometrics in Business-Cycle Analysis." In *Business Cycle and National Income*, by Alvin H. Hansen, 417–68. New York: W. W. Norton.

Hansen, Alvin H. 1941. *Fiscal Policy and Business Cycles*. New York: W. W. Norton.

Harrod, R. F. 1939. "An Essay in Dynamic Theory." *Economic Journal* 49 (193): 14–33.

Heims, Steve J. 1991. *The Cybernetics Group*. Cambridge, Mass.: MIT Press.

Hitch, Charles. 1950. "Planning Defense Production." *American Economic Review* 40 (2): 191–98.

Keynes, John Maynard. 1930. *A Treatise on Money*. Vol. 2. New York: Harcourt Brace.

Klaes, Matthias, and Esther-Mirjam Sent. 2005. "A Conceptual History of the Emergence of Bounded Rationality." *History of Political Economy* 37 (1): 27–59.

Klein, Judy L. 2000. "Economics for a Client: The Case of Statistical Quality Control and Sequential Analysis." In *Toward a History of Applied Economics*, edited by Roger E. Backhouse and Jeff Biddle. *History of Political Economy* 32 (supplement): 27–69.

——. 2012. "The Cold War Hot House for Modeling Strategies at the Carnegie Institute of Technology." Paper presented at Wake Forest University, November 29.

Koopmans, Tjalling C., ed. 1951. *Activity Analysis of Production and Allocation: Proceedings of a Conference*. New York: John Wiley and Sons.

Leslie, Stuart W. 1993. *The Cold War and American Science: The Military-Industrial-Academic Complex at MIT and Stanford*. New York: Columbia University Press.

Metzler, Lloyd A. 1941. "The Nature and Stability of Inventory Cycles." *Review of Economic Statistics* 23 (3): 113–29.
Mindell, David A. 2002. *Between Human and Machine: Feedback, Control, and Computing before Cybernetics*. Baltimore: Johns Hopkins University Press.
Mirowski, Philip. 2002. *Machine Dreams: Economics Becomes a Cyborg Science*. New York: Cambridge University Press.
Morgan, Mary. 2012. *The World in the Model: How Economists Work and Think*. New York: Cambridge University Press.
Morse, Philip M. 1955. "Where Is the New Blood?" *Journal of the Operations Research Society of America* 3 (4): 383–87.
———. 1977. *In at the Beginnings: A Physicist's Life*. Cambridge, Mass.: MIT Press.
Rancan, Antonella. 2013. "Modigliani's and Simon's Early Contributions to Uncertainty (1952–1961)." *History of Political Economy* 45 (1): 1–38.
Redmond, Kent C., and Thomas M. Smith. 2000. *From Whirlwind to MITRE: The R&D Story of the SAGE Air Defense Computer*. Cambridge, Mass.: MIT Press.
Samuelson, P. A. 1938. "A Note on the Pure Theory of Consumer's Behavior." *Economica* 5 (17): 61–71.
———. 1939. "Interactions between the Multiplier Analysis and the Principle of Acceleration." *Review of Economic Statistics* 21 (2): 75–76.
———. 1941. "The Stability of Equilibrium: Comparative Statics and Dynamics." *Econometrica* 9 (2): 97–120.
———. 1948. "Consumption Theory in Terms of Revealed Preference." *Economica* 15 (60): 243–53.
———. 1951. "Abstract of a Theorem concerning Substitutability in Open Leontief Models." In Koopmans 1951, 142–46.
———. (1962) 1972. "Stability and Growth in the American Economy." In *The Collected Scientific Papers of Paul A. Samuelson*, vol. 2, edited by Joseph E. Stiglitz, 1682–728. Cambridge, Mass.: MIT Press.
Sent, Esther-Mirjam. 2000. "Herbert A. Simon as a Cyborg Scientist." *Perspectives on Science* 8 (4): 380–406.
Simon, Herbert A. 1951. "Effects of Technological Change in a Linear Model." In Koopmans 1951, 260 77.
———. 1952. "On the Application of Servomechanism Theory in the Study of Production Control." *Econometrica* 20 (2): 247–68.
Solow, Robert M. 1956. "A Contribution to the Theory of Growth." *Quarterly Journal of Economics* 70 (1): 65–94.
Thiesmeyer, Lincoln R., and John E. Burchard. 1947. *Combat Scientists*. Boston: Little, Brown.
Thomas, William. 2012. "Operations Research vis-à-vis Management at the Massachusetts Institute of Technology and Arthur D. Little." *Business History Review* 86 (4): 99–122.
Thomas, William, and Lambert Williams. 2009. "The Epistemologies of Non-Forecasting Simulations, Part I: Industrial Dynamics and Management Pedagogy at MIT." *Science in Context* 22 (2): 245–70.

Tidman, Keith R. 1984. *The Operations Evaluation Group: A History of Naval Operations Analysis*. Annapolis, Md.: Naval Institute Press.

Wagner, Harvey M. 2004. Comments on "Dynamic Version of the Economic Lot Size Model." *Management Science* 50 (12) (supplement): 1775–77.

Whitin, Thomson M. 1953. *The Theory of Inventory Management*. Princeton, N.J.: Princeton University Press.

Wong, Stanley. 1978. *The Foundations of Paul Samuelson's Revealed Preference Theory: A Study by the Method of Rational Reconstruction*. Boston: Routledge and Kegan Paul.

Part 4
Inside MIT

The Desegregation of an Elite Economics Department's PhD Program: Black Americans at MIT

William Darity Jr. and Arden Kreeger

> Sam [Myers Jr.] feels the normal conflict between the desire to do good academic economics and the desire to be useful to the black community. I think he will succeed in both.
> —Robert Solow to Charles Leven (February 21, 1978)

> I understand what you're looking for, and I believe it is the right thing to look for. Unfortunately, there are very few really good people who meet the description. You have found nearly all of them. . . . Sad to say, I can't think of any female or black economists who belong on the list.
> —Robert Solow to Dwight Perkins (February 24, 197[?])

Rarely, if ever, have studies of desegregation examined doctoral programs at major universities. Instead, the emphasis has been placed on public schools, public accommodations, undergraduate and professional schools, particularly schools of law and medicine, and undergraduate admissions to previously all-white institutions of higher education. Our article breaks with the conventional pattern and examines desegregation through the lens of an elite economics PhD program. We explore how MIT's effort to desegregate its doctoral program in economics came to be seen, by some of its own faculty members, as a "failed experiment."

Correspondence may be addressed to William Darity Jr., Sanford School of Public Policy, Sanford 238, Duke University, Durham, NC 27708-0245; e-mail: william.darity@duke.edu.

History of Political Economy 46 (annual suppl.) DOI 10.1215/00182702-2716217

By 1970 MIT had the top-rated economics department in the world. The department was about twenty-five years old at that point. The faculty included the following scholars who had received or would receive the Nobel Prize in economics: Paul Samuelson, Robert Solow, Franco Modigliani, and Peter Diamond. Nobel Prize–winning alumni of the PhD program between the 1940s and 1970s included Lawrence Klein, Robert Mundell, George Akerlof, and Joseph Stiglitz. Yet unlike Harvard, Yale, the University of Pennsylvania, and Columbia, MIT had never produced a black American PhD in economics.

The department actually had two black graduate students who completed a PhD in the 1960s, both of whom were not from the United States. The Nigerian economist Lattee Fahm (1930–1998) completed his doctorate at MIT economics in 1963 and was serving as executive director of Economic Research Associates in Berkeley, California, at the time of his death. The Jamaican economist Alfred Francis earned his PhD in 1968 and served on the faculty at the University of the West Indies at Mona for more than forty years. In 2000 Francis received a distinguished professorship named in honor of George Beckford (1934–1990), the great development economist who developed the "plantation economy" model. Francis retired from teaching at Mona in 2006.

Affirmative Action in MIT's Economics Program

Affirmative action policy at MIT in the early 1970s explicitly distinguished US students and international students, and the objective at the time was to specifically bring in black, American students.[1] Samuelson, Solow, Richard Eckaus, and Peter Temin were among the MIT faculty members in economics who pushed the hardest to implement affirmative action to increase the presence of black Americans in the department's doctoral program.[2]

1. "Our only black graduate students prior to 1970 were foreign born. We now have 10 black graduate students making normal progress toward their Ph.D." (MIT Libraries Archives, AC 394 box 1, "Affirmative Action Plans of the Department of Economics," January 13, 1974, p. 20). The MIT Libraries Archives include a set of documents from the Department of Economics under the title Affirmative Action, AC 394 box 1. The documents consist primarily of papers on various aspects of efforts to recruit black American students and white women as graduate students and the department's formal affirmative action plans. We are grateful to Roger E. Backhouse and Beatrice Cherrier for alerting us to the existence of this box of papers.

2. MIT Libraries Archives, AC 394 box 1.

Eckaus, in particular, was especially steadfast in his support of the affirmative action program. Affirmative action in economics at MIT involved a number of actions by the Institute, by the department officially, and by individual faculty members. Once undertaken, affirmative action dramatically altered the demography of the PhD program.

By 1974 the department reached its peak enrollment of thirteen black American graduate students at various stages of progression through the program. (See table 1 for a complete list of black PhD students at MIT from 1960 to 2007.) That number has never been surpassed. Moreover, by 1979, when Susan Collins, a Jamaican national with permanent residency in the United States, enrolled in the PhD program, the previous concern over whether black students were US citizens or not had diminished significantly.

Beyond 1974, efforts to bring black American graduate students to MIT economics continued, but not with the same degree of effectiveness. In the spring of 1974, Harold Freeman, chair of the Graduate Admissions Committee in the department, sent letters to applicants for the National Fellowships Fund awards, urging them to apply to MIT's PhD program.[3] On August 15, 1974, Eckaus sent a memorandum to Freeman and E. Cary Brown attaching a booklet he had received from Samuel Myers Jr.—one of the first black American PhD students in the department—listing the recipients of Graduate Fellowships for Black Americans for 1974–75 and pointing out that Myers had "asked why we have not been more successful in getting black graduates from Harvard?"[4] John Turner, assistant dean of the Graduate School at MIT, sent the department head, Robert Bishop, contact information for the Black College Consortia directors in December 1974 to aid the department in seeking potential candidates for the PhD program.[5] By 1977 plans were under way to form a consortium of elite departments—Yale, MIT, Michigan, Northwestern, and Stanford—to promote graduate study in economics among "minority" students and to develop research capability among junior faculty at historically black institutions.[6] The consortium never was realized fully, and it was then that the momentum for transformation of the PhD program at MIT began to slow.

3. MIT Libraries Archives, AC 394 box 1, draft correspondence from Harold Freeman, March 19, 1974.

4. MIT Libraries Archives, AC 394 box 1, memorandum from Richard Eckaus to Harold Freeman and E. Cary Brown, August 15, 1974.

5. MIT Libraries Archives, AC 394 box 1, correspondence from John Turner to Robert Bishop, December 5, 1974.

6. MIT Libraries Archives, AC 394 box 1, documents and correspondence concerning a Minority Graduate Study Consortium in Economics.

Table 1 MIT Economics Black PhD Students, 1960–2007

Name	Year Started	Year Completed
Lattee Fahm	?	1963
Alfred Francis	1962	1968
Leland Dorman	1970	Did not finish
Hassan (Harry) Minor	1970	Did not finish
Richard Winstead	1970	Did not finish
Alvin Headen	1971	1981
James Karuga	1971	Did not finish
Samuel Myers Jr.	1971	1976
Valerie Williams (Williams-Pierre)	1971	Did not finish
Ronald Ferguson	1972	1981
Keith Hinch	1972	Did not finish
Glenn Loury	1972	1976
Barbara Purdom (Cottman)	1972	Did not finish
Barbara Becnel	1973	Did not finish
Ronald Mincy	1973	1980
Linda Datcher	1974	1978
Virgulino Duarte	1974	Did not finish
Julianne Malveaux	1974	1979
William Darity Jr.	1975	1978
Darius Mans	1975	1980
Sylvia Roberts	1975	Did not finish
Maurice Boissiere	1976	1980
Rhonda Williams	1978	1982
Eugene Flood	1979	1984
Susan Collins	1980	1984
Louis Hook	1980	Did not finish
Keith Hylton	1982	1986
Caroline Hoxby	1990	1994
Peter Henry	1993	1997
Allison McKie	2002	2007

The 1970s Cohort of Black Economics Students

When interviewed about his experiences at MIT, Samuel Myers Jr., who was one of the first two black American economics PhD recipients from the university, recalls MIT admitting a critical mass of black graduate students as it attempted to end its history of segregation: "So there were three in 1970, three in 1971, three in 1972—Glenn Loury, Ron Ferguson, and Keith Lynch [*sic*: Hinch], I think. I think Keith came in there too.

Then there were three in 1973. By 1975, you had fifteen [black graduate students]. The problem is we had fifteen, but still nobody had gotten the degree. Glenn and I finished in 1976, so we were the first two African-Americans to get their Ph.D.'s. Then in '76, '77, '78, Sandy Darity came and he finished up very quickly, faster than anybody had ever finished before. But by 1980, they had pretty much stopped admitting African-American students—maybe one here and one there, but not in any considerable mass" (quoted in Williams 2001, 553). At that point, Myers observes, "There had been an experiment, and they concluded from the experiment that it didn't work" (554).

Indeed, when Ronald Ferguson returned to MIT's economics department as a member of an alumni visiting committee in the early 1990s, he was struck by the absence of black graduate students. When he asked the department head at the time, Peter Temin, what had happened, Temin said that the department's attempt to bring in a significant number of black students simultaneously had not worked.[7] The Florida State University economist Patrick Mason reports that when he met with the American Economic Association's (AEA) executive committee in 2004, he asked why MIT had discontinued its efforts in the 1970s to have at least 10 percent of its economics students be black. Mason says that Peter Diamond, who was president of the AEA at the time, responded that it was a "failed experiment."[8] Indeed, the presence of black graduate students at MIT had become so sporadic at the start of the 1990s that when Rhodes Scholar Caroline Hoxby finished her degree in 1994, rumors circulated in the economics profession that she was the first black PhD in economics from MIT.

The idea of bringing three or four black students into the department at one time and of recruiting students from historically black colleges and universities (HBCUs) was a thing of the past by the start of the 1980s. The black PhD students themselves perceived Stanley Fischer and the late Rüdiger Dornbusch—two influential faculty members who became the key figures in macroeconomics research and teaching in the department in the 1970s—as particularly hostile toward the affirmative action program, and sensed the rest of the department had gravitated toward their perspective by the close of the decade.

Myers says that there were three black students who entered the program in 1970, none of whom finished the economics degree (quoted in

7. Telephone interview with Darity, August 9, 2012.

8. Personal conversation with Darity, American Economic Association meeting, 2011.

Williams 2001, 553). One of them, Hassan Minor, moved to MIT's urban studies and planning program and completed his degree in that field (553). He has since been on the faculty at Howard University. A second, Richard Winstead, who afterward taught for close to forty years at Morehouse College in Atlanta, never wrote the dissertation. All three had been undergraduates at HBCUs, and two of them eventually had careers at HBCUs, but none received a PhD in economics from MIT.

The 1971 cohort of black PhD students consisted of three students, two of whom were Myers himself and Alvin Headen. Myers finished his undergraduate degree at Morgan State University, and Headen had been an undergraduate at North Carolina A&T State University, both HBCUs. Myers took five years to finish the degree and completed it while serving as a lecturer at University College in Liberia during the 1975–76 academic year. Headen, on the other hand, took a full decade to finish the PhD, completing it in 1981. Myers and Headen were the last two black students from HBCUs to enter MIT's graduate program.

Myers does not recall the name of the third member of their class, but she did not complete the degree: "There was a woman from NYU who got married to somebody in the physics department. The two of them left. When he finished his Ph.D. they went down to New York. But she dropped out. She did real well on the exams, but she basically wasn't interested in doing what the MIT people were doing" (quoted in Williams 2001, 553).

The three black students who entered in 1972 were Ronald Ferguson, Keith Hinch, and Glenn Loury. Ferguson had been a Cornell undergraduate, Loury came from Northwestern University (where he later was to take his first post–graduate school job), and Hinch had done his undergraduate work at the University of Missouri at Kansas City. Loury was the first black graduate student in economics at MIT to finish within the standard four-year window. Ferguson, in contrast, did not finish the degree until 1981. Hinch never completed the PhD but went on to become the staff economist for the National Conference of Black Mayors. Loury is now one of the most prominent economists in America, holding a distinguished chair at Brown University, and Ferguson is one of the most well-known researchers on education policy and the racial achievement gap, holding a faculty position at Harvard's Kennedy School.

The 1973 cohort included Ronald Mincy, a Harvard undergraduate who finished his PhD seven years later. Today, Mincy is a distinguished professor at Columbia University's School of Social Work. In 1974 the class included Linda Datcher, Virgulino Duarte, and Julianne Malveaux. One of the coauthors of the present article (Darity) would have been in that class, but he won a Marshall Scholarship and went to the London School of Economics for a year before enrolling at MIT in 1975. Had Darity not studied in London, the class of 1974 would have had four black graduate students, the largest number to enter at one time in the history of the department.

Datcher, a Swarthmore undergraduate, finished her degree in "normal time" in 1978. She was the first black woman to earn the PhD in economics at MIT. Datcher died in October 2011 after a long bout with cancer. She taught for many years at Tufts University. Her research activity was devoted to various dimensions of labor market inequalities. She also was married to Glenn Loury.

Malveaux received her undergraduate degree from Boston College. She successfully completed the PhD in economics in 1979 and went on to have a career as a public intellectual, television personality, and served as president of Bennett College in Greensboro, North Carolina. Duarte never completed the PhD but went on to work as an economist for various public-sector agencies.

The cohort that entered MIT's PhD program in 1975 was the last to include three black graduate students—Darity, Darius Mans, and Sylvia Roberts. Roberts, who had been an undergraduate at Clark University in Atlanta, concluded that MIT's economics program was not for her and left after one semester. Mans, a Wayne State undergraduate, finished the degree in 1980 and went on to work at the World Bank and then as director of the Millennium Challenge Corporation. Today he serves as the CEO for Africare. Darity, a Brown undergraduate, completed the PhD in three years and is on Duke's faculty in public policy and African and African American studies with a secondary appointment in economics.

Following the 1975 cohort, no more than two black students entered MIT's PhD program at the same time. Frequently there were none; usually, when any entered, they were "Lone Rangers." No additional black students from HBCUs entered MIT's program. Virtually all the later entrants were students who had done their degrees at elite universities. Thus the MIT faculty adopted a signaling model for predicting black success in the program that relied on the premise that black scholars capable of succeeding in MIT's economics program are few and far between and so unlikely to come from HBCUs that it was not worth admitting students from those institutions.

Among the students entering MIT's economics program at different points after 1975 were the late Rhonda Williams (1957–2000), Susan Collins, Caroline Hoxby, and Eugene Flood—all Harvard undergraduates. Williams died while she was on the faculty at the University of Maryland at College Park in African American studies and in economics. Collins is now dean of the Ford School at the University of Michigan at Ann Arbor after establishing a career as a major scholar in international monetary economics. Hoxby, now a distinguished professor at Stanford, is one of the dominant scholars in the subfield of the economics of education. Flood has made a fortune in the investment banking world. Two current black PhD students at MIT, Isaiah Andrews and Conrad Miller, were Yale and Stanford undergraduates, respectively. Mild exceptions include Peter Henry and Allison McKie, both graduates of the University of North Carolina at Chapel Hill (UNC), a public institution; the two of them had studied with Darity when he was still on the faculty at UNC. Henry, like Hoxby, was a Rhodes Scholar and now is dean of the Stern School at NYU. McKie is a senior scholar at Mathematica.

While attrition or "late" completion of the degree was commonplace among MIT's black graduate students, the pattern is not consistent with the premise that black students were intrinsically inferior. Consider, for example, the case of Ronald Ferguson.

Before Ferguson fell in love with economics as an undergraduate student at Cornell University, he initially wanted to be a city planner so he could return to and improve his childhood neighborhood. However, after taking a series of independent study courses, Ferguson felt unfulfilled by his education and, in his senior year, decided to seek answers to his burning questions in graduate-level courses. In graduate-level microeconomics and econometrics, Ferguson discovered a passion for economics, earning A grades despite being an undergraduate.

His academic prowess led Cornell faculty to recommend that he pursue a graduate degree at MIT. Ferguson received graduate admissions offers from Princeton, Harvard, Northwestern, and MIT, much to the surprise and outrage of his white classmates, who were unaware of his success in his graduate-level coursework. Among the graduate programs, MIT recruited Ferguson the most persistently, with Paul Samuelson calling the department at Cornell on his behalf and MIT faculty flying Ferguson to Massachusetts to visit the school. Their recruitment efforts were effective, and Ferguson enrolled at MIT. While it took him nearly a decade to complete the degree, Ferguson clearly had an exceptional talent for economics prior to entering MIT.[9]

Ferguson says his inability to identify a research topic for his dissertation that was supported by an economics faculty member—a commonplace problem for graduate students—was the key factor delaying his completion of the PhD. He recalls William Wheaton rejecting every idea he had, but always being sent back to Wheaton by other faculty members.

The difficulty was so severe that he even took time away from MIT, teaching for one and a half years at Brown's African and African American studies program and several years at Brandeis. At Brown he designed two new courses: Comparative Perspectives on Economic Problems of the Poor and East African Economic Integration. At Brandeis he taught part-time in economics (courses in macroeconomics and statistics) and part-time in African American studies (urban economics). Finally, he got consent from Wheaton in 1979 for the dissertation topic that he finished in eighteen months under the title *Three Essays on Housing Inflation*.[10] Ferguson taught at Brandeis from 1978 through spring 1983, where he participated in John Kain's Urban Economics seminar at Harvard. Eventually, Kain invited him to apply to Harvard's Kennedy School, and that is how Ferguson made the transition to the position he now holds.[11]

Julianne Malveaux, prior to entering MIT, completed a BA and an MA in economics at Boston College in three years. Datcher had completed the challenging honors sequence in economics at Swarthmore before arriving at MIT. Loury was identified by several faculty members at Northwestern as the strongest student they had ever sent to a PhD program in economics.

Myers had a spectacular undergraduate record at Morgan State and contends that his experience attending a HBCU actually was critical in preparing him for MIT:

> If I had not gone to Morgan, I would have never gone to MIT. I think going to Morgan gave me an opportunity to focus more explicitly on using the tools and skills of economics in order to solve the problems of minority communities. . . . What Morgan did was instill the vision and the sense of commitment to use these skills and tools for a purpose. (quoted in Williams 2001, 551–52)

9. Telephone interview with Darity, August 9, 2012.
10. Telephone interview with Darity.
11. Telephone interview with Darity.

Nevertheless, collectively MIT's faculty appears to have reached the conclusion that students from HBCUs were not worth the investment of an admissions slot.

While apparently viewing Myers as the department's greatest success story among the black graduate students from HBCUs, Solow portrayed that success as a consequence of exceptional fortitude: "He [Myers] is something of a success story. He came here to start a Ph.D. with inadequate undergraduate training. By virtue of native ability, determination, and hard work he repaired those initial deficiencies and went through a very difficult program with flying colors."[12]

A Failed Project?

There were three key factors that led to the belief that the critical mass strategy was a failure: first, there was the perception that the completion rate for black PhD students was below the norm for MIT economics, a department where students customarily finished their degrees in four years. Indeed, it was widely understood that the culture of MIT's graduate program was the antithesis of the University of Chicago's: While Chicago brought in large classes and flunked out 60 to 70 percent after the first year, MIT brought in smaller classes—generally a maximum of thirty students a year—with the expectation that virtually all would complete the program.

The second factor that shaped the MIT faculty's conclusion that the experiment had failed was their impression that black graduate students—particularly when they entered the program in sufficiently large numbers to form a Black Graduate Economic Students Association—were too concerned with social issues and the black community to participate in "real" economics. MIT's faculty, which did not include any black faculty members (and *never* has included any black faculty members on tenure track), seemed to want its black graduate students to replicate their own interests and style of doing economics. There was little enthusiasm for black economists bringing a set of intellectual questions and perspectives to the field separate from their white mentors' interests and expertise. The experiment might have been deemed a success if black graduate students simply pursued economics in the same way as their more senior predecessors.

12. Robert Solow to Kenneth Haas, April 7, 1980 (Robert M. Solow Papers, David M. Rubenstein Rare Book and Manuscript Library, Duke University).

Clearly there was awareness among MIT faculty that black graduate students were not inclined to pursue economics in the same way as their white peers. In correspondence on February 21, 1978, with Charles Leven, Robert Solow expressed his opinion of Samuel Myers Jr.'s approach to economics: "Sam feels the normal conflict between the desire to do good academic economics and the desire to be useful to the black community. I think he will succeed in both."[13] Solow further echoed this sentiment in November 27, 1979, correspondence with Byron Brown in which he discusses Darity's academic performance: "Like any young black Ph.D. in economics, he feels powerfully driven to do things that are socially 'relevant.' He has no inclination whatever to water down his intellectual standards, however."[14]

Thus Solow suggests that the interest in "race" work on the part of many of the black PhD students potentially was a departure from doing "good" economics, although he indicates that neither Myers nor Darity would necessarily loosen the degree of intellectual rigor they brought to such problems. Even Loury, who receives Solow's most glowing recommendations, also drew comments in the letters indicating Solow's concern about Loury's interest in research that might be pertinent to understanding the problems confronting the black community in the United States.

Indeed, Glenn Loury's own description of the social conditions that led him to economics, instead of staying in mathematics, indicates that he brought a commitment to the study of social issues with him to MIT: "The year 1972 was a time of political upheaval, protest against the Vietnam War, advocacy for civil rights, black power radicalism and all of that. As a mathematics major, I felt that my study did not connect with the real world sufficiently. I found in economics a discipline that permitted one to employ sophisticated analytic technique while at the same time addressing oneself to core social and political issues."[15]

Darity compounded Solow's nervousness about the quality of black economists the department would produce not only by being interested in socially relevant topics but also by having a deep interest in heterodox economics: "To be honest, I have to say that I think his choice of thesis topics has not been the best. Motivated by a desire not to get swallowed up in the mainstream, he had originally chosen to work on what I think are

13. Solow Papers.
14. Solow Papers.
15. E-mail interview with Darity, August 1, 2012.

peripheral subjects—as exemplified by his paper on the Pasinetti model. He should have been steered toward topics of more permanent interest, and we are now doing this."[16]

Indeed, Rhonda Williams was the last black graduate student coming from MIT to have any leanings toward nonmainstream economics. At one point, she commented to Darity that she was exposed to Joseph Schumpeter in a class at MIT that explored technical change and that, plainly, Schumpeter did not understand competition. After a long conversation in which Darity proposed that Schumpeter was operating with a different concept of competition—dynamic, evolutionary, and rivalrous rather than market structure and state of affairs based—she dove fully into a critique of so-called neoclassical economics.

It was largely the first wave of black graduate students that was interested in doing economics to address the race problem. Indeed, two of the students were so convinced that they could not do work in the fashion that they felt would meet their personal standards of integrity that they left; one of them was Sylvia Roberts. Indeed, the post-1980 black PhD students in MIT economics largely have eschewed "race work"; at most, their research has only an indirect relationship to the problem of racial inequality in America.

Also, the post-1980 black PhD students at MIT generally express a greater level of comfort in their remembrances of their experiences in MIT's graduate program. While Ferguson says that he and Loury both felt a sense of uncertainty about their ability to navigate the program until they both did really well in a monetary economics course, he never really felt like he "belonged" in the program.[17] While Myers (1977, 749) describes his time at MIT as extremely happy, he also reports on incidents where other, nonblack graduate students explicitly made him feel as if they did not believe he should have been in the program, particularly by excluding him from study groups. Ferguson and Loury both describe themselves as being fortunate to have had each other to team with to study for their classes.

16. Solow to David Kendrick, February 3, 1978 (Solow Papers). Kendrick was chair of the search committee at Texas in 1978. Ironically, Darity's combination of MIT technical training and interest in heterodox economics made him especially attractive to Texas's economics department, which had a divide between neoclassical and institutional economists at the time. Darity took his first job there after completing his PhD. Indeed, there was one year, 1982–83, when Myers, Darity, and Williams all were on the faculty at the University of Texas at Austin simultaneously; all three were MIT PhDs.

17. Telephone interview with Darity, August 9, 2012.

In contrast, later black PhD recipients from MIT describe a smoother experience. For example, Susan Collins, who completed her economics PhD at MIT in 1984, described her experience in an e-mail interview on August 1, 2012: "Quite simply I had a wonderful experience at MIT, and am very thankful to be part of what seemed (and still seems) like a special extended family. While I was very aware of being one of only two black students in the class during my first year, I later learned that most first years were quite self-conscious and insecure. Faculty members were interested in and supportive of me professionally. If anything being black meant that more of the faculty were aware of me, and have continued to be supportive of my career."

Caroline Hoxby feels that by the time she entered the program race was not a factor in her experiences: "I had great relationships with my advisors and instructors. I liked every course that I took. . . . Being black played no perceptible role in my experiences while at MIT. I think that the department had completely absorbed whatever cultural changes it needed to absorb by then, and it did not arise."[18]

The third and final factor contributing to the conclusion that the experiment had failed was the general impression that the best of black economists still were not quite as good as the best of white economists. Indeed, in general it has proved much more difficult to desegregate faculty in the economics profession than to desegregate graduate programs. In a recent study, Gregory Price (2009) has demonstrated that, perversely, an increase in the supply of blacks with PhDs in economics is related inversely to the hiring of black economists by PhD-granting departments.

To this day, MIT's economics department has never had a black tenure-track faculty member. A. G. "Bertie" Hines was a visiting professor in the early 1970s, but never became a full-time faculty member. While MIT economics has a long history of hiring back their former PhD students as professors, no black alumnus of the PhD program has ever been appointed. The closest case of such an appointment apparently involved a substantive overture made to Glenn Loury that he describes as follows:

> The department at MIT talked to me with the idea of making me an offer to join the faculty in the early 1980s. I had several conversations, quite serious discussions, with people there. (I recall, for example, Linda [Datcher-Loury] and I traveling over to Martha's Vineyard to go sailing with Bob Solow and Bobbie Solow on their boat, while we explored the

18. E-mail interview with Darity, August 1, 2012.

> possibility . . .). I'm pretty sure that they would've made the offer if I had indicated that I was willing to come. (I was unhappy at Harvard at that time, having come in 1982 to a joint position in economics and Afro-American studies. I ended up moving over to the Kennedy school in 1984). It was at that time that I might have gone to MIT instead to the economics department there. I was told at the time that, while the department was enthusiastic about me joining them, there was an element of affirmative action involved. I don't remember exactly how this was said to me, but people wanted me to know that my being black was a part of what attracted them to me. This did not offend me at the time. But the most serious issue, and the reason ultimately that I decided not to go, is that it was made clear to me by my former teachers that the expectation if I came to the department would be that my main work would be in serious technical economics. I did not feel confident that I could honor that condition, as I was more and more being drawn at the time into public intellectual work. So, sometime in the spring of 1984 I told Bob Solow that I would be going to the Kennedy school, and that was the end of the conversation.[19]

Loury's attractiveness to the department was associated with his demonstrated success as a theorist. Richard Eckaus suggests that the department's failure to appoint a black faculty member, a condition that he "personally deplore[s]," is due to the department being "slow in expanding its coverage in a number of areas of applied economics"—that is, areas where black economists are concentrated. Eckaus writes:

> [The department] only appointed three or four years ago an economist specializing in environmental issues. It never has appointed one specializing in women's issues. After Rosenstein-Rodan's retirement, it was very slow to appoint another full time person in development economics. Peter Temin can tell you, if he has not already done so, about the failure to appoint another specialist in economic history. This might be considered a weakness of the Department, but it is not one which discriminates against black issues.[20]

Nevertheless there are a number of applied fields represented by the current faculty in MIT's Department of Economics. These include labor, eco-

19. E-mail from Glenn Loury to Darity, May 1, 2013.
20. E-mail from Richard Eckaus to Darity, April 30, 2013.

nomics of education, industrial organization, macroeconomic policy, demography, development economics, environmental economics, public finance, and health economics. Therefore, alleged field mismatch does not fully explain the absence of blacks from MIT's economics faculty. Since black economists participate in virtually all the fields listed above, their absence remains consistent with the interpretation that they simply have not been viewed as being "good enough" to be hired as tenure-track faculty.

It is noteworthy that just forty years ago, in 1973, the department's Affirmative Action Plans reported, "So far, blacks and women have been represented on our faculty only in visiting appointments. Beginning July 1, 1974, we plan to have our first woman appointment as an assistant professor to a regular faculty position [Anne F. Friedlaender]. We are eager to remedy our major defect: the absence of blacks and the underrepresentation of women on the faculty."[21] The "major defect" with respect to black faculty has yet to be remedied.

However, not all the faculty from the 1970s at MIT would label the experiment a "failure." Richard Eckaus, in particular, takes exception to that description of MIT's efforts to bring black American students into its doctoral program. He says explicitly, "As the person in the Department most closely associated with the program, I have never thought of it as being a failure. Peter Diamond never described it so to me and if he had, I would have disputed it."[22] He says further that the department did not expect the black graduate students to complete the program at the same pace and speed as their nonblack graduate students:

> The program produced a number of fine professionals. . . . Not every black applicant was admitted and, of those who were admitted, not every one finished. The Department faculty knew that would be the case when we started or would have known that had they listened to the discussion. We knew that not all would follow the usual time path and some would require special attention. The fact that so many required more than the four years that were standard at the time is not, I believe, a valid criticism of the program. None of the applicants came from Princeton or similar departments which gave a very strong undergraduate economics education and supplied most of our students.[23]

21. MIT Libraries Archives, AC 394 box 1, "Affirmative Action Plans of the Department of Economics" January 15, 1974, p. 1.

22. E-mail from Eckaus to Darity.

23. E-mail from Eckaus to Darity.

Eckaus goes on to observe: "There was never opposition to the program in the Department of Economics, at least none that was open and expressed to me, and the Department was prepared to keep it going, if there were applicants."[24] He says that the fundamental problem was the evaporation of applicants for the program:

> There simply were not enough applicants to keep it going. When I was Department Head I went two or three times to the AEA summer program for remedial economics and made talks inviting members of the program to apply to MIT. Not one did. I think that Peter Temin also went at least once, with the same result. We also circulated invitations to black colleges, with no results. My explanation for this was simply that the bright black undergraduates in economics recognized that they could make a lot more money with business administration degrees which they would take back to the business world, some parts of which was actively looking for black professionals.[25]

If Eckaus is correct in saying that the pool of black applicants for MIT's PhD program declined dramatically by the end of the 1970s, and that this constrained the department's ability to sustain its affirmative action efforts, then this leaves open the question why. When MIT first began its program, the MBA existed as an alternative in the world of business management, so it is worth exploring why that option became comparatively more attractive to potential black economics PhD candidates. Perhaps the greater problem contributing to an application decline was that the department's recruiting efforts became focused excessively on drawing applicants from the AEA's Summer Fellowship Program to the exclusion of students who did not go through the summer program at the same time. This may have led the wider community of economists to cease urging black students to do the PhD in economics at MIT or anywhere else.

Economics is the most retrograde of the social sciences in terms of changing its own demography. In that context, the effort pursued by MIT economics to increase the number of black American PhDs in economics was both unique and extraordinary. It clearly made a profound difference in the careers and lives of the black scholars who studied there. Although it was relatively short-lived, at least there was a period when it did take place.

24. E-mail from Eckaus to Darity.
25. E-mail from Eckaus to Darity.

Appendix: MIT Memories in the Black

William Darity Jr.

I finished my undergraduate training at Brown University in spring 1974. I had been a double concentrator in economics and political science, actually with two more courses in political science than economics. Friends of my family and my peers had expected from the time I was a first-year student that I would go to law school. But that never appealed to me, and my parents never pushed me in that direction. In fact, since both of them were academics—I do not have an "up from slavery" narrative to tell—their careers were moderately familiar models for me. I did not follow them to work and shadow them, but I did have a sense of what their professional world was like. From an early age I also had a deep commitment to trying to understand poverty and inequality and to find remedies for these injustices. I came to believe increasingly that I would find more pleasure and have a greater ability to address the phenomenon of gross disparities in human societies by becoming a professor. I may have been naive at the time, but I never felt that there was a sharp divide between activism and scholarship.

There was an attractive option after graduation, the highly selective and small PhD program in political economy at Harvard that offered a curriculum that integrated economics and political science. I arranged to visit and have an interview with the program's director. He asked me to send him my CV and a personal statement in advance of our meeting. When I entered the room for the interview, the director said, "Oh, you must be the young man from Dartmouth." I immediately decided that I was not going to go to that program even if they accepted me. My father's interpretation of the occurrence was consistent with my instincts: the director, upon seeing a black scholar who presumed that he had strong enough grades for the political economy PhD enter his office, assumed I had come from what was then viewed as the "softest" of the Ivies, Dartmouth, despite the fact that he had my CV in hand.

My experience visiting Harvard was vastly different from my visit to MIT. The faculty members whom I met there were warm and welcoming—and not confused about which undergraduate institution I attended. I also met with a group of six impressive black PhD students whose presence made it clear that I would not have to be a racial first there. I had had so many instances where I was the first and/or only black person in a program or activity that it was a relief to know that I would not have to go through that experience at MIT.

Ultimately I was accepted at the economics PhD programs at MIT, Harvard, Yale, Stanford, and Duke—and the political economy program at Harvard. I had won both a Danforth Fellowship and a Graduate Fellowship for Black Americans. Because the terms of support were better, I chose the Danforth Fellowship and took it to MIT. But I did not enter MIT immediately. I also had been awarded a Marshall scholarship, which enabled me to go to Britain to study. MIT's economics department told me that I could matriculate there in one, two, or three years. Had I entered MIT in fall 1974 I would have been one of four new black economics PhD students in the incoming class—the largest number in any cohort in the history of the program. Instead I entered in fall 1975 as one of three new black PhD students out of a class of about thirty students.

MIT's core theory courses were taught in eight half-semester modules. We were required to pass seven of the eight to complete the theory sequence. I recall that Robert Bishop's micro course provided us with a comparatively easy starting point. The content of the course was very similar to material most of us had had as undergraduates. I had had an excellent course in welfare economics at Brown taught by Alan Feldman, so I was able to test out of the module taught by Paul Samuelson, who was by all accounts, despite his sheer brilliance, an uninspired and uninspiring teacher. Robert Solow, on the other hand, was a marvelous lecturer. But I was told that it would be to my advantage to test out of the module and attend his macro lectures as a de facto auditor; the exam he would give at the end of the course would be notoriously more difficult because it would be the result of his working through fresh material during the half-semester. So I tested out of the Solow module and consistently attended his lectures. The only module that proved intractable for me was Martin Weitzman's linear programming class. I did take it a second time and pass it, although it was not necessary for me to do so, since I had passed the other seven modules.

The two heroes of my graduate school experience are Jerry Hausman and Lance Taylor. Despite the fact that I had taken a matrix algebra class at Brown and another at the London School of Economics, somehow Hausman correctly gauged that I did not have a sound grasp of the material. So before starting the econometrics sequence, Hausman arranged for Olivier Blanchard to tutor me in matrix algebra during the January 1976 break. I recall Olivier having me work carefully through Sam Perlis's *The-*

ory of Matrices. Blanchard was a superb tutor, and I went on to do the full econometrics sequence, earning an A in the second semester that was taught jointly by Franklin Fisher and Hausman. Our cohort of PhD students discovered that J. Johnston's *Econometric Methods*, out of all the texts, held the most accessible keys to the kingdom.

Lance Taylor was my dissertation supervisor. He was remarkably receptive to my unorthodox interests and allowed me fully to develop the topics that excited me. In a fundamental sense, he protected my passions. Robert Solow was my second reader and less enthusiastic about the various topics that I pursued. However, he was more concerned with the rigor of the analyses than the frame of the analyses, and when he was satisfied with the quality of the modeling, he was willing to sign off. Paul Krugman and I were the only MIT PhD students to finish in three years during that period. My third reader was Paul Samuelson, but it was the norm at MIT that the third reader deferred to the judgment of the first two and made limited suggestions.

Indeed, my first essay in my dissertation was a repudiation of the conclusions reached by Samuelson and Franco Modigliani in their treatment of Luigi Pasinetti's model of growth and income distribution. The second essay was a three by three international trade model to characterize the transatlantic slave trade that later was used by Ronald Findlay in his Princeton International Finance paper on the triangular trade and the Atlantic economy. The third was a formalization of Ester Boserup's model of agricultural intensification and growth. All three were published, the first in the *American Economic Review*, the second in *Research in Economic History*, and the third in the *Journal of Development Economics*.

None of my dissertation essays were on race or discrimination, although the second essay was on slavery and the slave trade. If they shared anything in common, they all dealt with various dimensions of the history of the evolution of international inequality. Not only did I float some of the ideas that went into these essays at the department's seminars where doctoral students tested their new projects, but I also floated them at the regular meetings held by our community of black graduate students. I remember that there was a deep divide among us over whether current or ongoing discrimination played a key role in explaining contemporary black-white inequality in the USA. Glenn Loury and I seemed to be the archetypal representatives of the polar positions. Glenn's dissertation attempted to demonstrate that past discrimination could lead to current deficiencies in human capital that would produce unequal earnings today. I argued that there was substantial evidence that blacks suffered substantial wage penalties even if they had comparable productivity with whites with similar levels of education.

As black graduate students, we received strong signals that research on race and discrimination was not valued by most of the economics faculty. This was not, in their view, the way to build a career in economics. In fact, there seemed to be more receptiveness to white economists doing work on the same topics than black economists. Nevertheless, most of us did do work that involved an exploration of racial inequality while at MIT or thereafter. We were stubborn.

In retrospect, I received a rich array of benefits from MIT economics. I received excellent training in mathematical model building and econometrics that has benefited me to this day even though there was no training or even readings in the history of economic thought. Big lessons that I retain until this day are that you never drop variables from your regression if your theory tells you they should be included, and always be cognizant of the possibility of endogeneity in any system of equations you might estimate. I also became acclimatized to the challenging culture of the seminar style in economics with its relentless demand for rigor and precision in the construction of your argument. For me at that time, MIT was a good "fit."

References

Myers, Samuel L., Jr. 1977. "Personal Testimony: The Agony of the Black Scholar in the White World." *Phi Delta Kappan*, June.

Price, Gregory N. 2009. "The Problem of the 21st Century: Economics Faculty and the Color Line." *Journal of Socio-Economics* 38:331–43.

Williams, Clarence G. 2001. *Technology and the Dream: Reflections on the Black Experience at MIT, 1941–1999.* Cambridge, Mass.: MIT Press.

The Rise and Fall of Economic History at MIT

Peter Temin

This article tells the story of economic history at MIT during the twentieth century, even though roughly half the century precedes the formation of the MIT economics department. Economic history was central in the development of economics at the start of the century, but it lost its primary position rapidly after the Second World War, disappearing entirely a decade after the end of the twentieth century. I taught economic history to MIT graduate students in economics for forty-five years during this long decline, and my account consequently contains an autobiographical bias.

The story begins with Davis Rich Dewey, older brother of John Dewey and professor of economics at MIT until 1940. He was one of several people who shaped the profession of economics, and the economics library at MIT is named after him. Best known for his writings on US economic history, his professional career spanned fifty years during the formative period of the modern economics profession.

Dewey received his doctorate from Johns Hopkins in 1886 with a thesis on the early history of American economics. He was appointed instructor in history and political science at MIT and published his first articles in 1887. He progressed steadily up the ranks to professor and department chairman. He also served as chairman of the MIT faculty in 1911–13.

Dewey was an associate of Francis Amasa Walker, who had become MIT's president in 1881, and he edited Walker's *Discussions in Economics*

Correspondence may be addressed to Peter Temin, Department of Economics, MIT, 77 Massachusetts Avenue, Room E18-276, Cambridge, MA 02139; e-mail: ptemin@mit.edu.

History of Political Economy 46 (annual suppl.) DOI 10.1215/00182702-2716226

and Statistics for publication in 1899 after Walker's sudden death. Dewey wrote his classic *Financial History of the United States* for Albert Bushnell Hart's American Citizen Series in 1902, and a volume titled *National Problems* for Hart's American Nation Series in 1907. *Financial History of the United States* won the John Marshall Prize offered by Johns Hopkins in 1904.

Dewey was influential in the internal affairs of two major professional organizations, the American Economic Association (AEA) and the American Statistical Association (ASA). He participated in the founding meeting of the AEA while still a graduate student, and he became its president in 1909. When the AEA's journal, the *American Economic Review*, was started in 1911, he served as its first editor, a post he held until 1940. The medal on the Dewey Library home page was awarded to him on the occasion of his retirement as editor of the *American Economic Review*. Also in his first year of service at MIT, he became a member and was elected secretary of the ASA, an office he held until 1906. Dewey helped edit the publications of that organization as well as serving as secretary and a member of the publications committee.

Dewey was above all a practitioner, insisting that applied knowledge was the true realm of the academic economist. He was indifferent to theorizing that had little to do with empirical fact. Dewey also maintained a lively interest in the politics of academic institutions and followed several academic freedom cases of his day.

At the time of Dewey's retirement in 1940, Paul Samuelson came onto the MIT scene. Receiving his PhD from Harvard in that year, he was snatched up by MIT when Harvard failed to make him a faculty appointment (Keller and Keller 2001, 81–82; Backhouse, this volume, "Samuelson's Move"; Weintraub, this volume, introduction). From this event came both the birth of the MIT economics department and a revolution of economics itself. Samuelson's thesis, published as *The Foundations of Economic Analysis* (1947), championed the use of mathematics in economics. He was hardly the first economist to use math, but he showed how math could be systematically employed to reformulate familiar and unfamiliar economic arguments. He was like Adam Smith, organizing various strands of existing economics into a new coherent synthesis.

The economics department started its graduate program after the war. The education was constructed like a three-legged stool, resting on required courses in economic theory, econometrics, and economic history. But while the legs of a stable stool are equal, these required courses were not. Economic theory and measurement were in their ascendancy, and economic history needed to find a way to coexist with the new theories and econometrics to survive.

This problem can be illuminated by another analogy: Marxian class struggles. Marx identified three classes that can be associated with the legs of MIT's three-legged stool. Aristocrats (landowners) are economic historians; capitalists (owners of capital) are theorists, and proletarians (owners of labor) are econometricians. Economic historians were being supplanted in economics as the aristocracy was in Europe after the Industrial Revolution. The question for power then was whom the econometricians would support. On the one hand, like economic historians, they regarded facts and data as primary inputs to their work. Dewey had helped form both the AEA and ASA. On the other hand, econometricians also were interested in new statistical and econometric theories. In the early years of the MIT economics department, they went with the theorists.

Dewey was succeeded initially by Karl Deutsch, who was at MIT, albeit not in the economics department. Deutsch taught economic history during the late 1940s and then was followed by Walt Rostow in 1950. Rostow served in the Office of Strategic Services during the war and became the assistant chief of the German-Austrian Economic Division in the Department of State immediately after the war. He was the Harmsworth Professor of American History at Oxford in 1946–47 and the assistant to the executive secretary of the Economic Commission for Europe in 1947. He was involved in the development of the Marshall Plan and was the Pitt Professor of American History and Institutions at Cambridge in 1949–50.

Rostow was professor of economic history at MIT from 1950 to 1961. I took Rostow's class when I began my graduate work at MIT in 1959. He had just written *The Stages of Economic Growth: A Non-Communist Manifesto* and was lecturing from it. My most vivid memory from his class was his frequent invocation of the maxim: "It's different in the South." A more widely repeated comment was made by Paul Samuelson to Walt Rostow over lunch one day. After Rostow made a claim that Samuelson disliked, Samuelson said, "Walt, you may be an economist among historians, but you are a historian when you are among economists."

The relationship between economics and economic history had changed dramatically from Dewey, who was a leader of both, to Rostow, who was marginal to economists. Economics in this interval became a mathematical social science under the leadership of Paul Samuelson. MIT was at the forefront of this process, and it became the leading proponent of mathematical growth theory under the leadership of Robert Solow in the 1960s.

Solow's seminal work was published while Rostow was at MIT, but he by then was moving into politics.

Rostow joined John Kennedy's campaign for the presidency in 1960, coining famous phrases like "The New Frontier" and "Let's get this country moving again." He left MIT to join the Kennedy administration in 1961, where he worked for McGeorge Bundy. President Lyndon B. Johnson appointed him to the post now called the National Security Advisor in 1966, "at a time when criticism and opposition to the war were beginning to crystallize, and he eventually served the purpose of shielding the president from criticism and from reality" (Halberstam 1972). He was not invited back to MIT when he completed his government service because—as Samuelson's quip illustrates—he was not considered enough of an economist. He was an "old economic historian" in the tradition of Dewey, and the faculty feared that he would not interact enough with the increasingly formal graduate students.

One effect of the change in the focus of economics was a shift in reasoning from inductive to deductive. Papers in economics went from being primarily narrative like Dewey's papers to starting with a model like Samuelson's papers. These new papers progressed from a model to data and then hypothesis tests. Economic historians responded to this change in economics by embracing the new tools of economic theory and measurement in what became known as the New Economic History.

This movement was led by the two recipients of the 1993 Nobel Prize in Economics, Douglass North and Robert Fogel. North was editor of the *Journal of Economic History* with William Parker in the 1960s, with the conscious aim of attracting papers using formal economics in their analysis. He gained the most fame by stimulating the growth of the New Institutional Economics through his many publications. Fogel burst onto this scene with his publications on the social savings of American railroads and then, with Stanley Engerman, his publications on American slavery. These contributions were first showcased at annual meetings of what later was called cliometricians held in the 1960s at Purdue University in the dead of winter.

The economics department at MIT participated in this reorientation of economic history by hiring me to replace Rostow in 1967. Like Deutsch in the 1940s, I had been teaching economic history in the economics department from outside the department for two years while a resident in MIT's Sloan School. My first graduate class in 1965 was extraordinary, containing such later luminaries as Robert Hall in macro and Richard Sutch in economic history. I had learned from Dewey (1903) and Frank Taussig (1910) while I was a student. As I started teaching, they were supplanted by Milton Friedman and Anna Schwartz (1963); I wrote my first book on the Great Depression in response to their views (Temin 1976).

In terms of the Marxian analogy, economic historians threw their lot in with the econometricians in the New Economic History. Most scholars interested in economic history are not very good and not very well-informed about current problems of economic theory. By contrast, the growing use of computers in economics rapidly reduced the cost of econometric work. New Economic Historians turned to the collection of historical data and their use in testing hypotheses about economic activity. In this way, the New Economic History brought itself into the mainstream of economics as it was developing, but it caused a growing problem for economic history at MIT, as the economics department turned to the new theories championed by Samuelson and Solow.

Economic history at MIT expanded in the 1970s as two economists already at MIT turned to economic history late in their careers and taught the subject during the years before they retired. They were Charles Kindleberger and Evsey Domar. Kindleberger had been involved with the war effort like Rostow and other members of the early department. He wrote prolifically about his experiences and turned to teaching and writing in economic history toward the end of his career. He wrote two books in the 1970s that have become classics. The first was the fourth volume in a series on the history of the world economy in the twentieth century, and it is safe to say that the series is remembered because of Kindleberger's book rather than the other way around. He championed an international view of the Great Depression and introduced the idea of an international hegemon, that is, a country that can lead the world economy to prosperity. Both ideas have had wide currency. The second was a more popular survey titled *Manias, Crashes, and Panics*. The two books appeared in 1973 and 1978, respectively; the first had a second edition in 1986, and the second had many revisions, the latest in 1996 (Kindleberger 1973, 1978).

Kindleberger made several points in his books. One important point of the first book was that the Great Depression was global, caused partly by the collapse of international raw-material cartels and the dramatic fall in trade. Another point was that the Depression took place in an interregnum when Britain had lost the ability to be a hegemon, largely by expending so many resources on the First World War and partly from the decay of its comparative advantage before the war. The United States, which might have been expected to become the new hegemon, was not yet ready to take on that role; only after the Second World War did the United States step forward as an international hegemon. In the second book, Kindleberger asserted that booms and busts are to be expected, not necessarily on the scale of the Great Depression, but still with enough force to disturb the progress of economic growth.

Domar was less prolific, but he left economic historians with the "Domar model": a trilemma that said you could not simultaneously have free land, free labor, and an aristocracy. This trilemma can be seen as an adaptation of the Marxian class struggle. Instead of foreseeing a winning combination of two out of three classes, Domar (1970) asserted only a combination of two out of three conditions he listed could exist in a world without capital. The idea of a trilemma has been used widely, and it has migrated into international economics to reveal that you can have only two of fixed exchange rates, free capital movements, and an independent monetary policy (Obstfeld and Taylor 2004). The trilemma was illustrated tragically in 1931 when Weimar Germany abandoned free capital movements, Britain abandoned fixed exchange rates, and monetary policy in the United States was dedicated to preserving the exchange rate. The resulting deflationary pressure sent the world into the Great Depression (Temin 1989).

The years of the late 1970s and early 1980s when students had a choice of three economic-history classes represented the high point of economic history at MIT. Kindleberger taught European economic history, Domar taught Russian economic history, and I taught American economic history. I had published my first book on the Great Depression in 1976, focusing on the United States, and Charlie and I spent many hours discussing among ourselves and with students the best way to understand that tragic phenomenon.

The most famous MIT graduate in economic history was Christina Romer, who in her 1985 dissertation analyzed the comparative severity of postwar and pre–First World War recessions. She wrote many papers about the Great Depression and was chair of the Council of Economic Advisers during the first year of Barack Obama's presidency. She is credited with advocating a larger stimulus as Obama took office that might have created more favorable economic conditions by the time of the midterm elections in 2010. It seems obvious to an outside observer that the claim of immediate politics—how large a stimulus could be passed by Congress—was weaker than the claim of electoral politics in less than two years. It must not have been as compelling in early 2009. There are no accounts that reproduce such a discussion if it actually took place (Scheiber 2011).

The abundance of economic history in MIT's graduate curriculum ended when Kindleberger and Domar retired in the early 1980s. I was the Pitt Professor at Cambridge in 1985–86, and I remember taking a long walk with Rudi Dornbusch at a conference in Puerto Rico soon after I returned, during which he persuaded me to teach world economic history. It seemed like a major challenge after teaching American economic history for twenty years, although it proved to be a great stimulus to my teaching and research. I published my second book on the Great Depression in 1989, building on Kindleberger's international approach in the Robbins Lectures at the London School of Economics (LSE) (Temin 1989).

I became head of the economics department in 1990. We had made appointments during the 1980s to replace Samuelson—many times—and the other retirees from the postwar cohort that built our department, but we had gotten out of the habit of hiring fresh PhDs. It was a problem of asymmetric information. We were happy to hire older scholars, but we seemed to need more information about younger ones. I launched a campaign to get us to hire freshly minted scholars, and found that it took some years before we relearned how to accomplish this task well. We made some bad choices in the first few years, and then had the opportunity to make a big score in 1993. There were many excellent students on the market that year, and we had the budget to hire several of them.

I decided to push our budget and hire a total of six new assistant professors, including Daron Acemoglu from the LSE and Dora Costa from Chicago. Acemoglu was very bright, but we were not sure what field he would fit into, while Costa was sharply focused on economic history. Hiring six junior faculty members in one year scared Philip Khoury, the dean of the School of Humanities and Social Sciences, and Jim Poterba and I had to calm him down over lunch one day in the spring of 1993.

That year also was busy among senior members of the MIT economics department when Harvard made offers to many of our senior people. Olivier Blanchard (macro) stayed at MIT, but we lost Oliver Hart and Drew Fudenberg (theorists) to Harvard. To counter this onslaught I hired Abhijit Banerjee from Harvard, a junior theorist with an interest in economic development, and started the process that brought Bengt Holmstrom, another theorist, to MIT the following year. Banerjee was one of the six junior hires in 1993.

The new junior faculty members were a good group, but Acemoglu and Costa were the only new PhDs who remained in the department, earned tenure, and took their place as senior members of the department. Acemoglu continued to work and publish in many fields of economics, and he rapidly emerged as a department leader with his broad interests and abilities. Costa proved to be an excellent scholar who published in leading economics journals as well as those in economic history and demography, but she remained at the edge of the department as an economic historian despite her prize-winning book on the evolution of retirement in America (Costa 1998).

It is probably not fair to either Acemoglu or Costa to use them as examples of trends, but it is instructive to see their development as chronicling the fate of economic history at MIT. I frame the argument using two slim volumes in the Oxford University Press series Very Short Introductions, one on economics and one on economic history (Dasgupta 2007; Allen 2011). Both books start by contrasting rich and poor nations, saying that explaining this difference is the topic of their brief books. Partha Dasgupta starts by contrasting conditions of two ten-year-old girls, one in America and one in Ethiopia, and goes on to contrast rich and poor nations. Robert Allen starts with the great divergence of incomes started by the Industrial Revolution and goes on to contrast rich and poor nations. Dasgupta explores differences in trust in the extremes of incomes, while Allen emphasizes the historical paths by which countries arrived to their present positions. They both end on the same note, however, as shown by their final sentences. For economics: "There is, alas, no magic potion for bringing about economic progress in either world" (Dasgupta 2007, 160). For economic history: "The best policy to effect economic development, therefore, remains very much in dispute" (Allen 2011, 147).

The two books are quite compatible. Neither claims to have a good answer for the question posed at the beginning. But only one of them is considered central to economics. In terms of the class struggle described earlier, the coalition of theory and econometrics left economic history out of power in the counsels of economics. Proponents of the New Economic History were using more and more econometrics in their work, but they were no match for theorists.

This is a loss to the department because economic history, even in Allen's short volume, adds to our understanding of economic growth in several ways. Most importantly, economic history contains a sense of time. Economic growth since the Industrial Revolution has continued over a long time, and the gaps we see today are the result of two centuries of varied experiences. In addition, politics and economics are intertwined in economic history. Nations make choices, even if only by default, and these choices affect growth. Demography and resources affect economic growth, but they do not determine it. And the study of history can expand the insights of formal economics, which provides detailed understanding of specific processes, into a narrative of people and choices. In particular, although not in Allen's small volume, it can acknowledge that history is not always monotonic.

Costa and I taught American and European economic history together for almost twenty years. She also taught econometrics, and I also taught macro, but we taught only undergraduates and were consumers rather than producers to these fields. Costa regularly published many papers and books in both economics and related journals. New graduates of other departments in economic history during these years lacked the technical skills she showed and were not considered by MIT. We did not have many graduate students in economic history, but several students rewrote and published their term papers (Berck 1978; Mishkin 1978; Frankel 1982; Johnson and Temin 1993; Head 1994; Slaughter 2001; Cole 2005; Gallego 2010; Hornbeck 2010).

The economic history paper was central to one leg of the three-legged stool supporting the economics department. The paper requirement began many years earlier when most field courses had term papers. It was by the turn of the century only a remnant of this pedagogical approach to graduate studies. The economic-history paper in the first year joined with the econometrics paper in the second year to help guide graduate students through the abrupt change from courses to thesis writing in the third year. We lack a test of the usefulness of these requirements, as we have neither random assignment nor a good measure of output for such a test. I remain convinced of the usefulness of having students write papers throughout their education despite the absence of a rigorous test.

The two surviving papers, the remnants of the omnipresent term papers in most courses in the 1950s and 1960s, shared several characteristics. Students had to select a question to answer or a hypothesis to test, drawing on their course work or their general knowledge. They had to answer their question or test their hypothesis using evidence from empirical data. And they had to write this up in the form of an article for an economics journal. They were, in short, two variants of an assignment in applied economics. In fact, they were hard to distinguish at the margin and sometimes overlapped.

The two papers also differed in important respects. The history paper drew from economic history—defined loosely to follow the economics convention of a quarter century or more past—for its questions and hypotheses. The aim was for the students to analyze events in a different institutional setting or with unfamiliar relative prices. Given the scarcity of historical data for many interesting historical questions, particularly those about foreign countries, many different quantitative techniques were used. The econometrics paper, by contrast, was focused on the econometric methodology being used and less on the context in which it was used. And of course the history paper came in the first year of graduate work, while the econometrics paper is a feature of the second year.

The emphasis on methodology was in tune with the development of economics at this time. Econometric theory advanced at the same time as growth theory. Given the outsize influence of Samuelson and Solow at MIT, it was only natural that the econometricians joined the theorists, leaving economic history behind. It was, extending the Marxian analogy, an intellectual revolution in modern economics.

This new power structure interacted with the perceived need for the students to learn more mathematics for modern economic theory and econometrics. Classes at MIT were set on a two-year basis, and there was only limited time available for students to learn all that appeared necessary. If there was to be more mathematics, preferably at the beginning of the graduate program, then something else in the first year would have to go.

Then, in rapid succession, Costa moved to California, and I retired. Late in the first decade of the twenty-first century the MIT economics department abandoned the graduate requirement of a course in economic history. The department made efforts to replace Costa and me, but the bar was set very high, and no appointment was made. The three-legged stool collapsed. In terms of class conflict, the new completely vanquished the old. Theory and econometrics joined to eliminate economic history, as the capitalists and workers joined earlier to exile aristocrats. The economic-history paper vanished.

What is the cost of not having economic history at MIT? It can be seen in Acemoglu and James Robinson's *Why Nations Fail* (2012). This is a deservedly successful popular book, making a simple and strong point that the authors made originally at the professional level over a decade before (Acemoglu, Johnson, and Robinson 2001). They assert that countries can be "ruled by a narrow elite that have organized society for their own benefit at the expense of the vast mass of people" or can have "a revolution that transformed the politics and thus the economics of the nation . . . to expand their economic opportunities" (Acemoglu and Robinson 2012, 3–4).

The book takes a shotgun approach to economic history, and many of the pellets go astray. In the areas I know about, their interpretations are out of date and misleading. For example, they quote research into the records of Hoare's Bank to illustrate that "loans would be available to all" as a result of Parliament's reform of finance after the Glorious Revolution (195). This inference has two problems. It was taken from a paper by me and Hans-Joachim Voth about the *micro*economics of what we called goldsmith banking (Temin and Voth 2008). But Acemoglu and Robinson ignored our earlier paper that used the records of Hoare's Bank to explore the *macro*-economics of British economic growth (Temin and Voth 2005). There we showed that financial changes in the early eighteenth century *retarded* the growth of incomes during the Industrial Revolution. In addition, goldsmith banks originated before the revolution noted by Acemoglu and Robinson. Their growth—like the country's growth a century later—was shackled by Parliament's financial actions after the Glorious Revolution.

Acemoglu and Robinson also pluck low-hanging fruit in Africa, Asia, and Latin America. They discuss China briefly in their discussion of current events, but they ignore the gorilla on the basketball court: the United States (Kahneman 2011). The United States is in danger of becoming a failed state, and Acemoglu and Robinson miss the chance to relate their survey of human history with an important lesson about the present. The distributions of income and wealth have been getting worse since the 1970s, and political power has been concentrating more and more in the very wealthy. The income Gini coefficient for American families moved slowly downward from the end of the Second World War until the late 1960s when it began to rise. The United States now has one of the highest national income Gini coefficients in the world (US Department of Commerce 2012). This process has gone on for a generation and was widely noticed in the literature, including major contributions by Thomas Piketty, one of the young economists hired with Acemoglu in 1993 (Piketty and Saez 2003, 2006).

The United States is not the only advanced country in trouble at the moment. Other countries are becoming failed states in the Acemoglu and Robinson sense, as their income inequality grows. Many countries have adopted policies that they should have avoided from their failures during interwar years, as recounted in my third book on the Great Depression (Temin and Vines 2013). When I taught the Great Depression at MIT, students asked me whether there could be another one. I replied that there would always be recessions and even possibly another depression, but I said it would not be like the Great Depression—because policymakers had learned to avoid the mistakes of the 1920s and 1930s. Alas, those who do not know history are condemned to repeat it (as Santayana famously noted).

The aim of history is to inform decisions in the present. *Why Nations Fail* indicates a desire in the MIT economics department to use economic history for this purpose, but the department is not now equipped to support this endeavor. The New Economic History, which adapted economic history to the MIT economics model described in this volume, is poised to fulfill this role at MIT if given an opportunity. The economics department started out in this direction by hiring me and then Costa, but we are gone without replacement. Anne McCants of MIT's history department continues to teach an undergraduate course in economic history that is cross-listed in economics. Undergraduates can get a taste of economic history, but the faculty and grad students are on their own.

I wish to close on a more positive note. Acemoglu plays a role in this ending, as this protean scholar has affected many things at MIT. Two of his recent students show how economic history might progress to rejoin economics more fully. Richard Hornbeck is now an assistant professor at Harvard, and Melissa Dell is a junior fellow at Harvard. They both are competent econometricians, and their research is based on the idea of natural experiments. In both cases, Hornbeck about the United States and Dell about Latin America, they find temporal and geographic boundaries where they can test the effects of various exogenous events. Some of these effects have proved highly durable and therefore important to economic history. Their papers are now appearing in prestigious economics journals. I hope that they will continue to do well and that the MIT economics department will invite one or both of them back at some time to teach economic history at MIT. In this way the three-legged stool could be reconstructed. Or, in the Marxian analogue, the three classes could learn to live cooperatively and supportively (Broadberry 2012).

References

Acemoglu, Daron, Simon Johnson, and James A. Robinson. 2001. "The Colonial Origins of Comparative Development: An Empirical Investigation." *American Economic Review* 91 (December): 1369–401.

Acemoglu, Daron, and James A. Robinson. 2012. *Why Nations Fail: The Origins of Power, Prosperity, and Poverty.* New York: Crown Business.

Allen, Robert C. 2011. *Global Economic History: A Very Short Introduction.* Oxford: Oxford University Press.

Berck, Peter. 1978. "Hard Driving and Efficiency: Iron Production in 1890." *Journal of Economic History* 38 (4): 879–900.

Broadberry, Stephen. 2012. "The Future of Economic History." *Scandinavian Economic History Review* 60 (3): 244–53. http://dx.doi.org/10.1080/03585522.2012.727766.

Cole, Shawn. 2005. "Capitalism and Freedom: Slavery and Manumission in Louisiana, 1770–1820." *Journal of Economic History* 65 (December): 1008–27.

Costa, Dora L. 1998. *The Evolution of Retirement: An American Economic History.* Chicago: University of Chicago Press.

Dasgupta, Partha. 2007. *Economics: A Very Short Introduction.* Oxford: Oxford University Press.

Dewey, Davis R. 1903. *Financial History of the United States.* New York: Longmans Green.

Domar, Evsey. 1970. "The Causes of Slavery or Serfdom." *Journal of Economic History* 30 (1): 18–32.

Frankel, Jeffrey A. 1982. "The 1807–1809 Embargo against Great Britain." *Journal of Economic History* 42 (June): 291–308.

Friedman, Milton, and Anna J. Schwartz. 1963. *A Monetary History of the United States, 1867–1960.* Princeton, N.J.: Princeton University Press.

Gallego, Francisco A. 2010. "Historical Origins of Schooling: The Role of Democracy and Political Decentralization." *Review of Economics and Statistics* 92 (2): 228–43.

Halberstam, David. 1972. *The Best and the Brightest.* New York: Random House.

Head, Keith. 1994. "Infant Industry Protection in the Steel Rail Industry." *Journal of International Economics* 37 (3–4): 141–65.

Hornbeck, Richard. 2010. "Barbed Wire: Property Rights and Agricultural Development." *Quarterly Journal of Economics* 125 (2): 767–810.

Johnson, Simon, and Peter Temin. 1993. "The Macroeconomics of NEP." *Economic History Review* 46 (November): 750–67.

Kahneman, Daniel. 2011. *Thinking Fast and Slow.* New York: Farrar, Straus and Giroux.

Keller, Morton, and Phyllis Keller. 2001. *Making Harvard Modern: The Rise of America's University.* New York: Oxford University Press.

Kindleberger, Charles P. 1973. *The World in Depression, 1929–1939.* London: Allen Lane.

———. 1978. *Manias, Panics, and Crashes: A History of Financial Crises.* New York: Basic Books.

Mishkin, Frederic S. 1978. "The Household Balance-Sheet and the Great Depression." *Journal of Economic History* 38 (December): 918–37.

Obstfeld, Maurice, and Alan M. Taylor. 2004. *Global Capital Markets: Integration, Crisis, and Growth.* Cambridge: Cambridge University Press.

Piketty, Thomas, and Emmanuel Saez. 2003. "Income Inequality in the United States, 1913–1998." *Quarterly Journal of Economics* 118 (1): 1–39.

——. 2006. "The Evolution of Top Incomes: A Historical and International Perspective." *American Economic Review* 96 (2): 200–205.

Rostow, Walt W. 1960. *The Stages of Economic Growth: A Non-Communist Manifesto.* Cambridge: Cambridge University Press.

Samuelson, Paul A. 1947. *Foundations of Economic Analysis.* Cambridge, Mass.: Harvard University Press.

Scheiber, Noam 2011. *The Escape Artists: How Obama's Team Fumbled the Recovery.* New York: Simon and Schuster.

Slaughter, Matthew. 2001. "Does Trade Liberalization Converge Factor Prices? Evidence from the Antebellum Transportation Revolution." *Journal of International Trade and Economic Development* 10 (3): 339–62.

Taussig, Frank W. 1910. *A Tariff History of the United States.* New York: G. P. Putnam's Sons.

Temin, Peter. 1976. *Did Monetary Forces Cause the Great Depression?* New York: Norton.

——. 1989. *Lessons from the Great Depression.* Cambridge, Mass.: MIT Press.

Temin, Peter, and David Vines. 2013. *The Leaderless Economy: Why the World Economic System Fell Apart and How to Fix It.* Princeton, N.J.: Princeton University Press.

Temin, Peter, and Hans-Joachim Voth. 2005. "Credit Rationing and Crowding Out during the Industrial Revolution: Evidence from Hoare's Bank, 1702–1862." *Explorations in Economic History* 42 (July): 325–48.

——. 2008. "Private Borrowing during the Financial Revolution: Hoare's Bank and Its Customers, 1702–24." *Economic History Review* 61:541–64.

US Department of Commerce. 2012. Census Bureau FRED data. research.stlouisfed.org/fred2/series/GINIALLRF.

On Kindleberger and Hegemony: From Berlin to MIT and Back

Stephen Meardon

> My instinct, or political prejudice, suggests that Nature abhors a vacuum, including one of power, and that the United States is assisting the work of Nature in its worldwide intervention.
> —Charles P. Kindleberger, *Power and Money* (1970)

In the large trove of Charles P. Kindleberger's "historical economics," comprising *The World in Depression, 1929–1939* (1973, 1986c), *Manias, Panics, and Crashes* (1978, 1989b, 1996, 2000), *A Financial History of Western Europe* (1984, 1993), and kindred contributions, the most conspicuous idea is the value of a single country acting as stabilizer of an international economy prone to instability.[1] "Hegemonic stability," the idea is called in the literature it inspired (see, e.g., Keohane 1984). The

Correspondence may be addressed to Stephen Meardon, Department of Economics, Bowdoin College, Brunswick, Maine 04011; e-mail: smeardon@bowdoin.edu. I thank Jeremy Lewis for his valuable research assistance, and Frank Ostrander and Tryntje Shapli for access to F. Taylor Ostrander's collections of papers, books, and photos. I have benefited much from conversations or correspondence with Roger E. Backhouse, Thomas Goda, Harold James, Robert Keohane, Perry Mehrling, Jill Smith, Peter Temin, E. Roy Weintraub, an anonymous referee, and participants in the Bowdoin College faculty seminar series, the *seminario* CEDE at the Universidad de los Andes, the HES/AEA session "Writing MIT's History" at the 2013 ASSA meetings, and the 2013 *HOPE* conference, "MIT and the Transformation of American Economics," Durham, North Carolina, April 26–28.

1. For corroborating views of the centrality of the idea in Kindleberger's oeuvre, see Kirshner, Gourevitch, and Eichengreen 1997 and Temin 1999, xi.

History of Political Economy 46 (annual suppl.) DOI 10.1215/00182702-2716235

present essay examines Kindleberger's attachment to the idea, which, as the epigraph shows, was more than an idea to him. It was an instinct. Yet the instinct was not innate: it developed from his personal experiences during the Second World War and its aftermath.

Kindleberger himself wrote occasionally about his wartime and early postwar experiences, including his tenure as chief of the State Department's Division of German and Austrian Economic Affairs from 1945 to 1947 and adviser to the European Recovery Program from 1947 to 1948 (Kindleberger [1968] 1987, 1987, 1989a, 1991, [1997] 1999). Here and there he gives a glimpse of their importance to the big idea (see, e.g., Kindleberger 1987, 181–84). One set of experiences of special importance to his subsequent career was his indirect participation in the 1948 German monetary reform. With the reform, the United States impelled Germany's conversion of old currency and other paper assets to new currency at a fraction of their former nominal value, to the end of dismantling price controls without fomenting price inflation. This, too, Kindleberger wrote about—fifty years later, at the back end of his octogenary decade, and in collaboration with a longtime friend and fellow economist whose acquaintance with him dated back to the early 1930s.

In the collaboration, Kindleberger emphasized the relevance of the German monetary reform to the idea of hegemonic stability and other timely questions, not to *development* of the idea through his own life and work. This essay shifts the emphasis. The materials of Kindleberger's research and collaboration—notes, correspondence, printed materials, published and unpublished manuscripts—help explain, as Kindleberger himself did not, how he got his "instinct" and what it meant for the hegemonic stability idea. They also reveal the difficulty Kindleberger had in developing the idea during his career at MIT.

Early Careers of Kindleberger and F. Taylor Ostrander

Kindleberger's collaborator was Frank Taylor Ostrander Jr., an economist of exactly the same vintage (b. 1910). The two first crossed paths at a Students International Union conference in New York City in the spring of 1931, Kindleberger representing the University of Pennsylvania and Ostrander Williams College. Both were in the class of '32, and both would be elected Phi Beta Kappa. From the strength of their conference participation, both won scholarships to the Geneva School of International Studies in the summer of '31, where they got better acquainted with each other and the nexus of economics and international affairs. After Geneva they followed parallel routes for the better part of two decades. For starters, Kindleberger went back to Penn and on to graduate studies in economics at Columbia University, Ostrander to Williams and then the same at Oxford and the University of Chicago.[2]

Unlike Kindleberger, Ostrander did not finish his PhD. He succumbed first to an offer of an instructorship at Williams and then to Aaron Director's call from Washington to run a US Treasury–sponsored project to collect tax data. But the two young men were situated similarly once again by the latter half of 1936. From that time until the United States' entry into World War II, both were economists in government service (or, in Kindleberger's case, quasi-government service): Ostrander mostly at the Treasury Department's Division of Monetary Research, working under Harry Dexter White, and Kindleberger mostly at the New York Federal Reserve and at the Bank of International Settlements in Basel.

The war drew Kindleberger into the Office of Strategic Services in Washington, DC, and London, then into the Twelfth Army Group in Europe, where he held the rank of captain and later major. The end of the war in 1945 drew him into the State Department, which set up a new Office of Economic Security (OES) with three divisions. Each division concentrated on the economic and legal affairs of a different set of defeated or neutral countries. Here the abbreviations proliferate: Kindleberger became chief of the Division of German and Austrian Affairs (GA) and in that capacity devised economic policy for the Office of the Military Government, US (OMGUS). In broadest terms his charge was making the Allied agreement on reparations operational while fostering the recovery of the countries under his purview (Kindleberger 1991, 112–20). Fostering the recovery of Europe at-large became his charge after Secretary of State George Marshall's famous speech at Harvard on June 5, 1947; the event occasioned his transfer inside the State Department to an advisory role for the European Recovery Program (ERP), a.k.a. the Marshall Plan (122). From these positions Kindleberger made his wartime and postwar observations on the German economy and participated in planning the monetary reform of 1948. In the summer of that year, just as the reform was carried out, he decamped for his new career at MIT.

2. The biographical material in this paragraph and the following one is drawn from Kindleberger 1991 and Ostrander 2009a, 2009b.

Kindleberger's work at GA reconnected him with Ostrander, who, after his tenure at Treasury and subsequent positions in and out of government, had migrated to OMGUS in Berlin in late 1945 (Ostrander 2009a, 92).[3] Ostrander was chief of price control in OMGUS and the US member of the Price Control Committee at the four-power Allied Control Council (ACC). In February 1948 he was appointed deputy for negotiations at the ACC Economic Directorate (Ostrander [1996] 2001, 2), where the terms of the monetary reform were under dispute. Physical control over printing the new money was the stickiest point (Tenenbaum ca. 1958, 13:11). The Soviets wanted it; the Americans did not want them to have it. In March, soon after Ostrander's appointment, the top Soviet member of the ACC abandoned the council, signaling the rupture between the Soviet Union and the Western Allies. The rupture suspended the work of all the ACC directorates. In its sequel, in late June, the Soviets blockaded Berlin. But before that, and more to the point of this essay, the rupture ended the Allied impasse over monetary reform. Like Kindleberger, only more so, Ostrander was an indirect participant in the reform.

The German Monetary Reform

What Ostrander and Kindleberger alike observed in postwar Germany was an economy still beset by wartime monetary impairments.[4] Although the Hitler government had resorted to the usual expedients of war finance, namely, explicit taxation and seigniorage, it had preferred "noiseless" methods. It had compelled the deposit of workers' wages in savings banks that were compelled in turn to buy government debt. Insurance and social security funds had been under similar compulsion. Corporations had been ordered to use retained earnings to buy Treasury bills. At the same time, businesses had been prohibited from replacing prewar stocks of merchandise, and any other business and consumer spending had been impeded by price controls and rationing (Tenenbaum ca. 1958, 4:13–16). By war's end, the result was a plethora of paper and account-book claims in a prostrate country producing few goods to be claimed.

The fix was monetary reform. What that entailed in general was clear enough. New money with a new name would have to be printed and then

3. Kindleberger's contemporary report on his meeting with Ostrander in Berlin may be found in CPK to John DeWilde, August 3, 1946, in Kindleberger 1989a, 6.

4. Kindleberger's and Ostrander's observations are spelled out in detail in a longer version of this essay. See Meardon 2013.

exchanged for old money at an appropriately small ratio of new units to old. Then, sooner or later, people would be allowed to trade money for goods and goods for money.

Stated that way, monetary reform may have seemed like a logistical question. The better way to state it was as a question of "bring[ing] total outstanding money and monetary claims against the government into some approximate balance with the reduced wealth and national income" (Stolper 1948, 102). Logistics, however complicated, were as yet the lesser part of it. Monetary reform entailed figuring out whose claims would be honored and whose repudiated. The destruction of wealth and income wrought by the war were so vast—perhaps one-third of real wealth had been wiped out, and income reduced by half from the prewar level (Colm, Dodge, and Goldsmith 1946, 1)—that, when the figuring was done, the effects of monetary reform would be "tantamount to a social revolution" (Stolper 1948, 102).

Finding consensus among either Allies or Germans on questions of revolutionary scope was unlikely. Numerous proposals for monetary reform, embodying equally numerous priorities, circulated from 1945 to 1948 (Tenenbaum ca. 1958, chap. 12). As early as January 1946, Ostrander and Raymond Goldsmith, a German émigré and US State Department economist, discussed the possibility of outside consultants studying the proposals and making recommendations to OMGUS. Their discussion gave impetus to a commission ultimately comprising three men: Goldsmith; Gerhard Colm, another German-born US government economist; and Joseph M. Dodge, a Detroit banker and financial adviser to the chief of OMGUS, General Lucius D. Clay (Kindleberger and Ostrander 2003, 170, 176–77). The Colm-Dodge-Goldsmith report, submitted to General Clay on May 20, 1946, was the main reference point for official discussions of monetary reform for the next two years. It did not reflect consensus among Allies or Germans but helped guide a decision.

The report's recommendations boiled down to three: (1) The creation of a new currency, the deutsche mark (DM), to replace the old reichsmark (RM), and the writing down of all monetary claims including private debts to 10 DM = 100 RM, except that Reich debt would be totally invalidated; (2) The mortgage of half the value of each person's real estate, plant, equipment, and inventories beyond 1,000 DM, with title to the mortgage being vested in the government, the aim being to help equalize war losses; (3) The levying of a progressive capital tax ranging from 10 to 90 percent on each person's net worth after accounting for (1) and (2), so as to go yet farther toward equalization of losses.

Two men spearheaded the efforts to turn the recommendations into policy and get the Allies and the Germans to acquiesce. They were Jack Bennett, director of the OMGUS Finance Division, and his deputy, Edward A. Tenenbaum. The latter was a young man of twenty-five, already accomplished beyond his years. His undergraduate senior thesis on the Nazi economy was published by Yale University Press; his wartime service as a US Air Force intelligence officer earned him a bronze star.[5] As much as Kindleberger and Ostrander, the rest of the story turns on him.

Tenenbaum's purport was parsimony, decisiveness, and indifference to complaints about the currency reform's distributive effects. "The monetary reform, however much it may have met the yearnings and needs of the German public," he later recalled (Tenenbaum ca. 1958, 13:19), "was in fact dictated by a Military Government that professed to be trying to introduce democracy. It would be ridiculous to deny this." Aiding the ability of Tenenbaum and his superiors to dictate the terms of reform was the Soviet break from the Allies at the ACC on March 20, 1948. With the Soviets excluded from Allied deliberations and the die cast for a divided Germany, the way was cleared for assertion of American leadership. The reform that resulted was a good deal more parsimonious, more likely to reduce the quantity of money to a level commensurate with official prices and the growth of money to a rate commensurate with Germany's capacity to produce, than either the Colm-Dodge-Goldsmith proposal or the competing French, British, and German ones. The final ratio for substituting deutsche marks for reichsmarks was 6.5:100. In addition, recommendations (2) and (3) of Colm-Dodge-Goldsmith were vetoed. Collectivizing war losses and capital taxation, especially at progressive rates ranging up to practical confiscation, were measures the United States would *not* dictate. They would be left for Germany to decide.

To Kindleberger the results were of "the nature of a miracle." In June 1948 German industrial production was 50 percent of the 1936 average; by February 1949 it was at 80 percent. In 1946 exports had been valued at $160 million; by the end of 1948 they were at $850 million annually (Kindleberger [1949] 1987, 34). Kindleberger did not credit monetary reform alone for the miracle: other changes in German economic administration, especially the simultaneous scrapping of wartime price controls by

5. Tenenbaum's senior thesis is given in the bibliography as Tenenbaum 1942. His wartime accomplishment is cited in his obituary: "E.A. Tenenbaum, Overseas Economist, Dies," *Washington Post*, October 31, 1975.

Ludwig Erhard, the Bizonal economic director, also helped (35; Van Hook 2004, 139). Nevertheless, he saw monetary reform as the main cause.

From August 1948, Kindleberger watched the miracle unfold from his new position as associate professor of economics at MIT. From that perspective he might have seen a deeper cause in the circumstances that made reform possible: the dominant leadership of a nation, say, like the United States absent effective Soviet opposition, or that of an individual, like Tenenbaum absent a rival with comparable authority and will. The reader will perceive that the story as told here invites one to see it that way. But the telling is informed by Kindleberger's work during a prolific career, and also during a productive retirement, in which he revisited the German monetary reform with a different purpose than he had early in his tenure at MIT. For him to adopt that purpose took a while.

Leadership

Indeed Kindleberger wrote little about the monetary reform that he watched unfold in 1948–49 until the 1980s. He mentioned it now and then. Like the Marshall Plan, it was an episode in the "clash between the United States and the Soviet Union over economic recovery in Europe" (Kindleberger [1968] 1987, 101). European recovery after World War II was not a major subject of his writing between the 1950s, when it was effected, and the early 1970s, when he published *The World in Depression, 1929–1939*. Still, it was in this period that he developed his ideas about leadership in the international economy that came to be seen as the core of "hegemonic stability" theory.

In the ideas' later stages of development, they spurred Kindleberger's reconsideration of immediate postwar events. The question to be taken up now is, What about their early stages of development? What were the nature and application of Kindleberger's ideas about leadership before, and then during, his writing *The World in Depression*?

From the mid-1950s to the early 1970s, and even before, Kindleberger wrote of the importance of building international economic institutions and coordinating economic policy. He even pondered the prospects for US "dominance" of the international economy. Yet few of his ponderings resembled a theory, and what did was markedly different from his later writings. In *The Dollar Shortage* (Kindleberger 1950, 254), he determined that "a cooperative effort . . . unique in world experience" was required to address the balance-of-payments problem of countries in urgent need of US goods and capital. But the determination only concluded his analysis of the problem. The analysis was economic, not political. A few years later, in "The Role of the United States in the European Economy, 1919–1950," he seized on François Perroux's theory of economic domination. But as far as Kindleberger ([1954] 1966, 230) was concerned, its relevance lay only in the implication that "whether it wills it or not, the United States by all its actions affects what goes on in Europe." This was how he understood US domination of Europe. International economics, not international political economy, was his province.

In the late 1950s and 1960s he moved toward the other province, albeit haltingly and with a twist. In an article tellingly titled "International Political Theory *from Outside*" (1959; italics added), Kindleberger sketched a US role in the international economy more aptly described as collaboratorship than leadership.[6] He elaborated the sketch in an essay for Perroux's own journal, *Cahiers de l'Institut de Science Économique Appliquée* (1961). Kindleberger beheld "la fin du rôle dominant des États-Unis" (as he began the essay's title). In contrast to his later idea in *The World in Depression*, he seemed unperturbed by the prospect of the United States' diminished role. The responsibility of maintaining equilibrium in the balance of international payments should lie first with each particular country, said Kindleberger, then with the International Monetary Fund (IMF), and then some institution of broader international cooperation. Only then should the United States be responsible, and even then not uniquely (Kindleberger 1961, 97). Ditto for the responsibility of aiding economic development (104). The United States should exercise "*leadership*," but only on the basis of equality and economic symmetry: its interventions should take the character of "le *do as I do*," not "le *do as I say*" (105). This notion of leadership was a far cry from his later one.

It would appear that Kindleberger entered the realm of international political economy as an outsider, speaking pidgin, because he was unsure he belonged there—or unsure that he wanted to belong. Considering the "MIT tradition of an intimate interplay between basic theory and practical application," in the words of his colleague Max Millikan (memo, April 4, 1950, quoted in Blackmer 2002, 10), such an appearance seems strange on its face. Upon closer inspection it gives insight into Kindleberger's role at MIT and his character as a scholar.

6. "The United States cannot shift to the long-run basis of maximization by itself. But if the Soviet Union were to extend its horizon, and the United States to follow . . ." (Kindleberger 1959, 82).

Kindleberger was hired by MIT as an international economist (Cherrier, this volume). The work entailed teaching undergraduate and graduate courses and supervising dissertations on the subject. Through the 1950s and 1960s he supervised to the tune of about 1.5 students per year, a high number by the economics department's standards (Svorenčík, this volume; Duarte, this volume). He also wrote a textbook on the subject and revised it through several editions (Kindleberger 1953; see Teixeira, this volume). Thus the obvious explanation of Kindleberger's uncertainty in the province of international political economy as opposed to international economics is that he lacked time to explore it deeply. His role at MIT prevented the exploration.

But the obvious explanation can hardly satisfy, because there existed an institution within MIT that could have bought him the time and changed his role: the Center for International Studies (CIS). Other authors (Needell 1998; Blackmer 2002) have told the story of the CIS's origins in the CIA-sponsored "Project Troy," its direction under Millikan beginning in 1952, the large grants it garnered, and its increasingly controversial association with the CIA (along with the Ford Foundation and other granters) for fourteen of Millikan's eighteen years as director. Beatrice Cherrier (this volume) tells of, among other things, the CIS's influence on the MIT economics department by way of the faculty lines it brought and the fields it promoted. For present purposes, what is notable in these particular stories is how little they involve Kindleberger—and rightly so.

One might suppose Kindleberger was involved in the CIS from the start. His professional profile was similar to Millikan's: intelligence and strategic work for the US government during the war, more government work afterward in service of European reconstruction and the Marshall Plan (Blackmer 2002, 8). If, during the 1950s, one sought an early-to-mid-career MIT economist with a proven ability for interdisciplinary dialogue who was doing policy-relevant research on topics of international scope, one might just as well have turned to Kindleberger as Millikan or any other. The fact is manifest in a weighty CIS planning document, "A Program of Research in Economic and Political Studies," from February 1953.[7] The program aimed to involve more than two dozen affiliated staff members in identifying obstacles to growth and social change in democracies

7. MIT Center for International Studies (1955–80), AC 236 box 2, Records of the Center for International Studies, MIT Institute Archives and Special Collections, AC 236. In the text proper, the next two page citations are also to this document. See also Blackmer 2002, 68–82.

around the world, the better to "hasten the trend in the desired direction" in the "larger power struggle" between the United States and the Soviet Union (1). Kindleberger is named second on the participants' roster after Millikan himself—yet with the admission that he would not stay on, as he was "required by a prior commitment to turn his attention to other matters" (54). Thereafter he appears occasionally on distribution lists of CIS memos, but not on lists of project contributors. By Kindleberger's reckoning, Walt Rostow, Paul Rosenstein-Rodan, Everett Hagen, and (mostly later) Richard Eckaus were the CIS's mainstays among MIT economists (Kindleberger to Assistant Director Donald L. M. Blackmer, February 10, 1967).[8] Kindleberger looked on cordially "from the outside," as it were.

By remaining a CIS outsider, Kindleberger guarded the eclecticism of his scholarship. His work was no less international in scope and no less relevant to policy, but it was more decidedly the work of a free agent unencumbered by group allegiances.[9] At the same time, to be a CIS outsider was to be that much more an economist than an interdisciplinary social scientist. Here lies the fuller explanation of his ambivalence about international political economy.

During the 1950s and most of the 1960s, his ideas on leadership showed the ambivalence. On a Treasury Department consultative committee during the administrations of Presidents John F. Kennedy and Lyndon B. Johnson, Kindleberger expressed concern about the state of "Franco-American rivalry for political leadership . . . and their relative prestige." He confessed that "as a technical economist, I am perhaps not competent" to speak to the issue.[10] And then he proceeded to try. Consistent with his other efforts during these years, he suggested that the United States should muffle rather than amplify its pretentions to leadership.[11]

8. MIT Records of the Department of Economics (1947–82), AC 394 box 1, Records of the Department of Economics, MIT Institute Archives and Special Collections, AC 394.

9. Kindleberger once responded to a memo from then Senator John F. Kennedy by professing his general support but also his deep disappointment in respect to Kennedy's "efforts on behalf of Massachusetts interests which are subversive of international trade" (Kindleberger to Kennedy, March 20, 1958, Charles P. Kindleberger Papers [1934–95] [MC 299], box 2, MIT Institute Archives and Special Collections; hereafter cited as Papers). He valued highly the freedom to disagree without worry of disloyalty.

10. "Issues and Positions in International Monetary Arrangements," p. 1, July 26, 1965, Papers, box 4, folder "Treasury Dept."

11. In Kindleberger's words, "the most productive stance we can take is to ignore considerations of prestige entirely. Prestige can best be served in these matters [of international monetary arrangements] by contributions to common goals. . . . I believe it would be a mistake to try to preserve the dollar as a reserve currency, except on grounds of efficiency, if this be the efficient path" ("Issues and Positions," p. 1).

Kindleberger's famous thesis of the indispensability of leadership in *The World in Depression* (1973) was therefore a significant turn from where he had stood less than a decade before. He signaled it early in *Power and Money: The Economics of International Politics and the Politics of International Economics* (1970)—the source of the epigraph at the beginning of this essay. He signaled it more tellingly in correspondence with Gunnar Myrdal in the same year. Piqued by Myrdal's *Challenge of World Poverty* (1970), Kindleberger told him, "I am particularly interested in what you say about leadership." He was working on the 1929 World Depression, he continued, and took "as a basic explanation the inability of the British to furnish economic leadership to the system, and the unwillingness of the United States." He thought Myrdal was right to say that US leadership in international economic affairs was currently crumbling, but wrong to rejoice in it, as "there will be chaos when it is gone unless it is replaced by some other." Replacement by any party was hardly likely; replacement by any party more enlightened than the United States was even less so. Myrdal was rooting for such replacement, but did not say how it would happen. Kindleberger ended pointedly, "Does a social scientist like you think it likely to be forthcoming as a result of preaching?" (CPK to Myrdal, July 24, 1970).[12]

The leadership thesis appeared in *The World in Depression*'s culminating fourteenth chapter. For present purposes, its summary in the foregoing letter to Myrdal will do (although see also Temin, this volume). Not coincidentally, by this time Kindleberger was nearing retirement. His role in the economics department had begun to change from international economist to economic historian (or "historical economist," as he preferred), and his duties as a dissertation supervisor slowed (Mehrling, this volume; Svorenčík, this volume; Duarte, this volume). The CIS was unnecessary to buy him the time for international political economy, which, to Kindleberger, was couched in economic history. Under the circumstances, his pursuit of the subject had become an expression of his eclecticism, not a suppression of it. The rest of the present essay is about what happened to the leadership thesis afterward—through Kindleberger's elaborations, other authors' responses, and his rejoinder.

Hegemonic Stability

Kindleberger's first major elaboration was in *Manias, Panics, and Crashes* (1978). By extending his canvas temporally to the start of the eighteenth

12. Myrdal answered, "Yes" (Myrdal to CPK, August 4, 1970). Both letters are in Papers, box 2, folder "M, correspondence, 1946–87."

century and geographically to Western Europe, he could discuss more and varied financial crises. To Kindleberger, what the history of the Great Depression showed vividly, a larger sampling of financial crises confirmed unmistakably. Responsibility for stability was a public good. The greater the benefits conferred by the public good, the smaller the incentive to provide it privately. Enter the "international lender of last resort." For somebody or some nation to step forward in that role even when private incentives counseled otherwise was the function of leadership (Kindleberger 1978, 3–4, 220–26).

But the canvas of *Manias, Panics, and Crashes* did not extend as far as the Second World War. From postwar Western Europe Kindleberger drew no lessons. By his own account, it was invitations to help commemorate the 1947 Harvard speech of Secretary George C. Marshall, first in 1977 and then again in 1982, that got him started in that direction (Kindleberger [1978] 1987, 120). His reflections informed his next major monograph, *A Financial History of Western Europe* (1984).

Part 5 of *Financial History* concentrated on the postwar period. The Marshall Plan got major billing: it allowed Kindleberger (1984, 403) to show distinctly the difference between, on the one hand, the "key-currency and key-region philosophy" that he advocated for relief, rehabilitation, reconstruction, and payments stability, and, on the other, the "worldwide approach" proposed by champions of the UN, World Bank, and IMF. The German monetary reform had its place in the book, too, although it did less work. Whereas the Marshall Plan was unambiguously a case of US leadership, monetary reform was apparently a case of shared responsibility between the United States, Great Britain, and France. Whereas the Marshall Plan had direct repercussions to international economic stability, monetary reform's repercussions were felt directly in Western Germany. Still, in a minor way the story of monetary reform supported the leadership thesis. It illustrated the "political vacuum in which policy in the general interest was possible" (Kindleberger 1984, 419). Which was to say, the general interest was served by economic policy leadership—and, as the German monetary reform showed, leadership was more likely to emerge from a political vacuum than from a bunch of contending equals.

By this time Kindleberger's leadership thesis had garnered popularity for kindred ideas in the field of international relations (e.g., Gilpin 1975; Krasner 1976). Other authors developed the thesis and rebranded it.[13]

13. Eichengreen (1990) offers a survey and evaluation. For the survey, see footnotes 2 and 3 (271–72).

Robert Keohane (1980, 132) dubbed it "the theory of hegemonic stability," and although Kindleberger (1986c, 289n1; 1986a, 841) did not care for the name, it stuck. Timothy McKeown (1983), Fred Lawson (1983), Arthur Stein (1984), and Joanne Gowa (1984), among others, wrote articles in direct reference to the theory so dubbed, all of them citing Kindleberger as well as Keohane. Keohane himself surveyed the growing literature and plotted its course in his book, *After Hegemony: Cooperation and Discord in the World Political Economy* (1984). But the course Keohane proposed spelled trouble for the theory as Kindleberger understood it.

Kindleberger's (1973, 105) "main lesson" in *The World in Depression* was that "for the world economy to be stabilized, there has to be a stabilizer—one stabilizer." The one stabilizer, he admitted, need not necessarily be a nation (the United States) or even a tightly integrated bloc of nations (Europe). It could be a nexus of international regimes: "a world central bank, a world capital market, and an effective General Agreement on Tariffs and Trade" (308). He conceded that the latter was "the most attractive"; but, he added, "because difficult, the least likely" (308). The implication was that the world would do best with the United States or Europe in the lead, and if the reader wondered whether it was realistic to expect Europe to take the role, then he was left with one viable option. Kindleberger did not hazard to spell it out.

The concession that leadership by international regimes was "the most attractive" option was an affirming nod to those, like Myrdal, who blanched at the thought of US hegemony. It probably made Kindleberger's thesis more palatable outside the United States and in circles friendly to international regimes, not least in academe. The trouble was that it encouraged inquiry along different lines than Kindleberger had in mind: not "How can a revival of US leadership be fostered?" but instead "How can the option that is 'most attractive' but 'least likely' be made *more* likely? In what forms is it *most* likely?" Such were Keohane's lines of inquiry. His conclusion was that hegemony was useful to establish regimes, but, when that work was done, could very well be supplanted by them. In his words, "cooperation does not necessarily require the existence of a hegemonic leader after international regimes have been established. Post-hegemonic cooperation is also possible" (Keohane 1984, 32).

Kindleberger's presidential address to the American Economic Association two years later offered a prominent stage for a rejoinder. "I am a realist when it comes to regimes," he said. "It seems to me that the momentum set in motion by hegemonic power . . . runs down pretty quickly unless it is sustained by powerful commitment" (Kindleberger 1986b, 10).

The most fruitful course lay in persuading the nation that had the power to provide international public goods to wield it, not devolve it. Anyway, hegemony was hardly as *un*attractive as the boosters of "post-hegemonic cooperation" supposed.

This was the point that Kindleberger, now in his seventy-sixth year, wished to contribute to the literature that he had inspired but that had gotten away from him. To support the point, he would need new evidence, or maybe a new take on old evidence.

Octogenarian Collaboration

The spark for Kindleberger's reconnection with Ostrander in their octogenary decade, followed by their collaboration on a new study of the German monetary reform, was not anybody's conviction that such a study would support Kindleberger's interpretation of hegemonic stability. That came later. It was Ostrander's reading *A Financial History of Western Europe* and finding two small discrepancies between his own memory of the reform and Kindleberger's.

The discrepancies concerned the original inspiration of the Colm-Dodge-Goldsmith commission. In *Financial History* Kindleberger credited one Manuel Gottlieb of the OMGUS Finance Division for suggesting the currency reform; Ostrander denied that Gottlieb mattered much. Kindleberger credited his own State Department for having appointed the commission (not for having "proposed" it, as Ostrander construed him incorrectly to mean); Ostrander insisted that he and Goldsmith together cooked up the idea (Kindleberger 1984, 412; FTO to Samuel I. Katz, May 24, 1990, 4). These were insignificant details in the big picture. Ostrander himself considered them personally fascinating but worth maybe "a footnote" in history books (4). Nevertheless, after Ostrander settled into retirement in 1990 with a spacious basement library and a lifetime's collection of papers, he had time and means to write for whatever purpose pleased him, even footnotes. In 1992 he wrote up a friendly memo to Kindleberger to set the record straight.[14]

14. "F. Taylor Ostrander—Experience in Post-War Germany," typescript, March 10, 1992. Receipt acknowledged by Kindleberger in CPK to FTO, March 14, 1992 (F. Taylor Ostrander [1945–2003], box "Dept. of Defense Conference," folder "FTO Papers prepared for Dept. of Defense Conference," German Monetary Reform/Kindleberger Papers and Correspondence, in author's possession).

Kindleberger accepted the correction thankfully. It impelled him to change no more than ten words in the second edition of *Financial History*.[15] More significantly, he probed Ostrander's memories. He asked about Ludwig Erhard's role, which he thought was overhyped by the likes of Milton Friedman, Gottfried Haberler, and even Paul Samuelson. He asked for information about Tenenbaum, and also about the US War Department's veto of steps 2 and 3 of Colm-Dodge-Goldsmith. And he suggested that Ostrander keep to the subject and add to his account (CPK to FTO, March 14, 1992).[16]

Ostrander answered the queries. Erhard's role was the lifting of most price controls, but he "had *nothing at all* to do with M[onetary] R[eform]" per se. Tenenbaum was a "strange, unlikable type," although "brilliant" and capable of working out the fine details of the reform; "but he does not deserve a larger place in history than this." About the US veto of the collectivization of war losses and capital taxation, Ostrander knew nothing firsthand. The answers earned Kindleberger's thanks and another nudge to pursue the subject at length (FTO to CPK, April 4, 1992; CPK to FTO, April 10, 1992).[17]

But the larger purpose of Ostrander's specific answers, let alone the purpose of a lengthier account of the German monetary reform, was as yet unclear. Kindleberger's nudging did nothing to clarify it; his own notion seems to have been muddled. Was it merely an exercise of fact checking for erudite retirees with (post) war stories to tell?

The reconsideration of the German monetary reform lay dormant for five more years. Then Kindleberger revived it in vexation. In 1997 Amity Shlaes published a story in the *New Yorker* celebrating the success of the deutsche mark and asking, "Can the Euro take its place?" It depends, was her answer. What miffed Kindleberger was not her answer but the historical sketch behind it. Shlaes (1997, 188) said that the "priest" of the German economic miracle, which began with the monetary reform, was Ludwig Erhard.

Shlaes's article was the "straw that broke the camel's back." It prompted Kindleberger to suggest again that Ostrander should undertake a study of

15. Cf. Kindleberger 1984, 412; 1993, 401.

16. F. Taylor Ostrander (1945–2003), box "Dept. of Defense Conference," folder "FTO Papers prepared for Dept. of Defense Conference," German Monetary Reform/Kindleberger Papers and Correspondence, in author's possession.

17. Ibid.

the monetary reform, now imagined as a collaborative effort led by Kindleberger. "Only some part of the story would be to knife Erhard further," he wrote. "I did that in Fin[ancial] Hist[ory] of Western Europe" (CPK to FTO, May 3, 1997).[18] The rest of the aim he did not explain—indeed, did not appear to know, as shortly thereafter he wrote an aide-mémoire for the collaboration that stated its "particular focus" to be "on the fable that [the monetary reform] was the work of Ludwig Erhard" (CPK, May 8, 1997).[19] Anyway, Ostrander accepted the proposition, and the two men got to work swapping ideas and references as preliminaries for the first draft.

Kindleberger finished the draft on July 24. Its stated purposes were multiple. "The initial purpose in writing this paper was to disabuse many scholars in the United States who call the monetary reform of June 1948 the work of Ludwig Erhard," it began. Some "limited personal interest in how the so-called Colm-Dodge-Goldsmith report . . . got its start" was acknowledged. But "of far greater importance" were several other questions the paper promised to address. What was the effect of monetary reform compared with the effects of other policies and events on the German recovery? How important was government action compared with the autonomous action of financial markets in effecting reform? "Was a military occupation necessary to effect a drastic monetary reform that the Germans would not have been able to accomplish by themselves?" Was the years-long delay in implementing reform helpful or harmful? Was the plan for the equalization of war losses that the US War Department vetoed truly important for reform? And beside those big questions were some smaller "technical" ones: whether for purposes of monetary reform it is appropriate to treat private and public debts differently; whether blocking part of the converted currency is a good idea; what sort of banking, tax, and government-expenditure policies should go along with the reform.[20] It was not Kindleberger's finest introduction, and it would remain a jumble even in the final product. But there would be some signal changes along the way.

18. F. Taylor Ostrander (1945–2003), binder 1, German Monetary Reform/Kindleberger Papers and Correspondence, in author's possession.

19. Ibid.

20. "The 1948 Monetary Reform in Western Germany," first draft of July 24, 1997, FTO copy, pp. 1–3 (F. Taylor Ostrander [1945–2003], box "G.M.R.-1948, CPK Early Drafts 1, 2, 3, 4," folder "CPK 1st Draft 7/24/97," German Monetary Reform/Kindleberger Papers and Correspondence, in author's possession).

A few days after finishing the first draft, Kindleberger received a much-awaited delivery. Earlier in July he had read an article by Eckhard Wandel (1979) that resulted in his "raising [his] valuation of the shares of Tenenbaum" (CPK to FTO, ca. July 5, 1997). He had seen Wandel's mention of Tenenbaum's (ca. 1958) unfinished history of the German mark, cited earlier in this essay but not then widely known. Following Wandel's trail, he had sent away for it from the Truman Presidential Library. The photocopied manuscript arrived on July 29 (CPK to FTO, July 29, 1997). Kindleberger dove into it. On July 31 he reported to Ostrander, "I have finished reading Tenenbaum and I must say I think it remarkable. . . . As far as I'm concerned, it's back to the drawing board" (CPK to FTO, July 31, 1997).

Parts of Tenenbaum's account of the negotiations for monetary reform in late 1947 and the first half of 1948 have already been quoted. "The monetary reform . . . was in fact dictated by a Military Government that professed to be trying to introduce democracy," he observed (Tenenbaum ca. 1958, 13:19). What bears noting is the shade of difference between Tenenbaum's observation and Kindleberger's original inkling that "a military occupation [was] necessary to effect a dramatic monetary reform." The difference lay in Tenenbaum's word, "dictated." In several parts of the unfinished manuscript, he elaborated with vivid detail. With some assistance, including Ostrander's, Tenenbaum quashed one plan that would have addressed repressed inflation with open inflation followed by a decrease in money growth rather than with an absolute decrease of the money stock (Tenenbaum ca. 1958, 12:21, 45). He quashed other disfavored plans by his own devices. At a secret conclave of the Western Allies at a military installation in Rothwesten, near Kassel in Hessen, and with the German, French, and British representatives all favoring one element or another of the relatively mild German proposal, only the American representative spoke all three languages. "There are allegations that I took advantage of my position as interpreter to force American views on my colleagues, as well as on the Germans," he deadpanned. "At this late date it may be safe to confess that these allegations are correct" (13:22–23).

Tenenbaum felt no compunction about using "force" to see American views prevail, for monetary reforms were "by their very nature citatorial and conspiratorial." To avoid a wave of speculation, the public had to be kept in the dark. Parliamentary deliberation was out of the question. But, what was more, why give Germans much of a say even in secretive deliberations out of the public eye? "We seriously doubted the wisdom of saddling the weak German government with the enormous responsibility and onus of currency reform." Deliberating with the other Western allies was more necessary, but even so, the United States was the preeminent power among them and had the responsibility to use that power for "reestablishing law and order in the economic field," for "liquidating economic dictatorship." Any democratic state could rightfully use "emergency police powers" to those ends. It went without saying that the US military government could, too (13:17–19).

With these revelations from Tenenbaum's manuscript in mind, Kindleberger began rewriting. On August 14 he sent Ostrander the second draft (CPK to FTO, August 14, 1997). With thirty-one pages of text, it was about three times longer than the first, contained a substantially modified introduction, and had an utterly different conclusion. Whereas the first draft had merely asked (among other questions) whether military government was necessary for dramatic reform, the second inquired whether "an autocratic benevolent *despot* from outside" was necessary.[21] Whereas the first draft had concluded with some bland technical remarks about the Colm-Dodge-Goldsmith report, the second was replete with observations about Tenenbaum and the implications of what he did. "Tenenbaum writes that currency reforms are inherently conspiratorial," wrote Kindleberger, adding that "perhaps it is less inflammatory to suggest that in complex financial matters which may roil economic and financial behavior there is something to be said for benevolent *despotism*."[22] In this case, "the *despot* . . . was Edward Tenenbaum."[23] Finally, Kindleberger challenged the view that a monetary reform like the one Tenenbaum delivered "must be 'unpopular, unfair, arbitrary, and ineffective'":

> Unpopular, perhaps and requiring *despotic* powers to cut through. Arbitrary, perhaps, and mistakes would inevitably be made. Unfair? Not necessarily. . . . Ineffective seems clearly wrong in the German case. It is sad for the social sciences that democratic institutions sometimes fail at drastic financial surgery. It is consoling, however, that a successful operation, even one that fell a bit short of fairness in the German case, can strengthen democratic habits and institutions.[24]

21. CPK/FTO, Draft 2, p. 4; emphasis added.
22. CPK/FTO, Draft 2, p. 27; emphasis added.
23. CPK/FTO, Draft 2, p. 28; emphasis added.
24. CPK/FTO, Draft 2, p. 31; emphasis added.

Despot, despotism, despotic. For initiates to hegemonic stability theory, there could have been little doubt about what Kindleberger had seen in Tenenbaum's manuscript and how it had changed the project. To Kindleberger, it was "sad for the social sciences" that democracy was not always fit for the economic tasks at hand, but so it went, and social scientists had to face the fact. Leadership was necessary, as he had observed all along. Doyens of the academic field of international relations could not skirt around the fact by fostering deliberative "regimes" to provide leadership without hegemony. Deliberation was unreliable. The fact remained. It had to acknowledged forthrightly—even when the alternative to deliberation was "despotism."

Ostrander, however, was not among the initiates.[25] He was puzzled by the sudden appearance and insistent repetition of "despot" and its variants. The word was absent in the first draft. Something was amiss. He lay awake at night trying to work it out—then rose in the wee hours to register his qualms (FTO to CPK, September 10, 1997). "What is the intended *audience*," Ostrander asked Kindleberger, and "what is the *purpose* of the piece?" As to purpose, was it to show that despotism could be benevolent if it had positive effects? "If one intends to praise American Military Government action," Ostrander averred, "'despot' seems an inappropriate word in this context" (FTO to CPK, September 10, 1997).

To this, Kindleberger responded with his own softish despotism. Ostrander had asked about purpose, Kindleberger acknowledged a few days later. "Here is where we may have different ideas that must be resolved for the collaboration to work," he replied. The second draft, he said pointedly, stated the purposes clearly: to disabuse scholars about Erhard's role, to say something about the origins of the Colm-Dodge-Goldsmith report,

25. That is not to say that Ostrander was unversed in the political and economic debates to which hegemonic stability theory contributed. He had been a member of the Council on Foreign Relations since 1957 and taught evening courses in international business and economics as an adjunct professor at Pace University from 1975 to 1990 (Ostrander 2009a, 97–98). His marked-up copy of the third edition of Joan Edelman Spero's *The Politics of International Relations* (1985; in the present author's possession), which he used at Pace, bears evidence of his opinions in the debates. "*Nonsense*," he wrote of Spero's claim that, after détente, "the United States was no longer willing to bear the economic costs of leadership for reasons of security" (Spero 1985, 30); "Oh boy," he scribbled next to her sketch of the emerging view that an "open international system" required "new forms of international management that would assume responsibilities and prerogatives formerly undertaken by the state" (32). In these matters his opinions dovetailed with Kindleberger's. But he did not know the academic literature well enough to see how characterizing past US policies as "despotic" might, in a roundabout way, promote his opinions.

and, above all, to ask and answer a series of questions about currency reform. Then going from pointed to cutting: "These are scholarly interests. I pretend to be a scholar. . . . Your interest Taylor, it seems to me is to educate a wider public, those who read for example, the NYTimes M[a]gazine Section, The Atlantic, or Harpers" (CPK to FTO, September 15, 1997).

Kindleberger opportunely avoided the "despotism" question and thereby missed the point. He did not answer the question, did not even admit it. Nor did he need to, as scholarship was ostensibly his bailiwick, not Ostrander's. "Despot" would stay, whether Ostrander liked it not.

The word stayed because it served the deeper purpose that the collaboration had taken on. The purpose did not relate particularly to Erhard or Colm-Dodge-Goldsmith or even monetary reform—although it did relate, as Kindleberger said, to "scholarly interests." It was to turn the scholarly conversation away from posthegemonic cooperation and toward the restoration of leadership, as Kindleberger understood it.

Conclusion

After beginning their collaborative work but before wrapping it up, Kindleberger and Ostrander found its outlet (CPK to FTO, October 7, 1997).[26] They presented it at a conference, "The International Financial System, Past and Present," organized by the German Historical Institute and held at Princeton University, in April 1998. The conference yielded a volume edited by Marc Flandreau, Carl-Ludwig Holtfrerich, and Harold James and published in 2003. Kindleberger and Ostrander's contribution is titled "The 1948 Monetary Reform in Western Germany," and modified but little from the second draft. The inset quotation from the section above appears in its entirety, with only trivial changes, as the chapter's concluding sentences (Kindleberger and Ostrander 2003, 192).

The published volume reached Kindleberger the month before he died at age ninety-two (CPK to FTO, June 13, 2003).[27] In the decade since, Kindleberger and Ostrander's contribution has not registered in the literature of international relations and political economy.[28] But it may yet. In

26. F. Taylor Ostrander (1945–2003), binder 1, German Monetary Reform/Kindleberger Papers and Correspondence, in author's possession.

27. F. Taylor Ostrander (1945–2003), binder 3, German Monetary Reform/Kindleberger Papers and Correspondence, in author's possession.

28. As of July 3, 2013, the essay has two recorded citations in the Social Science Citation Index, both in the field of policy history and both by the same author: Madsen (2012a, 2012b).

their new foreword for the fortieth-anniversary reprint of *The World in Depression*, Barry Eichengreen and J. Bradford DeLong (2013, 9, 11) remark on the continuing relevance of "'Kindleberger's theory of hegemonic stability'" under conditions of world financial distress and US political dysfunction. Harold James (2011, 531) sees China responding to such conditions as if its leaders "were 'A' students in one of Kindleberger's courses." Inquiry into Kindleberger's version of the theory may arouse curiosity about how he conceived it, stated it, changed it, and treated other scholars' variations of it over the course of his career.

The course began in Berlin and finally returned there, if only vicariously, a half-century later. In the interim it wound through the economics department of MIT. There Kindleberger developed the theory only as he neared retirement because of what economics was understood to mean at MIT and what deviating from that understanding would have cost. In the MIT tradition, he valued the policy relevance of his research. But he also valued his free agency in undertaking the research and interpreting its relevance without concern for project commitments and group allegiances. The difficulty he had in maintaining both values at once is another part of the history of economics at MIT.

References

Blackmer, Donald L. M. 2002. *The MIT Center for International Studies: The Founding Years, 1951–1969.* Cambridge, Mass.: MIT Press.

Colm, Gerhard, Joseph M. Dodge, and Raymond W. Goldsmith. 1946. "A Plan for the Liquidation of War Finance and the Financial Rehabilitation of Germany." Office of the Military Government for Germany (U.S.), May 20. In F. Taylor Ostrander, OMGUS-Berlin/Marshall Plan Papers, 1945–2005 (2 boxes), box 1 (in author's possession).

Eichengreen, Barry. 1990. "Hegemonic Stability Theories of the International Monetary System." In *Elusive Stability: Essays in the History of International Finance, 1919–1939*, edited by Barry Eichengreen, 271–311. New York: Cambridge University Press.

Eichengreen, Barry, and J. Bradford DeLong. 2013. Foreword to *The World in Depression, 1929–1939.* 40th anniversary ed. Berkeley: University of California Press.

Gilpin, Robert. 1975. *U.S. Power and the Multinational Corporation: The Political Economy of Foreign Direct Investment.* New York: Basic Books.

Gowa, Joanne. 1984. "Hegemons, IOs, and Markets: The Case of the Substitution Account." *International Organization* 38 (Autumn): 661–83.

James, Harold. 2011. "International Order after the Financial Crisis." *International Affairs* 87 (3): 525–37.

Keohane, Robert O. 1980. "The Theory of Hegemonic Stability and Changes in International Economic Regimes, 1967–1977." In *Change in the International System*, edited by Ole R. Holsti, Randolph M. Siverson, and Alexander L. George, 131–62. Boulder, Colo.: Westview.

———. 1984. *After Hegemony: Cooperation and Discord in the World Political Economy*. Princeton, N.J.: Princeton University Press.

Kindleberger, Charles P. (1949) 1987. "Germany and the Economic Recovery of Europe." In *Marshall Plan Days*, 33–45. Winchester, Mass.: Allen and Unwin.

———. 1950. *The Dollar Shortage*. New York: Wiley and Sons.

———. 1953. *International Economics*. Homewood, Ill.: Irwin.

———. (1954) 1966. "The Role of the United States in the European Economy, 1919–1950." In *Europe and the Dollar*, 202–34. Cambridge, Mass.: MIT Press.

———. 1959. "International Political Theory from Outside." In *Theoretical Aspects of International Relations*, edited by William T. R. Fox, 69–82. Notre Dame, Ind.: University of Notre Dame Press.

———. 1961. "La fin du rôle dominant des États-Unis et l'avenir d'une politique économique mondiale." *Cahiers de l'Institut de Science Économique Appliquée*, no. 113 (serie P, no. 5): 91–105.

———. (1968) 1987. "The Marshall Plan and the Cold War." In *Marshall Plan Days*, 92–105. Winchester, Mass.: Allen and Unwin.

———. 1970. *Power and Money: The Economics of International Politics and the Politics of International Economics*. New York: Basic Books.

———. 1973. *The World in Depression, 1929–1939*. London: Lane.

———. 1978. *Manias, Panics, and Crashes: A History of Financial Crises*. New York: Basic Books.

———. (1978) 1987. "The OECD and the Third World." In *Marshall Plan Days*, 120–40. Winchester, Mass.: Allen and Unwin.

———. 1984. *A Financial History of Western Europe*. London: Allen and Unwin.

———. 1986a. "Hierarchy versus Inertial Cooperation." *International Organization* 40 (4): 841–47.

———. 1986b. "International Public Goods without International Cooperation." *American Economic Review* 76 (1): 1–13.

———. 1986c. *The World in Depression, 1929–1939*. Revised and enlarged ed. Berkeley: University of California Press.

———. 1987. "Toward the Marshall Plan: A Memoir of Policy Development in Germany, 1945–47." In *Marshall Plan Days*, 161–208. Winchester, Mass.: Allen and Unwin.

———. 1989a. *The German Economy, 1945–1947: Charles P. Kindleberger's Letters from the Field*. Westport, Conn.: Meckler.

———. 1989b. *Manias, Panics, and Crashes: A History of Financial Crises*. Rev. ed. New York: Basic Books.

———. 1991. *The Life of an Economist*. Cambridge, Mass.: Basil Blackwell.

———. 1993. *A Financial History of Western Europe*. 2nd ed. New York: Oxford University Press.

———. 1996. *Manias, Panics, and Crashes: A History of Financial Crises*. 3rd ed. New York: Wiley.

———. (1997) 1999. "Legislating the Marshall Plan: A Memoir." In *Essays in History: Financial, Economic, Personal*, 204–20. Ann Arbor: University of Michigan Press.

———. 2000. *Manias, Panics, and Crashes: A History of Financial Crises*. 4th ed. New York: Wiley.

Kindleberger, Charles P., and F. Taylor Ostrander. 2003. "The 1948 Monetary Reform in Western Germany." In *International Financial History in the Twentieth Century: System and Anarchy*, edited by Marc Flandreau, Carl-Ludwig Holtfrerich, and Harold James, 169–96. Cambridge: Cambridge University Press.

Kirshner, Jonathan, Peter A. Gourevitch, and Barry Eichengreen. 1997. "Crossing Disciplines and Charting New Paths: The Influence of Charles Kindleberger on International Relations." *Mershon International Studies Review* 41 (2): 333–45.

Krasner, Stephen D. 1976. "State Power and the Structure of International Trade." *World Politics* 28 (April): 317–47.

Lawson, Fred H. 1983. "Hegemony and the Structure of International Trade Reassessed: A View from Arabia." *International Organization* 37 (2): 317–37.

Madsen, Grant. 2012a. "Becoming a State-in-the-World: Lessons Learned from the American Occupation of Germany." *Studies in American Political Development* 26 (2): 163–79.

———. 2012b. "The International Origins of Dwight D. Eisenhower's Political Economy." *Journal of Policy History* 24 (4): 675–708.

Meardon, Stephen. 2013. "On Kindleberger and Hegemony: From Berlin to M.I.T. and Back" (version of September 29). dx.doi.org/10.2139/ssrn.2304466.

McKeown, Timothy J. 1983. "Hegemonic Stability Theory and Nineteenth-Century Tariff Levels in Europe." *International Organization* 37 (1): 73–91.

Myrdal, Gunnar. 1970. *The Challenge of World Poverty: A World Anti-Poverty Program in Outline*. New York: Pantheon Books.

Needell, Allan A. 1998. "Project Troy and the Cold War Annexation of the Social Sciences." In *Universities and Empire: Money and Politics in the Social Sciences during the Cold War*, edited by Christopher Simpson, 3–38. New York: New Press.

Ostrander, F. Taylor. (1996) 2001. "How I Came to Work in the Marshall Plan in Paris." Typescript, February 13, 1996, revised January 15, 2001, F. Taylor Ostrander (1945–2005), box 2, folder: "FTO Memoirs of Marshall Plan," OMGUS-Berlin/Marshall Plan Papers, in author's possession.

———. 2009a. "F. Taylor Ostrander: His Long and Wide-Ranging Career." *Research in the History of Economic Thought and Methodology* 27–C: 89–107.

———. 2009b. "My Wonderful Summer of Study in Geneva in 1931." *Research in the History of Economic Thought and Methodology* 27–C: 45–52.

Shlaes, Amity. 1997. "Loving the Mark." *New Yorker*, April 28, 188–93.

Spero, Joan Edelman. 1985. *The Politics of International Economic Relations*. 3rd ed. New York: St. Martin's Press.

Stein, Arthur A. 1984. "The Hegemon's Dilemma: Great Britain, the United States, and the International Economic Order." *International Organization* 38 (Spring): 355–86.

Stolper, Wolfgang. 1948. *German Realities*. New York: Reynal & Hitchcock.

Tenenbaum, Edward A. 1942. *National Socialism vs. International Capitalism*. Undergraduate Prize Essays, vol. 4. New Haven, Conn.: Yale University Press.

———. ca. 1958. "The German Mark." Unpublished manuscript. Boxes 2–3, Papers of Edward A. Tenenbaum, Harry S. Truman Library, Independence, Missouri. Reproduction in box "G.M.R. 1948/Studies by Others," folder: "Biographical Detail, Colm/Goldsmith/Tenenbaum." In Ostrander 1945–2003.

Temin, Peter. 1999. Foreword to *Essays in History: Financial, Economic, Personal*, by Charles P. Kindleberger, ix–xvi. Ann Arbor: University of Michigan Press.

Van Hook, James C. 2004. *Rebuilding Germany: The Creation of the Social Market Economy, 1945–1957*. New York: Cambridge University Press.

Wandel, Eckhard. 1979. "Historical Developments Prior to German Currency Reform of 1948." In "Currency and Economic Reform in West Germany after World War II," edited by Rudolph Richter. *Zeitschrift für die gesamte Staatswissenschaft* 135 (3): 320–31.

Contributors

Roger E. Backhouse is professor of the history and philosophy of economics at the University of Birmingham, UK, and Erasmus University Rotterdam. He holds a Leverhulme Major Research Fellowship to write an intellectual biography of Paul Samuelson. He is the author of *The Puzzle of Modern Economics* (2010) and *Transforming Modern Macroeconomics: Exploring Disequilibrium Microfoundations, 1956–2003* (2013) and is coeditor, with Philippe Fontaine, of *The History of the Social Sciences since 1945* (2010) and *A Historiography of the Modern Social Sciences* (2014).

Mauro Boianovsky is professor of economics at Universidade de Brasilia, Brazil, where he teaches history of economic thought and growth economics. He has published a number of articles in professional journals and chapters in edited volumes. Along with Roger E. Backhouse, he is the author of *Transforming Modern Macroeconomics: Exploring Disequilibrium Microfoundations, 1956–2003* (2013).

Beatrice Cherrier is assistant professor in economics at the University of Caen, France. She is interested in what economists thought, practiced, debated, wrote, publicized, denied, and popularized after World War II. This includes, among others, looking at specific communities (MIT, Chicago), figures (Marschak, Friedman, Myrdal), and themes (sunspots, large macromodels, economic classifications, urban economics, public economics, and social choice). Many of these research lines have recently converged in a unified enterprise: studying how economics became applied in the last decades of the twentieth century.

History of Political Economy 46 (annual suppl.) DOI 10.1215/00182702-2734588

William Darity Jr. is Samuel DuBois Cook Professor of Public Policy, African and African American Studies, and Economics at Duke University. His research focuses on inequality by race, class, and ethnicity; stratification economics; schooling and the racial achievement gap; North-South theories of trade and development; skin shade and labor market outcomes; the economics of reparations; the Atlantic slave trade and the Industrial Revolution; the history of economics; and the social psychological effects of exposure to unemployment. He was recently a fellow at the Center for Advanced Study in the Behavioral Sciences (2011–12) at Stanford University, and he received the Samuel Z. Westerfield Award in 2012 from the National Economic Association, the organization's highest honor. He served as editor in chief of the latest edition of the *International Encyclopedia of the Social Sciences* (2008) and as an associate editor of the new edition of the *Encyclopedia of Race and Racism* (2013).

Pedro Garcia Duarte is professor of economics at the University of São Paulo (FEA-USP), Brazil. His research interests are the history of postwar economics, in particular macro and monetary economics, with an emphasis on how modeling strategies and techniques had their use stabilized over time. He has published articles on this subject in leading journals of the field and a few book chapters. In 2012 he coedited with his colleague Gilberto Tadeu Lima a volume on the history of microfoundations of macroeconomics, titled *Microfoundations Reconsidered: The Relationship of Micro and Macroeconomics in Historical Perspective* and published by Edward Elgar.

Yann Giraud is associate professor of economics at the University of Cergy-Pontoise, France. His PhD dissertation, on the history of economics, studied the changing place of visual representation in the discipline throughout the twentieth century. He has published several articles and book chapters examining how economists and social scientists have used diagrams, graphs, and pictorial representations at the crossroads between theorizing, teaching, and policymaking.

Verena Halsmayer is completing her PhD in the history and philosophy of science at the University of Vienna (DK program "The Sciences in Historical, Philosophical, and Cultural Contexts"). Her research interests lie at the crossroads of the history and philosophy of economic modeling, historical epistemology, and the history of economic governance. Of special importance to her dissertation is the question of how to relate the concrete research practices of economists to the authoritative role of economic knowledge in society.

Kevin D. Hoover is professor of economics and philosophy at Duke University. He is the author of *Causality in Macroeconomics* (2001) and *The Methodology of Empirical Macroeconomics* (2001). He is a past editor of the *Journal of Economic Methodology* and current editor of *History of Political Economy.*

Arden Kreeger is an undergraduate at Duke University. She will graduate with a BA in public policy in 2015. In 2012 she began working with William Darity Jr. on the history of black graduate students at MIT. She is interested in international development and urban policy and governance.

Harro Maas is associate professor at Utrecht University. He has published widely in the history and methodology of economics, from the early modern period to the econometric revolution in the interwar period, and especially in the history of political economy in Victorian Britain. His book on one of the founders of modern economics, *William Stanley Jevons and the Making of Modern Economics* (2005), was awarded the Joseph J. Spengler prize by the (American) History of Economics Society. A historical introduction into economic methodology was published by Routledge in 2014. With Mary S. Morgan (LSE) he coedited *Observing the Economy: Historical Perspectives*, the 2012 supplement of *History of Political Economy*.

Stephen Meardon is assistant professor of economics at Bowdoin College. His recent research examines connections between the history of American economics from the eighteenth to the twentieth century and the politics of international trade. That research has produced essays in *History of Political Economy*, the *European Journal of the History of Economic Thought*, the *Journal of Economic Issues*, *History of Economic Thought and Policy*, *Early American Studies: An Interdisciplinary Journal*, and the *Journal of the History of Economic Thought*, of which he is editor.

Perry Mehrling is professor of economics at Barnard College, Columbia University, where he teaches Money and Banking, now online through Coursera. His most recent book is *The New Lombard Street: How the Fed Became the Dealer of Last Resort* (2010). His research has focused on the historical development of economic thought about money and finance in the twentieth century, which he uses as a foundation for understanding the financial globalization of the twenty-first century.

Andrej Svorenčík is a postdoctoral scholar at the Department of Economics, University of Mannheim, where he manages the local experimental economics laboratory. The overarching theme of his research is the emergence, diffusion, and reception of scientific communities, their related ideas and practices that make these epistemic groups distinct. His current book project is on the history of experimental economics.

Pedro Teixeira is associate professor at the Department of Economics (University of Porto) and Director of CIPES (Centre of Research on Higher Education Policies). His research interests focus on the economics of higher education, notably on markets and privatization, and the development of human capital as a research program. He has also published several articles and book chapters on the history of economic thought and on the economics of higher education.

Peter Temin is the Elisha Gray II Professor Emeritus of Economics at the Massachusetts Institute of Technology (MIT). His research interests include macroeconomic history, the Great Depression, industry studies in both the nineteenth and twentieth centuries, and ancient Rome. His most recent books are *The Roman Market Economy* (2013), *Prometheus Shackled: Goldsmith Banks and England's Financial Revolution after 1700* (2013, with Hans-Joachim Voth), and *The Leaderless Economy: Why the World Economic System Fell Apart and How to Fix It* (2013, with David Vines).

William Thomas is a senior historian at History Associates in Rockville, Maryland. He has previously worked at the American Institute of Physics and as a Junior Research Fellow at Imperial College London. His forthcoming book, *Rational Action: The Sciences of Policy in Britain and America, 1940–1960*, addresses the early history of operations research, systems analysis, statistical decision theory, and related areas. He is a member of the History and Traditions Committee of the Institute for Operations Research and the Management Sciences.

E. Roy Weintraub is professor of economics and Fellow of the Center for the History of Political Economy at Duke University. A former president of the History of Economics Society, and a Distinguished Fellow of that society, his most recent book, coauthored with Till Düppe, is *Finding Equilibrium: Arrow, Debreu, McKenzie, and the Problem of Scientific Credit* (2014).

Index

History of Political Economy 46 (annual suppl.) DOI 10.1215/00182702-2734600